AAT UNIT 11

Drafting Financial Statements

COMBINED TEXTBOOK AND WORKBOOK

Technician (NVQ Level 4)

ISBN 1 84390 2036

British Library Cataloguing-in-Publication data

A catalogue record for this book is available from the British Library.

We are grateful to the Association of Accounting Technicians for permission to reproduce past assessment materials. The solutions have been prepared by The Financial Training Company.

Published by

The Financial Training Company
22J Wincombe Business Park
Shaftesbury
Dorset
SP7 9QJ

P.S. For All Past Central Exam Papers - See Page 345 onwards.

Contents

Notes: (D.F. Central Assessment – Dec. 1999 Exam Paper
See Page 404 for Same Questions
see Page 476 for Same ANSWERS.

Preface

This is a combined textbook and workbook for Unit 11 (Drafting Financial Statements) of the AAT's Technician syllabus (NVQ Level 4).

Textbook

The textbook is written in a practical and interactive style:

- key terms and concepts are clearly defined
- all topics are illustrated with practical examples with clearly worked solutions
- frequent practice activities throughout the chapters ensure that what you have learnt is regularly reinforced
- 'pitfalls' and 'examination tips' help you avoid commonly made mistakes and help you focus on what is required to perform well in your examination.

Icons

Throughout the text we use symbols to highlight the elements referred to above.

Key facts

Examination tips and techniques

Pitfalls

Practice activities

Workbook

The workbook comprises three main elements

(a) A question bank of key techniques to give additional practice and reinforce the work covered in each chapter. The questions are divided into their relevant chapters and students may either attempt these questions as they work through the textbook, or leave some or all of these until they have completed the textbook as a sort of final revision of what they have studied.

(b) A mock examination which closely reflect the type of examination they may expect.

(c) The AAT specimen paper.

Syllabus

Unit 11 Drafting Financial Statements (Accounting Practice, Industry and Commerce)

Unit commentary

This unit is about drafting and interpreting financial statements of limited companies. The first element in this unit is about drafting limited company year-end financial statements from a trial balance. You are responsible for ensuring that the financial statements comply with any relevant domestic legislation and *either* the relevant UK standards (Statements of Standard Accounting Practice, Financial Reporting Standards and other relevant pronouncements) *or* the International Accounting Standards. You also need to show that you ensure that confidentiality procedures are followed. The second element requires you to interpret the financial statements of companies and the relationships between the elements using ratio analysis.

Elements contained within this unit are:

Element 11.1	Draft limited company financial statements
Element 11.2	Interpret limited company financial statements

		Chapter
Knowledge and Understanding		
To perform this unit effectively you will need to know and understand:		
The Business Environment:		
1	The elements and purposes of financial statements of limited companies as set out in the conceptual framework for financial reporting *(Element 11.2)*	1, 2
2	The general legal framework of limited companies and the obligations of Directors in respect of the financial statements *(Element 11.1)*	1, 3, 4, 5
3	The statutory form of accounting statements and disclosure requirements *(Element 11.1)*	5, 10
4	The UK regulatory framework for financial reporting and the main requirements of relevant Financial Reporting Standards or The relevant requirements of the International Accounting Standards *(Element 11.1)*	6, 10 to 17
5	The forms of equity and loan capital *(Element 11.1)*	4
6	The presentation of Corporation Tax in financial statements *(Element 11.1)*	4, 5
Accounting Techniques:		
7	Preparing financial statements in proper form *(Element 11.1)*	Throughout
8	Analysing and interpreting the information contained in financial statements *(Element 11.2)*	18
9	Computing and interpreting accounting ratios *(Element 11.2)*	18
Accounting Principles and Theory:		
10	Generally accepted accounting principles and concepts *(Element 11.1)*	2
11	The general principles of consolidation *(Element 11.1)*	7, 8, 9
The Organisation:		
12	How the accounting systems of an organisation are affected by its roles, organisational structure, its administrative systems and procedures and the nature of its business transactions *(Elements 11.1 & 11.2)*	Throughout

Unit 11 Drafting Financial Statements (Accounting Practice, Industry and Commerce)

Element 11.1 Draft limited company financial statements

Performance criteria

In order to perform this element successfully you need to:

A Draft **limited company financial statements** from the appropriate information

B Correctly identify and implement subsequent adjustments and ensure that discrepancies, unusual features or queries are identified and either resolved or referred to the appropriate person

C Ensure that **limited company financial statements** comply with **relevant accounting standards** and **domestic legislation** and with the organisation's policies, regulations and procedures

D Prepare and interpret a limited company cash flow statement

E Ensure that confidentiality procedures are followed at all times

Range statement

Performance in this element relates to the following contexts:

Limited company financial statements:

- Income statement
- Balance sheet
- Cash flow statement (not consolidated)
- Statement of total recognised gains and losses
- The supplementary notes required by statute
- Unitary
- Consolidated

Domestic legislation:

- Companies Act

Relevant accounting standards:

- Relevant Statements of Standard Accounting Practice, Financial Reporting Standards and other relevant pronouncements

or

- International Accounting Standards

Unit 11 Drafting Financial Statements (Accounting Practice, Industry and Commerce)

Element 11.2 Interpret limited company financial statements

Performance criteria

In order to perform this element successfully you need to:

A Identify the general purpose of financial statements used in limited companies

B Identify the **elements** of financial statements used in limited companies

C Identify the **relationships between the elements** within financial statements of limited companies

D Interpret the relationship between elements of limited company financial statements using ratio analysis

E Identify unusual features or significant issues within financial statements of limited companies

F Draw valid conclusions from the information contained within financial statements of limited companies

G Present issues, interpretations and conclusions clearly to the appropriate people

Range statement

Performance in this element relates to the following contexts:

Financial statements:

- Balance sheet
- Income statement

Elements:

- Assets
- Liabilities
- Ownership interest
- Gains
- Losses
- Contributions from owners
- Distributions to owners

Relationship between elements:

- Profitability
- Liquidity
- Efficient use of resources
- Financial position

TEXTBOOK

CHAPTER 1

The regulatory framework

ASSESSMENT FOCUS

In this initial chapter we will be covering background information that is essential for your understanding of the preparation of financial statements for many types of organisation but in particular for limited companies.

This chapter covers the following Knowledge and Understanding of the AAT Syllabus:

> The elements and purposes of financial statements of limited companies as set out in the conceptual framework for financial reporting *(Element 11.2)*
>
> The general legal framework of limited companies and the obligations of Directors in respect of the financial statements *(Element 11.1)*

In order to cover these the following topics are included:

> The purpose of financial statements
> The legal framework
> Accounting standards

Key definitions

Balance sheet	Accounting statement showing an entity's financial position at a particular date.
Profit and loss account	Accounting statement showing an entity's financial performance over a particular period of time.
Cash flow statement	Accounting statement showing an entity's receipts and payments of cash over a particular period of time.
Accounting standards	Official statements describing how accounts should be prepared if they are to give a true and fair view. In the UK, accounts are prepared in compliance with SSAPs and FRSs. There are also IASs that some countries choose to adopt.

1 Introduction

1.1 Background knowledge

In Unit 5 your accounting studies took you from ledger accounts to a trial balance to an extended trial balance. On the extended trial balance you will have put through a number of adjustments for stock, accruals, prepayments, depreciation and bad and doubtful debts. Each account on the extended trial balance was then balanced and extended into either the profit and loss account columns or the balance sheet columns depending upon whether the balance was income, expenditure, an asset or a liability.

For this Unit your accounting knowledge must be taken further.

1.2 Drafting financial statements

Element 1 of this Unit involves the drafting of the relevant financial statements for limited companies. You must be able to prepare a balance sheet, profit and loss account and cash flow statement in accordance with all the applicable regulations (the Companies Act 1985, accounting standards, etc).

1.3 Interpretation of financial statements

Element 2 of this Unit is entitled "Interpret limited company financial statements". It is concerned with being able to analyse and understand the structure and purpose of financial statements of limited companies. It requires a sound understanding of the elements of financial statements and an ability to interpret the relationships between these elements of financial statements by using ratio analysis.

In order to understand and interpret limited company financial statements you must be able to understand how they have been prepared. Therefore in the first few chapters of this text we will consider the preparation of simple accounts for a sole trader and then transfer these principles to gaining an understanding of how the financial statements of limited companies are prepared.

In this chapter and the next however we will consider the background to the preparation of financial statements for limited companies firstly by considering the regulatory framework and then the conceptual framework within which these financial statements must be prepared.

2 The purpose of financial statements

2.1 Introduction

The main purpose of financial statements is to provide information to a wide range of users.

The *balance sheet* provides information on the financial position of a business (its assets and liabilities at a point in time).

The *profit and loss account* provides information on the performance of a business (the profit or loss which results from trading over a period of time).

The *cash flow statement* provides information on the financial adaptability of a business (the movement of cash into and out of the business over a period of time).

2.2 Stewardship

Financial statements also show the results of the *stewardship* of an organisation. Stewardship is the accountability of management for the resources entrusted to it by the owners or the Government. This applies to the financial statements of limited companies as well as to central and local government and the National Health Service.

2.3 Needs of users

All users of financial statements need information on financial position, performance and financial adaptability. However, many different groups of people may use financial statements and each group will need particular information. Users of financial statements may include investors, management, employees, customers, suppliers, lenders, the government and the public. Investors need to be able to assess the ability of a business to pay dividends and manage resources. Management need information with which to assess performance, take decisions, plan, and control the business. Lenders, such as banks, are interested in the ability of the business to pay interest and repay loans. The Inland Revenue uses financial statements as the basis for tax assessments. The detailed needs of users of financial statements will be considered further in Chapter 2.

2.4 Legal requirements

The law requires limited companies to prepare financial statements annually. These financial statements must be filed with the Registrar of Companies and are then available to all interested parties. Most businesses, whether incorporated or not, are required to produce financial statements for submission to the Inland Revenue.

In the UK, the form and content of limited company accounts is laid down within the Companies Acts. The preparation of limited company accounts is also subject to regulations issued by the Accounting Standards Board.

3 Legal framework

3.1 Introduction

The financial statements of limited companies must be prepared within the legal framework of the Companies Acts. The Companies Act 1985 contains guidance and rules on:

- Formats for the financial statements
- Fundamental accounting principles
- Valuation rules

3.2 Formats

Companies must prepare their annual financial statements in accordance with certain formats. There is a choice of two formats specified for the balance sheet and four formats specified for the profit and loss account. These formats specify the items which must be disclosed in the financial statements and the order in which they must be shown, although they do provide some flexibility in relegating details to the notes to the accounts. We shall study these formats in the chapter on limited company accounts.

3.3 Fundamental accounting principles

The law embodies five accounting principles:

- going concern
- consistency
- prudence
- accruals
- separate valuation

These accounting principles are well known to accountants and will be considered in the next chapter.

If the financial statements of a limited company depart from these accounting principles, a note to the accounts must provide particulars of the departure, the reasons for it and its effect.

3.4 Valuation rules

The Companies Act 1985 embodies a choice between two sets of valuation rules for assets: the historical cost accounting rules and the alternative accounting rules.

- *Historical cost accounting rules*

  Under these rules, assets are shown on the basis of their purchase price or production cost. Fixed assets with a finite useful economic life must be depreciated on a systematic basis over their useful economic life. Current assets (eg stocks) must be written down if the net realisable value is lower than the cost.

- *Alternative accounting rules*

  Under these rules, fixed assets (other than goodwill), stocks and short-term investments may be shown at their current cost.

These alternative accounting rules allow companies to revalue their fixed assets to current market value if the directors wish this.

3.5 Companies Act 1989

The Companies Act 1989 has to some extent increased the volume of disclosure that companies are required to make in their financial statements. These disclosures are dealt with in later chapters on limited company accounts.

One of the most significant requirements is that accounts of public and large private companies must state whether they have been prepared in accordance with applicable accounting standards (eg SSAPs and FRSs – see below) and give details of, and the reasons for, any material departures.

4 UK accounting standards

4.1 SSAPs and FRSs

Accounting standards give guidance in specific areas of accounting. There are two types of accounting standard currently in issue in the UK:

- *Statements of Standard Accounting Practice (SSAPs)*

  SSAPs were created by a body known as the Accounting Standards Committee (ASC). The ASC was abolished in July 1990, but several of the SSAPs still remain in force.

- *Financial Reporting Standards (FRSs)*

  The Accounting Standards Board (ASB) took over the role of setting accounting standards from the ASC in August 1990. One of the ASB's first acts was to adopt all 22 existing SSAPs. The SSAPs therefore continue to be applicable to all sets of accounts until they are replaced or withdrawn.

  The accounting standards created by the ASB are known as *Financial Reporting Standards.* In preparing company accounts, both SSAPs and FRSs should be complied with. Failure to do so can lead to the company being ordered to redraft its accounts (*S12 CA 1989*).

4.2 Accounting Standards Board (ASB) and Financial Reporting Council (FRC)

The Accounting Standards Board is the body responsible for developing UK accounting standards – it consists of ten qualified accountants and is monitored and funded by a supervisory body called the Financial Reporting Council, whose members are drawn from accounts user groups (eg Stock Exchange, CBI) as well as the accounting profession.

4.3 Financial Reporting Review Panel (FRRP)

The Financial Reporting Review Panel is also guided and monitored by the FRC. It enquires into apparent material departures from the requirements of the Companies Act or of accounting standards in the annual accounts of public and large private companies. The Review Panel can require companies to amend their accounts and has the power to prosecute them under the Companies Act if they refuse to do so voluntarily. Although a number of public companies have agreed to amend their accounts since the Review Panel was set up in 1990, no case has yet reached the courts.

4.4 Urgent Issues Task Force (UITF)

This is a committee of the ASB. It deals with urgent and emerging issues, particularly where the normal standard setting process would be too slow to implement changes. It issues consensus pronouncements which are known as *UITF Abstracts*.

4.5 The Public Sector and Not for Profit Committee

This is another sub-committee of the ASB. It maintains contact between the ASB and public sector accounting by advising the ASB on ways of minimising differences between public sector and private sector accounting practices. It also comments on FRSs before they are issued from the point of view of public sector and 'not for profit' organisations.

4.6 Aims of UK accounting standards

The aim of the ASB is to establish and improve standards of financial accounting and reporting for the benefit of users, preparers and auditors of financial information.

Accounting standards:

- are authoritative statements of how particular types of transaction and other events should be reflected in financial statements
- are applicable to all financial statements that are intended to give a true and fair view
- need not be applied to immaterial items.

4.7 The standard setting process

There are several stages in the development of a new FRS:

1. A topic is identified and a member of the ASB's staff carries out research.
2. The ASB issues a Discussion Paper, which sets out the issues and discusses the possible alternative approaches. This is circulated to interested parties, who comment.
3. A Financial Reporting Exposure Draft (FRED) is published. This is a draft version of the new FRS. Again, this is circulated to interested parties. The proposals may be amended as a result of their comments.
4. The FRS is published.

The ASB issues standards on its own authority. Although it does take comments into account, the ultimate content of an FRS depends on its own judgement based on research, public consultation and careful deliberation about the benefits and costs of providing the resulting information in the financial statements.

5 International Accounting Standards

The current requirement is that UK companies must produce their accounts in compliance with UK law (the Companies Acts 1985 and 1989) and UK accounting standards (SSAPs and FRSs). However, you should also be aware of the existence of the International Accounting Standards Board (IASB) which has published a complete suite of International Accounting Standards (IASs).

As business throughout the world becomes more global in outlook, there is increasing pressure for similar accounting principles to be applied internationally. Thus, the IASB was born. IASs have no authority of their own; it is up to the governments in each country and trading bloc to decide on their applicability. An increasing number of countries have decided not to develop their own domestic accounting standards, but simply to adopt IASs wholesale.

The Council of Ministers of the European Union (EU) have decided that any company which is listed on a European Stock Exchange must prepare their consolidated accounts in line with IASs with effect from 1 January 2005. Thus, while IASs currently have no authority in the UK, from 2005 all companies listed on the London Stock Exchange will have to prepare their consolidated accounts in accordance with IASs. In the future, therefore, IASs will be very important in the UK. For now, you should concentrate on studying the rules contained in the Companies Acts and UK accounting standards since it is these rules that are currently relevant.

6 Quick quiz *(The answers are in the final chapter of this book)*

1 What is the main Act of Parliament governing the conduct and financial statements of companies in the UK?

2 What five accounting principles are required by this Act?

3 What are the two sorts of mandatory accounting standards in force in the UK?

4 What is the name of the body that issues accounting standards in the UK?

5 Are International Accounting Standards currently mandatory in the UK?

7 Summary

The regulatory framework for preparing financial statements in the UK consists of:

- the Companies Acts (which apply to limited company financial statements).
- UK accounting standards (which apply to all financial statements giving a true and fair view).

CHAPTER 2

The conceptual framework

ASSESSMENT FOCUS

This chapter provides some essential background knowledge of the principles and concepts that underlie the preparation of financial statements for limited companies. It also considers the Statement of Principles which amongst other things defines the elements of financial statements which are an important area of element 11.2.

This chapter covers the following Knowledge and Understanding of the AAT Syllabus:

> The elements of financial statements of limited companies as set out in the conceptual framework for financial reporting *(Element 11.2)*
>
> Generally accepted accounting principles and concepts *(Element 11.1)*

In order to cover these the following topics are included:

> Fundamental accounting concepts
> Other accounting concepts
> The Statement of Principles
> FRS 18: Accounting policies

Key definitions

Accounting concepts	Also called **accounting principles**, these are the broad basic assumptions underlying the preparation of financial statements that give a true and fair view.
The Statement of Principles	The ASB's conceptual framework document, identifying the basic building blocks of accounting.
Qualitative characteristics	The Statement of Principles identifies four characteristics that make financial information useful: relevance, reliability, comparability and understandability.
Elements of financial statements	The Statement of Principles identifies seven elements, the classes of items that financial statements comprise: assets, liabilities, ownership interest, gains, losses, contributions from owners and distributions to owners.

1 Fundamental accounting concepts

1.1 Introduction

The Companies Act 1985 outlines five fundamental accounting concepts or principles which underlie the preparation of financial statements. These are:

- the going concern concept
- the accruals concept

- the consistency concept
- the prudence concept
- the non-aggregation (or separate valuation) principle

The first four of these concepts were described as 'Fundamental' and defined in SSAP 2. However SSAP 2 was replaced by FRS 18 in December 2000. FRS 18 has moved its emphasis away from these four fundamental concepts but they are enacted in legislation and underpin best accounting practice, therefore they are still named as being fundamental to the preparation of financial statements.

1.2 The going concern concept

The going concern concept assumes that the enterprise will continue in operational existence for the foreseeable future. This means that assets should be valued at cost or valuation less depreciation where applicable rather than on a break-up or forced sale basis.

1.3 The accruals concept

The accruals or matching concept is that revenues and costs are 'matched' with one another in the period to which they relate rather than the period in which the cash is received or paid.

1.4 The consistency concept

Like items are treated in a similar manner within each accounting period and from one period to the next. This aids comparison of results over time.

1.5 The prudence concept

Revenues and profits are not included in the accounts until they are realised but provision is made for losses and liabilities immediately, even if the loss will not occur until the future. Although FRS 18 is moving away from the prudence concept, in some measure financial statements should still be prepared on a 'conservative' basis.

1.6 Non-aggregation principle (CA 1985)

In determining items in the accounts, assets and liabilities should not be offset against one another. So for example compensating inaccuracies in individual accounts should not be lost in one large total or if a company borrows money to buy a building, the building should be shown in fixed assets and the loan in creditors.

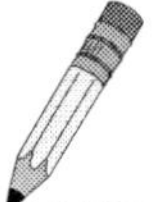

Activity 1 *(The answer is in the final chapter of this book)*

Give a brief example of the application of each of the five accounting concepts or principles considered so far in the preparation of financial statements.

---

2 Other accounting concepts

2.1 The concept of 'true and fair'

The Companies Act 1985 requires the directors of a company to prepare for each financial year of the company a balance sheet as at the last day of the year and a profit and loss account.

It continues, insisting that the balance sheet shall give a *true and fair* view of the state of the affairs of the company as at the end of the financial year and the profit and loss account shall give a *true and fair* view of the profit or loss of the company for the financial year.

So, where accounts are drawn up to comply with the Companies Acts, the concept of *true and fair* is a legal one.

The phrase 'true and fair view' is not defined in the Companies Act but it is generally believed to mean the following.

Truth implies that the figures are mathematically accurate and factually correct.

Fairness implies that the information is presented in a manner which is free from bias.

2.2 Substance over form

Under this concept, transactions and other events are accounted for and presented in financial statements in accordance with their economic substance and financial reality and not merely with their legal form.

For example, leasehold buildings are owned by the landlord rather than the occupier, but the occupier is using them for his business in the same way as if they were freehold. Thus it is appropriate to treat them as a fixed asset in the occupier's balance sheet, provided that it is made clear that the premises are leasehold.

2.3 Materiality concept

There is no precise definition of materiality but it is generally felt that an item in the financial statements is material if its omission or mis-statement would affect decisions made by users of the financial statements.

There is no rigid mathematical definition. Very small mis-statements are immaterial so do not have to be adjusted. Large mis-statements are material and therefore must be adjusted. Accounting standards do not apply to immaterial items.

2.4 Realisation concept

Transactions are normally recorded when there is a legal requirement to accept liability for them; that is, when the legal title is transferred.

This means that a transaction may be included in an earlier accounting period than the one in which cash is eventually exchanged. The realisation concept is that revenues and profit can be treated as realised when the receipt of cash or other assets is reasonably certain.

2.5 Historical cost concept

Quantitative information recorded in monetary values is normally retained at its historical cost.

In the case of goods and other assets purchased, this will be at the price originally paid for them and, in the case of sales, at the agreed price for which the goods were eventually sold.

2.6 Objectivity

The preparation of accounting statements involves a considerable amount of individual discretion and judgement. They should be prepared with the minimum amount of personal bias and the maximum amount of overall objectivity.

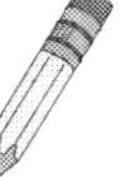

Activity 2 *(The answer is in the final chapter of this book)*

The normal accounting treatment of sales on credit is an example of the application of which two accounting concepts?

---

3 The Statement of Principles

3.1 Introduction

The ASB has published a Statement of Principles, which is intended to lay out the conceptual underpinning of the accounting standards that are issued. The idea is that, if we can all agree on a uniform set of basic accounting principles, then there should be less disagreement on the contents of accounting standards developed from those principles.

The Statement of Principles is split up into eight chapters, each of which deals with a particular topic.

- Chapter 1: The objective of financial statements
- Chapter 2: The reporting entity
- Chapter 3: The qualitative characteristics of financial information
- Chapter 4: The elements of financial statements
- Chapter 5: Recognition in financial statements
- Chapter 6: Measurement in financial statements
- Chapter 7: Presentation of financial information
- Chapter 8: Accounting for interests in other entities

3.2 Chapter 1: The objective of financial statements

The objective is stated as to provide information useful to a wide range of users. Information is required on:

- financial position – balance sheet
- performance – profit and loss account and statement of total recognised gains and losses
- financial adaptability – cash flow statement and certain notes to the accounts

Each category of user has a different set of interests:

Users	Need information to assess ability of enterprise to
Investors (primary users)	pay dividends, manage resources
Employees	provide employment/remuneration
Customers	continue in operational existence
Suppliers	repay debts, continue in operational existence
Lenders	pay interest, repay loans
Government	pay tax, manage and account for resources
Public	provide goods and services, provide employment
	Need information on
All	financial position, performance and financial adaptability

3.3 Chapter 2: The reporting entity

This chapter considers the issue of which entities should be required to prepare and publish their financial statements, so that the users of accounts (as previously identified) can be satisfied. It is clearly important that those entities that ought to publish their financial statements do in fact do so.

The chapter concludes that an entity should prepare and publish financial statements if there is a legitimate demand for the information, and it is a cohesive economic unit.

3.4 Chapter 3: The qualitative characteristics of financial information

Threshold quality

Information is only useful if it is *material* (ie if its omission or mis-statement could influence economic decisions taken by users on the basis of the information).

Subject to the threshold quality of materiality, the chapter identifies four characteristics that make financial information useful to users:

- relevance
- reliability
- comparability
- understandability

Relevance	**Reliability**
relevant = can influence decisions Information is relevant if - it possesses predictive and/or confirmatory value; and - it is provided in time to influence the decisions	reliable = a complete and faithful representation Information is reliable if it is - faithful representation (reflecting the substance of the transactions) - neutral (free from bias) - free from material error - complete, and - prudent
Comparability	**Understandability**
comparable →for an enterprise over time and between enterprises Aspects of comparability: - consistency - disclosure (eg accounting policies, corresponding amounts) - compliance with accounting standards	understandable → to a user with - a reasonable knowledge of business, economic activities and accounting; and - a willingness to study the information with diligence. Aspects of understandability: - users' abilities - aggregation and classification

3.5 Chapter 4: The elements of financial statements

This chapter identifies seven elements of financial statements:

Assets

= Rights or other access to future economic benefits controlled by an entity as a result of past transactions or events.

Liabilities

= An entity's obligations to transfer economic benefits as a result of past transactions or events.

Ownership interest

= The residual amount found by deducting all liabilities of the entity from all of the entity's assets.

Gains

= Increases in ownership interest other than those relating to contributions from owners.

Losses

= Decreases in ownership interest other than those relating to distributions to owners.

Contributions from owners

= Increases in ownership interest resulting from investments made by owners in their capacity as owners.

Distributions to owners

= Decreases in ownership interest resulting from transfers made to owners in their capacity as owners.

The performance criteria for element 2 of this Unit requires that the elements of the financial statements should be identified and that the relationships between these elements are also identified.

Earlier in your studies you will have learned the accounting equation:

Assets - liabilities = Capital + profits - drawings

The Statement of Principles restates this as:

Assets - liabilities = Ownership interest; or

Assets - liabilities = Contributions from owners + Gains - Losses - Distributions to owners

3.6 Chapter 5: Recognition in financial statements

An item should be recognised in financial statements if:

- the item meets the definition of an element of financial statements (asset, liability, gain, loss etc), and
- there is sufficient evidence that the *change in assets or liabilities* inherent in the item has occurred (including where appropriate, evidence that a future inflow or outflow of benefit will occur); and
- the item can be *measured* at a monetary amount with sufficient *reliability*.

Reliable measurement

Methods of reliable measurement include transaction price (historic cost), market-based measures (eg replacement costs, net realisable value) and the expected value of a group of items.

Recognition in profit and loss account

For gains to be recognised in the profit and loss account rather than in the statement of total recognised gains and losses, certain additional criteria must be satisfied:

- the gain must be earned;
- the gain must be realised.

The idea is that a gain which is earned but not yet realised will be dealt with in the statement of total recognised gains and losses. When such a gain is subsequently realised, it will still not feature in the profit and loss account as it has already been reported in the statement of total recognised gains and losses.

3.7 Chapter 6: Measurement in financial statements

When preparing financial statements, a measurement basis has to be chosen for each category of assets and liabilities. Possible bases are:

- historical cost
- replacement cost
- present value of future cashflows (= economic value = value in use)
- net realisable value

This chapter does not specify a single measurement basis which must be adopted, but states that the basis chosen should be the one that best meets the objective of financial statements and the demands of the qualitative characteristics of financial information.

Historical cost is usually more reliable than measures of current value, though arguably current values are more relevant.

3.8 Chapter 7: Presentation of financial information

Financial statements comprise the primary financial statements plus supporting notes.

Individual primary statements

These comprise:

- the profit and loss account;
- the statement of total recognised gains and losses;

} statements of financial performance

- the balance sheet; and
- the cash flow statement.

Statements of financial performance

Statements of financial performance contribute to financial reporting by:

- giving an account of the results of the stewardship of management to enable users to assess the past performance of management and to form a basis for developing future expectations about financial performance; and
- providing feedback to users so that they can check the accuracy of their previous assessments of the financial performance for past periods and, if necessary, modify their assessments for future periods.

Balance sheet

The balance sheet and notes provide information on and the interrelationships between its:

- **resource structure** - major classes and amounts of assets; and
- **financial structure** - major classes and amounts of liabilities and ownership interest.

It is helpful to users if assets, liabilities and ownership interest are reported in classes.

Presentation of information in the balance sheet can help a user to assess future cash flows. For example, assets held for sale should be reported separately from those held on a continuing basis.

A balance sheet does not purport to show the value of a business enterprise. However, together with other financial statements and other information, balance sheets should provide information that is useful to those who wish to make their own assessment of a company's value.

Cash flow statement

A cash flow statement reports cash receipts classified by major sources and cash payments classified by major uses. It provides useful information on a company's activities in:

- generating cash through operations;
- using cash to repay debt;
- using cash to distribute dividends; and
- re-investing to maintain or expand operations.

This helps in the assessment of a company's risk, liquidity, viability, adaptability and the way in which profits are converted to cash. Assessment of prospects for future cash flows is hindered by the effect of timing differences between, for example, cash receipts and sales. Therefore, cash flow statements should be useful in conjunction with the other primary statements when assessing future cashflow prospects.

Features of financial statements that help them to communicate clearly

- **Aggregation** - the simplification, condensation and structuring of voluminous transactions and other events into amounts and totals in the financial statements.
- **Classification** - the grouping of items by their nature or function.
- **Structure** - the presentation of the components resulting from the process of aggregation and classification in individual statements of financial performance, financial position and cashflows along with related notes.
- **Articulation** - the interrelation of the financial statements because they reflect different aspects of the same transactions or events.
- **Accounting policies –** should be disclosed clearly
- **Notes to financial statements** - amplifying or explaining items in the primary statements. The notes and primary statements provide an integrated whole, but misrepresentation in the primary statements corrected by disclosure in the notes will not give a true and fair view.
- **Supplementary information** - such as alternative asset values from those in the financial statements and statistical information, positioned outside the primary statements and notes.

3.9 Chapter 8: Accounting for interests in other entities

This chapter reiterates the standard method of accounting for investments owned by the parent company, when preparing the parent's individual accounts and the parent's group accounts.

In the individual accounts, investments are shown as assets, with dividends receivable credited to the profit and loss account.

In consolidated financial statements the way in which the interests in other entities are dealt with depends on the degree of influence involved. This will be covered in more detail in later chapters of this text.

3.10 The impact of the Statement of Principles

The Statement of Principles is not an accounting standard, so its provisions are persuasive rather than mandatory. Nothing in the Statement of Principles can overrule any rule contained in an accounting standard (SSAP or FRS).

The relationship of the Statement of Principles to the standard setting process is therefore indirect. The aim is that the ASB should consider the contents of the Statement of Principles when deciding between possible alternative treatments to go in an FRS. Whether the Statement is actually any practical use to the ASB in developing FRSs is unproven. The ASB seem more driven by the desire to harmonise UK accounting with IASs than by the desire to align accounting with the Statement of Principles, but it is possible that in future the Statement will have a more influential role.

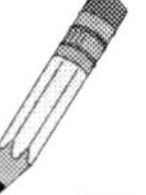

Activity 3 *(The answer is in the final chapter of this book)*

What are the seven elements of financial statements identified in the Statement of Principles?

---

4 FRS 18: Accounting policies

4.1 Introduction

After the Statement of Principles was issued in 1999, it was clear that there were inconsistencies between the Statement's approach promoting relevance, reliability, comparability and understandability, and SSAP 2 which identified going concern, consistency, accruals and prudence as fundamental concepts. SSAP 2 has therefore been withdrawn and replaced by FRS 18 which is consistent with the Statement of Principles.

The SSAP 2 concepts must still be applied when preparing accounts, since the CA 1985 specifically requires their application, but they are no longer singled out in FRS 18 as being more important than other principles. Just to remind you again the meaning of each of the SSAP 2 concepts is given below:

(a) The **going concern concept** - accounts are prepared on the assumption that the entity will continue in operational existence for the foreseeable future.

(b) The **accruals concept** (also called the **matching concept**) - costs and revenues should be matched in the profit and loss account in the period in which they arise, rather than when the cash is received or paid.

(c) The **consistency concept** - similar items should be treated similarly in each accounting period, and from one period to the next.

(d) The **prudence concept** - profits should not be recognised until they are realised. Losses should be recognised as soon as they are foreseen.

4.2 Purpose of FRS 18

FRS 18 sets out the principles to be followed in selecting accounting policies, and the disclosures needed to help users to understand the accounting policies adopted and how they have been applied.

The overriding requirement is for accounting policies to be selected to enable the financial statements to give a true and fair view. Accounting policies should normally be chosen to comply with accounting standards and UITF Abstracts. However where in exceptional circumstances following an accounting standard or Abstract would not give a true and fair view, the standard or Abstract should be departed from to the extent necessary to give a true and fair view.

4.3 Pervasive concepts

FRS 18 identifies the going concern concept and the accruals concept as playing a pervasive role in the process of selecting accounting policies:

- an entity should prepare its financial statements on a going concern basis, unless the entity is being liquidated or the directors have no realistic alternative but to cease trading. In such circumstances the financial statements should not apply the going concern basis.
- an entity should prepare its balance sheet and profit and loss account on an accruals basis rather than a strict cash basis.

4.4 Four objectives

When choosing accounting policies, an entity should judge possible policies against the objectives of relevance, reliability, comparability and understandability. (Note how this is directly consistent with the wording of the Statement of Principles.)

4.5 Reviewing and changing accounting policies

Accounting policies should be reviewed regularly to ensure that they remain the most appropriate to the particular circumstances.

Changes in accounting policies should be accounted for as a prior period adjustment in accordance with FRS 3 (see later). This should be differentiated from changes in accounting estimates, which should be reflected in the current (and future) year's results.

For example, a company might have an accounting policy of depreciating its machines on a straight line basis over five years. A machine is bought for £10,000 with an expected scrap value after five years of £2,000. The depreciation charge for the first year is £8,000/5 = £1,600.

In the second year it is felt that although the total life of the machine remains at five years (ie, there are still four years to go), the scrap value of the machine is now only £600. This is a change in accounting estimate, not a change in accounting policy. The policy remains to depreciate the historical cost less scrap value, on a straight line basis over its useful life. There is no prior year adjustment. The depreciation charge for the second year will be:

$$\frac{\text{NBV b/f} - \text{scrap value}}{\text{Remaining life}} = \frac{£8{,}400 - £600}{4 \text{ years}} = £1{,}950$$

FRS 18 draws the distinction between estimation techniques and accounting policies. Estimation techniques are used to implement the measurement aspects of accounting policies. A change to an estimation technique should not be accounted for as a prior period adjustment, unless it represents the correction of a fundamental error, or such accounting is required by statute, accounting standard or Abstract.

4.6 Disclosures

An entity should disclose a description of all the accounting policies used for material items in the financial statements.

Where a change in accounting policy has been made the entity should disclose the particulars of the change and the reasons why it is believed that the new policy is more appropriate.

The directors should disclose any uncertainties which cast doubt on whether the entity is a going concern.

Where the statutory true and fair view override has been invoked, the entity should disclose the particulars of the matter, the reasons and the effect.

4.7 Commentary on FRS 18

FRS 18 is broadly uncontroversial. It is widely recognised that SSAP 2 was no longer tenable once the Statement of Principles had been issued. The main discussion area has been the alleged downgrading of the prudence concept. SSAP 2 identified prudence as a fundamental concept; in FRS 18 it is only part of the reliability characteristic. Some commentators believe that there will be less emphasis placed on prudent accounting in the future as a result of this downgrading. It remains to be seen whether these fears are well grounded.

4.8 Example of disclosure

FRS 18 requires entities to disclose their accounting policies selected. This disclosure is normally given in Note 1 to the accounts, immediately following the financial statements themselves (profit and loss account, balance sheet, cash flow statement and STRGL).

As an illustrative example, consider the following (abridged) Note 1 to the 2000 Accounts of Pacific Media plc, a cinema, television and e-commerce company.

> **'1 Accounting Policies**
>
> The principal accounting policies are set out below and have been applied consistently throughout the year and the preceding year. The accounts are prepared under the historical cost convention and in accordance with applicable UK Accounting Standards.
>
> As stated in the Corporate Governance Statement the directors have formed a judgement, at the time of approving the financial statements, that there is a reasonable expectation that the Company will have adequate resources to continue for the next 12 months.
>
> **Intangible assets**
>
> Goodwill arising on the acquisition of subsidiary undertakings is amortised over its useful life or 20 years whichever is the lesser.
>
> **Turnover**
>
> Turnover, which excludes value added tax and discounts allowed, comprises the value of sales of goods and services to outside customers.
>
> **Tangible fixed assets and depreciation**
>
> Tangible fixed assets are shown at original historical cost. Depreciation is provided on a straight line basis in order to write down the cost of each asset over its expected useful life to an estimate of residual value, as follows:

Leasehold improvements	15 years
Cinema equipment	10 years
Plant, equipment and vehicles	3 - 5 years

Fixed asset investments

Investments held as fixed assets are stated at cost less provision for impairment.

Stocks

Stocks consist of finished trading goods and cinema concession inventory and are stated at the lower of cost and net realisable value.

Current asset investments

Current asset investments are stated at the lower of cost and net realisable value.

Leasing and hire purchase commitments

Rentals paid under operating leases are charged to the profit and loss account on a straight line basis. Assets held under finance leases and hire purchase contracts, which are those where substantially all the risks and rewards of ownership of the asset have passed to the Group, are capitalised in the balance sheet and are depreciated over their estimated economic lives. The finance charges are allocated over the period of the lease in proportion to the capital amount outstanding and are charged to the profit and loss account.'

5 Quick quiz *(The answers are in the final chapter of this book)*

1 What is the going concern concept?

2 Give an example of application of the substance over form concept.

3 What is the objective of financial statements?

4 How is ownership interest calculated?

5 State the names of the four primary statements in a set of accounts.

6 Which two concepts does FRS 18 identify as having a pervasive role?

6 Summary

The Companies Act 1985 sets out five fundamental accounting concepts or principles:

- going concern
- accruals
- consistency
- prudence
- non-aggregation of assets and liabilities

The Statement of Principles was published by the ASB as a conceptual framework for accounting practice and development.

The objective of financial statements is to provide information about the reporting entity's financial performance and financial position that is useful to a wide range of users for assessing the stewardship of management and for making economic decisions.

The qualitative characteristics of financial information are:

- relevance;
- reliability;
- comparability; and
- understandability.

The elements of financial statements are:

- assets;
- liabilities;
- ownership interest;
- gains;
- losses;
- contributions from owners; and
- distributions to owners.

FRS 18 has now been issued in place of SSAP 2. FRS 18 only recognises the going concern and accruals concepts as fundamental to the preparation of financial statements. Prudence and consistency now appear to be less important but are still enacted in law. FRS 18 requires that accounting policies should be chosen to meet the objectives of relevance, reliability, comparability and understandability.

CHAPTER 3

Drafting financial statements

ASSESSMENT FOCUS

For element 1 of this Unit you need to be able not only to draft a set of limited company financial statements but also to understand the structure of profit and loss accounts and to explain how these tie in with the balance sheet. This can only be achieved by a detailed knowledge of how to prepare a set of financial statements. Therefore in this chapter we will concentrate on the preparation of a set of financial statements initially for a sole trader and then in later chapters we will consider the preparation of financial statements for a limited company.

This chapter covers the following Knowledge and Understanding of the AAT Syllabus.

> The general legal framework of limited companies and the obligations of Directors in respect of the financial statements *(Element 11.)*
>
> Preparing financial statements in proper form *(Element 11.1)*

In order to cover these the following topics are included.

> Types of profit making organisation
> Types of non-profit making entities
> Preparing final accounts
> Making adjustments
> The extended trial balance
> From trial balance to final accounts

Key definitions

Limited company	Business structure in which the shareholders are not legally responsible for the debts owed by their company. A limited company is a distinct 'person' in law so can sue or be sued in its own name.
Books of prime entry	Accounting records in which entries are made individually, before being totalled to be entered in the ledgers. Examples are the sales day book and the purchases day book.
Trial balance	List of the balances on all the ledger accounts at a particular date. The total debit balances should equal the total credit balances.
Extended trial balance	Working sheet in which the trial balance is analysed into the profit and loss account and balance sheet of the business.

1 Types of profit making organisation

1.1 Introduction

There are three main types of profit making business organisation:

- sole trader (sole proprietor)
- partnership
- limited company

1.2 Sole trader

As the name suggests, this is an organisation owned by one person.

Accounting conventions recognise the business as a *separate entity* from its owner. However, legally, the business and personal affairs of a sole trader are not distinguished in any way. The most important consequence of this is that a sole trader has complete personal unlimited liability. Business debts which cannot be paid from business assets must be met from the sale of personal assets, such as a house or car.

Sole trading organisations are normally small because they have to rely on the financial resources of their owner.

The advantages of operating as a sole trader include flexibility and autonomy. A sole trader can manage the business as he or she likes and can introduce or withdraw capital at any time.

1.3 Partnership

A partnership is two or more persons associated for the purpose of a business or a profession. Like a sole trader, a partnership is not legally distinguished from its members. Personal assets of the partners may have to be used to pay the debts of the partnership business.

The advantages of trading as a partnership stem mainly from there being many owners rather than one. This means that:

- more resources may be available, including capital, specialist knowledge, skills and ideas;
- administrative expenses may be lower for a partnership than for the equivalent number of sole traders, due to economies of scale; and
- partners can substitute for each other.

Partners can introduce or withdraw capital at any time, provided that all the partners agree.

1.4 Limited company

A limited company is a distinct, artificial 'person' created in order to separate legal responsibility for the affairs of a business (or any other activity) from the personal affairs of the individuals who own and/or operate the business.

The owners are known as *shareholders* (or members) and the people who run the business are known as *directors*. In a small corporation, owners and directors are often the same people.

1.5 Limited liability

The concept of limited liability is based on the premise that the company's debts and liabilities are those of the company and not those of the members.

Each member of a limited company is liable to contribute if called on to do so only the amount he has agreed to pay on his shares.

Limited liability refers to the liability of each shareholder being limited to any unpaid amount on their shares.

1.6 Comparison of limited companies to sole traders and partnerships

The fact that a company is a separate legal entity means that it is very different from a sole trader or partnership in a number of ways.

- **Property holding**

  The property of a registered company belongs to the company. A change in the ownership of shares in the company will have no effect on the ownership of the company's property. (In a partnership the firm's property belongs directly to the partners who can take it with them if they leave the partnership.)

- **Transferable shares**

  Shares in a registered company can usually be transferred without the consent of the other shareholders. In the absence of agreement to the contrary, a new partner cannot be introduced into a firm without the consent of all existing partners.

- **Contracts with members**

  A registered company can contract with its members and can sue and be sued on such contracts. A partner cannot enter into contracts with his own firm, nor can a sole trader.

- **Suing and being sued**

  As a separate legal person, a company can sue and be sued in its own name. Judgements relating to companies do not affect the members personally.

- **Number of members**

  There is no upper limit on the number of members in a company.

  In a partnership, except in certain restricted categories, such as accountants and stockbrokers, the maximum number of partners is 20. This limitation on numbers makes it difficult for a partnership to raise large amounts of capital.

- **Security for loans**

  A company has greater scope for raising loans by, for example, borrowing on debentures (long-term borrowings) and may secure them with floating charges.

  A floating charge is a mortgage over the constantly fluctuating assets of a company providing security for the lender of money to a company. It does not prevent the company dealing with the assets in the ordinary course of business. Such a charge is useful when a company has no fixed assets such as land, but does have a large and valuable stock in trade.

  The law does not permit partnerships or individuals to secure loans with a floating charge.

- **Taxation**

  Because a company is legally separate from its members, it is taxed separately from its members. Tax payable by companies is known as *corporation tax*. Partners and sole traders are personally liable for income tax on the profits made by their businesses.

1.7 Disadvantages of incorporation

The disadvantages of being a limited company arise principally from the restrictions imposed by the *Companies Act 1985*.

- **Formalities, publicity and expenses**

  When they are being formed, companies have to register and to file a Memorandum and Articles of Association (formal constitution documents) with the Registrar. Registration fees and legal costs have to be paid.

The accounts of larger limited companies are subject to an annual audit inspection (this requirement has been lifted for small companies). The costs associated with this can be high. Partnerships and sole traders are not subject to this requirement unless as members of professional bodies whose own rules apply.

A registered company's accounts and certain other documents are open to public inspection. The accounts of sole traders and partnerships are not open to public inspection.

- **Capital maintenance**

  Limited companies are subject to strict rules in connection with the introduction and withdrawal of capital and profits.

- **Management powers**

  Members of a company may not take part in its management unless they are directors, whereas all partners are entitled to share in management, unless the partnership agreement provides otherwise.

2 *Types of non-profit making entities*

2.1 *Introduction*

The main types of non-profit making entity are:

- clubs and societies
- charities
- public sector organisations (including central government, local government and National Health Service bodies).

2.2 *Objectives of profit making and 'not for profit' entities compared*

The main objective of sole traders, partnerships and limited companies is normally assumed as being to make a profit.

The main objective of charities, clubs and societies is to carry out the activities for which they were created. In order to do this, they need to attract or generate sufficient income to cover their expenditure, including administration costs. A large surplus of income over expenditure in the accounts of a charity is normally regarded as a bad sign, as it suggests that donors' money is not being used for the purpose for which it was intended.

The main objective of public sector organisations is to provide services to the general public. Like charities, their long term aim is normally to break even, rather than to generate a surplus. Most public sector organisations aim to provide value for money which is usually analysed into the three Es – economy, efficiency and effectiveness.

2.3 Other differences between profit making and non-profit making entities

These are summarised in the table below:

	Profit making	Clubs, societies, charities	Public sector
Managed by:	Sole traders, partners, directors (who may also be shareholders)	Depends on constitution/other internal regulations	Elected officials, eg MPs, councillors
Main sources of finance	Personal capacity, equity, debt	Donations, membership fees	Taxation
Stewardship responsibilities to: (likely to be main users of financial statements)	Shareholders	Members, donors, beneficiaries	The general public
Financial statements used to assess:	Financial performance, whether to hold or sell investment	Whether resources have been used efficiently to achieve objectives	Level of spending in relation to services provided, whether services provide value for money, whether services have been provided economically efficiently, effectively

2.4 Accounts of non-profit making entities

Most non-profit making entities prepare a statement of financial performance (the equivalent of a profit and loss account for a profit making entity) and a balance sheet. Many entities also prepare a cash flow statement. Increasingly, non-profit making entities are adopting commercial style accounting practices, so that the basic principles used to prepare accounts are very similar to those used by a profit making entity. This is particularly true of the public sector. Many charities are companies and must therefore comply with the accounting requirements of the Companies Act.

3 Preparing final accounts

3.1 Introduction

Final accounts are the end result of a process of summarising, classifying and structuring large quantities of data. The objective of preparing final accounts is to turn individual transactions into useful information.

3.2 Process of preparing final accounts

Whether the accounts are being prepared for a sole trader, a partnership or a limited company, the steps in the process are basically the same.

Stage 1	Source documents	♦ Invoices, cheques, petty cash vouchers, other
Stage 2	↓ Summarise in books of prime entry	♦ Day books, cash books, journal book, wages book
Stage 3	↓ Enter totals in ledgers	♦ Nominal ledger, cash account, debtors' ledger control account, creditors' ledger control account, individual accounts in sales and purchases ledger
Stage 4	↓ Reconciliations	♦ Cash book to bank statement, control accounts to list of balances, fixed asset accounts to fixed asset register
Stage 5	↓ Prepare a trial balance	
Stage 6	↓ Adjustments	♦ To clear suspense account, to correct any other errors
Stage 7	↓ Extended trial balance	♦ Adjustments for depreciation, accruals, pre-payments, closing stock, correction of errors
Stage 8	↓ Adjustments	♦ For corporation tax, dividends, revaluations, to change accounting treatment of items, to provide for any further accruals/prepayments, to correct any further errors discovered
Stage 9	↓ Draft profit and loss account and balance sheet	

The first few stages should be familiar to you as you have covered them in your earlier studies. In this chapter we will concentrate on the later stages, in particular:

- making final adjustments
- drafting the final accounts

3.3 The profit and loss account of a sole trader

The *profit and loss account* is a summary of a business' transactions for a given period. In practice, as you will see from the following pro forma, it is commonly split into two parts and referred to as a *trading and profit and loss account.*

Pro forma trading and profit and loss account for the year ended ...

			£	£
①	**Sales**			X
	Less:	**Cost of sales**		
		Stock, at cost on 1 January (opening stock)	X	
		Add: Purchases of goods	X	
			X	
	Less:	Stock, at cost on 31 December (closing stock)	(X)	
				(X)
②	**Gross profit**			X
	Sundry income:			
		Discounts received	X	
		Commission received	X	
		Rent received	X	
				X
				X
	Less:	Other expenses:		
		Rent	X	
		Rates	X	
		Lighting and heating	X	
		Telephone	X	
		Postage	X	
		Insurance	X	
		Stationery	X	
		Office salaries	X	
		Depreciation	X	
		Accountancy and audit fees	X	
		Bank charges and interest	X	
		Bad and doubtful debts	X	
		Delivery costs	X	
		Van running expenses	X	
		Advertising	X	
		Discounts allowed	X	
				(X)
	Net profit			X

① - **Trading account**
② - **Profit and loss account**

3.4 Explanations

- The *trading account* discloses the *gross profit* generated by the business by comparing sales with the cost of those sales. A shopkeeper, for example, will purchase for resale items from various suppliers (wholesalers); by adding a profit margin to this cost, the selling price of the goods will be computed and this margin is the *gross profit*.
- *Cost of sales* is calculated by taking the cost of the goods available for sale during the year (ie opening stock plus purchases) and deducting the cost of the goods which were unsold (ie closing stock). Sales and cost of goods sold relate to the *same* number of units.
- The *profit and loss account* shows other items of income and expenditure earned or incurred by the business, in order to arrive at *net profit*.
- In a manufacturing industry, further analysis is needed of the figure for cost of sales. This is dealt with later in this book. Similarly, service industries may have different ways of defining goods and net profit.

3.5 The balance sheet of a sole trader

The *balance sheet* is a statement of the financial position of a business at a given date, usually the end of the period covered by the *profit and loss account*. It is a snapshot at one given moment.

Pro forma balance sheet at ......

	Cost	Depreciation	
	£	£	£
Fixed assets			
Freehold factory	X	X	X
Machinery	X	X	X
Motor vehicles	X	X	X
	X	X	X
Current assets			
Stocks		X	
Debtors	X		
Less: Provision for doubtful debts	(X)	X	
Prepayments		X	
Cash at bank		X	
Cash in hand		X	
		X	
Current liabilities			
Trade creditors	X		
Accrued charges	X		
		(X)	
Net current assets			X
			X
Long-term liabilities			
12% loan			(X)
Net assets			X
Representing:			
Capital at 1 January			X
Profit for the year			X
			X
Less: Drawings			(X)
Proprietor's funds			X

3.6 Explanations

- *Fixed assets:* Assets acquired for use within the business with a view to earning profits, but not for resale. They are normally valued at cost less accumulated depreciation.
- *Current assets:* Assets acquired for conversion into cash in the ordinary course of business; they should not be valued at a figure greater than their realisable value.
- *Current liabilities:* Amounts owed by the business, payable within one year.
- *Net current assets:* Funds of the business available for day-to-day transactions. This can also be called *working capital.*
- *Long-term liabilities:* Funds provided for the business on a medium to long-term basis by an individual or organisation other than the proprietor. Long-term liabilities are repayable in more than one year.

4 Making adjustments

4.1 Introduction

Adjustments to the initial trial balance, the extended trial balance and the draft accounts are made by drawing up and posting a *journal entry*.

4.2 Journals

In practice, journals may be used in several ways:

- to record major or unusual transactions;
- to record period-end adjustments (eg depreciation, stock, doubtful debts); and
- to facilitate the correction of errors, and to explain the nature of the errors.

Journals are recorded in the journal book. This is a book of prime entry and is not part of the double entry. From the journal book, the journals are posted to the relevant accounts in the nominal ledger.

4.3 Example

On 31 March 20X5 a company purchased a new motor vehicle for £20,000 in cash. How would this be recorded in the journal?

4.4 Solution

The double entry for this would be:

Debit:	Motor vehicles	£20,000	
Credit:	Cash		£20,000

This statement of the double-entry is itself known as a *journal*.

In the journal book, the transaction would be recorded as follows:

Date	*Narrative*	*Account No*	*Dr*	*Cr*
			£	£
31.3.X5	Dr Motor Vehicles	M1	20,000	
	Cr Cash	C41		20,000
	Purchase of new motor vehicle			
	(registration P666 BLR)			

4.5 Posting the journal

When period-end adjustments are made, the journal is drawn up and the trial balance or draft accounts are adjusted. These journals are not normally posted to the nominal ledger until the accounts have been finalised. The nominal ledger accounts are then balanced off and the new balances brought down for the start of the next accounting period.

4.6 Example

Flagg extracted the following trial balance from his ledgers at 31 March 20X4:

	£	£
Petty cash	48	
Capital		3,830
Drawings	3,360	
Sales		49,457
Purchases	37,166	
Purchases returns		504
Stock (1 April 20X3)	5,057	
Fixtures and fittings	1,704	
Debtors	4,366	
Sundry creditors		4,987
Carriage on purchases	262	
Carriage on sales	442	
Rent and rates	1,104	
Light and heat	180	
Postage and telephone	204	
Sundry expenses	456	
Cash at bank	4,328	
	58,677	58,778

The trial balance did not agree. On investigation, Flagg discovered the following errors:

(1) In extracting the schedule of debtors, the credit side of a debtor's account had been overcast by £24.

(2) An amount of £10 for carriage on sales had been posted in error to the carriage on purchases account.

(3) A credit note for £41 received from a creditor had been entered in the purchase returns book but no entry had been made in the creditor's account.

(4) £84 charged for repairs to Flagg's private residence had been charged, in error, to the sundry expenses account.

(5) A payment of a telephone bill of £51 had been entered correctly in the cash book but had been posted, in error, to the postage and telephone account as £15.

Required

Show the journal entries to correct the errors and set up the suspense account and show how it is cleared. Finally show the corrected trial balance.

4.7 Solution

The adjustments are as follows:

		Dr	Cr
		£	£
1	Debit Debtors	24	
	Credit Suspense account		24
	Being correction of undercast in debtor's account		
2	Debit Carriage on sales	10	
	Credit Carriage on purchases		10
	Being correction of wrong posting		
3	Debit Creditors	41	
	Credit Suspense account		41
	Being correction of omitted entry		
4	Debit Drawings	84	
	Credit Sundry expenses		84
	Being payment for private expenses		
5	Debit Postage and telephone	36	
	Credit Suspense account		36
	Being correction of transposition error		

Journals 1, 3 and 5 clear the suspense account:

Suspense account

	£		£
Difference per trial balance	101	Debtors	24
		Creditors	41
		Postage	36
	101		101

The trial balance is then corrected:

	Opening	*Adjustments*	*Dr*	*Cr*
	£	£	£	£
Petty cash	48		48	
Capital	(3,830)			3,830
Drawings	3,360	84	3,444	
Sales	(49,457)			49,457
Purchases	37,166		37,166	
Purchases returns	(504)			504
Stock at 1 April 20X3	5,057		5,057	
Fixtures and fittings	1,704		1,704	
Debtors	4,366	24	4,390	
Creditors	(4,987)	41		4,946
Carriage on purchases	262	(10)	252	
Carriage on sales	442	10	452	
Rent and rates	1,104		1,104	
Light and heat	180		180	
Postage and telephone	204	36	240	
Sundry expenses	456	(84)	372	
Cash at bank	4,328		4,328	
	(101)	101	58,737	58,737

5 The extended trial balance

5.1 Introduction

A **trial balance** is simply a list of all the balances on the ledger accounts *before* year-end adjustments are made. These adjustments need to be made before the preparation of the profit and loss account and balance sheet and they normally include the following:

- correction of errors
- recognition of accruals and prepayments
- provision of the year's depreciation charge
- review of the charge for bad and doubtful debts
- inclusion of closing stock

The **extended trial balance** is a worksheet which takes us from the trial balance to the profit and loss account and balance sheet.

Layout of a typical extended trial balance

Account	*Trial balance*		*Adjustments*		*Profit and loss account*		*Balance sheet*	
	Dr	*Cr*	*Dr*	*Cr*	*Dr*	*Cr*	*Dr*	*Cr*
	£	£	£	£	£	£	£	£

The names of the ledger accounts and the corresponding amounts per the trial balance are entered into the first three columns.

The adjustments columns are used for all of the year-end adjustments mentioned above.

5.2 Example

Trial balance at 31 December 20X6

	Dr	Cr
	£	£
Shop fittings at cost	2,000	
Depreciation provision at 1 January 20X6		100
Leasehold premises at cost	12,500	
Depreciation provision at 1 January 20X6		625
Stock in trade at 1 January 20X6	26,000	
Debtors at 31 December 20X6	53,000	
Provision for doubtful debts at 1 January 20X6		960
Cash in hand	50	
Cash at bank	2,250	
Creditors for supplies		65,000
Proprietor's capital at 1 January 20X6		28,115
Drawings to 31 December 20X6	2,000	
Purchases	102,000	
Sales		129,000
Wages	18,200	
Advertising	2,300	
Rates for 15 months to 31 March 20X7	1,500	
Light and heat	1,800	
Bank charges	200	
	223,800	223,800

The following adjustments are to be made:

(1) Depreciation of shop fittings £100
Depreciation of leasehold premises £625

(2) A debt of £500 is irrecoverable and is to be written off; the doubtful debts provision is to be increased to 2% of the debtors.

(3) Advertising fees of £200 have been treated incorrectly as wages.

(4) The proprietor has withdrawn goods costing £1,000 for his personal use; these have not been recorded as drawings.

(5) The stock in trade at 31 December 20X6 is valued at £30,000.

(6) The electricity charge for the last three months of 20X6 is outstanding and is estimated to be £400.

Prepare the extended trial balance at 31 December 20X6.

5.3 Solution

Step 1: The balances per the trial balance are recorded in the correct columns and the total of the debit balances is agreed to the total of the credit balances.

Step 2: We shall now deal with the adjustments (apart from accruals and prepayments).

- **Correction of errors**

  Two errors need to be corrected. One of the errors concerns the drawings of the proprietor, ie the fact that some of the purchases were bought for his own use. To correct this, we should decrease the purchases and increase the drawings, ie:

		£	£
Debit	Drawings	1,000	
Credit	Purchases		1,000

The other error concerns the mis-classification of advertising fees as wages. To correct this, the following adjustment is necessary:

Debit	Advertising	200	
Credit	Wages		200

- **Provision of the year's depreciation charge**

  The charge for the year is £725 and we need to charge this to the *depreciation expense* account and also to increase the *provision for depreciation,* ie. the accumulated depreciation carried forward. The double-entry is:

Debit	Depreciation expense: shop fittings	100	
Debit	Depreciation expense: leasehold premises	625	
Credit	Provision for depreciation: shop fittings		100
Credit	Provision for depreciation: leasehold premises		625

  We will need to set up the depreciation expense account as none exists.

- **Provision for doubtful debts**

  The debtors amount to £52,500 after the write-off of the bad debt of £500. A provision of £1,050 (£52,500 × 2%) is therefore required at 31.12.X6. The provision brought forward at the beginning of the year was £960; therefore it should be increased by £90 (1,050 - 960). The total charge to the profit and loss account is £590 (the debt written off plus the increase in the provision). The double-entry is:

Debit	Bad and doubtful debts expense	590	
Credit	Provision for doubtful debts		90
Credit	Debtors		500

  The bad debt expense account will need to be created.

- **Inclusion of closing stock**

  Closing stock appears in both the profit and loss account and the balance sheet.

  - In the profit and loss account, it is a reduction of cost of goods sold and hence is a *credit.*
  - In the balance sheet, it is an asset and hence is a *debit.*

  Accordingly we set up two stock accounts: one for the balance sheet and one for the profit and loss account. The adjustment is:

Debit	Stock (balance sheet)	30,000	
Credit	Stock (profit and loss account)		30,000

If you turn to the extended trial balance on the next page, you will see that each of these pairs of double-entry has been recorded in the adjustment columns. As the debit entries should always equal the credit entries, it is a useful check to cast the debit and credit adjustment columns to see that the totals are equal.

Step 3: We now have to deal with the last adjustments, ie. the accruals and prepayments.

- **Electricity**

  The profit and loss account charge for the year needs to be increased by £400 and a creditor for £400 must be established. The double-entry is:

Debit	Light and heat	400	
Credit	Accruals		400

  The accruals account will need to be set up.

- **Rates**

  The profit and loss account charge for the year should be £1,200 (12/15 × £1,500), and therefore there should be a prepayment of £300. The double-entry is:

Debit	Prepayments	300	
Credit	Rates		300

Step 4: We have now recorded all of the adjustments and we need to prepare the trading and profit and loss account and balance sheet columns. This is achieved by the following:

- Cross-cast each account and enter the total in the appropriate column of the profit and loss account or balance sheet columns. Some examples are as follows:

  - Fittings (2,000 + 0 = £2,000) are recorded in the *debit* column of the balance sheet.

  - Provision for depreciation on fittings (100 + 100 = £200) is recorded in the *credit* column of the *balance sheet.*

  - Purchases (102,000 – 1,000 = £101,000) is recorded in the *debit* column of the *profit and loss account.*

  Note: Accruals are added to the original trial balance amount whereas prepayments are subtracted.

- Add the debit and credit sides of the profit and loss account. The differences between these two columns is a profit (if the credits exceed the debits) or a loss (if the debits exceed the credits). The difference is recorded in the correct column of the profit and loss account (so that the two sides now balance) and the double-entry is with the balance sheet.

- Add the debit and credit columns of the balance sheet. These should agree unless you have made any errors.

Step 5: The trading and profit and loss account and balance sheet are then prepared from the relevant columns.

The completed extended trial balance is shown below:

Extended trial balance at 31 December 20X6

Account	*Trial balance*		*Adjustments*		*Profit and loss account*		*Balance sheet*	
	Dr	*Cr*	*Dr*	*Cr*	*Dr*	*Cr*	*Dr*	*Cr*
	£	£	£	£	£	£	£	£
Shop fittings	2,000						2,000	
Provision for depreciation 1.1.X6		100		100				200
Leasehold premises	12,500						12,500	
Provision for depreciation 1.1.X6		625		625				1,250
Stock 1.1.X6	26,000		30,000	30,000	26,000	30,000	30,000	
Debtors	53,000			500			52,500	
Provision for doubtful debts 1.1.X6		960		90				1,050
Cash in hand	50						50	
Cash at bank	2,250						2,250	
Creditors		65,000						65,000
Capital		28,115						28,115
Drawings	2,000		1,000				3,000	
Purchases	102,000			1,000	101,000			
Sales		129,000				129,000		
Wages	18,200			200	18,000			
Advertising	2,300		200		2,500			
Rates	1,500			300	1,200			
Light and heat	1,800		400		2,200			
Bank charges	200				200			
Depreciation - shop fittings			100		100			
Depreciation - leasehold premises			625		625			
Bad debts expense			590		590			
Prepayments			300				300	
Accruals				400				400
					152,415	159,000		
Net profit					6,585			6,585
	223,800	223,800	33,215	33,215	159,000	159,000	102,600	102,600

The trading and profit and loss account and balance sheet are now drafted from the extended trial balance. (For the purpose of this example, we are assuming that there are no further adjustments to the extended trial balance; in practice, this might not be the case. Any further adjustments would be made by drawing up and posting journal entries, exactly as before.)

Trading and profit and loss account for the year ended 31 December 20X6

		£	£
Sales			129,000
Less:	Cost of sales		
	Opening stock	26,000	
	Purchases	101,000	
		127,000	
	Closing stock	(30,000)	
			(97,000)
Gross profit			32,000
Less:	Expenses		
	Wages	18,000	
	Advertising	2,500	
	Rates	1,200	
	Light and heat	2,200	
	Bank charges	200	
	Depreciation (100 + 625)	725	
	Bad debts	590	
			(25,415)
Net profit			6,585

Balance sheet at 31 December 20X6

		Cost	*Accumulated depreciation*	*Net book value*
		£	£	£
Fixed assets				
	Shop fittings	2,000	200	1,800
	Leasehold premises	12,500	1,250	11,250
		14,500	1,450	13,050
Current assets				
	Stocks		30,000	
	Debtors (52,500 – 1,050)		51,450	
	Prepayments		300	
	Cash at bank		2,250	
	Cash in hand		50	
			84,050	
Current liabilities				
	Creditors	65,000		
	Accruals	400		
			(65,400)	
Net current assets				18,650
				31,700
Represented by:				
Capital				28,115
Add:	Net profit for the year			6,585
				34,700
Less:	Drawings			(3,000)
				31,700

Activity 1 (The answer is in the final chapter of this book)

Sandro Venus

Data

You have been asked by Sandro Venus to assist in the preparation of the year end financial statements of his business. He is a sole trader who runs a trading business which specialises in ornaments decorated with sea shells. The trial balance as at 31 March 20X7 is set out below, and the extended trial balance is continued on the next page.

Description	*Trial balance*	
	Debit	*Credit*
	£	£
Wages and National Insurance Contributions	28,996	
Capital as at 1 April 20X6		83,696
Postage and stationery	524	
Accumulated depreciation - Motor vehicles		8,125
Accumulated depreciation - Office equipment		1,375
Accumulated depreciation - Fixtures & fittings		2,780
Purchases	103,742	
Trade creditors		17,725
Carriage inwards	923	
Motor vehicles (cost)	32,500	
Office equipment (cost)	13,745	
Fixtures & fittings (cost)	27,800	
Sales		187,325
Returns outwards		1,014
Trade debtors	18,740	
Drawings	14,400	
Depreciation - Motor vehicles		
Depreciation - Office equipment		
Depreciation - Fixtures & fittings		
Prepayments		
Accruals		
Stock	27,931	
Returns inwards	1,437	
Cash at bank	9,473	
Cash in hand	166	
Bank deposit interest		972
Carriage outwards	657	
Rent, rates and insurance	8,041	
Bad debts	830	
Discounts allowed	373	
Bank charges	693	
Telephone	3,524	
Lighting and heating	3,755	
Motor expenses	4,762	
Profit		
	303,012	303,012

Adjustments		*Profit and loss*		*Balance sheet*	
Debit	*Credit*	*Debit*	*Credit*	*Debit*	*Credit*
£	£	£	£	£	£
348		29,344			
					83,696
		524			
	6,094				14,219
	1,375				2,750
	2,780				5,560
		103,742			
					17,725
		923			
				32,500	
				13,745	
				27,800	
			187,325		
			1,014		
				18,740	
				14,400	
6,094		6,094			
1,375		1,375			
2,780		2,780			
320				320	
	1,131				1,131
30,229	30,229	27,931	30,229	30,229	
		1,437			
				9,473	
				166	
			972		
		657			
	320	7,721			
		830			
		373			
		693			
783		4,307			
		3,755			
		4,762			
		22,292			22,292
41,929	41,929	219,540	219,540	147,373	147,373

You are given the following further information.

1 A general provision for doubtful debts is to be set up at 5% of the year end debtors' balance.

2 During the year Sandro Venus took goods which had cost £500 for his own personal use in decorating his flat.

3 At the end of the year, one of the motor vehicles which had cost £5,500 and on which there was accumulated depreciation of £2,400 was sold for £3,500. Payment for the vehicle sold has not yet been received by Sandro Venus and no entry to reflect the sale has been made in the extended trial balance.

Task 1

Make additional adjustments you feel necessary to the balances in the extended trial balance as a result of the matters set out in the further information above. Set out your adjustments in the form of journal entries.

Note

Narratives are not required.

Task 2

Draft a profit and loss account for the year ended 31 March 20X7.

Task 3

Sandro Venus is considering whether to incorporate the business and has said that he will telephone you tomorrow for advice.

Prepare notes for the telephone conversation that will enable you to explain the difference between the legal status of a sole trader and that of a company in respect of:

(i) the liability of the owners for the debts of the business;
(ii) the legal identity of the business;
(iii) the regulation of the production of the financial statements for the business.

---

6 From trial balance to final accounts

6.1 Introduction

In the last paragraphs we saw how to prepare a profit and loss account and balance sheet from an extended trial balance. However it is more likely in an assessment that you will be required to prepare a set of final accounts from a trial balance and a given set of adjustments to the trial balance figures.

6.2 Additional problems

There are no major additional problems in doing this as the adjustments are the same as those encountered with an extended trial balance. However there are two aspects that you must be able to deal with:

- you must be able to work out which balances from the trial balance appear in the profit and loss account and which appear in the balance sheet;
- you must be able to put through the adjustments required without the adjustment column of the extended trial balance - this will either be done in workings or on the face of the profit and loss account and balance sheet if they are fairly straightforward.

6.3 Example

Set out below is the trial balance of Lyttleton, a sole trader, extracted at 31 December 20X5.

	Dr	*Cr*
	£	£
Capital account		7,830
Cash at bank	2,010	
Fixed assets at cost	9,420	
Provision for depreciation at 31 December 20X4		3,470
Debtors	1,830	
Stock at 31 December 20X4	1,680	
Creditors		390
Sales		14,420
Purchases	8,180	
Rent	1,100	
Electricity	940	
Rates	950	
	26,110	26,110

On examination of the accounts, the following information is obtained.

1 Depreciation for the year of £942 is to be charged.

2 A provision for doubtful debts of 3% of total debts is to be set up.

3 Purchases include £1,500 of goods which were bought for the proprietor's personal use.

4 Stock at 31 December 20X5 was £1,140.

5 The rent account shows the monthly payments of £100 made from 1 January to 1 November 20X5 inclusive. Owing to an oversight the payment on 1 December 20X5 was not made.

6 The rates account shows the prepayment of £150 brought forward at the beginning of 20X5 (and representing rates from 1 January 20X5 to 31 March 20X5) together with the £800 payment made on 1 April 20X5 and relating to the period from 1 April 20X5 to 31 March 20X6.

7 The electricity charge for the last three months of 20X5 is outstanding and is estimated to be £400.

Required

Prepare a trading and profit and loss account for the year ended 31 December 20X5 and a balance sheet as at that date.

Step by step approach

1 Read the requirements at the end of the question to see what it is you are required to do.

2 Draft out working papers as per the requirements, one complete page for each including a working paper.

Trading and profit and loss account for	**Balance sheet as at .....**	**Working Paper**

3 Now read through the information available using a highlighter to pick out key points. You may want to write down adjustments as you go.

4 Start with the profit and loss account. It is essential that you know the proforma off by heart. This will guide you through the information you need rather than letting all the information bombard you.

Lyttleton trading and profit and loss account for the year ended 31.12.X5

	£	£
Sales		14,420

Sales will always be the first figure. Pull it from the trial balance, put it in your trading account and tick the figure on your question to show you've used it.

Extract	*Dr* £	*Cr* £
Creditors		390
Sales		14,420 ✓
Purchases	8,180	

Repeat this to complete the trading account.

Remember that closing stock will come from your additional information and opening stock from the trial balance.

Also figures in the trial balance are affected by subsequent information as in note 3. Purchases in the trial balance include goods used by the proprietor – drawings. Use a bracket to show your adjustment - as below.

Lyttleton trading and profit and loss account for the year ended 31.12.X5

	£	£
Sales		14,420
Cost of sales		
Opening stock	1,680	
Purchases (8,180 – 1,500)	6,680	
	8,360	
Closing stock	(1,140)	
		(7,220)
Gross profit		7,200

Make sure you have ticked the figures you have used.

5 **Expenses**

Put a ruler on the first line of the trial balance. Is the balance an expense?

If no - move down a line.

If yes - refer to the additional information for adjustments, accruals and prepayments and include the total in the profit and loss account. Tick off and move down a line.

Repeat this until you have got to the bottom of the trial balance.

	£
Less: Expenses	
Rent (1,100 + 100)	1,200
Electricity (940 + 400)	1,340
Rates (950 - ¼ × 800)	750

As you can see, each trial balance figure had an adjustment – accruals for rent (note 5) and electricity (note 7) and a prepayment for rates (note 6).

6 Now go through the additional information for further expenses.

	£
Depreciation	942
Bad debt expense (3% × 1,830)	55

Your final trading and profit and loss account should look like:

Lyttleton trading and profit and loss account for year ended 31 December 20X5

	£	£
Sales		14,420
Cost of sales		
Opening stock	1,680	
Purchases (8,180 – 1,500)	6,680	
	8,360	
Less: Closing stock	(1,140)	
		(7,220)
Gross profit		7,200
Less: Expenses		
Rent (1,100 + 100)	1,200	
Electricity (940 + 400)	1,340	
Rates (950 - ¼ × 800)	750	
Depreciation	942	
Bad and doubtful debts (3% × 1,830)	55	
		(4,287)
Net profit		2,913

7 Now check your question.

The only balances not ticked should be balance sheet accounts and all of the additional information has been dealt with – or has it?

Remember every transaction has two impacts: one debit, one credit. Consider the opposite side of each of those adjustments before we move onto the balance sheet.

The link between the profit and loss account and the balance sheet is the profit for the year. Transfer this figure across first.

	£
Capital at 1.1.X5	
Profit for the year	2,913
Less: Drawings	

It is now easy to slot in the two remaining figures to get the total for your balance sheet.

Remember the purchases adjustment.

	£
Capital as at 1.1.X5	7,830
Profit for the year	2,913
	10,743
Less: Drawings	(1,500)
	9,243

8 Start at the top of the balance sheet with fixed assets and follow the proforma down pulling information from the question as you need it.

Lyttleton balance sheet as at 31.12.X5

	Cost £	*Depn* £	£
Fixed assets	9,420	4,412 (W1)	5,008

Working Paper

W1 *Depreciation*

Trial balance	3,470
Charge for the year	942
	4,412

It is important to show how figures are made up. Using brackets, as in the profit and loss account, is a good option where space allows. Where it would clutter an answer, use your working paper but remember to cross reference.

Lyttleton balance sheet as at 31.12.X5

	Cost £	*Depn* £	£
Fixed assets	9,420	4,412	5,008
Current assets			
Stocks		1,140	
Debtors	1,830		
Provision for doubtful debts	(55)		
		1,775	
Prepayments		200	
Cash		2,010	
		5,125	
Current liabilities			
Creditors	390		
Accruals (100 + 400)	500		
		(890)	
Net current assets			4,235
			9,243

As you can see, a lot of the balance sheet figures come from the additional information.

Your complete balance sheet should be as below.

Lyttleton balance sheet as at 31 December 20X5

	Cost	*Depn*	
	£	£	£
Fixed assets	9,420	4,412	5,008
Current assets			
Stocks		1,140	
Debtors	1,830		
Provision for doubtful debts	(55)		
		1,775	
Prepayments		200	
Cash		2,010	
		5,125	
Current liabilities			
Creditors	390		
Accruals (100 + 400)	500		
		(890)	
Net current assets			4,235
			9,243
Capital as at 1.1.X5			7,830
Profit for the year			2,913
			10,743
Less: Drawings			(1,500)
			9,243

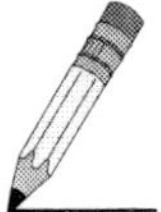

Activity 2 *(The answer is in the final chapter of this book)*

Given below is the trial balance of a sole trader's business as at 31 March 20X5:

	£	£
Motor vans	25,700	
Motor vans - accumulated depreciation		6,460
Sales		106,080
Purchases	58,760	
Debtors	8,840	
Creditors		4,940
Capital		20,740
Opening stock	5,460	
Discount received		130
Discount allowed	160	
Carriage inwards	570	
Carriage outwards	800	
Rent	1,250	
Heat, light and power	1,400	
Loan		5,000
Telephone	1,670	
Wages	25,220	
Motor expenses	1,700	
Drawings	10,400	
Bank	1,420	
	143,350	143,350

You also have the following additional information:

- the motor vans are being depreciated at a rate of 15% per annum straight line
- the stock at 31 March 20X5 is £6,100
- a bad debt of £240 is to be written off
- a provision for doubtful debts of 3% is to be set up
- purchases include £400 of goods which the owner has used for personal purposes
- the rent in the trial balance is for the 15 months ending 30 June 20X5
- a £200 bill for electricity was received just after the year end and has not been accounted for.

You are required to prepare the profit and loss account for the year ending 31 March 20X5 and the balance sheet at that date.

Activity 3 *(The answer is in the final chapter of this book)*

Given below is the trial balance at 30 June 20X4 for a sole trader.

	£	£
Motor vehicles at cost	75,000	
Fixtures and fittings at cost	18,400	
Motor vehicles - provision for depreciation		26,000
Fixtures and fittings - provision for depreciation		4,160
Bank	4,960	
Electricity	1,490	
Loan		12,500
Loan interest paid	550	
Capital		79,100
Carriage outwards	500	
Discount received		1,730
Sales		272,800
Opening stock	14,880	
Debtors	24,800	
Provision for doubtful debts		400
Wages	64,400	
Discount allowed	2,720	
Creditors		14,880
Rent	3,750	
Insurance	1,980	
Carriage inwards	990	
Drawings	22,000	
Purchases	175,150	
	411,570	411,570

You are also given the following information:

- closing stock has been valued at £19,800
- £50 of loan interest is to be accrued
- no depreciation charge has yet been accounted for for the year. The rates of depreciation are:
  - motor vehicles 20% reducing balance
  - fixtures and fittings 10% straight line

- a bad debt of £1,800 is to be written off and the provision for doubtful debts is to remain at 2% of debtors
- the rent is £250 per month payable quarterly in advance
- there is an insurance prepayment at the end of the year of £280

You are required to prepare the profit and loss account for the year ended 30 June 20X4 and a balance sheet at that date.

---

7 Quick quiz *(The answers are in the final chapter of this book)*

1 Is a limited company a separate legal entity?

2 What is meant by limited liability?

3 The top section of a profit and loss account, from sales to gross profit, has what name of its own?

4 Give four examples of current assets.

5 What is represented in the two most right-hand columns of an extended trial balance?

8 Summary

The journal is used to record period-end adjustments. Each journal entry must be accompanied by a narrative stating the nature of the transaction.

The extended trial balance is simply a worksheet showing the adjustments made to the figures in the trial balance to lead to the profit and loss account and balance sheet.

Procedure:

- Set out initial trial balance.
- Deal with adjustments.
- Deal with accruals and prepayments.
- Add the columns across into the 'profit and loss' and 'balance sheet' columns.
- Add the columns down and determine the net profit for the period.
- Prepare the profit and loss account and balance sheet from the relevant columns.

You must be ready to be required to prepare financial statements from a trial balance with a number of required adjustments. The trick here is to recognise which balances appear in the profit and loss account and which in the balance sheet.

CHAPTER 4

Preparing limited company accounts

ASSESSMENT FOCUS

For element 1 of this Unit you need to be able to draft the financial statements of a limited company. In this chapter we will consider the preparation of financial statements for limited companies and in the next chapter consider the legal and regulatory requirements for the presentation of those financial statements.

This chapter covers the following Knowledge and Understanding of the AAT Syllabus.

> The general legal framework of limited companies and the obligations of Directors in respect of the financial statements *(Element 11.1)*
>
> The forms of equity and loan capital *(Element 11.1)*
>
> The presentation of Corporation Tax in financial statements *(Element 11.1)*

In order to cover these the following topics are included.

> Types of limited company
> Proforma accounts for a limited company
> Debentures
> Share capital
> Types of share issue
> Types of reserves
> The profit and loss account
> Drafting limited company accounts

Key definitions

Debenture	Borrowings incurred by a company, acknowledged in writing, and normally carrying a fixed rate of interest and secured against assets owned by the company.
Ordinary shares	The normal type of shares. Dividends vary in size according to the profits available.
Preference shares	An unusual type of shares. A fixed dividend is paid, in priority to any ordinary dividends.
Share premium	Amount for which a share is issued over and above its nominal value.
Revaluation reserve	Reserve arising on revaluation of a company's fixed assets (usually property).

1 Distinctive features of limited companies

1.1 Differences between a sole trader and a limited company

A limited company is a separate legal entity and is distinct from its owners. This is in contrast to a sole trader who in law is *not* a separate entity from his business, even though he is treated as such for accounting purposes.

The key advantage of this is the *limited liability* that an investment in shares offers the shareholder. While a sole trader has unlimited liability for the debts of his business, shareholders have limited liability for the debts of the company in which they hold shares.

1.2 Types of limited company

There are two types of limited company, public and private. A public company must include in its name the letters 'plc' standing for public limited company. Private companies must include Limited or Ltd in their name. The main difference is that a private company may not offer its shares to the public and so all companies listed on the Stock Exchange are public companies.

1.3 Advantages and disadvantages of incorporated status

There are certain advantages and disadvantages associated with trading as a company rather than as a sole trader.

The advantages are as follows.

- If a company goes into liquidation the owners of the company (the shareholders) are only liable to pay any amounts that they have not yet paid for the shares that they hold. A sole trader would be personally liable for any outstanding debts of the business.
- The shareholders can share in the profits of the business without necessarily having to work day-to-day for the business.
- Companies are in a better position when borrowing money; for example they can issue debentures.
- The company will continue in existence even if shareholders die. If a sole trader dies the business will only continue if the business is sold.

The disadvantages are as follows.

- A large company must normally have an audit of its accounts and therefore must pay auditors' fees. However an audit also offers benefits to the company.
- A company must prepare its accounts in a format prescribed by legislation.
- A company suffers a greater administrative burden than a sole trader. For example, it must file its accounts each year with the Registrar of Companies and must hold an Annual General Meeting of its shareholders.

1.4 Accounting distinctions between a limited company and a sole trader

There are three main differences between the final accounts of a company and those of a sole trader.

- The way in which profit and tax are dealt with in the profit and loss account
- The composition of capital in the balance sheet
- The statutory requirements of the Companies Act 1985

We will look first at the non-statutory requirements, ie the accounts of a company ignoring the statutory formats. The accounts prepared by a company for its own internal use can be in any format that the managers choose. It is only the accounts filed publicly with the Registrar of Companies each year that have to follow the statutory formats. The statutory formats will be considered in the following chapter.

1.5 Proforma accounts

PROFORMA PROFIT AND LOSS ACCOUNT FOR A LIMITED COMPANY (FOR INTERNAL USE)

		£	£
Sales			X
Opening stock		X	
Add	Purchases of goods/transfers from factory	X	
		X	
Less	Closing stock	(X)	
Cost of sales			(X)
Gross profit			X
Sundry income			X
			X
Expenses (classified/listed as appropriate)			(X)
Operating profit			X
Interest payable			(X)
Profit before taxation			X
Taxation			(X)
Profit after taxation			X
Dividends	Paid	(X)	
	Proposed	(X)	
			(X)
Retained profit for the financial year			X
Retained profit brought forward			X
Retained profit carried forward			X

PROFORMA BALANCE SHEET FOR A LIMITED COMPANY (FOR INTERNAL USE)

		Cost	*Depreciation*	
		£	£	£
Fixed assets				
Freehold factory		X	X	X
Machinery		X	X	X
Motor vehicles		X	X	X
		X	X	X
Current assets				
Stocks			X	
Debtors		X		
Less	Provision for doubtful debts	(X)		
			X	
Prepayments			X	
Cash at bank and in hand			X	
			X	

Current liabilities			
Trade creditors	X		
PAYE, NIC and VAT	X		
Corporation tax	X		
Proposed dividends	X		
Accruals	X		
		(X)	
Net current assets			X
Total assets less current liabilities			X
Long-term liabilities			
Debenture loans			(X)
			X
Capital and reserves			
Share capital			X
Share premium account			X
Other reserves			X
Profit and loss account			X
			X

2 The balance sheet

2.1 Introduction

The major difference in the balance sheet of a company lies in the capital section, reflecting the differences in the nature of ownership of a company as compared with an unincorporated business.

2.2 Debentures

When we first met the balance sheet of a sole trader we saw that the proprietor was not necessarily the only person to invest in the business. It is quite common for such a business to have a medium or long-term loan provided by some person or organisation other than the proprietor.

The same will happen with a limited company in that it may well have a medium-term loan from the bank. However, in addition, a limited company can issue debentures.

A debenture is a written acknowledgement of a debt by a company. The debt referred to will be the borrowing of money usually for a number of years. This loan will normally carry a fixed rate of interest and may be secured against assets owned by the company.

The main difference between debentures and other long-term borrowings is that debentures may well be held by (ie the monies are owed to) a large number of people rather than one person or organisation. In that respect, they are similar to the share capital of a limited company which, as we will see, can be held by more than one person. Debentures are also similar to share capital in that a certificate will be held by the debenture holder saying that he owns £100 (say) of debentures in the company. This means that, like the share capital of a company, debentures can more easily be bought and sold, ie transferred.

2.3 Share capital

The ownership of a company is through shares, which have been issued by the company. For example, a company may have issued 1,000 shares for £1,000 to each of two businessmen who wish to operate their trading through a limited company. So far as the company is concerned the bookkeeping entries will be as follows.

Debit Cash
  Credit Share capital account

One important point, before we move on to a more detailed look at the different types of share capital, is that although the owners of those shares may change (for example one of the two businessmen may sell his shares to ten other members of his family) the company will not subsequently make any accounting change in its balance sheet although it does of course keep a register of shareholders.

2.4 Types of share

A company may issue different types (classes) of shares, by far the most important of which are as follows.

- *Ordinary shares*. The majority of companies will have only this type of share. Ordinary shareholders are effectively the owners of the company. If the company does well and makes profits, the ordinary shareholders can be paid dividends limited only by the amount of profits that have been made.
- *Preference shares*. Preference in this context means that the owners of these shares will have priority over the ordinary shareholders in the payment of their dividend, which is usually of a fixed amount.

  In addition, if the company winds up (ceases to exist as a legal entity) the preference shareholders will normally be repaid their capital before the ordinary shareholders.
- *Deferred shares*. These are rare. They have their dividends deferred until the preference shares are paid their fixed dividend and the ordinary shareholders have received a stated minimum dividend.

The difference between these three classes of shares is in essence the difference between the risk takers (the ordinary shareholders) whose reward will be geared to how well the company performs, and the non–risk takers (the preference shareholders) whose entitlement is fixed.

Companies with borrowings (such as long-term loans or debentures) or preference shares in their capital structure are said to have 'gearing', meaning that they have taken on a degree of financial risk. Even if the company's financial performance deteriorated badly, the company would still have to pay the annual interest charge and the preference dividend each year. If it was unable to pay these amounts, the company could be wound up. There is less risk associated with ordinary share capital, since there are no penalties directly associated with not paying an ordinary dividend in one year. Gearing is looked at in more detail in the later chapter covering the interpretation of financial statements.

2.5 Other definitions

There are various accounting terms to describe share capital: authorised, issued, called up and paid up.

(a) When a company is first established it must prepare a Memorandum of Association which will state the maximum amount of shares which the company is allowed to issue to its shareholders. This is the *authorised share capital* of the company.

(b) There is nothing to compel the company to issue to shareholders all of the shares which it is authorised to issue. The number of shares actually issued is known as the *issued share capital*.

(c) Once the company has asked its shareholders to pay for the shares it has issued to them, the shares are said to be *called up*.

(d) Once those shareholders have paid the company for the shares they are said to be *paid up*.

2.6 Share premium account

Each share in the UK has a nominal value, eg a company might have in issue 1,000 £1 shares. The share premium is the amount for which a share is issued over and above its nominal value. Thus if a share has a nominal value of £1 and it is issued for £1.50, 50p will be the share premium.

The amounts of share premium received by a company must be credited to a share premium account on the balance sheet.

2.7 Example

Enterprise Limited makes an issue of 10,000 £1 ordinary shares for £1.60 each. What are the accounting entries?

2.8 Solution

Debit Cash account £16,000

Credit Share capital account £10,000
Credit Share premium account £6,000.

The share capital account is only ever credited with the nominal value of the shares issued. Any excess over this nominal value must be credited to the share premium account.

2.9 Share capital and reserves

The share premium account is an example of a reserve on the balance sheet (see the proforma balance sheet above).

The total of share capital and reserves in a company's balance sheet is described as shareholders' funds. This is directly comparable with the proprietor's capital figure in a sole trader's balance sheet and represents the amount of capital subscribed and owned by the proprietors (in this case the shareholders).

2.10 Nominal value and market value

In the above example the nominal value (or par value or face value) of each share is £1.00 and the issue price is £1.60. This amount of £1.60 is probably the amount that each share is being traded at between individuals buying and selling the company's shares, ie the market value of each share.

There is no direct connection between the nominal value and the market value. The nominal value is fixed, while the market value varies.

A company will be concerned about its market value since the market value represents the value that the shareholders could get if they sold their shares.

The aim of any company should be to increase the value of its shares so as to increase the wealth of its shareholders. The market value of a share will reflect the value of the company's assets and its future profit generating capabilities.

Since shareholders who buy the shares of a company could have invested their money in a bank or building society account they will be interested to compare the return they can get from the bank or building society with that being given by the share.

The annual return on a share can be calculated as $\frac{\text{annual dividend}}{\text{current market value}} \times 100\%$

3 Types of share issue

3.1 Introduction

Once the initial shares in a company have been issued the company may, at a later date, wish to make further share issues.

3.2 Bonus issues

Sometimes, extra shares may be issued to existing shareholders without any more money having to be paid for them. Such an issue of shares is known as a bonus issue (or capitalisation issue). The extra shares will be issued to existing shareholders in proportion to their present shareholdings. Since no cash changes hands, the exercise is merely a bookkeeping one.

The accounting entries are as follows.

Debit		Reserves
	Credit	Ordinary share capital

With the nominal value of the bonus shares issued.

Advantages of a bonus issue are:

- As the market price of a share will fall after a bonus issue it can make the shares more marketable and so promote share purchases.
- Issued share capital is increased giving creditors greater protection.

The disadvantage of a bonus issue is that no cash is raised.

3.3 Example

AB plc has an authorised share capital of 2,000,000 ordinary shares of £1 each, and an issued and fully paid share capital of 600,000 ordinary £1 shares. At 30 June 20X8 its reserves amounted to £900,000. The company proposes to make a bonus issue of one share for every share held (a one for one bonus issue).

Required

Prepare an extract of AB plc's balance sheet immediately before and immediately after the issue of the bonus shares.

3.4 Solution

AB PLC BALANCE SHEET AT 30 JUNE 20X8

	Before	*After*
	£000	*£000*
Net assets (balancing figure)	1,500	1,500
Share capital		
Issued and fully paid: ordinary shares £1 each	600	1,200
Reserves	900	300
Shareholders' funds	1,500	1,500

3.5 Effect of a bonus issue

It can be seen from the above example that shareholders' funds are not changed by the bonus issue. However, the number of shares in issue and their total nominal value has increased by £600,000 (from £600,000 to £1,200,000), but the reserves have decreased by an equivalent amount (from £900,000 to £300,000). No change has taken place in the total value of the net assets.

The value per share on an asset basis has changed as a result of the bonus issue from

$$£2.50 = \frac{£1{,}500{,}000}{600{,}000 \text{ shares}}$$

to

$$£1.25 = \frac{£1{,}500{,}000}{1{,}200{,}000 \text{ shares}}$$

In this particular case (a one for one bonus issue) the asset value per share has halved. Each shareholder holds twice as many shares after the bonus as before the bonus and this means that, in terms of asset value, he has neither gained nor lost as a result of the bonus.

For example, a holder of 100 shares has a holding valued at £250 before the bonus issue (ie 100 shares at £2.50 each); after the bonus issue his holding is still worth £250 (200 shares at £1.25 each).

In practice the market value of a share is not linked exclusively to its asset value (asset backing) and it is probable that the market value will not fall to half of its original value as a bonus issue is often regarded favourably by the market. The resulting market value will therefore probably be slightly higher than half of the market value of the original shares.

3.6 Rights issues

A rights issue differs from a bonus issue in that the company actually raises cash through an additional issue of shares at a favourable price to the existing shareholders.

Existing shareholders are given the exclusive right to take up a new issue of shares at a specific price. The number of shares that they are entitled to take up will be in proportion to their existing holdings; for example, with a one for five rights issue, a shareholder with one hundred shares has the right to subscribe for twenty new shares. The issue price will normally be below the market price.

Advantages of a rights issue are:

- it is the cheapest way for a company to raise new finance using a share issue.
- it has a greater guarantee of acceptance than issuing to the public.

The disadvantage of a rights issue is the possibility that the issue may not raise all the capital required if the shareholders choose not to take up their rights.

3.7 Example

Z Ltd has 400,000 50p ordinary shares in issue and makes the following issues:

(i) Bonus issue of 100,000 50p ordinary shares.

The only available reserve is the profit and loss reserve of £460,000.

(ii) A rights issue of 100,000 50p ordinary shares at 80p per share. The issue is fully taken up.

Required

Show the entries in the relevant ledger accounts.

3.8 *Solution*

Share capital

	£		£	
		b/f (400,000 × 50p)	200,000	
		P&L account (100,000 × 50p)	50,000	W1
c/f	300,000	Bank (100,000 × 50p)	50,000	W2
	300,000		300,000	
		b/f	300,000	

Profit and loss reserve

	£		£
Share capital (100,000 × 50p)	50,000	b/f	460,000
c/f	410,000		
	460,000		460,000
		b/f	410,000

Bank

	£		£
Share capital	50,000		
Share premium	30,000		

Share premium

	£		£	
c/f	30,000	Bank (100,000 × 30p)	30,000	W2
	30,000		30,000	
		b/f	30,000	

Workings

1 Bonus issue: 100,000 shares at £0.50 = £50,000; transferred from the profit and loss account reserve.

2 Rights issue: 100,000 × £0.50 = £50,000 is entered in the share capital account.
100,000 × £0.30 = £30,000 is entered in the share premium account.

3.9 *Example*

XYZ plc has 2,000,000 25p ordinary shares in issue and its summarised balance sheet is given below.

	£000
Net assets	2,300
Capital and reserves	
Share capital	500
Reserves	1,800
	2,300

The company decides to make a rights issue of one for every five held at £1 each.

Required

Show the balance sheet after the rights issue is complete.

3.10 Solution

The rights issue will be 400,000 shares at £1 each and will raise cash of £400,000 which can be split between nominal value and premium as follows.

	£
Nominal value 400,000 × 25p	100,000
Share premium (75p each)	300,000
Cash	400,000

The new balance sheet will be as follows.

	£000
Net assets (2,300 + 400)	2,700
Capital and reserves	
Share capital (500 + 100)	600
Share premium	300
Other reserves	1,800
	2,700

3.11 Share issues compared to borrowing

The advantage is that no additional profits are required immediately to cover interest on financing.

The disadvantage is that a rights issue is usually more expensive to carry out than issuing debt.

3.12 Shareholders' options

A shareholder who receives a rights offer has three options open to him. These are as follows.

(a) Take up the rights and pay the required amount to the company, increasing his shareholding.

(b) Sell his rights to a third party who may then buy the shares from the company.

(c) Do nothing and let his rights lapse.

Option (a) above may be considered the normal course for a shareholder to follow, but shareholders may not wish to take up the offer, or may not be in a position to do so. In this case they would adopt (b) as their course of action.

3.13 Example

Mr Q owns 500 shares in XYZ plc which is making a rights issue on a one for five basis at £1 each.

The value of each share before the rights issue is £1.15 but this is expected to fall to £1.12½ after the rights issue has occurred. The rights can be sold for 12½p each (£1.12½ - £1.00).

Required

Show the options open to Mr Q.

3.14 Solution

Mr Q is entitled to 100 new shares in XYZ plc. He has the following options.

(a) Pay XYZ plc £100 for the new shares, increasing his holding to 600 shares.

(b) Sell his rights to 100 shares for £12.50 leaving his holding at 500 shares.

(c) Do nothing, leaving his holding at 500 shares (note that under this option he will lose the £12.50 available under option (b)).

4 Types of reserves

4.1 Introduction

Having looked at share capital we will now consider the different types of reserves a company might have.

4.2 Reserves

The assets and liabilities are shown on the top half of a balance sheet; the share capital and reserves are shown on the bottom half. 'Reserves' are therefore the excess of a company's net assets over its issued capital.

Reserves comprise:

- Revenue reserves
- Capital reserves

4.3 Revenue reserves

These comprise the cumulative total of the company's retained profits. In respect of each accounting period the retained profit for the year (at the bottom of the profit and loss account) will be added to revenue reserves; the double entry will be as follows.

Debit Profit and loss account
  Credit Reserves account

The company may well have more than one revenue reserve depending on the purpose for which the fund is intended, eg plant replacement reserve, general reserve etc. However, they all have one feature in common, namely that they represent the *retention* of an amount of profit by the company, as opposed to the *distribution* of that amount by way of dividend to its shareholders.

Appropriation of profits in a limited company

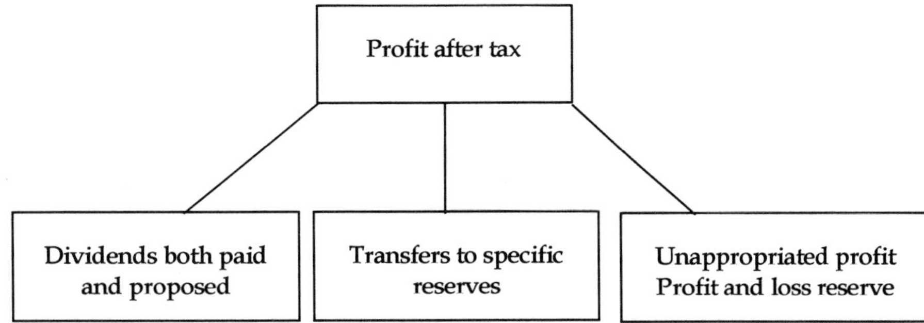

This shows the appropriation of profits firstly to shareholders then to specific named reserves and then finally the retained profits which go to the profit and loss reserve.

The heading 'profit and loss account' among the reserves on a balance sheet refers to the unappropriated profits balance to date.

4.4 Capital reserves

Some reserves are established in certain circumstances by law, for example:

(a) Share premium account.
(b) Revaluation reserve.

These may also be referred to as statutory reserves.

The balances on these capital or statutory reserves cannot legally be paid out in dividends, as opposed to revenue reserves which could legally be paid out in dividends if the directors wished.

5 The profit and loss account

5.1 Corporation tax

The figure for the corporation tax charge in a company's profit and loss account is a provision for tax based on the profits for the year. It does not represent the tax paid because, as you will see later in your studies, corporation tax is not payable immediately but nine months or more after the year end.

The accounting entries for the corporation tax payable for the year are as follows:

Debit Profit and loss account
Credit Corporation tax account (shown as a current liability in the balance sheet)

In the next year, when the tax is paid, the entry will be as follows:

Debit Corporation tax account
Credit Cash

5.2 Under or over provision for Corporation Tax

The tax charge for the year is an estimate of the tax charge that is due to be paid next year. If the amount actually paid in the following year is different to the estimate then there will be an under or over provision which remains on the corporation tax account and must be dealt with in the following year.

5.3 Example

For the year ended 31 December 20X1 the estimated corporation tax charge was £20,000. The actual payment made in 20X2 was only £18,000. Show the accounting entries relevant to this.

5.4 Solution

Corporation Tax

	£		£
20X2 Bank	18,000	31 Dec 20X1 P&L	20,000
Bal c/d	2,000		
	20,000		20,000
		Bal b/d	2,000

This was an over provision in 20X1 which will be used to reduce the 20X2 tax charge. The double entry being

		£	£
DR	Corporation tax	2,000	
CR	P&L		2,000

The reverse entry would be made for an under provision.

5.5 Dividends

As far as a sole trader is concerned, when they drew money from the business, the double-entry was as follows:

Debit Drawings account
  Credit Cash

However for a company, where there may be many hundreds of shareholders, it would be far from practical for each one of them to have a drawings account. A system of dividend payments is therefore used. The actual amount of dividend to be paid by a company will be determined by many factors, the main one being the need to retain sufficient profits to provide for the future working capital and fixed assets requirements of the company.

5.6 Interim dividend

Some companies pay an amount on account of the total dividend before the end of the year. This is known as an interim dividend. The bookkeeping entry is as follows:

Debit Dividend account
  Credit Cash

(The dividend account is closed off to the profit and loss account at the year end.)

5.7 Final dividend

It will only be at the end of the year, when the company's results for the whole accounting period are known, that the directors can declare a final dividend. As this event takes place after the year end the figure in the accounts will represent a provision or current liability. The entries for a proposed final dividend are therefore as follows:

Debit Profit and loss account
  Credit Dividends proposed account (shown as current liability)

Hence we will have two debits for dividends in the profit and loss account – one paid and one proposed.

6 Drafting accounts for internal purposes

6.1 Introduction

The example below allows you to apply all your knowledge of company accounting learnt to date, to prepare a set of accounts for a company for internal purposes (ie not in statutory formats).

6.2 Example

The following is the trial balance of Transit Ltd at 31 March 20X8.

	£	£
Issued share capital (ordinary shares of £1 each)		42,000
Leasehold properties, at cost	75,000	
Motor vans, at cost (used for distribution)	2,500	
Provision for depreciation on motor vans to 31 March 20X7		1,000
Administration expenses	7,650	
Distribution expenses	10,000	
Stock, 31 March 20X7	12,000	
Purchases	138,750	
Sales		206,500

Directors' remuneration (administrative)	25,000	
Rents receivable		3,600
Investments at cost (short-term)	6,750	
Investment income		340
7% Debentures		15,000
Debenture interest	1,050	
Bank interest	162	
Bank overdraft		730
Debtors and creditors	31,000	23,000
VAT control		1,100
Interim dividend paid	1,260	
Profit and loss account, 31 March 20X7		17,852
	311,122	311,122

You are given the following additional information.

- All the motor vans were purchased on 1 April 20X5. Depreciation has been, and is to be, provided at the rate of 20% per annum on cost from the date of purchase. On 31 March 20X8 one van, which had cost £900, was sold for £550, as part settlement of the price of £800 of a new van, but no entries with regard to these transactions were made in the books. Depreciation is charged on assets in the year of their disposal.
- The estimated corporation tax liability for the year to 31 March 20X8 is £12,700.
- It is proposed to pay a final dividend of 10% for the year to 31 March 20X8.
- Stock at the lower of cost and net realisable value on 31 March 20X8 is £16,700.

Required

Prepare, without taking into account the relevant statutory provisions:

(a) a profit and loss account for the year ended 31 March 20X8
(b) a balance sheet at that date.

6.3 Solution

Step 1

Get yourself organised. The requirements are a profit and loss account and balance sheet for Transit Limited. Draft proformas for both, leaving plenty of space to slot in detail and any missed headings. You will also probably need a page for workings.

TRANSIT LIMITED
PROFIT AND LOSS ACCOUNT FOR THE YEAR ENDED 31 MARCH 20X8

	£	£
Sales		
Cost of sales		
Gross profit		
Less: Distribution costs		
Administrative expenses		
Operating profit		
Investment income		

Profit before taxation
Corporation tax
Profit after taxation
Dividends
    Interim - paid
    Final – proposed

Retained profits for the year
Profit and loss account 1 April 20X7

Profit and loss account 31 March 20X8

BALANCE SHEET AT 31 MARCH 20X8

	Cost	*Dep'n*	
	£	£	£
Fixed assets			
Leasehold properties			
Motor vans			
Current assets			
Stock			
Debtors			
Investments			
Current liabilities			
Bank overdraft			
Creditors			
Corporation tax			
Proposed dividend			
Net current assets			
Total assets less current liabilities			
Long term liabilities			
Capital and reserves			
Share capital			
Reserves			

Workings

(W1) *Expenses*

Cost of sales	*Distribution costs*	*Administration expenses*
£000	*£000*	*£000*

Step 2

Read the question to establish the information available.

Step 3

Start with the profit and loss account and let the proforma guide you through the information you require.

Start with sales. Slot the figure in the proforma and tick it off on the trial balance.

Cost of sales will come from the expenses working so you will need to enter the cost of sales items from the information into the table.

TRANSIT LTD
PROFIT AND LOSS ACCOUNT FOR THE YEAR ENDED 31 MARCH 20X8

	£	£
Sales		206,500
Cost of sales (W1)		134,050
Gross profit		72,450
Less: Distribution costs (W1)	10,500	
Administrative expenses (W1)	32,650	
		43,150
Operating profit		29,300
Profit on sale of van (W3)		190
Investment income		340
Rental income		3,600
		33,430
Interest payable		
Bank interest	162	
Debenture interest	1,050	
		1,212
Profit before taxation		32,218
Corporation tax		12,700
Profit after taxation		19,518
Dividends		
Interim - paid	1,260	
Final – proposed (10% × £42,000)	4,200	
		5,460
Retained profits for the year		14,058
Profit and loss account 1 April 20X7		17,852
Profit and loss account 31 March 20X8		31,910

Note that when a dividend is expressed as a percentage the amount of the dividend is the percentage of the nominal value of the share capital.

Workings

(W1) *Expenses*

	Cost of sales £	*Distribution costs* £	*Administration expenses* £
Opening stock	12,000		
Purchases	138,750		
Closing stock	(16,700)		
Distribution costs		10,000	
Administration expenses			7,650
Depreciation (W2)		500	
Directors' remuneration			25,000
	134,050	10,500	32,650

(W2) *Depreciation*

	£
Motor vans cost	2,500
Disposal at cost	(900)
	1,600
Charge at 20%	320
Depreciation on disposed asset (£900 × 20%)	180
Total charge for year	500

(W3) *Profit on disposal of fixed assets*

Disposal account

	£		£
Motor van cost	900	Accumulated depreciation (£900 × 20%) × 3 years	540
Profit on disposal	190	Cash	550
	1,090		1,090

Step 4

Repeat the process for the balance sheet.

BALANCE SHEET AT 31 MARCH 20X8

	Cost £	*Dep'n* £	£
Fixed assets			
Leasehold properties	75,000	-	75,000
Motor vans (1,600 (W2) + 800)	2,400	960 (W4)	1,440
	77,400	960	76,440
Current assets			
Stock		16,700	
Debtors		31,000	
Investments		6,750	
		54,450	
Current liabilities			
Bank overdraft		730	
Creditors (W5)		23,250	
VAT control		1,100	
Corporation tax		12,700	
Proposed dividend		4,200	
		41,980	
Net current assets			12,470
Total assets less current liabilities			88,910
Long term liabilities			
7% Debentures			15,000
			73,910
Capital and reserves			
Ordinary shares of £1 each			42,000
Profit and loss account			31,910
			73,910

(W4) *Accumulated depreciation*

	£
Balance b/d	1,000
Disposed asset (W3)	(540)
	460
Charge for year (W2)	500
	960

(W5) *Creditors due within one year*

	£
Trade creditors	23,000
Balance due on new motor vehicle (£800 - £550)	250
	23,250

Activity 1 *(The answer is in the final chapter of this book)*

Pirbright

The bookkeeper of Pirbright Precision Ltd has extracted the following trial balance at 31 March 20X8.

	£	£
Administrative expenses	8,474	
Bank balance per cash book	715	
Creditors and accruals		7,855
Debentures		4,000
Debtors and prepayments	12,390	
Fixtures and fittings	2,280	
Motor vehicles	17,284	
Plant and machinery	16,327	
Premises	12,000	
Profit and loss account - balance at 1 April 20X7		7,613
Provision for depreciation:		
Fixtures and fittings		1,250
Motor vehicles		7,212
Plant and machinery		9,557
Premises		1,200
Purchases	66,751	
Sales		102,142
Selling and distribution expenses	2,610	
Share capital		20,000
Share premium account		5,000
Stock	9,880	
Taxation due at 1 April 20X7		1,400
Wages and salaries (all administrative)	18,518	
	167,229	167,229

The directors of the company suspect that some of the figures are incorrect, and further enquiry reveals the following.

(1) The bookkeeper has admitted that, originally, the trial balance did not agree, and to make it balance the difference has been entered in the administrative expenses account.

(2) Fixtures and fittings, which were purchased on 1 April 20X6 for £1,000, were sold for £400 on 12 January 20X8. The sale proceeds were credited to the fixtures and fittings account and the only other entry made in the books in respect of this disposal was to debit cash.

(3) No depreciation has been charged for the year ended 31 March 20X8. The company's depreciation policy is to take a full year's depreciation in the year of acquisition and none in the year of disposal at the following rates.

Fixtures and fittings	20% per annum on cost
Motor vehicles	25% per annum on reducing balance
Plant and machinery	10% per annum on cost
Premises	2% per annum on cost

Of the plant and machinery, items costing £4,000 in total had been acquired more than 10 years before 31 March 20X8.

(4) Payments of sales commission of £1,385 had been entered in the cash book, but not posted to the expense account. At 31 March 20X8 commission due but unpaid amounted to £230.

(5) The taxation liability for the year ended 31 March 20X7 was eventually agreed at £1,560. This amount was paid on 1 January 20X8 and debited to administrative expenses. The directors estimate the current year's liability to be £10,400.

(6) No account has been taken of bank charges debited to the company's bank statement on 31 December 20X7 of £187.

(7) The stock figure of £9,880 shown on the trial balance represented stock at cost at 31 March 20X8. This figure included £500 which had been taken by the company on sale or return and treated as a credit purchase. Stock at 1 April 20X7 was valued at £8,220.

After these adjustments had been made the final balance agreed.

Required

(a) Show by means of a suspense account how the original trial balance difference was made up.

(b) Prepare a profit and loss account for the year ended 31 March 20X8, together with a balance sheet at that date. **(22 marks)**

Activity 2 *(The answer is in the final chapter of this book)*

Collins

The following trial balance was extracted from the books of Collins Ltd at 31 December 20X8.

	£	£
Share capital authorised and issued:		
80,000 ordinary shares of £1 each		80,000
Freehold premises at cost	59,000	
Motor vans at cost (1 January 20X8)	15,000	
Additions less sale proceeds in year	650	
Provision for depreciation of motor vans to 31 December 20X7		6,750
Stock in trade 31 December 20X7	13,930	
Balance at bank	6,615	
Provision for doubtful debts 31 December 20X7		275
Trade debtors and creditors	12,395	11,380
Directors' remuneration	4,000	
Wages and salaries	13,127	
Motor and delivery expenses	3,258	
Rates	700	
Purchases	108,440	
Sales		142,770
Legal expenses	644	
General expenses	5,846	
Profit and loss account at 31 December 20X7		2,430
	243,605	243,605

You are given the following information.

(1) Stock in trade, 31 December 20X8, £14,600.

(2) Rates paid in advance, 31 December 20X8, £140.

(3) Debts of £1,075 to be written off and the provision to be increased to £350.

(4) On 1 January 20X8, a motor van which had cost £680 was sold for £125. Depreciation provided for this van up to 31 December 20X7 was £475.

(5) Provide for depreciation of motor vans (including additions) at 20% of cost.

(6) The balance on the legal expenses account included £380 in connection with the purchase of one of the freehold properties.

(7) The directors have decided to recommend a dividend of 5%.

Required

Prepare a trading and profit and loss account for the year 20X8 and a balance sheet at 31 December 20X8 ignoring taxation. **(24 marks)**

7 Quick quiz *(The answers are in the final chapter of this book)*

1 What is the difference between a private company and a public company?

2 What are the accounting entries for an issue of shares at their nominal value?

3 What are the accounting entries for an issue of 1,000 ordinary £1 shares for £3 each?

4 What are the accounting entries for a rights issue that involves issuing 10,000 new £1 ordinary shares raising a total of £18,000?

8 Summary

The accounts of a limited company differ in several ways from those of a sole trader.

- The inclusion of a tax charge
- The way in which profit is appropriated in the profit and loss account
- The composition of capital in the balance sheet
- The statutory requirements

You need to be familiar with the various types of share issues.

- Bonus issues
- Rights issues

CHAPTER 5

Statutory formats

ASSESSMENT FOCUS

For element 1 of this Unit you are required to draft a set of limited company financial statements so in this chapter we will consider how the financial statements of a limited company are prepared and the form and content of these financial statements.

This chapter covers the following Knowledge and Understanding of the AAT Syllabus.

> The general legal framework of limited companies and the obligations of Directors in respect of the financial statements *(Element 11.1)*
>
> The statutory form of accounting statements and disclosure requirements *(Element 11.1)*
>
> The presentation of Corporation Tax in financial statements *(Element 11.1)*
>
> Preparing financial statements in proper form *(Element 11.1)*

In order to cover these the following topics are included.

> The content of company financial statements
> The balance sheet
> Notes to the balance sheet
> The profit and loss account
> Notes to the profit and loss account
> Approach to preparing company accounts
> The directors' report
> Summary financial statements and abbreviated accounts

Key definitions

Statutory formats	Formats for the balance sheet and profit and loss account that companies must use in their published accounts, as required by the Companies Act 1985.
Turnover	Sales revenues, excluding VAT.
Directors' report	Commentary on the financial performance for the period, required by CA 85 to be included with the financial statements in the annual report.
Summary financial statements	Simplified set of statements that shareholders of listed companies can choose to receive rather than a full set of accounts.
Abbreviated accounts	Simplified set of statements that small and medium-sized companies can choose to file at Companies House rather than a full set of accounts.

1 Introduction to company accounts

1.1 The content of company accounts

The financial statements of a company comprise the following elements.

- Balance sheet and notes
- Profit and loss account and notes
- Statement of total recognised gains and losses
- Cash flow statement and notes
- Accounting policies note
- Comparative figures

1.2 Regulations governing company accounts

The main sources of regulations are the Companies Act 1985 (CA 85) and accounting standards.

CA 85 (Schedule 4) is the main source for the required formats and disclosures in the published profit and loss account and balance sheet.

Relevant accounting standards include FRS 1 (requirement for cash flow statement) and FRS 3 (requirement for statement of total recognised gains and losses). Additional disclosures are specified by other standards.

In this chapter, all balance sheet and profit and loss account requirements are from the Companies Act 1985 unless otherwise stated. Requirements of standards are indicated as such.

2 The balance sheet

2.1 Introduction

The CA 85 gives preparers a choice of two formats for the published balance sheet:

- Format 1 is a so-called vertical format, as illustrated below. This is by far the more common format, and should always be used unless you are instructed otherwise.
- Format 2 lists out first all the assets, then the capital and reserves, then the liabilities. This would allow the balance sheet to be presented in a horizontal format, with the assets and the credit balances shown side-by-side of each other.

2.2 Format 1

Note		£	£
	Fixed assets		
1 (a)	Intangible assets		X
1 (b)	Tangible assets		X
2	Investments		X
			X
	Current assets		
3	Stocks	X	
4	Debtors	X	
2	Investments	X	
	Cash at bank and in hand	X	
		X	
5	*Creditors: amounts falling due within one year*	(X)	
	Net current assets		X
	Total assets less current liabilities		X

6	*Creditors: amounts falling due after more than one year*	(X)
8	*Provisions for liabilities and charges*	(X)
9	*Accruals and deferred income*	(X)
		X
	Capital and reserves	
10	Called up share capital	X
11	Share premium account	X
11	Revaluation reserve	X
11	Other reserves	X
11	Profit and loss account	X
		X

2.3 Further requirements

(i) As well as the balance sheet figures for this year, comparative figures as at the previous year-end must also be shown in a statutory balance sheet. Any line item with a nil value this year and the previous year need not be shown on the balance sheet.

(ii) Prepayments could either be shown amongst debtors or as a separate line item after "Cash at bank and in hand".

(iii) FRS 4 requires the total of shareholders' funds (ie the total at the bottom of the balance sheet) to be split between equity funds (belonging to ordinary shareholders) and non-equity funds (belonging to preference shareholders, if any).

(iv) SSAP 17 requires that the date on which the directors approved the accounts must be disclosed. This information is normally provided immediately following the balance sheet.

(v) The numbers of the notes to the balance sheet are not fixed. Notes are included to give additional details of the composition of any of the amounts included in the balance sheet.

3 Notes to the balance sheet

3.1 Introduction

In this section we list the notes required and, where relevant, provide an illustration of each.

3.2 Intangible fixed assets

Capitalised development costs – disclose:

- reasons for capitalisation
- write-off period.

Acquired goodwill – disclose:

- write-off period
- reason for period chosen.

3.3 Tangible fixed assets

The following details of cost or valuation must be disclosed.

- Opening balance
- Movements (additions, disposals, revaluations, transfers)
- Closing balance

The following details of accumulated depreciation must be disclosed.

- Opening balance
- Movements (disposals, charge for year, transfers, revaluations)
- Closing balance

Land and buildings: disclose the following categories separately.

- Freeholds
- Long leaseholds (at least 50 years to run)
- Short leaseholds (less than 50 years to run)

In relation to fixed assets at valuation, disclose the following.

- Years and amounts of valuation
- If valued during the year, the name or qualification of the valuers and the basis of valuation
- Comparable historical cost (HC) amounts or differences between HC and carrying amounts

3.4 Investments

In relation to *all types of investments*, disclose:

- amounts written off
- amounts written back
- fixed asset details, if the investments rank as fixed assets (short-term investments rank as current assets).

Investments in participating interests must be shown separately. These are broadly investments comprising 20% to 50% of the shares in the investee. If an investment comprises more than 50% of the investee's shares, that investee is a subsidiary of the investing company.

In relation to *listed investments* only, disclose:

- market value, if this is different from book value
- stock exchange value, if this is less than market value
- the amount of tax that would be payable if the investments were sold at valuation

3.5 Illustration

These requirements relating to fixed assets are exemplified in the following illustration.

Intangible assets

	Goodwill	*Licences*	*Total*
	£000	£000	£000
Cost			
At 1 April 20X5 and 31 March 20X6	X	X	X
Amortisation			
At 1 April 20X5	X	X	X
Provision for year	X	X	X
At 31 March 20X6	X	X	X
Net book amount			
At 1 April 20X5	X	X	X
At 31 March 20X6	X	X	X

Tangible assets

	Land and buildings				
	Freehold	Long Lease	Short Lease	Plant and Machinery	Total
	£000	£000	£000	£000	£000
Cost or valuation					
At 1 April 20X5	X	X	X	X	X
Revaluation	X	-	-	-	X
Additions	X	X	X	X	X
Disposals	(X)	(X)	(X)	(X)	(X)
At 31 March 20X6	X	X	X	X	X
Depreciation					
At 1 April 20X5	X	X	X	X	X
Disposals	(X)	(X)	(X)	(X)	(X)
Provision for year	X	X	X	X	X
At 31 March 20X6	X	X	X	X	X
Net book amount					
At 1 April 20X5	X	X	X	X	X
At 31 March 20X6	X	X	X	X	X

A freehold site was revalued during the year by Messrs Tottitup Chartered Surveyors, on the basis of its current use as a parking lot. If the site were sold for its revalued amount, it is estimated that tax of £X would be payable on the gain.

The historical cost of the site was £Z and it was revalued to £Y. No provision for depreciation has been made.

Investments

	Shares in group undertakings	Participating Interests	Loans to undertakings in which the company has a participating interest	Other investments other than loans	Total
	£000	£000	£000	£000	£000
Cost					
At 1 April 20X5	X	X	-	X	X
Transfers	X	(X)	-	-	-
Additions	X	-	X	-	X
Disposals	(X)	-	-	-	(X)
At 31 March 20X6	X	X	X	X	X
Listed investments at cost					X
Market value of listed investments					X

Taxation of £X would be payable if the investments were sold at market value.

3.6 Stocks

Separate disclosure is required of raw materials, work in progress and finished goods. Disclose also the difference between carrying value and replacement costs for each category, if material.

3.7 Illustration

Stocks

	£000
Raw materials	X
Work in progress	X
Finished goods	X
	X

3.8 Debtors

The main categories to be disclosed separately are: trade debtors, other debtors, and prepayments and accrued income. Distinguish between debts falling due within one year of the balance sheet date and debts due more than one year after the balance sheet date.

3.9 Illustration

Debtors

	£000
Trade debtors	X
Other debtors	X
Prepayments and accrued income	X
	X

Included in other debtors is an amount of £X which is not recoverable until 30 September 20X8.

3.10 Creditors

The main categories are shown in the illustration below. Creditors falling due within one year are shown separately from those falling due after more than one year.

Under 'other creditors including tax and social security', show amounts for tax and social security separately.

Show the following details in relation to secured creditors.

- Type
- Amount
- Nature of security.

In relation to debts not wholly payable within five years, disclose:

- the amount payable by instalment
- the amount payable otherwise than by instalment
- the repayment terms
- the rates of interest.

In relation to debentures issued in the year, state:

- the classes issued
- the amount issued and the consideration received by class.

Debentures which are convertible should be disclosed as such.

3.11 Illustration

Creditors: amounts falling due within one year

	£000
Debenture loans	X
Bank loans and overdrafts	X
Payments received on account	X
Trade creditors	X
Bills of exchange payable	X
Amounts owed to group undertakings	X
Amounts owed to undertakings in which the company has a participating interest	X
Other creditors including taxation and social security	X
Obligations under finance leases and hire purchase contracts	X
Accruals and deferred income	X
	X

Loans not wholly repayable within five years

	£000
Repayable by instalments	X
Repayable otherwise	X
	X

Details of loans not wholly repayable within five years are as follows.

	£000
X% debentures repayable in annual instalments of £X commencing 31 December 20XX	X
X% secured loan repayable in annual instalments of £X commencing 31 December 20XX	X
X% secured US dollar loan repayable on 31 May 20XX	X
	X

The long-term bank loans are secured by fixed charges over various of the group's properties. Bank loans wholly repayable within five years include £X secured by a floating charge over the company's assets.

3.12 Provisions for liabilities and charges

Disclose the deferred tax balance and any other provisions.

3.13 Illustration

Provisions for liabilities and charges

	Deferred tax	*Other provisions*	*Total*
	£000	£000	£000
At 1 April 20X5	X	X	X
Movement	X	(X)	X
At 31 March 20X6	X	X	X

3.14 Called up share capital

Disclose the amount of *authorised* share capital.

For each class of *allotted* share capital, disclose:

- number of shares
- total nominal value

In relation to redeemable shares, disclose:

- earliest and latest redemption dates
- whether redemption is at shareholder's or company's option.
- premium payable on redemption.

In relation to shares allotted during the year, disclose:

- the classes of shares allotted
- for each class, the number of shares, their nominal value and the consideration received.

In relation to share options, disclose:

- the number, description and amount of shares under option
- the period of option
- the price.

3.15 Illustration

Called up share capital

	Authorised	*Allotted, called up, and fully paid*
	£000	£000
10% preference shares of £1 each	X	X
Ordinary shares of 50p each	X	X
	X	X

During the year, X ordinary shares with an aggregate nominal value of £X were issued fully paid for cash of £X.

The following options to acquire ordinary shares under the executive share option scheme were outstanding at 31 March 20X6.

	Number	*Price*
20X8	X	X
20X9	X	X

3.16 Example

The following trial balance has been extracted from the books of account of Oscar plc as at 31 March 20X8.

	£000	£000
Called up share capital (ordinary shares of £1 fully paid)		600
Debtors	400	
Prepayments	70	
Bank overdraft		80
Provision for pension costs		180
Listed fixed asset investments	560	
Plant and machinery		
At cost	750	
Accumulated depreciation (at 1 April 20X7)		145
Profit and loss (at 1 April 20X7)		180
Trade creditors		260
Profit for the year (subject to any items appearing in the following notes)		335
	1,780	1,780

Additional information

(1) Stock at 31 March 20X8 was valued at £150,000 and has been valued consistently at the lower of cost and net realisable value.

(2) Annual depreciation on plant and machinery is to be calculated at the rate of 10% on cost.

(3) The corporation tax charge based on the profit on ordinary activities is estimated to be £74,000.

(4) The provision for pension costs is to be increased by £16,000.

(5) The company's authorised ordinary share capital consists of 1,000,000 ordinary shares of £1 each.

(6) A final dividend of 50p per share is proposed.

(7) Additions have been made to plant costing £10,000.

(8) The market value of the listed fixed asset investments as at 31 March 20X8 was £580,000. There were no purchases or sales of such investments during the year.

(9) The directors have placed contracts for new plant costing £5,000 and have authorised further expenditure costing £10,000.

Required

Insofar as the information permits, prepare the company's published balance sheet at 31 March 20X8 in accordance with the Companies Act 1985. (Relevant notes are required, including a statement of accounting policies.)

3.17 Approach to the example

Read the requirements at the end of the question first of all.

Depending on the requirements, get yourself organised. You need to draw up a separate sheet of paper for each of the following.

- The balance sheet
- Notes to the balance sheet
- Workings

Remember to use the Companies Act 1985 format.

Leave plenty of empty space in case you miss something.

Let the format dictate the order of your workings.

To show you how the figures are built up, we begin by presenting the notes to the accounts.

Notes to the accounts

1 *Statement of accounting policies*

(i) The accounts have been prepared in accordance with applicable accounting standards.

(ii) Depreciation

Plant and machinery depreciation is charged at 10% per annum on cost.

(iii) Stock

Stock has been valued at the lower of cost and net realisable value.

2 *Tangible fixed assets*

Cost	*Plant and machinery*	*Total*
	£000	£000
Cost at 1 April 20X7	740	740
Additions	10	10
Cost at 31 March 20X8	750	750
Accumulated depreciation		
At 1 April 20X7	145	145
Charge for year (750 × 10%)	75	75
Accumulated depreciation at 31 March 20X8	220	220
Net book value at 1 April 20X7	595	595
Net book value at 31 March 20X8	530	530

Future capital expenditure

	£
Contracted for but not provided in the accounts	5,000
Authorised by the directors but not contracted for	10,000
	15,000

3 *Investments*

	£000
Listed investments at cost	560
Market value of listed investments	580

4 *Debtors*

	£000
Trade debtors	400
Prepayments and accrued income	70
	470

5 *Creditors: amounts falling due within one year*

	£000
Bank overdraft	80
Trade creditors	260
Tax	74
Dividend accrual (600 × 50p)	300
	714

The corporation tax and the proposed dividend must be accrued for in the balance sheet as they will be paid in the coming year.

6 *Provisions for liabilities and charges*

	Pension provision
	£000
At 1 April 20X7	180
Movement in year	16
At 31 March 20X8	196

7 *Called up share capital*

	Authorised	*Allotted and fully paid*
Ordinary shares of £1 each	1,000,000	600,000

8 *Profit and loss account*

	£000
Retained profit as at 1 April 20X7	180
Profit for the year (W1)	20
Retained profit as at 31 March 20X8	200

Workings

(W1) *Profit for the year*

		£000
As per trial balance		335
Add closing stock		150
Less:	Depreciation charge	(75)
	Increase in pension	(16)
	Dividend	(300)
	Tax	(74)
Retained profit for the year		20

You are now in a position to prepare the balance sheet.

BALANCE SHEET AS AT 31 MARCH 20X8

	Notes	£000	£000
Fixed assets			
Tangible assets	2		530
Investments	3		560
			1,090
Current assets			
Stocks		150	
Debtors	4	470	
		620	
Creditors: amounts falling due within one year	5	(714)	
Net current liabilities			(94)
Total assets less current liabilities			996
Provisions for liabilities and charges	6		(196)
			800
Capital and reserves			
Called up share capital	7		600
Profit and loss account	8		200
			800

Activity 1 *(The answer is in the final chapter of this book)* Homework for 19-11-03

Suzanne plc

Suzanne plc is a quoted company with an authorised share capital of £500,000 consisting of ordinary shares of £1 each. The company prepares its accounts as at 31 March each year and the trial balance extracted on 31 March 20X5 before final adjustments is as follows.

	£000	£000
Ordinary share capital, issued and fully paid		400
Retained profits on 1 April 20X4		122
6% debenture stock (secured on leasehold factory)		120
Leasehold factory	400	
Accumulated depreciation at 1 April 20X4		152
Plant and machinery	180	
Accumulated depreciation at 1 April 20X4		60
Creditors and accruals		340
Debtors	200	
Prepayments	160	
Bank	180	
Loss for the year (subject to any items in the following notes)	98	
Sale proceeds of plant		24
	1,218	1,218

Additional information

1 Plant was acquired in the year costing £20,000. This is included in the trial balance figure for plant and machinery.

2 Annual depreciation is to be calculated as follows.

Leasehold factory	2% on cost
Plant and machinery	20% reducing balance

A full year's charge is to be made on additions in the year with no charge in the year of disposal.

3 Plant was sold in the year. It had originally cost £32,000. Depreciation charged at the date of disposal was £6,400.

4 Stock at 31 March 20X5 is £320,000 and has been valued at the lower of cost and net realisable value.

5 A final dividend of 20% is proposed.

Required

Prepare a balance sheet as at 31 March 20X5, in a form suitable for publication. Notes to the accounts (including a statement of accounting policies) are required.

4 The profit and loss account

4.1 Introduction

The Companies Act permits four alternative formats for the profit and loss account: two vertical formats (Formats 1 and 2) and two horizontal formats (Formats 3 and 4, which are not commonly used in the UK). Format 1 is set out below, amplified where necessary by the requirements of FRSs.

4.2 Format 1

Notes		Continuing operations £	Acquisitions £	Discontinued operations £	Total £
1 (a)	Turnover	X	X	X	X
	Cost of sales	(X)	(X)	(X)	(X)
	Gross profit	X	X	X	X
	Distribution costs	(X)	(X)	(X)	(X)
	Administrative expenses	(X)	(X)	(X)	(X)
	Other operating income	X	X	X	X
2	Operating profit	X	X	X	X
	Profit on sale of fixed assets	X	X	X	X
	Loss on disposal of discontinued operations			(X)	(X)
	Profit on ordinary activities before interest	X	X	X	X
	Income from shares in group undertakings				X
	Income from participating interests				X
5	Income from other fixed asset investments				X
6	Other interest receivable and similar income				X
6	Interest payable and similar charges				(X)
1 (b)	Profit on ordinary activities before taxation				X
7	Tax on profit on ordinary activities				(X)
10	Profit for the financial year				X
8	Dividends				
	Preference dividend on non-equity shares			X	
	Ordinary dividend on equity shares			X	
					(X)
11	Retained profit for the financial year				X
9	Earnings per share				X

Tutorial notes on the above profit and loss account

(i) FRS 3 requires the profit and loss account from turnover to operating profit to be analysed between continuing operations, acquisitions and discontinued operations.

(ii) FRS 3 requires that any profit or loss on the sale of fixed assets, profit or loss on the sale of an operation, and costs of a fundamental reorganisation must be shown separately on the face of the profit and loss account after operating profit and before interest.

(iii) FRS 14 requires the earnings per share to be disclosed by listed companies on the face of the profit and loss account (normally as a figure of pence per share shown immediately below the profit and loss account).

4.3 Alternative presentation of Format 1

An alternative version of format 1 incorporates the FRS 3 analysis in part by way of a note – see below.

	£	£
Turnover		
Continuing operations	X	
Acquisitions	X	
	X	
Discontinued operations	X	
		X
Cost of sales		(X)
Gross profit		X
Distribution costs		(X)
Administrative expenses		(X)
Other operating income		X
Operating profit		
Continuing operations	X	
Acquisitions	X	
	X	
Discontinued operations	(X)	
Less provision in previous year	X	
		X
Profit on sale of fixed assets in continuing operations		X
Loss on disposal of discontinued operations	(X)	
Less provision in previous year	X	
		X
Profit on ordinary activities before interest		X

The profit and loss account then continues as previously. The analysis of cost of sales and expenses is provided in a note to the accounts using the familiar four-column layout.

4.4 Format 2

Format 2 of the profit and loss account is set out below.

Notes		*Continuing operations*	*Acquisitions*	*Discontinued operations*	*Total*
		£	£	£	£
1 (a)	Turnover	X	X	X	X
	Change in stocks of finished goods and work in progress	X	X	X	X
	Own work capitalised	X	X	X	X
	Other operating income	X	X	X	X
	Raw materials and consumables	(X)	(X)	(X)	(X)
	Other external charges	(X)	(X)	(X)	(X)
	Staff costs	(X)	(X)	(X)	(X)
	Depreciation and other amounts written off tangible and intangible fixed assets	(X)	(X)	(X)	(X)
2	Operating profit	X	X	X	X
	Profit on sale of fixed assets	X	X	X	X
	Loss on disposal of discontinued operations	-	-	(X)	(X)
	Profit on ordinary activities before interest	X	X	X	X

The profit and loss account then continues as previously. With regard to the FRS 3 analysis, the same alternative is available as for Format 1.

Tutorial notes on Format 2

(i) The analysis of staff costs between wages and salaries, social security costs and other pension costs can either be given on the face of the profit and loss account or in a note.

(ii) In practice Format 1 is more commonly used than Format 2, but it is possible that the assessor might require knowledge of Format 2.

4.5 Combining items in the profit and loss account

In both profit and loss account formats, the line items in the Act are preceded by arabic numerals (not Roman numerals). This means that they can be combined on the face of the profit and loss account and disclosed separately in the notes if this facilitates better presentation.

Despite this, some items must be disclosed on the face of the profit and loss account.

- Profit or loss on ordinary activities before taxation
- Transfers to reserves
- Dividends paid and proposed (aggregate amount)
- Earnings per share (listed companies only – a requirement of FRS 14).

Certain disclosures required by FRS 3 must also be shown on the face of the account (not by way of a note).

- Analysis of turnover and operating profit
- Profit or loss on sale or termination of operations
- Costs of a fundamental reorganisation
- Profit or loss on fixed asset disposal

Activity 2 *(The answer is in the final chapter of this book)*

List the advantages and disadvantages of prescriptive formats for company accounts.

---

5 Notes to the profit and loss account

5.1 Introduction

In this section we list the notes required and, where relevant, provide an illustration of each.

5.2 Accounting policies

The following disclosures are required by the CA 85 and FRS 18:

- Accounting policies for all material areas, eg depreciation, leased assets, stock valuation.
- Particulars and reasons for any changes in accounting policies adopted.

5.3 Illustration

Depreciation

Depreciation is provided on tangible fixed assets, other than freehold land, at rates calculated to write off the cost or valuation, less estimated residual value, of each asset evenly over its expected useful economic life, as follows.

Freehold buildings	-	over 50 years
Leasehold land and buildings	-	over the lease term
Plant and machinery	-	over 5 to 15 years

5.4 Turnover

The CA 85 and SSAP 25 together require disclosure of the analysis of turnover by class of business and by geographical market.

5.5 Illustration

Turnover comprises the value of contracting work carried out during the year and the invoiced value of goods and services provided, net of value added tax and trade discounts.

The analysis of turnover is as follows.

	£000
Class of business	
Property development and investments	X
Retailing	X
Other trading activities	X
	X
Geographical analysis	
UK	X
South America	X
Europe	X
USA	X
	X

5.6 Operating costs and revenues

Income: disclose any exceptional income (plus description).

Expenditure: disclose the following.

- Depreciation
- Auditors' remuneration (all remuneration to the auditor, whether for audit or other services)
- Exceptional charges (plus description)

5.7 Illustration

Operating profit

Profit is stated after charging the following.

	£000	£000
Depreciation of owned assets		X
Depreciation of leased assets		X
Amounts written off intangible assets		X
Hire of plant and machinery		X
Other operating lease rentals		X
Auditors' remuneration		X
In capacity as auditor	X	
In other capacities	X	
		X
Exceptional bad debt		X
Research and development costs written off		X
Amortisation of goodwill		X

Items in italics are disclosure requirements of accounting standards rather than of CA 85. SSAP 25 additionally requires the result (normally the operating profit) of each business segment and geographical segment to be disclosed, further to the analysis of turnover described above.

5.8 Employees

Disclose the following.

- Average number of employees in year
- Average number in each category
- Total wages and salaries
- Social security costs
- Other pension costs

5.9 Directors

Disclose the aggregate of directors' emoluments*.

- Include salary, fees, bonuses, benefits in kind.
- Exclude share options, pensions, long-term incentive schemes.

Disclose gains on exercise of share options (listed companies only)*.

Disclose assets (excluding share options and, for non-listed companies, shares) receivable under long-term incentive schemes*.

Disclose pension contributions paid by the company.

Disclose the number of directors covered by each of two types of pension schemes.

- Money purchase schemes
- Defined benefit schemes

For non-listed companies only, disclose the number of directors who:

- exercised share options
- received or became entitled to shares under a long-term incentive scheme.

Where the items marked * total more than £200,000 the following additional disclosures are required in relation to the highest paid director.

- How much of the above amounts are attributable to him
- If covered by a defined benefit pension scheme, the amount of accrued retirement benefits (excluding money purchase benefits or those from his own voluntary contributions)
- Whether he exercised share options or received or became entitled to shares under a long-term incentive scheme (non-listed companies only)

Finally, disclose excess retirement benefits paid to directors or past directors, and compensation for loss of office, including payments in connection with breach of contract.

5.10 Illustration

Employees and directors

Staff

The average monthly number of employees during the year was as follows.

	Number
Office and management	X
Retailing	X
Distribution	X
	X

Salaries, wages and other costs

	£000
Wages and salaries	X
Social security costs	X
Other pension costs	X
	X

Directors

	£000
Emoluments	X
Gains made on exercise of share options	X
Company contributions to money purchase pension schemes	X
Compensation for loss of office	X

All X directors are accruing pension benefits under money purchase schemes.
X directors exercised share options during the year.
The above details include the following amounts in respect of the highest paid director:

	£000
Emoluments	X
Gains on exercise of share options	X
Company contributions to money purchase pension scheme	X

5.11 *Interest payable*

Disclose the amount of interest payable, analysed between interest payable on:

- bank loans and overdrafts
- other loans

Disclose the amount of interest capitalised (ie not written off to profit and loss account as incurred, but added to the cost of an asset).

5.12 *Illustration*

Interest payable and similar charges

	£000
On bank loans and overdrafts	X
On other loans	X
Interest charges in respect of hire purchase and finance leases	X
Less amount capitalised on properties in course of construction	(X)
	X

5.13 *Tax on profit on ordinary activities*

Disclose any special circumstances affecting the tax liability.

5.14 *Illustration*

Tax on profit on ordinary activities

	£000
Corporation tax *(at 30%) based on profits of the year*	X
Under/(over) provision for corporation tax in previous year	X (X)
Transfer to/(from) deferred tax	X (X)
	X

5.15 Dividends

Disclose the total amount paid and proposed, per share and in total.

5.16 Illustration

Dividends

	£000	£000
Preference dividend		
5% (5p per share paid)	X	
5% (5p per share proposed)	X	
		X
Ordinary dividend		
5p interim (paid)	X	
6p final (proposed)	X	
		X
		X

5.17 Prior year items

Disclose the effect of amounts included in the profit and loss account relating to previous years. Under/over provisions from a prior year in the tax charge note are an example.

Disclose prior year adjustments (per FRS 3) shown as adjustments to retained earnings brought forward.

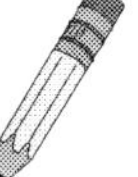

Activity 3 *(The answer is in the final chapter of this book)*

Readycut

The draft accounts of Readycut Toys plc, a toy manufacturer, have been prepared for the year ended 30 September 20X2 and are shown below.

The authorised share capital is 6,000,000 8% preference shares of 50p each and 36,000,000 ordinary shares of 25p each.

Extract from the trial balance for the year ended 30 September 20X2

	£000	£000
Sales		318,000
Increase in provision for bad debts	131	
Auditors' remuneration	93	
Loan interest	405	
Dividends - interim preference	120	
- interim ordinary	370	
Corporation tax (over-provision)		20
Directors' emoluments	400	
Administration costs	7,500	
Distribution costs	29,250	
Stock at 1 October 20X1	9,000	
Purchases	267,662	
Creditors		2,160
Profit and loss at 1 October 20X1		5,467
Loan		6,000
Preference shares (50p)		3,000
Ordinary shares (25p)		4,500

Plant and machinery	2,580	
Depreciation – plant and machinery		774
Land	2,400	
Buildings	3,900	
Depreciation – buildings		462
Fixtures and fittings	720	
Depreciation – fixtures and fittings		144
Debtors	6,315	
Bank	9,681	
	340,527	340,527

The following information was available at the time the accounts were drafted.

(1) The policy of the company is to provide depreciation at the following rates.

Buildings	2% per annum on cost
Plant and machinery	20% per annum on cost
Fixtures and fittings	10% per annum on cost

(2) The loan is unsecured and repayable in the year 20X4. It carries interest at 9% per annum.

(3) The charge for corporation tax for the year is estimated to be £4,360,000. An over-provision of £20,000 had been made in the previous year.

(4) The directors' emoluments of £400,000 comprise the following.

	Salary £	*Fees* £
Managing director	146,000	10,000
Chairman	120,000	-
Four other directors, each receiving	25,000	6,000

M Leggo, one of the four other directors, was based in Paris and only returned to London for board meetings.

(5) The following dividends are proposed.

Preference shares	Payment of second half year's dividend
Ordinary shares	Payment of a dividend of 24%

(6) The closing stock is £9,828,000 when valued at the lower of cost and net realisable value.

Required

Prepare the profit and loss account for the year ended 30 September 20X2 and the relevant notes for publication in accordance with the *Companies Act 1985.*

6 Preparing company accounts

6.1 Introduction

We now show how all of this information is brought together.

6.2 Example

The following trial balance at 30 September 20X2 relates to V Ltd, a manufacturing company.

	£000	£000
Sales		430
Stock at 1 October 20X1	10	
Purchases	75	
Advertising	15	
Administrative salaries	14	
Manufacturing wages	60	
Interest paid	14	
Dividends received		12
Audit fee	7	
Bad debts	10	
Taxation	37	
Dividend	60	
Grant received		30
Premises (cost)	450	
Plant (cost)	280	
Premises (depreciation)		40
Plant (depreciation)		160
Investments (long-term)	100	
Debtors	23	
Bank	169	
Creditors		7
Deferred taxation		62
Debenture loans at 10%		140
Share capital		100
Profit and loss at 1 October 20X1		343
	1,324	1,324

Further information

(a) Stock was worth £13,000 on 30 September 20X2.

(b) Premises consist of land costing £250,000 and buildings costing £200,000. The buildings have an expected useful life of 50 years.

(c) Plant includes an item purchased during the year at a cost of £70,000. A government grant of £30,000 was received in respect of this purchase. These were the only transactions involving fixed assets during the year.

Depreciation of plant is to be charged at 10% per annum on a straight-line basis.

(d) The balance on the corporation tax account comprises the under provision for corporation tax brought forward from the year ended 30 September 20X1.

(e) The provision for deferred tax is to be reduced by £17,000.

(f) The directors have estimated that corporation tax of £57,000 will be paid on the profits of the year, based on a tax rate of 30%.

(g) The directors have proposed a final dividend for the year of £67,000.

Required

Prepare a profit and loss account for V Ltd for the year ended 30 September 20X2 and a balance sheet at that date. These should be in a form suitable for presentation to the shareholders in accordance with the requirements of the Companies Act 1985 and be accompanied by notes to the accounts so far as is possible from the information given above.

You are *not* required to prepare the note relating to accounting policies.

6.3 Solution

Bear in mind the following points of assessment technique.

Get yourself organised: you will need to prepare a sheet for the profit and loss account and a separate sheet for the balance sheet

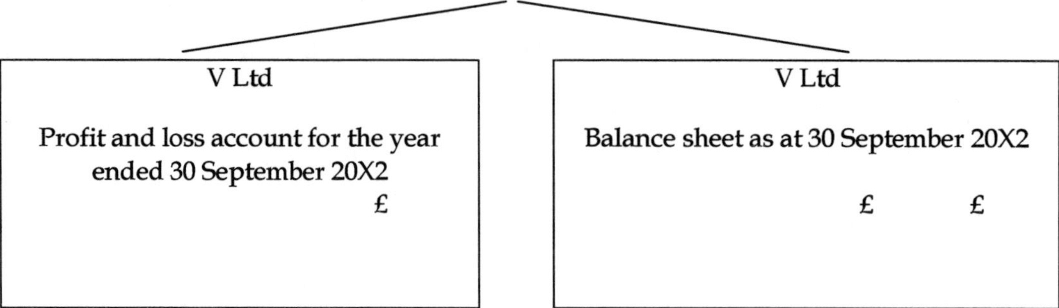

You will also need a sheet for notes to the accounts and a sheet for workings.

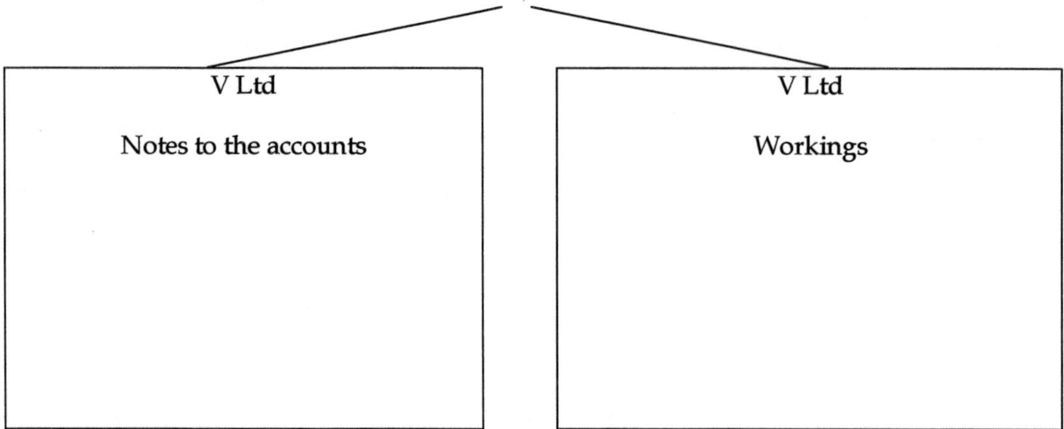

You must let the format dictate the order of working. Slot sales in as the starting point on the profit and loss account (turnover). Cost of sales, distribution costs and administrative expenses will then become (W1) on your working paper.

(W1) Cost of sales etc

	Cost of sales	*Distribution costs*	*Administrative expenses*
	£000	£000	£000
Opening stock	10		
Purchases	75		
Advertising		15	
Administrative salaries			14
Manufacturing wages	60		
Audit fee			7
Bad debts		10	
Grant (see below)	(3)		
Closing stock	(13)		
Depreciation – buildings (200/50)	4		
Depreciation – plant (280 × 10%)	28		
	161	25	21

In this case the treatment of the capital grant is in compliance with SSAP 4 which requires that the grant is treated as a deferred credit and brought into the profit and loss account over the expected useful life of the asset which it was used to buy.

The plant has an expected life of ten years and the grant will therefore be brought into the profit and loss account over ten years. In the current year we transfer £3,000 (£30,000 ÷ 10 = £3,000) to the profit and loss account; the remainder (£27,000) is deferred income.

You can then continue to work through the profit and loss account picking up the information as you go. So far, it looks as follows.

V LTD
PROFIT AND LOSS ACCOUNT FOR THE YEAR ENDED 30 SEPTEMBER 20X2

Notes		£000
	Turnover	430
	Cost of sales (W1)	(161)
	Gross profit	269
	Distribution costs (W1)	(25)
	Administrative expenses (W1)	(21)
	Operating profit	223
	Income from fixed asset investments	12
	Interest payable and similar charges	(14)
	Profit on ordinary activities before tax	221
	Taxation	

When you get as far as taxation, you can then turn your attention to any required notes to the accounts.

Remember: you can only provide notes if there is information available to you.

Note 1 usually deals with accounting policies but we are told *not* to provide this note in the present question.

Note 2 (analysis of turnover) cannot be completed as we are given no information. Our first note will therefore be set against operating profit.

1 Operating profit

Profit is stated after charging the following

	£000
Depreciation of owned assets (28 + 4)	32
Auditors' remuneration	7
Wages and salaries (60+14)	74

There are detailed disclosure requirements on employees and directors but as we only know total wages and salaries that is all we can disclose.

You can then cross-reference operating profit to note 1.

Our next note would be the analysis of *interest payable* but again we have not enough information to provide this analysis. This will bring us on to the taxation disclosure.

2 Tax on profit on ordinary activities	£000
Corporation tax (at 30%) based on profits of the year	57
(Over)/under provision for corporation tax in previous year	37
Transfer to/(from) deferred tax	(17)
	77

The corporation tax charge for the year is given in the additional information in the question. This is however only an estimate of the tax for the year – the final figure will be determined by the Inland Revenue after the year-end and this figure may be different to this estimated charge of £57,000.

This is what happened last year as we still have a debit balance on the taxation account of £37,000, being an under-provision from last year.

This must be included in this year's tax charge.

Finally the deferred tax provision is being reduced. As the provision is a credit balance, to reduce it we debit the deferred tax account and credit the profit and loss account with £17,000.

You can then continue down your profit and loss account. The next required note is dividends.

3 Dividends		£000
Ordinary dividend:	interim (paid)	60
	final (proposed)	67
		127

Your profit and loss account is then complete.

V LTD - PROFIT AND LOSS ACCOUNT FOR THE YEAR ENDED 30 SEPTEMBER 20X2

Notes		£000
	Turnover	430
	Cost of sales (W1)	(161)
	Gross profit	269
	Distribution costs (W1)	(25)
	Administrative expenses (W1)	(21)
1	Operating profit	223
	Income from fixed asset investments	12
	Interest payable and similar charges	(14)
	Profit on ordinary activities before tax	221
2	Taxation	(77)
	Profit on ordinary activities after tax	144
3	Dividends paid and proposed	(127)
	Retained profit for the year	17
	Retained profit brought forward	343
	Retained profit carried forward	360

You are now in a position to prepare the balance sheet using exactly the same approach. Allow the format to take you through the question.

We will continue the balance sheet notes directly on from the profit and loss notes. Note 4 will therefore be fixed assets – tangible assets. This note will also form the working for the figure on the balance sheet.

Note 4 Tangible assets	*Land and buildings*	*Plant and machinery*	*Total*
	£000	£000	£000
Cost at 1 October 20X1	450	210	660
Additions	-	70	70
Cost at 30 September 20X2	450	280	730

Depreciation at 1 October 20X1	40	160	200
Charge for year	4	28	32
Depreciation at 30 September 20X2	44	188	232
NBV at 1 October 20X1	410	50	460
NBV at 30 September 20X2	406	92	498

This can then be taken to the balance sheet and cross referenced to Note 4. ↑

You can then continue to work down the rest of the balance sheet. Remember you will not need a note if there are no details given in the question.

V LTD
BALANCE SHEET AS AT 30 SEPTEMBER 20X2

Note		£000	£000
	Fixed assets		
4	Tangible assets		498
	Investments		100
			598
	Current assets		
	Stocks	13	
	Debtors	23	
	Cash at bank and in hand	169	
		205	
5	*Creditors: amounts falling due within one year*		

You will need a note against Creditors: amounts falling due within one year. This note will again form the basis of your working.

Note 5 Creditors: amounts falling due within one year

	£000
Trade creditors	7
Other creditors including taxation and social security	
Corporation tax (estimated charge for the year)	57
Proposed dividend	67
Accruals and deferred income (government grant, 30-3)	27
	158

Add this in to your balance sheet and continue to work down. Your next disclosure will be for provisions for liabilities and charges – deferred tax.

Note 6 Provisions for liabilities and charges

	Deferred tax £000
At 1 October 20X1	62
Transfer to profit and loss account	(17)
At 30 September 20X2	45

You are now in a position to complete the balance sheet.

V LTD - BALANCE SHEET AS AT 30 SEPTEMBER 20X2

Note		£000	£000
	Fixed assets		
4	Tangible assets		498
	Investments		100
			598
	Current assets		
	Stocks	13	
	Debtors	23	
	Cash at bank and in hand	169	
		205	
5	*Creditors: amounts falling due within one year*	(158)	
	Net current assets		47
	Total assets less current liabilities		645
	Creditors: amounts falling due after more than one year		
	Debenture loans		(140)
6	*Provisions for liabilities and charges*		(45)
			460
	Capital and reserves		
	Called up share capital		100
	Profit and loss account		360
			460

You should now have completed:

- a profit and loss account
- a balance sheet
- notes to the accounts
- your working paper.

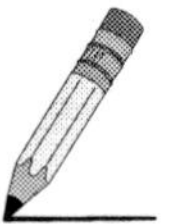

Activity 4 *(The answer is in the final chapter of this book)*

KL plc

KL plc is a manufacturing company. On 31 December 20X4 the following trial balance was extracted from the records of the company.

KL PLC TRIAL BALANCE AT 31 DECEMBER 20X4	£000	£000
Sales		7,000
Purchase of raw materials	1,280	
Wages		
Manufacturing	800	
Administration	420	
Distribution	340	
Administrative costs	400	
Selling and advertising	480	
Manufacturing overhead	740	
Opening stocks		
Raw materials	370	
Work in progress	410	
Finished goods	640	
Interim dividend	36	
Dividends received		6
Taxation	14	

Factory building		
Cost	1,200	
Accumulated depreciation		440
Plant and machinery		
Cost	1,820	
Accumulated depreciation		570
Disposal		24
Investments (short-term)	28	
Bank		280
Overdraft interest	34	
UJ Ltd	350	
Debtors	580	
Bad debts	44	
Provision for doubtful debts		20
Creditors		320
Deferred taxation		110
Share capital		600
Share premium		200
Profit and loss account		416
	9,986	9,986

Notes

(1) Stocks at 31 December 20X4 were valued as follows.

	£000
Raw materials	390
Work in progress	255
Finished goods	615

(2) Plant and machinery is to be depreciated by 20% of cost.

The factory building is to be depreciated by 2% of cost.

(3) The balance on the disposal account represents the proceeds from the sale of a machine which had cost £50,000 in 20X1. No further entries have been made in respect of this transaction.

KL plc charges a full year's depreciation in the year of acquisition and none in the year of disposal.

(4) On 31 December 20X4 the factory building was valued at £1,500,000 by S and J, a firm of Chartered Surveyors. The directors have decided to bring this valuation into the balance sheet.

(5) The following expenses have to be accrued.

	£000
Audit fee	14
Fees payable to three non-executive directors (£12,000 each)	36

(6) The production director's salary of £27,000 is included in manufacturing overhead.

(7) The sales director's salary of £24,000 is included in selling and advertising.

(8) The managing director's salary of £32,000 and the chairman's salary of £18,000 are included in administrative costs.

(9) The provision for doubtful debts is to be increased by £2,000.

(10) The balance on the UJ Ltd account is the cost of liquidating a loss-making subsidiary which had manufactured an obsolete product line which was unrelated to that of KL plc.

(11) The balance on deferred tax is to be increased by £27,000.

(12) Corporation tax of £920,000 is to be provided in respect of the total taxable profit earned during the year.

(13) The directors have proposed a final dividend of £72,000.

Required

Prepare a profit and loss account for KL plc for the year ended 31 December 20X4 and a balance sheet at that date. These should be in a form suitable for publication.

The accounting policies note is *not* required, nor is a statement of total recognised gains and losses, nor a reconciliation of movements in shareholders' funds.

7 The directors' report and other matters

7.1 Introduction

In addition to a balance sheet and profit and loss account, shareholders must also receive a report prepared on behalf of the directors. Although the Companies Act specifies the contents of this report no formal layout is included in the Act.

Remember that in assessments the term financial statements does not include the directors' report. If a directors' report is required the assessor will ask for it specifically.

7.2 Contents

The directors' report must contain:

- a fair review of the development of the business of the company during the year;
- its position at the end of the year;
- principal activities during the year and significant changes in those activities;
- significant changes in fixed assets;
- difference, if significant, between the book value of land and its market value;
- proposed dividends and transfers to reserves;
- names of directors who served at any time during the year;
- directors' interests (including nil holdings) in the shares or debentures of the company or any other company in the group; there must be shown for each director at the year end:
  - the number held in each company at the beginning of the year, or, if he became a director during the year, at that date; and
  - the number held at the year-end;
- particulars of important events affecting the company or its subsidiary undertakings which have occurred since the end of the year;
- an indication of likely future developments in the business;
- an indication of the activities in the field of research and development;

- the separate totals of political and charitable contributions, if, taken together, these exceed £200;
- the amount and name of recipients of individual political contributions exceeding £200;
- particulars of purchases of its own shares by the company during the year;
- a statement of the company's policy on the employment, training and career development of disabled people where the average number of employees exceeds 250;
- a statement describing the action that has been taken during the financial year to introduce, maintain or develop arrangements aimed at employee communication, consultation, involvement and awareness, where the average number of employees exceeds 250; and
- details of the company's policy on the payment of creditors (required for public companies and large companies only).

7.3 *Illustration of a directors' report*

Directors' Report
Drake Limited

The directors present herewith their report and accounts of Drake Limited for the year ended 31 December 20X4.

Activities and business review of the company

The principal activity of the company is that of manufacturing television and video equipment. Both the level of business and the year end financial position were satisfactory and the directors expect that the level of activity will continue to grow for the foreseeable future.

Post balance sheet events

Subsequent to the 31 December 20X4 balance sheet date, the company has purchased a large retail outlet, and intends to sell a substantial proportion of its manufacture to the public direct.

Research and development

Company policy is to invest in product innovation and manufacturing improvement to enable it to retain and enhance its market position. Such research and development expenditure is written off in the year in which it is incurred.

Fixed assets

Details of the company's fixed assets are set out in Notes 12 and 13 to the accounts. The market value of the freehold land and buildings at 31 December 20X4 was estimated by the directors at £150,000.

Directors

The company's directors during the year were as follows:

M R Worbbs
F E Gines
D G Thimms
G A Tison
C G Donker (appointed 1 July 20X4)

Their interests, including those of their family in the ordinary shares of the company were as follows:

Number of shares held	*31 December 20X4*	*1 January 20X4*
M R Worbbs	31,000	30,000
F E Gines	30,000	30,000
D G Thimms	20,000	20,000
G A Tison	31,300	30,000
C G Donker	16,500	Nil*

*At date of appointment.

In addition to the above holdings, Mr M R Worbbs was the non-beneficial holder of 1,000 ordinary shares (20X3 1,000 shares). No director held any interest in the company's debenture stock.

Dividends

The directors recommend the payment of a final ordinary dividend of 15p per share for the year ended 31 December 20X4 (20X3 13.25p) which, together with the interim dividend of 5p (20X3 5p) already paid, makes a total of 20p per share. A full preference dividend is recommended.

Transfers to reserves

The directors recommend a transfer to the debenture redemption reserve of £50,000 (20X3 £50,000).

Disabled persons

The policy of the company is to recruit disabled persons on a fair basis, to provide training and career development facilities on the same basis as for other staff, and to make every effort to retain and assist any individuals disabled in the course of their employment.

Political and charitable contributions

During the year, charitable contributions by the company were £4,290 (20X3 £2,550). No political contributions were made.

7.4 Summary financial statements

The Companies Act 1989 introduced summary financial statements. These may be produced by public limited companies which have a full Stock Exchange Listing as an alternative to publishing full accounts.

This recognises that the vast amount of detail as required by full Companies Act formats and disclosures may not be of relevance or interest to all shareholders.

Public limited companies must always file a full set of accounts with the Registrar of Companies.

If the company decides to produce summary financial statements, the company must ascertain whether its shareholders wish to receive full or summary financial statements. This will usually be achieved by writing to each shareholder. Once a shareholder's preference has been ascertained, it is up to the shareholders to notify the company of any change in future years. The shareholders will always have the right to demand a full set of accounts.

The contents of the summary financial statements must be derived from the full accounts. No additional information can be included which is not in the full accounts.

The summary financial statements must carry a 'health warning' to advise shareholders not to take investment decisions based on the contents of these statements.

7.5 Abbreviated accounts

Certain small and medium-sized companies can take advantage of accounting exemptions in section 247 of Companies Act 1985 permitting them to prepare two sets of accounts, normal full accounts for their shareholders and abbreviated accounts which are filed at Companies House. The benefit of preparing abbreviated accounts is that companies can keep details, for example profit margins, secret from their competitors.

7.6 Qualifying conditions for abbreviated accounts

- At least two to be satisfied for the current and immediately preceding financial years.

		Small	*Medium*
1	**Turnover** not more than:	£2,800,000	£11,200,000
2	**Assets** not more than:	£1,400,000	£5,600,000
3	**Average number of employees** not more than:	50	250

- If the qualifying conditions are met, the company will be entitled to the same status in the following financial year irrespective of whether the criteria are met.

- If the qualifying conditions are met in the company's first financial year, it can file abbreviated accounts in that year.

- Whatever their size there are some companies which can never file abbreviated accounts. These are as follows:

  (i) public companies;

  (ii) banking and insurance companies;

  (iii) companies authorised to carry out investment business;

  (iv) companies in a group which contains a public company, a banking or insurance company, or a company authorised to carry out investment business.

7.7 Exemptions permitted for medium-sized companies

- No requirement to state whether the accounts have been prepared in accordance with applicable accounting standards.

  This exemption applies regardless of whether abbreviated accounts are prepared.

- **Profit and loss account**

  (i) Start with gross profit (ie no figures for turnover and cost of sales need to be disclosed).

  (ii) No analysis of turnover by class of business or geographical destination.

7.8 Exemptions permitted for small-sized companies

- No requirement to state whether the accounts have been prepared in accordance with applicable accounting standards.

  This exemption applies regardless of whether abbreviated accounts are prepared.

- **Profit and loss account**

  Not required.

- **Balance sheet**

  Only the figures for the main headings (fixed assets, current assets, etc).

- **Notes to the accounts**

  Only the following notes are required:

  (i) accounting policies;

  (ii) share capital;

  (iii) debtors recoverable after more than one year;

  (iv) creditors due after more than five years;

  (v) secured creditors;

  (vi) the movements (in total) on intangible fixed assets, tangible fixed assets and fixed asset investments.

- **Directors' report**

  Not required.

7.9 Other exemptions for small companies

Regardless of whether a small company (as previously defined) has chosen to *file* abbreviated accounts, it may take advantage of certain additional exemptions when *preparing* full accounts for distribution to shareholders.

These exemptions result in a simplified balance sheet format, with some of the more minor items being combined – for example:

(a) tangible assets have only two sub-categories
(b) all categories of stock are combined, with the exception of payments made on account;
(c) the nine separate headings under creditors in the full format are reduced to four.

The profit and loss account remains the same.

There is also a considerable reduction in the number of notes required, eg security of creditors, particulars of staff, emoluments of directors, taxation notes are all not required.

8 Quick quiz *(The answers are in the final chapter of this book)*

1 Which statutory format for the balance sheet is normally used?

2 Which statutory format for the profit and loss account is normally used?

3 Does the directors' report have to name all directors who held office at any time during the year?

4 A company has turnover of £3m, total assets of £1m and 20 employees. Is it a small company?

9 Summary

In order to prepare limited company financial statements you need:

- a detailed knowledge of the disclosure requirements of the Companies Acts and the Accounting Standards; and
- the ability to get the knowledge onto paper quickly and neatly.

Therefore, you must learn the requirements and test that knowledge by practising questions.

Published accounts is primarily a practical subject, so take the opportunity to learn from financial statements which you come across in practice.

CHAPTER 6

Cash flow statements

ASSESSMENT FOCUS

A typical task in the second section of a Central assessment might be to draft a cash flow statement and a reconciliation between cash flow from operating activities and operating profit from information provided in the balance sheets, profit and loss account and additional information.

This chapter covers the following Knowledge and Understanding and Performance Criteria of the AAT Syllabus.

> Prepare and interpret a limited company cash flow statement *(Performance Criteria Element 11.1)*
>
> The UK regulatory framework for financial reporting and the main requirements of relevant Financial Reporting Standards *(Knowledge and Understanding Element 11.1)*

In order to cover these the following topics are included.

> FRS 1: Cash flow statements
> The elements of a cash flow statement
> Preparing a cash flow statement
> Dealing with interest and dividends paid
> Dealing with fixed assets and depreciation
> Dealing with provisions

Key definitions	
Cash flow statement	Accounting statement showing the cash receipts and cash payments of the business during a stated period of time.
Equity dividends	Dividends paid on equity shares such as ordinary shares.
Liquid resources	Short-term investments held as current assets.
Net debt	Borrowings less cash and liquid resources.

1 FRS 1: Cash flow statements

1.1 The need for a cash flow statement

The original (September 1991) FRS 1 standard was introduced because it was generally felt that the financial statements required an additional primary statement with the same importance as a profit and loss account and balance sheet – to emphasise the difference between profit and cash.

The October 1996 revised version of FRS 1 placed greater emphasis on net debt – borrowings less cash resources – that the company uses to finance its current and future operations. FRS 1 now requires all financial statements (except those of small companies as defined in the CA 85) to include a cash flow statement, showing the generation of cash and the uses of cash in the period.

One reason why a cash flow statement was considered necessary is that final profit figures are relatively easy to manipulate. There are many items in a profit and loss account involving judgement, including:

- Stock valuation
- Depreciation policy
- Provision for doubtful debts.

This makes it difficult to interpret a company's results with confidence. An FRS 1 statement showing merely inflows and outflows of cash is easier to understand and more difficult to manipulate.

Cash flows, including net present value calculations, have always been a popular management accounting tool and the requirement to produce a cash flow statement as part of the financial statements helps to form a basis for any future decision making process.

1.2 The FRS 1 proforma

The standard headings shown in the FRS 1 cash flow statement are as follows.

- Operating activities
- Dividends from joint ventures and associates
- Returns on investments and servicing of finance
- Taxation
- Capital expenditure and financial investment
- Acquisitions and disposals
- Equity dividends paid
- Management of liquid resources
- Financing
- Increase/decrease in cash.

The key to producing an accurate cash flow statement in the assessment is to know which cash flows go under which heading. Below is a typical FRS 1 statement showing many of the cash flows one would normally expect to see.

PROFORMA CASH FLOW STATEMENT FOR THE YEAR ENDED 31 DECEMBER 20X6

	£000	£000
Net cash flow from operating activities (Note 1)		X
Returns on investments and servicing of finance		
Dividends received	X	
Interest received	X	
Preference dividends paid	(X)	
Interest paid	(X)	
		X
Taxation		(X)
Capital expenditure		
Payments to acquire intangible fixed assets	(X)	
Payments to acquire tangible fixed assets	(X)	
Receipts from sale of tangible fixed assets	X	
		(X)
Equity dividends paid		(X)

Management of liquid resources		
Purchase of treasury bills	(X)	
Sale of other short-term investments	X	
		(X)
Financing		
Issue of ordinary share capital	X	
Repurchase of debenture loan	(X)	
Expenses paid in connection with share issue	(X)	
		X
Increase in cash		X

There are also three analyses which are required by FRS 1 which can conveniently be shown as notes to the cash flow statement. Proforma examples are set out below.

1.3 Proforma notes to the cash flow statement

(1) *Reconciliation of operating profit to net cash flow from operating activities*

	£000
Operating profit	X
Depreciation charges	X
Increase in stocks	(X)
Increase in debtors	(X)
Increase in creditors	X
Net cash inflow from operating activities	X

(2) *Reconciliation of net cash flow to movement in net debt*

	£000	£000
Increase in cash in the period	X	
Cash to repurchase debenture	X	
Cash used to increase liquid resources	X	
Change in net debt		X
Net debt at 1 January 20X6		(X)
Net funds at 31 December 20X6		X

(3) *Analysis of changes in net debt*

	At 1 January 20X6	*Cash flows*	*Other changes*	*At 31 December 20X6*
	£000	£000	£000	£000
Cash in hand and bank	X	X		X
Overdrafts	(X)	X		-
Long-term debt	(X)	X		(X)
Current asset investments	X	X		X
Total	(X)	X		X

2 The elements of a cash flow statement

2.1 Net cash flow from operating activities

This is the first line of the cash flow statement in the proforma shown above. It can be derived by adjusting the operating profit shown in the profit and loss account, as demonstrated in the analysis shown in Note 1 above. The profit figure is adjusted for any transactions not involving the movement of cash, eg depreciation or profit/loss on disposal of fixed assets.

This reconciliation from operating profit to operating cash flow can be shown as Note 1 to the cash flow statement. Apart from the depreciation adjustment, note the increase/decrease in stock, debtors and creditors. An increase in stock involves an outflow of cash and is, hence, a negative figure. The main problem here is to get the signs right.

2.2 Returns on investments and servicing of finance

Note that any dividends received and non-equity dividends paid would be included here whilst equity dividends paid are disclosed separately, lower down the cash flow statement.

Preference dividends are non-equity dividends, while ordinary dividends are equity dividends.

2.3 Taxation

This is corporation tax *paid* during the year, not the tax *charged* in the profit and loss account.

2.4 Dividends

The same rule applies to dividends: we show the amount *paid* in the year, not usually the same as the appropriation shown in the profit and loss account. Typically, the profit and loss account will include an interim dividend already paid plus a final dividend accrued at the year end. By contrast, the amount paid in the year will usually not include this year's final dividend, but may well include last year's final dividend.

2.5 Management of liquid resources

Liquid resources are short-term or current asset investments. Current asset investments are investments held for less than a year with a view to trading in them.

It is possible for the net movement only to be shown on the cash flow statement instead of the purchase outflow and sales inflow.

2.6 Financing

This will include any or all of the following elements.

- Proceeds of share issues
- Proceeds on taking out a new loan or debenture
- Payments to redeem a loan or debenture

2.7 Increase/decrease in cash

This includes cash in hand plus bank deposits repayable on demand, less any overdrafts.

2.8 Notes 2 and 3

The additional two notes – reconciliation of cash flow to movement in net debt, and the analysis of changes in net debt – are relatively easy to produce and will be illustrated later in this chapter.

3 Preparing a cash flow statement

3.1 Direct and indirect methods

In principle, there are two main ways of calculating the first item in an FRS 1 cash flow statement (the net cash inflow from operating activities). Both methods are permitted by FRS 1.

The *indirect method* begins with operating profit from the profit and loss account and adjusts this figure for non-cash items and for increases and decreases in working capital. This is the method we have already seen in action.

The *direct method* uses the actual trading cash flows to arrive at the net cash flow from operating activities. These cash flows – cash actually received from customers, cash actually paid to suppliers etc – can be derived by inspecting the company's detailed books of account, but cannot usually be found from inspection of the profit and loss account and balance sheet.

For this practical reason, the indirect method is much more common in assessment tasks. However, as an illustration of how the direct method might be used see the comparison below.

Direct method	£000	*Indirect method*	£000
Cash received from customers	15,424	Operating profit	6,022
Cash payments to suppliers	(5,824)	Depreciation charges	899
Cash paid to and on behalf of employees	(2,200)		
Other cash payments	(511)	Increase in stocks	(194)
		Increase in debtors	(72)
		Increase in creditors	234
Net cash inflow from operating activities	6,889		6,889

3.2 Example

The summarised balance sheets of Grasmere Ltd at 31 December 20X4 and 20X5 were as follows.

	20X4	*20X5*
	£	£
Plant and machinery, at cost	15,000	16,500
Less depreciation	8,000	10,000
	7,000	6,500
Stock	20,000	23,500
Debtors	10,000	15,000
Cash	5,000	2,000
	42,000	47,000
Share capital	20,000	20,000
Reserves	17,000	21,000
Creditors	5,000	6,000
	42,000	47,000

No fixed assets have been sold during the period under review. Depreciation provided for the year amounted to £2,000. There is no interest paid, dividends paid or taxation paid.

Required

Prepare a cash flow statement for the year ended 31 December 20X5 using the indirect method.

3.3 Solution

FRS 1 questions usually appear in the same format: you are given two balance sheets plus additional information.

To tackle these questions, work down the balance sheets identifying the movements between the two and then decide where each movement should be disclosed on the cash flow statement or the notes (or sometimes both).

In the present example, there is a £1,500 increase in plant and machinery at cost. This goes under capital expenditure (as payments to acquire fixed assets). This is a cash outflow.

When you have dealt with a line on the balance sheet, tick it off.

The movement in stock and debtors goes into Note 1.

Stock levels have risen which results in a decrease in cash resources available.

Debtors have also increased, so less cash has been received.

The overall cash decrease of £3,000 should form the bottom figure on the cash flow statement.

Share capital has not changed. Reserves have risen by £4,000 which represents the operating profit (in the absence of interest, dividends and taxation) – the operating profit is the first line of Note 1.

An increase in creditors results in £1,000 more cash available and also goes into Note 1. We are now in a position to produce Note 1 in full.

1 *Reconciliation of operating profit to net cash outflow from operations*

	£
Operating profit for the year (21,000 - 17,000)	4,000
Depreciation (10,000 - 8,000)	2,000
Increase in stock	(3,500)
Increase in debtors	(5,000)
Increase in creditors	1,000
Net cash outflow from operating activities	(1,500)

The rest of the statement now follows very quickly if you have the format clear in your head.

GRASMERE LIMITED
CASH FLOW STATEMENT FOR THE YEAR ENDED 31 DECEMBER 20X5

	Notes	£
Net cash outflow from operating activities	1	(1,500)
Capital expenditure		
Payments to acquire tangible fixed assets		(1,500)
Decrease in cash		(3,000)

3.4 Interpreting a cash flow statement

Despite the fact that this is a simple example, with few figures, it is still possible to gain valuable information concerning the company's current and future financing strategy.

Payments to acquire fixed assets (£1,500) and the increase in working capital (stock and debtors) have resulted in an overall decrease in the company's cash resources.

The preparation of a cash flow statement highlights the drain on cash as a potential future problem that perhaps would not have been identified by the standard profit and loss account and balance sheet.

3.5 Example

The following information relates to X plc. The company's accounting year ends on 30 September.

BALANCE SHEETS	*30 September 20X6*		*30 September 20X7*	
	£000	£000	£000	£000
Tangible fixed assets (Note 1)		945		1,662
Current assets				
Stocks	1,225		1,488	
Debtors	700		787	
Short-term liquid investments	175		262	
Cash at bank	184		186	
	2,284		2,723	
Creditors: amounts falling due within one year				
Bank overdraft	52		105	
Trade creditors	525		735	
Expense creditors	9		10	
Taxation	140		228	
Proposed dividends	140		175	
	866		1,253	
Net current assets		1,418		1,470
Total assets less current liabilities		2,363		3,132
Creditors: amounts falling due after more than one year				
Long-term loan		(525)		(700)
		1,838		2,432
Capital and reserves				
Called up ordinary share capital		1,225		1,400
Share premium account		-		87
General reserve		525		787
Profit and loss account		88		158
		1,838		2,432

SUMMARY PROFIT AND LOSS ACCOUNT FOR THE YEAR ENDED 30 SEPTEMBER 20X7

	£000	£000
Profit on ordinary activities before taxation		735
Corporation tax		228
Profit on ordinary activities after taxation		507
Proposed dividend	175	
Transfer to general reserve	262	
		(437)
Retained profit for the year		70
Retained profit brought forward		88
Retained profit carried forward		158

Note 1. Tangible fixed assets

	Freehold premises	Plant and machinery	Freehold premises	Plant and machinery
	20X6		20X7	
	£000	£000	£000	£000
At cost	560	455	560	718
Additions during the year	-	263	280	700
	560	718	840	1,418
Less depreciation	35	298	53	543
Net book value	525	420	787	875

Required

Prepare a cash flow statement and related notes for X plc for the year ended 30 September 20X7, conforming to the requirements of FRS 1, in so far as this is possible from the information given.

3.6 Solution

We begin our answer by looking at Notes 2 and 3 because we have not examined them in any great detail so far. You should complete Note 3 first, then Note 2.

In an assessment task it is advisable to start with the reconciliation of operating profit to net cash flow from operations (Note 1) and then the cash flow statement. Leave Notes 2 and 3 until the end.

2 *Reconciliation of net cash flow to movement in net debt (Note 3)*

	£000	£000
Decrease in cash in the period (186 - 184) – (105 – 52)	(51)	
Cash from loan issue (700 – 525)	(175)	
Cash used to increase liquid resources (262 – 175)	87	
Change in net debt		(139)
Net debt at 1 October 20X6 (Note 3)		(218)
Net debt at 30 September 20X7 (Note 3)		(357)

3 *Analysis of changes in net debt*

	At 1 October 20X6 £000	Cash flows £000	At 30 September 20X7 £000
Cash in hand and at bank	184	2	186
Bank overdraft	(52)	(53)	(105)
		(51)	
Debt repayable after more than one year	(525)	(175)	(700)
Current asset investments	175	87	262
Net debt	(218)	(139)	(357)

Note 3 has three columns and requires four straightforward calculations using the four figures that comprise net debt.

- Cash
- Bank overdrafts
- Short-term investments
- Long-term debt

In each case put the opening balance sheet amount in column one, the closing balance sheet amount in column three and the difference in column two. You must ensure that the signs are the right way around.

Note 2 is simply a summary of the information produced in Note 3.

The movement or change column is produced first with the cash and overdraft movement being combined and the current asset investment change and long term debt change being shown separately.

Note that all the Note 2 figures can be taken from Note 3.

Having completed Notes 2 and 3 you have some of the figures to start the cash flow statement.

We can then fill in the rest of the cash flow statement and Note 1 by working down the balance sheet line by line.

In this case, the rest of the question is relatively straightforward. The fixed assets information is all provided and tax paid and dividends paid are equal to the prior year profit and loss amounts.

The full solution is as follows.

X PLC - CASH FLOW STATEMENT FOR THE YEAR ENDED 30 SEPTEMBER 20X7

	£000	£000
Net cash inflow from operating activities (Note 1)		859
Returns on investments and servicing of finance		-
Taxation		(140)
Capital expenditure		
Purchase of tangible fixed assets (280 + 700)		(980)
Equity dividends paid		(140)
Management of liquid resources		(87)
Financing		
Issue of ordinary share capital (1,400 + 87 – 1,225)	262	
New loans issued	175	
		437
Decrease in cash		(51)

Notes to the cash flow statement

1 *Reconciliation of operating profit to net cash inflow from operating activities*

		£000
Operating profit		735
Depreciation	– freehold premises (53 – 35)	18
	– plant and machinery (543 – 298)	245
Increase in stock		(263)
Increase in debtors		(87)
Increase in creditors (735 + 10) – (525 + 9)		211
Net cash inflow from operating activities		859

2, 3 *As already printed*

4 More complex areas

4.1 Introduction

In many cases the figures for the cash flow statement can be found simply by comparing the opening and closing balance sheets. However in other instances a slightly more involved approach is required.

4.2 Interest paid

The first point to note is that interest paid is treated as a separate cash flow in the cash flow statement (in 'Returns on investments and servicing of finance') therefore the operating profit figure used in Note 1 must be the profit before any interest paid has been deducted.

Care must be taken as the interest charge in the profit and loss account may not always be the amount of cash paid in interest. If there are accruals for interest payable in the balance sheet then a T account working will be required in order to determine the interest paid.

4.3 Example

The interest charge in a company's profit and loss account is £300. The balance sheet shows the following figures under the heading of creditors: amounts falling due within one year.

	Opening balance sheet	Closing balance sheet
	£	£
Interest payable	120	150

What is the amount of interest paid in the year?

4.4 Solution

Open up a T account putting in the opening and closing balance sheet figures and the profit and loss account charge for interest. The balancing figure is the cash paid for interest in the year.

Interest payable

	£		£
Cash paid (bal fig)	270	Opening balance	120
Closing balance	150	P&L account	300
	420		420

The amount to appear in the cash flow statement for interest paid is therefore £270.

4.5 Dividends paid and tax paid

A similar method is used in order to determine the amount of equity dividends paid and the amount of tax paid during a year.

A T account is opened for each of dividends and tax. The opening and closing creditors for tax and proposed dividend are entered together with the relevant profit and loss account figures and the amount of cash paid is the balancing figure.

4.6 Example

Given below are extracts from the profit and loss account and balance sheets for a business.

Profit and loss account

	£000
Profit before tax	1,300
Tax	400
Profit after tax	900
Dividends paid and proposed	600
Retained profit	300

	Opening balance sheet £000	*Closing balance sheet* £000
Creditors: amounts falling due within one year		
Corporation tax	360	400
Proposed dividends	250	450

What figures should appear in the cash flow statement for tax paid and equity dividends paid?

4.7 Solution

Corporation tax

	£000		£000
Cash paid (bal fig)	360	Opening balance	360
Closing balance	400	P&L account	400
	760		760

Dividend

	£000		£000
Cash paid (bal fig)	400	Opening balance	250
Closing balance	450	P&L account	600
	850		850

4.8 Fixed assets and depreciation

Further calculation problems can arise when trying to find the relevant figures for fixed assets and depreciation.

The depreciation charge for the year is required in order to add back to operating profit in Note 1. Any additions to fixed assets are also cash outflows and they may also have to be calculated.

Again the technique is to use a T account for fixed assets at cost and for accumulated depreciation and to enter into these accounts all of the relevant figures from the question.

4.9 Example

Given below are extracts from the opening and closing balance sheets for a company.

	Opening balance sheet £000	*Closing balance sheet* £000
Fixed assets at cost	1,000	1,100
Accumulated depreciation	400	480
Net book value	600	620

You are also told that an asset which had cost £150,000 and on which £90,000 of accumulated depreciation had been charged was sold during the year for £50,000.

What are the figures for depreciation, profit or loss on disposal and additions to fixed assets for the cash flow statement?

4.10 Solution

Open up a T account for fixed assets at cost. Enter the opening and closing balances and the cost of the asset disposed of. The additions will then be the balancing figure.

Fixed assets at cost

	£000		£000
Opening balance	1,000	Disposals	150
Cash paid (bal fig)	250	Closing balance	1,100
	1,250		1,250

Now to find the depreciation charge for the year by using the same technique with an accumulated depreciation T account.

Accumulated depreciation

	£000		£000
Disposals	90	Opening balance	400
Closing balance	480	P&L account (bal fig)	170
	570		570

Therefore the depreciation charge for the year is £170,000 to be added back to operating profit.

Finally any profit or loss on disposal can be found using a disposal account.

Disposal account

	£000		£000
Fixed assets at cost	150	Accumulated depreciation	90
		Cash proceeds	50
		Loss on disposal (bal fig)	10
	150		150

4.11 Fixed assets at net book value

In some tasks you are only given the net book value of the fixed assets rather than separate cost and accumulated depreciation information. In such questions you may need to find either the depreciation charge for the year or the additions. Again this is done by drawing up a T account showing all of the fixed asset entries as follows:

Fixed assets at NBV

	£		£
Opening NBV	X	Disposals @ NBV	X
Additions	X	Depreciation charge	X
		Closing NBV	X
	X		X

4.12 Example

Given below is an extract from the opening and closing balance sheets of a company.

	Opening balance sheet	*Closing balance sheet*
	£000	*£000*
Fixed assets at net book value	3,000	3,200

During the year fixed assets with a net book value of £100,000 were sold and fixed assets costing £650,000 were purchased. What is the depreciation charge for the year?

4.13 Solution

Fixed assets at NBV

	£000		£000
Opening NBV	3,000	Disposals @ NBV	100
Additions	650	Depreciation charge (bal fig)	350
		Closing NBV	3,200
	3,650		3,650

4.14 Provisions

In some tasks you might find a provision in the balance sheet. Any increase or decrease in a provision is not a cash flow and therefore the increase or decrease should be dealt with by adjusting the operating profit in Note 1.

An increase in provision will be added back to profit and a decrease will be deducted.

Activity 1 *(The answer is in the final chapter of this book)*

Fallen plc

Fallen plc has prepared the following draft accounts for the year ended 31 December 20X8.

PROFIT AND LOSS ACCOUNT	£000
Turnover	11,563
Cost of sales	(5,502)
Gross profit	6,061
Distribution costs	(402)
Administrative expenses	(882)
Interest payable	(152)
Profit before tax	4,625
Taxation	(1,531)
Profit after tax	3,094
Dividends	(700)
Retained profit	2,394

BALANCE SHEETS	*31 December*	
	20X8	*20X7*
	£000	£000
Leasehold premises (net)	6,600	5,700
Plant, machinery and equipment (net)	5,040	3,780
Investments at cost held as liquid resources	2,406	2,208
Stock	2,880	1,986
Debtors	2,586	1,992
Bank	-	576
	19,512	16,242

Share capital (25p ordinary)	2,280	1,800
Share premium	2,112	1,800
Profit and loss account	9,108	6,714
Debentures (10%)	1,240	1,800
Provision for deferred repairs	1,202	1,016
Creditors	1,026	702
Overdraft	222	-
Taxation	1,932	2,176
Proposed dividends	390	234
	19,512	16,242

The following data is relevant.

1 The 10% debentures redeemed during the year were redeemed at par.

2 Plant and equipment with a written down value of £276,000 was sold for £168,000. New plant was purchased for £2,500,000.

3 Leasehold premises costing £1,300,000 were acquired during the year.

Required

Prepare the cash flow statement and supporting notes for 20X8 in accordance with FRS 1.

Activity 2 *(The answer is in the final chapter of this book)*

Oxford Ltd

Oxford Ltd has been trading for five years using a patented recipe for apple sauce. You are given the following information.

		30 June 20X8			*30 June 20X7*	
	Cost	*Depn*	*NBV*	*Cost*	*Depn*	*NBV*
Fixed assets	£	£	£	£	£	£
Freehold factory	142,000	-	142,000	142,000	-	142,000
Plant and machinery	121,800	(47,500)	74,300	99,000	(48,300)	50,700
Patents	2,000	-	2,000	2,000	-	2,000
	265,800	(47,500)	218,300	243,000	(48,300)	194,700
Current assets						
Stocks		11,100			10,000	
Debtors		11,000			7,500	
Short-term investments		13,000			-	
Balance at bank		7,100			2,100	
		42,200			19,600	
Creditors: amounts falling due within one year						
Creditors		13,400			12,600	
Taxation		900			700	
Proposed dividends		7,700			6,000	
		(22,000)			(19,300)	
Net current assets			20,200			300
			238,500			195,000
Creditors: amounts falling due after more than one year (8% debentures)			(40,000)			(40,000)
			198,500			155,000

Capital and reserves		
Called up share capital	115,000	100,000
Share premium account	15,000	10,000
Profit and loss account	68,500	45,000
	198,500	155,000

PROFIT AND LOSS ACCOUNT FOR THE YEAR ENDED 30 JUNE 20X8

	£
Turnover	253,600
Cost of sales	(160,900)
Gross profit	92,700
Administrative expenses	(53,800)
Operating profit	38,900
Interest payable and similar charges	(3,200)
Profit before taxation	35,700
Taxation	(1,300)
Profit after taxation	34,400
Dividends paid and proposed	(10,900)
Retained profit for the year	23,500

During the year the company disposed of five apple-bashing machines for a total of £4,200 and replaced them with more modern machinery. The old machines were standing in the books at a cost of £14,000 with accumulated depreciation of £12,600. The profit made on the sale has been credited to the profit and loss account.

All purchases and disposals of plant and machinery were settled in cash during the year.

The short-term investment is a one-month bank deposit.

Required

Prepare a cash flow statement for the year ended 30 June 20X8 (only Note 1 is required).

4 Quick quiz *(The answers are in the final chapter of this book)*

1 Does FRS 1 require all companies to publish a cash flow statement?

2 Is a preference dividend an equity dividend or a non-equity dividend?

3 When using the indirect method of reporting the cash flow from operating activities, is the depreciation charge added to the operating profit or subtracted?

4 A company has loans payable of £10m, a bank overdraft of £2m and short-term investments of £1m. What is the company's net debt?

5 Summary

A cash flow statement provides information additional to that contained in the profit and loss account and balance sheet. It is an obligatory disclosure for all except small companies.

The content of a cash flow statement is governed by FRS 1. You must commit to memory the main headings required by FRS 1, and the format of the three notes to a cash flow statement.

CHAPTER 7

Consolidated accounts – balance sheet

ASSESSMENT FOCUS

For this Unit you may have to draft a consolidated balance sheet using the financial statements of a parent and a subsidiary undertaking.

This chapter covers the following Knowledge and Understanding of the AAT Syllabus.

Generally accepted accounting principles and concepts *(Element 11.1)*
The general principles of consolidation *(Element 11.1)*

In order to cover these the following topics are included.

Group accounts
The mechanics of consolidation
Minority interests
Accounting for reserves
The treatment of goodwill
Intra-group balances
Dividends
Unrealised intra-group profit
Fair values
Other considerations

Key definitions

Group of companies	A parent company together with its subsidiaries.
Parent company	A company that controls another company (its subsidiary), normally by owning more than half of that company's ordinary share capital.
Goodwill	Difference between the cost of shares acquired and the fair value of net assets acquired.
Minority interest	The stake in a subsidiary not owned by the parent company. For example, if P Ltd owns 80% of S Ltd, then there is a 20% minority interest.
Consolidated balance sheet	Balance sheet prepared for a group as though the group were a single economic entity.
Pre-acquisition reserves	Reserves of a subsidiary at the date of acquisition by a parent company.
Post-acquisition reserves	Reserves of a subsidiary that have been earned subsequent to acquisition by a parent company.

1 Group accounts

1.1 Introduction

Until now, we have only dealt with the accounts of a single company. In this and the following chapters, we cover the major topic of group accounts.

In this chapter, we meet the basic principles of consolidation whilst preparing a consolidated balance sheet. This will provide us with the foundation for studying the area in more detail in later chapters. In studying these chapters, you should always keep in mind these basic principles.

1.2 Groups

A group comprises a parent company and the undertakings (usually companies) under its control, which are called subsidiaries. The full legal definitions of a parent and subsidiaries are dealt with later and are not important at this stage. For now, we shall assume that a parent has control of another company if it holds more than 50% of that company's ordinary shares.

1.3 Group accounts

The Companies Act 1985 requires a parent company to produce group accounts which show a true and fair view of the group to the parent's shareholders. The group accounts provide the parent's shareholders with information about the parent and the investments which it has made. Group accounts are intended for the parent's shareholders and are therefore prepared from the perspective of the parent company.

The parent's own individual balance sheet shows the investment in the subsidiary, usually at cost, and its profit and loss account shows dividend income from the subsidiary in investment income. Where the investing company has a controlling interest in another company, it is not sufficient merely to show the investment in this way as this does not reflect the substance of the relationship between a parent and its subsidiaries.

1.4 Control

As the parent has control, it can decide how a subsidiary's assets are used to generate income in the same way that it can decide how to manage its own resources. Hence, the Companies Act requires group accounts to be in the form of consolidated accounts, which combine the results and net assets of the group members into a single set of figures.

Group accounts comprise the following:

- a consolidated balance sheet, which is presented in addition to the parent's own balance sheet as an individual company
- a consolidated profit and loss account, which is usually presented instead of the parent's own individual profit and loss account, although the parent may choose to publish its own individual profit and loss account as well
- a consolidated cash flow statement and statement of total recognised gains and losses (preparation of these for group accounts is beyond the scope of this Unit)
- notes to the accounts, including accounting policies

The requirement to produce group accounts is subject to exemptions, which are dealt with later.

Note that, although the parent does not need to publish its own profit and loss account as an individual company since it is publishing a consolidated profit and loss account instead, it must still publish its own individual balance sheet, in addition to the consolidated balance sheet.

1.5 Single entity concept

Group accounts *consolidate* the results and net assets of the individual group members to present the group to the parent's shareholders as a single economic entity.

This contrasts with the legal form that each company is a separate legal person. This is called the **single entity concept** and is an example of reflecting economic substance in financial statements rather than strict legal form.

Single entity concept

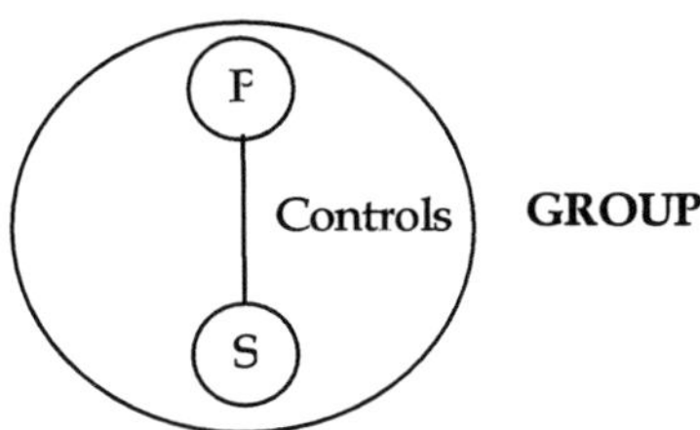

The group is viewed as a single entity.

To present the group as a single entity, the net assets and results of subsidiaries are added to those of the parent line by line to show the group's financial position and performance.

2 The mechanics of consolidation

2.1 Introduction

A standard group accounting assessment task will present you with the accounts of the parent company and the accounts of the subsidiary and will require you to prepare consolidated accounts.

To tackle tasks of this kind we will use a formal pattern of five workings. These are listed below. In a complex example all five of these workings may be needed, but we will begin with simpler cases.

2.2 Standard workings

We are going to use this formal pattern of workings to illustrate the approach to these questions, starting with basic examples and gradually building in complications.

(W1) Establish the group structure

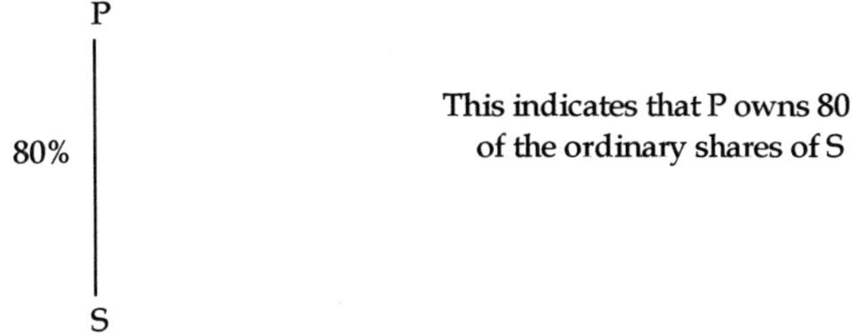

(W2) Set out the net assets of S

	At date of acquisition	*At the balance sheet (B/S) date*
	£	£
Share capital	X	X
Profit and loss account	X	X
	X	X

(W3) Calculate the goodwill on acquisition

	£
Cost of shares acquired	X
Less share of net assets at acquisition (see W2)	(X)
	X

(W4) Calculate the minority interest

	£
Share of net assets at balance sheet date (see W2)	X

(W5) Calculate the profit and loss reserve

	£
P Ltd profit and loss reserve (100%)	X
S Ltd – group share of post-acquisition profits	X
Less goodwill amortised to date	(X)
	X

2.3 *Buying shares in another company*

When one company buys shares in another company the cash paid is recorded as an investment in the acquiring company's balance sheet. When the consolidated balance sheet is prepared this investment is substituted by the net assets of the subsidiary which are included in the consolidated balance sheet on a line by line basis.

2.4 *Example*

Draft balance sheets of Polar and Squirrel on 31 December 20X1 are as follows.

	Polar Ltd	*Squirrel Ltd*
	£000	£000
Tangible fixed assets	90	80
Investment in Squirrel at cost	110	
Current assets	50	30
	250	110
Creditors: amounts falling due within one year	(30)	(10)
	220	100
Capital and reserves		
Share capital	100	100
Profit and loss account	120	-
	220	100

Polar Ltd has just bought 100% of the shares of Squirrel on the balance sheet date.

Required

Prepare a consolidated balance sheet as at 31 December 20X1.

2.5 Solution

Step 1

- Get organised
- Always present the answer first, supported by workings
- Set up two sheets of A4 paper

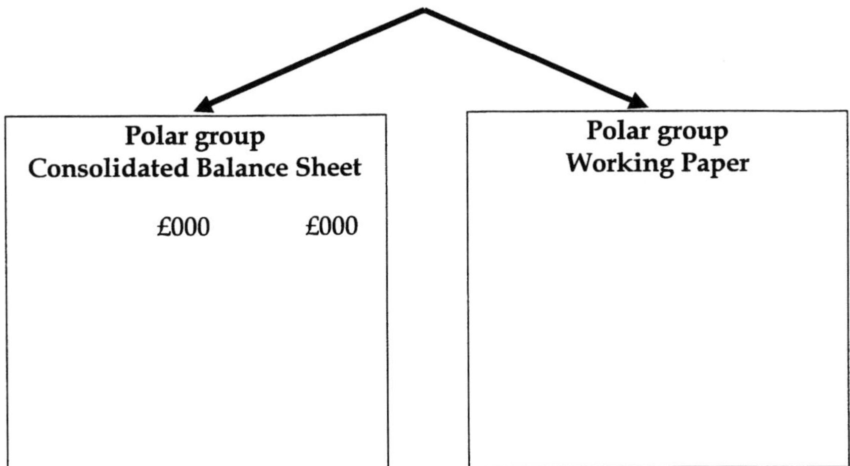

- Start with the workings. Then use your workings to construct the balance sheet.

Step 2

The starting point is to establish the group structure. We are told that Polar owns 100% of Squirrel and therefore (W1) will look like this.

(W1) Group structure

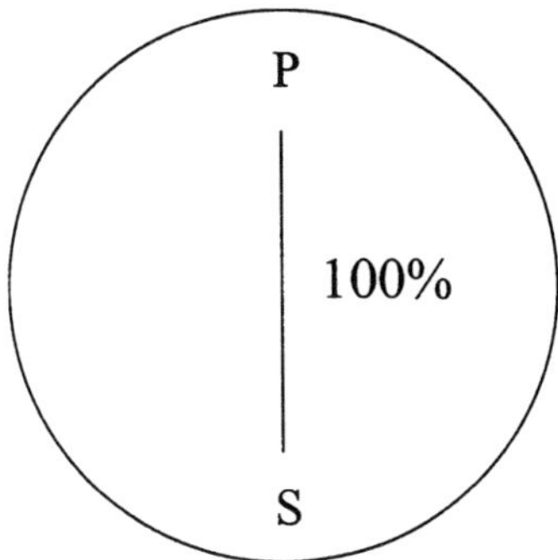

(*Tutorial note.* P controls S and therefore we need to prepare group accounts.)

Step 3

Our next step is to focus on the net assets of the subsidiary. We calculate net assets by remembering that:

Net assets = Share capital + reserves

Squirrel Ltd has no reserves and so net assets = share capital. The balance sheet date is the same as the date of acquisition.

(W2) will look like this.

Net assets of Squirrel Ltd

	At date of acquisition	*At balance sheet date*
	£000	£000
Share capital	100	100

The reason for preparing (W2) is so that we can go on to calculate the goodwill arising on consolidation. This is a key mark-earning calculation.

Step 4

The difference between the amount P paid to acquire S ('the purchase consideration') and the share of the net assets acquired is the amount P paid for goodwill. This is normally, but not always, a positive figure. In other words, P usually pays an amount greater than the value of the tangible net assets, the excess being the amount paid for the intangible asset 'goodwill'.

We use (W3) to calculate the goodwill.

(W3) Goodwill	£000
Purchase consideration (from P's balance sheet)	110
For 100% of net assets (£100,000) acquired (W2)	(100)
Goodwill	10

The positive goodwill is a further asset which P has paid for. It will appear as an intangible fixed asset in the consolidated balance sheet and will be amortised over its useful life. In the given case the investment has only just been acquired, so no amortisation is necessary.

Step 5

We are now in a position to produce a consolidated balance sheet.

Watch out for the following key points.

- The investment in S at cost will *never* appear in the consolidated balance sheet.
- The share capital of S will *never* appear in the consolidated balance sheet.
- The investment in S has been cancelled against the share capital on consolidation and it is only the difference between the two (ie goodwill) which appears in the consolidated balance sheet as an intangible fixed asset.

We include 100% of the assets and liabilities of both the parent and subsidiary in a consolidated balance sheet because by definition we control these net assets. They belong to the group and must be disclosed in full in the consolidated balance sheet.

You can now produce an answer which is cross-referenced to the workings.

POLAR GROUP CONSOLIDATED BALANCE SHEET AS AT 31 DECEMBER 20X1

	£000	£000
Goodwill (W3)		10
Tangible fixed assets (90 + 80) 100% P + S		170
		180
Current assets (50 + 30) 100% P + S	80	
Creditors: amounts due within one year (30 + 10) 100% P+S	(40)	
Net current assets		40
		220
Capital and reserves		
Share capital (100% P only)		100
Profit and loss reserve (100% P)		120
		220

Workings

(W1) Group structure

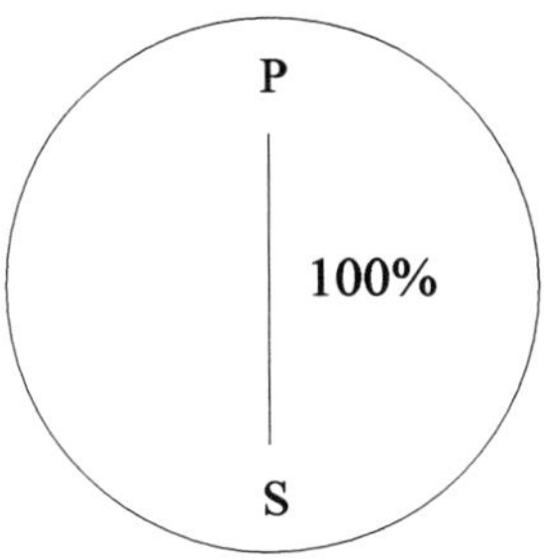

(W2) Net assets of S	*At date of acquisition* £000	*At balance sheet date* £000
£1 shares	100	100

(W3) Goodwill	£000
Purchase consideration	110
For 100% net assets acquired	(100)
Goodwill	10

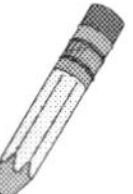

Activity 1 *(The answer is in the final chapter of this book)*

Puffin (I)

Draft balance sheets of Puffin and Seagull on 31 December 20X1 are as follows.

	Puffin Ltd £000	*Seagull Ltd* £000
Tangible fixed assets	146	35
Investment in Seagull at cost	90	
Current assets	24	15
	260	50
Creditors: amounts falling due within one year	(30)	(10)
	230	40
Capital and reserves		
Share capital	100	40
Profit and loss account	130	-
	230	40

Puffin Ltd has just bought 100% of the shares of Seagull on the balance sheet date.

Required

Prepare a consolidated balance sheet as at 31 December 20X1.

3 Minority interests

3.1 Control

We said earlier that we can 'control' a company without necessarily owning it 100%. In fact any holding of more than 50% of the equity shares is usually sufficient to give control. If we own more than 50%, but less than 100%, of the equity shares of another company we need an additional working: (W4) minority interest. This calculation is necessary to reflect the third-party ownership in the net assets of the subsidiary.

3.2 Example

Suppose that Polar's investment in Squirrel represents only 80% of Squirrel's equity, not 100%. All other details remain the same.

Required

Prepare a consolidated balance sheet as at 31 December 20X1.

3.3 Solution

We use exactly the same technique as before, following our standard pattern of workings.

Step 1

(W1) Group structure

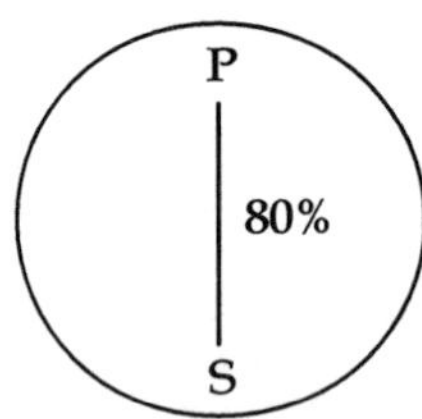

Step 2

(W2) Net assets of Squirrel	*At date of acquisition* £000	*At balance sheet date* £000
£1 shares	100	100

Step 3

(W3) Goodwill	£000
Purchase consideration	110
For 80% of net assets (£100,000) acquired	(80)
Goodwill	30

Note that the application of the 80% in (W3) gives us a different goodwill figure.

Step 4

We now move on and calculate the third-party ownership in the net assets of Squirrel. Again, (W2) is a sub-working which will feed into (W4), minority interest. This time however it is the net assets at the balance sheet date which concern us.

(W4) Minority interest	£000
20% of net assets at balance sheet date (£100,000) (W2)	20

Tutorial note. If we own 80% of the shares of Squirrel, third parties own the rest (20%). In other words 20% of Squirrel's net assets at the balance sheet date are 'owned' by third parties and this will need to be reflected in the consolidated balance sheet.

Step 5

We are now in a position to prepare a consolidated balance sheet. Note the position of the minority interest figure.

POLAR GROUP CONSOLIDATED BALANCE SHEET AS AT 31 DECEMBER 20X1

	£000	£000
Fixed assets		
Intangible assets (W3)		30
Tangible assets (90 + 80)		170
		200
Current assets (50 + 30)	80	
Creditors: amounts falling due within one year (30 + 10)	(40)	
Net current assets		40
		240
Capital and reserves		
£1 shares (100% P only)		100
Profit and loss reserves (100% P)		120
Shareholders' capital		220
Minority interest (W4)		20
		240

Make sure that you include 100% of all S's net assets in order to reflect 'control' and reflect 'ownership' by the minority interest line.

Activity 2 *(The answer is in the final chapter of this book)*

Puffin (II)

Using Activity 1, facts as before, but now assume that Puffin's investment in Seagull represents only a 90% interest.

Required

Prepare a consolidated balance sheet as at 31 December 20X1.

4 Accounting for reserves

4.1 Pre-acquisition reserves

The reserves which exist in a subsidiary company at the date when it is acquired are called its 'pre-acquisition' reserves. These are capitalised at the date of acquisition by including them in the goodwill calculation.

To see what this means, remember that we calculate the value of net assets acquired not by totalling the value of individual assets, but instead (as a short cut) by referring to the other side of the balance sheet (capital and reserves). Thus the value of net assets acquired is the value of share capital acquired plus the value of (pre-acquisition) profits acquired. By comparing this total with the amount of the purchase consideration we arrive at the value of goodwill.

4.2 Example

Draft balance sheets of Piper and Swans on 31 December 20X1 are as follows.

	Piper Ltd	*Swans Ltd*
	£000	*£000*
Fixed assets	90	100
Investment in Swans at cost	110	
Current assets	50	30
	250	130
Creditors: amounts falling due within one year	(30)	(10)
	220	120
Capital and reserves		
Share capital	100	100
Profit and loss account	120	20
	220	120

Piper Ltd had bought 80% of the shares of Swans on 1 January 20X1 when the profit and loss account of Swans had stood at £15,000.

Required

Prepare a consolidated balance sheet as at 31 December 20X1, ignoring the amortisation of goodwill.

4.3 Solution

We use our standard workings as before, but when we calculate net assets at the date of acquisition we include share capital and *reserves at the date of acquisition.*

(W2) will look like this.

Net assets of Swans Ltd	*At date of acquisition*	*At balance sheet date*
	£000	£000
£1 shares	100	100
Profit and loss account	15	20
	115	120

If we follow our standard workings our answer will be as follows.

PIPER GROUP CONSOLIDATED BALANCE SHEET AS AT 31 DECEMBER 20X1

	£000	£000
Fixed assets		
Intangible assets (W3)		18
Tangible assets (90 + 100)		190
		208
Current assets (50 + 30)	80	
Current liabilities (30 + 10)	(40)	
Net current assets		40
		248
Capital and reserves		
£1 shares (100% P only)		100
Profit and loss reserves (W5)		124
Shareholders' capital		224
Minority interest (W4)		24
		248

Workings

(W1) Group structure

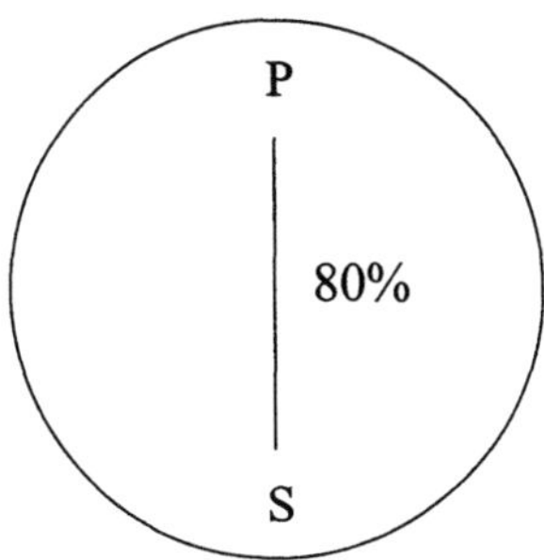

(W2) Net assets of Swans	*At date of acquisition* £000	*At balance sheet date* £000
£1 shares	100	100
Reserves	15	20
	115	120

(W3) Goodwill	£000
Purchase consideration	110
For 80% of net assets (£115,000) acquired	(92)
Goodwill	18

(W4) Minority interests

20% of net assets at balance sheet date (£120,000)	24

(W5) Group Profit and Loss reserve

Profits earned by the subsidiary after the date of acquisition are called 'post-acquisition reserves'. We include the group's share of the subsidiaries' post-acquisition reserves in the consolidated balance sheet, which gives us our final standard working (W5): the group profit and loss account.

	£000
100% Parent	120

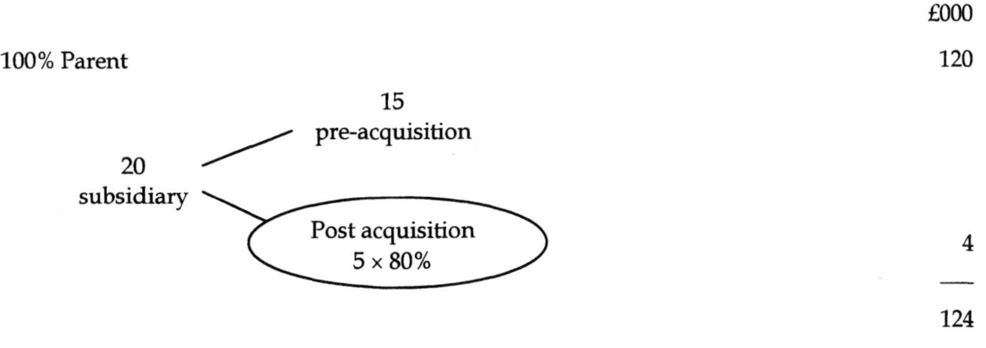

	4
	124

If the subsidiary has other reserves (eg, a revaluation reserve, a share premium, a general reserve) we use the same basic calculation for each reserve separately.

Activity 3 *(The answer is in the final chapter of this book)*

Pluto

Draft balance sheets of Pluto and Snoopy on 31 December 20X8 are as follows.

	Pluto Ltd	*Snoopy Ltd*
	£000	£000
Fixed assets	120	150
Investment in Snoopy at cost	140	-
Current assets	40	50
	300	200
Creditors: amounts falling due within one year	(40)	(30)
	260	170
Capital and reserves		
Share capital	100	100
Profit and loss account	160	70
	260	170

Pluto purchased 75% of the shares of Snoopy on 1 January 20X7, when the profit and loss account of Snoopy stood at £40,000.

Required

Prepare a consolidated balance sheet as at 31 December 20X8, ignoring the amortisation of goodwill.

5 The treatment of goodwill

5.1 FRS 10: Goodwill and Intangible Assets

FRS 10 requires that non-purchased goodwill (or inherent goodwill), should never be shown in the accounts at all.

Purchased goodwill (including goodwill arising on consolidation) is required to be shown as an asset on the balance sheet and amortised over its useful economic life, a straight line basis is the preferred option.

Negative goodwill is shown as a negative asset in the fixed assets section of the balance sheet, just below any positive goodwill. (Negative goodwill arises if a subsidiary is purchased for an amount *less than* the total value of its separable net assets).

5.2 Amortisation of goodwill

The standard contains a presumption that the useful life of goodwill is a maximum of 20 years. If the estimated useful economic life of goodwill is *20 years or less,* the goodwill is required to be amortised over its estimated useful economic life. The amortisation should be charged in the profit and loss account.

If the estimated useful economic life of goodwill is *more than 20 years* the goodwill is required to be written off over its estimated useful economic life, with the amortisation charged in the profit and loss account. If the estimated useful economic life is indefinite, the goodwill should not be amortised.

In both the cases described in the previous paragraph, at the end of each financial year, a full impairment review must be performed. When the estimated life is 20 years or less an impairment review is normally only required at the end of the first full year after acquisition.

5.3 Example

Consider the example of Faye Ltd below.

BALANCE SHEETS AT 31 DECEMBER 20X9

	Faye Ltd		*Garbo Ltd*	
	£	£	£	£
Fixed assets				
Tangible assets		33,000		20,000
Investments: shares in Garbo Ltd at cost		12,000		
Current assets	5,000		15,000	
Creditors: amounts falling due within one year	(9,000)		(10,000)	
Net current (liabilities)/assets		(4,000)		5,000
Total assets less current liabilities		41,000		25,000
Creditors: amounts falling due after more than one year				
8% Debenture loans		20,000		9,000
		21,000		16,000
Capital and reserves				
Called up share capital (£1 ordinary shares)		10,000		4,000
Share premium account		5,000		-
Profit and loss account		6,000		12,000
		21,000		16,000

On 1 January 20X3 Faye Ltd acquired 3,000 shares of Garbo Ltd. At that date the balance on Garbo Ltd's profit and loss account was £8,000.

Required

Prepare the consolidated balance sheet of Faye Ltd at 31 December 20X9, assuming the group policy is to amortise goodwill arising on consolidation over a period of ten years.

5.4 Solution

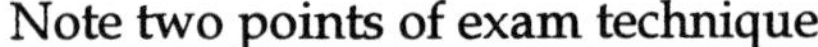

Note two points of exam technique.

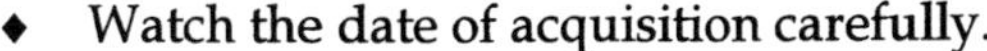

- Watch the date of acquisition carefully.
- Make sure you use the correct number of years for the amortisation charge.

We use our standard workings.

(W1) Group structure

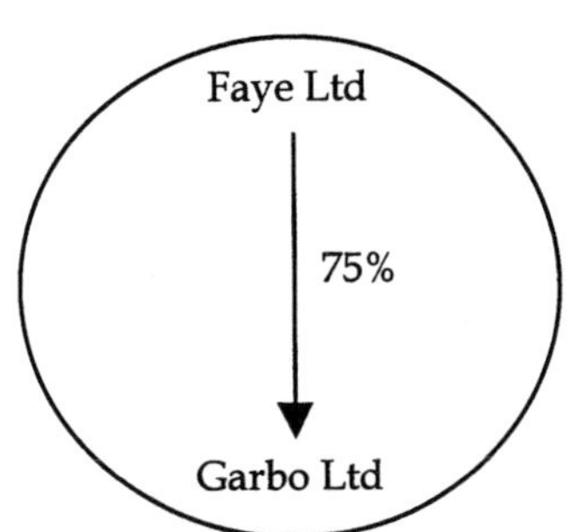

(W2) Net assets of Garbo Ltd

	At date of acquisition	*At balance sheet date*
	£	£
Share capital	4,000	4,000
Profit and loss account	8,000	12,000
	12,000	16,000

(W3) Goodwill

	£
Purchase consideration	12,000
Net assets acquired (75% × £12,000) (W2)	(9,000)
Goodwill	3,000
Amortised to date (7/10)	(2,100)
Intangible fixed asset remaining	900

We must recognise that at 31 December 20X9, seven years' worth of the purchased goodwill (ie 70%) would have been written off to the profit and loss account, leaving three years' worth (ie 30%) as an asset in the balance sheet.

(W4) Minority interest

	£
Minority interest (25% × 16,000 (W2))	4,000

But now (W3) will feed into (W5) showing the write-off of the goodwill to the profit and loss account.

(W5) Profit and loss account

	£
Faye Ltd	6,000
Less accumulated amortisation of goodwill (70% × 3,000)	(2,100)
	3,900
Garbo Ltd (75% × (12,000 – 8,000) (W2)) group share of post acquisition reserves	3,000
	6,900

The consolidated balance sheet will now look as follows.

FAYE LTD - CONSOLIDATED BALANCE SHEET AT 31 DECEMBER 20X9

	£	£
Fixed assets		
Intangible asset: goodwill (30% × £3,000)		900
Tangible assets (33,000 + 20,000)		53,000
Current assets (5,000 + 15,000)	20,000	
Creditors: amounts falling due within one year (9,000 + 10,000)	(19,000)	
Net current assets		1,000
Total assets less current liabilities		54,900
Creditors: amounts falling due after more than one year		
8% Debenture loans (20,000 + 9,000)		(29,000)
		25,900
Capital and reserves		
Called up share capital		10,000
Share premium account		5,000
Profit and loss account (W5)		6,900
		21,900
Minority interest (W4)		4,000
		25,900

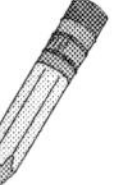

Activity 4 *(The answer is in the final chapter of this book)*

Dublin

The following are the summarised balance sheets of Dublin and Shannon at 31 December 20X9.

	Dublin Ltd	Shannon Ltd
	£	£
Fixed assets		
Tangible assets	100,000	60,000
Investments:		
24,000 shares in Shannon Ltd	50,000	
Current assets	215,000	50,000
	365,000	110,000
Creditors: amounts falling due within one year	(150,000)	(20,000)
	215,000	90,000
Capital and reserves		
Called up share capital (£1 ordinary)	190,000	40,000
Profit and loss account	25,000	50,000
	215,000	90,000

Dublin Ltd purchased its shares in Shannon Ltd on 1 January 20X9, when there was a credit balance on that company's profit and loss account of £40,000.

The accounting policy of Dublin Ltd is to amortise goodwill over 5 years.

Required

Prepare the consolidated balance sheet as at 31 December 20X9.

Activity 5 *(The answer is in the final chapter of this book)*

Prince plc

On 1.1.20X4 Prince plc acquired 100% of the share capital of Madonna Ltd and Jackson Ltd, paying £60,000 and £40,000 respectively.

The balance sheets of the three companies are as follows at 31.12.X4:

		Prince	Madonna	Jackson
		£	£	£
Fixed assets:	Tangible	60,000	40,000	32,000
	Investments	100,000	-	-
		160,000	40,000	32,000
Current assets		90,000	86,000	52,000
Creditors: Amounts falling due within one year		(50,000)	(41,000)	(40,000)
Net current assets		40,000	45,000	12,000
Total assets less current liabilities		200,000	85,000	44,000
Creditors: Amounts falling due after more than one year		(18,000)	(30,000)	(10,000)
		182,000	55,000	34,000

Share capital	60,000	50,000	30,000
Profit and loss account	122,000	5,000	4,000
	182,000	55,000	34,000

Profit for the year:

	£
Jackson Ltd	3,000
Madonna Ltd	1,000

Goodwill arising on acquisition is amortised through the profit and loss account over three years from the date of acquisition.

Required

Show how the consolidated balance sheet would look at 31 December 20X4.

6 Intra-group balances

6.1 Introduction

When consolidating we need to cancel out items which are assets in one group company and liabilities in another.

This is an application of the single entity concept, which we met earlier in the chapter.

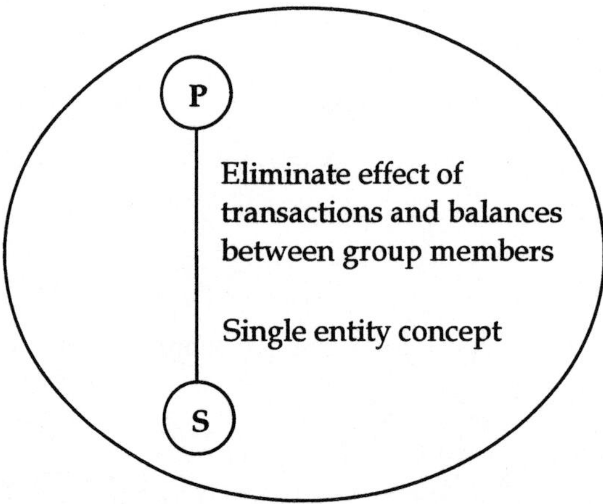

Where the group companies trade with each other, there are several ways in which balances with each other can arise. The most common of these are:

- loans and debentures
- current accounts

6.2 Loans and debentures

This is where one company in the group has made a loan to another. In one company there is a creditor and in the other a debtor. The cancellation process is very simple in that the credit balance of one company is offset against the debit balance of the other company, eliminating both balances from the consolidated balance sheet.

6.3 *Current accounts*

Current accounts are intra-group trading balances. The treatment of current accounts is the same as for loans. However, inter-company current accounts may not agree.

For example, the following balances appeared in the books of P Ltd and S Ltd in their balance sheets dated 31 December 20X0:

	Books of P Ltd	*Books of S Ltd*
	£	£
Current account with S Ltd	10,700 Dr	
Current account with P Ltd		10,000 Cr

On 31 December 20X0 S Ltd had sent a cheque for £700 to P Ltd which the latter company did not record until 2 January 20X1. This is called cash-in-transit.

The necessary consolidation adjustment will be to follow the transaction to its natural conclusion by recording the receipt of the cash in P Ltd's books, thus decreasing its current account balance by £700 to £10,000, and increasing its cash balance by £700. The current account balances of £10,000 can then be cancelled out.

6.4 *Example*

Laura plc acquired 100% of the share capital of Ashley Ltd for £40,000 on 1 January 20X4, when the balance on the profit and loss account reserve of Ashley Ltd stood at £8,000. The following draft balance sheets were drawn up at 31 December 20X7.

	Laura plc		*Ashley Ltd*	
	£	£	£	£
Fixed assets				
Tangible assets		88,000		39,000
Investments				
Shares in Ashley Ltd		40,000		-
6% debentures in Ashley Ltd		4,000		-
		132,000		39,000
Current assets				
Trade debtors	84,000		26,000	
Due from Laura plc	-		15,000	
Cash at bank and in hand	-		16,000	
	84,000		57,000	
Creditors: Amounts falling due within one year				
Trade creditors	46,000		28,000	
Due to Ashley Ltd	10,000		-	
Bank overdraft	14,000		-	
	70,000		28,000	
Net current assets		14,000		29,000
Total assets less current liabilities		146,000		68,000
Creditors: Amounts falling due after more than one year				
6% debentures		-		(12,000)
		146,000		56,000

Capital and reserves		
Called-up share capital	100,000	24,000
Profit and loss account	46,000	32,000
	146,000	56,000

You discover that Laura plc sent a cheque for £5,000 to Ashley Ltd on 30 December 20X7, which was not received until 3 January 20X8.

Goodwill arising on the acquisition is to be amortised over its useful economic life of four years.

Required

Prepare the consolidated balance sheet of Laura plc as at 31 December 20X7.

6.5 Solution

Consolidated balance sheet of Laura plc at 31 December 20X7

	£	£
Fixed assets		
Tangible assets (88 + 39)		127,000
Current assets		
Trade debtors (84 + 26)	110,000	
Cash (16 + 5)	21,000	
	131,000	
Creditors: Amounts falling due within one year		
Trade creditors (46 + 28)	74,000	
Bank overdraft	14,000	
	88,000	
Net current assets		43,000
Total assets less current liabilities		170,000
Creditors: Amounts falling due after more than one year		
6% debentures (12 – 4)		(8,000)
		162,000
Capital and reserves		
Called-up share capital		100,000
Profit and loss account (W5)		62,000
		162,000

Workings

- Current accounts

  Adjust the receiving company's books, as if Ashley Ltd had received the cheque before the end of the year.

  Ashley Ltd's books

			£	£
Dr	Cash		5,000	
	Cr	Intra-group – due from Laura		5,000

Therefore the balance on its intra-group debtor is reduced to £10,000 and is equal to the amount shown as a creditor in Laura plc's accounts. We cancel these £10,000 balances and increase the consolidated cash balance by £5,000.

- 6% debentures

  Laura plc owns £4,000 of the debentures issued by Ashley Ltd. This asset in Laura plc's accounts must be cancelled with the liability in Ashley Ltd's books, leaving a liability due to the other debenture holders of £8,000.

- Consolidation workings

(W1) Group structure

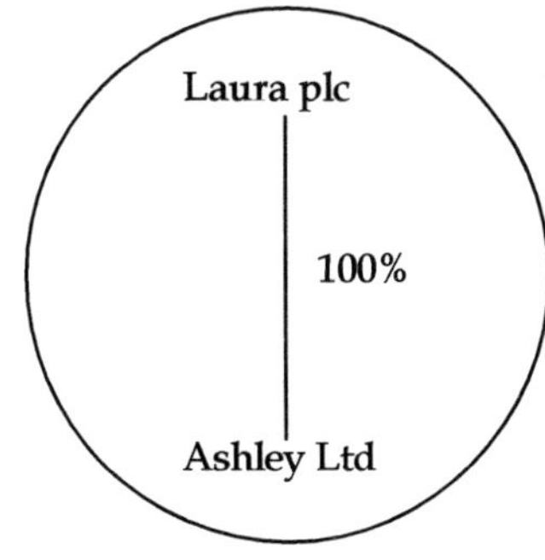

(W2) Net assets of Ashley Ltd

	Acquisition date	*Balance sheet date*
	£	£
Share capital	24,000	24,000
Profit and loss account	8,000	32,000
	32,000	56,000

(W3) Goodwill schedule

	£
Costs of shares acquired	40,000
Net assets acquired (W2)	(32,000)
Goodwill, fully written off	8,000

(W4) No minority interest

(W5) Profit and loss account schedule

	£
Laura plc	46,000
Ashley Ltd post-acquisition	
[32,000 – 8,000 (W2)] × 100%	24,000
Less: Goodwill (W3) (fully amortised)	(8,000)
	62,000

7 Dividends

7.1 Individual companies

If a subsidiary proposes a dividend, the effects will be as follows:

- Subsidiary company books

Dr Profit and loss	X	
Cr Dividend creditor		X

with the dividend payable

- Parent company books

Dr Dividend debtor	X	
Cr Profit and loss account		X

with its share of the dividend receivable from the subsidiary company

7.2 Consolidation adjustment

The dividend debtor in the parent company's books is receivable from another group company, and should be cancelled out against all (if 100% owned) or part (if less than 100% owned) of the dividend creditor in the subsidiary company's books. Any balance left on the dividend creditor of the subsidiary company represents the dividend owed to the minority shareholders of the company.

The only figure that will appear in the consolidated net assets will be any dividend payable by the subsidiary to the minority shareholders.

7.3 Example

The following are draft balance sheets as at 31 December 20X9 for Wells Ltd and its subsidiary, Christie Ltd:

	Wells Ltd	*Christie Ltd*
	£000	£000
Fixed assets		
Tangible assets	300	100
Investment in Christie Ltd - 24,000 shares at cost	45	-
Current assets	300	168
Creditors: Amounts falling due within one year		
Trade creditors	(80)	(100)
Proposed dividends	(20)	-
Long-term loans	(175)	(60)
	370	108
Called up share capital - £1 ordinary shares	90	30
Profit and loss account	280	78
	370	108

Wells Ltd acquired its shares in Christie Ltd when the latter's reserves stood at £20,000. Christie Ltd wishes to propose a dividend of £8,000. Goodwill arising on the acquisition has been fully amortised.

Required

Prepare the consolidated balance sheet as at 31 December 20X9.

7.4 Solution

Wells Ltd consolidated balance sheet at 31 December 20X9

		£000	£000
Fixed assets			
Tangible assets (300 + 100)			400.0
Current assets (300 + 168 + 6.4 – 6.4)*		468.0	
Creditors: Amounts falling due within one year			
Trade creditors (80 + 100)		180.0	
Proposed dividends:	Parent company	20.0	
	Minority interests (20% × 8,000)	1.6	
		201.6	
Net current assets			266.4
Total assets less current liabilities			666.4
Creditors: Amounts falling due after more than one year (175 + 60)			(235.0)
			431.4
Capital and reserves			
Called-up share capital			90.0
Profit and loss account (W5)			321.4
			411.4
Minority interest (W4)			20.0
			431.4

*£6,400 represents the parent company's share of the subsidiary's dividend (80% of £8,000). This will be added to the parent's current assets as 'dividend receivable'. It will also be added to the subsidiary's current liabilities as 'dividend payable', forming part of the total liability of £8,000.

Workings

(W1) Group structure

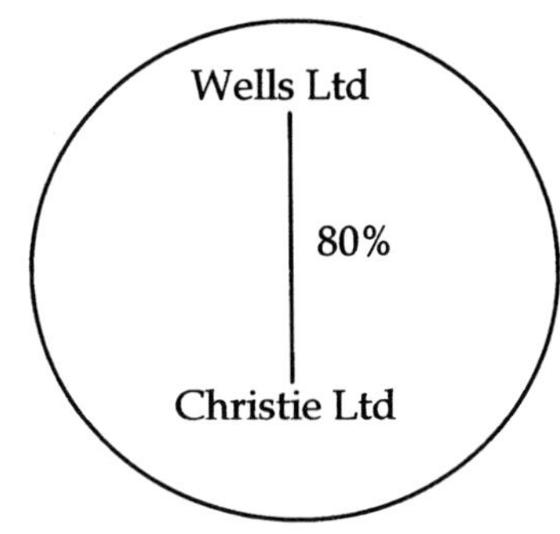

(W2) Net assets of Christie:

	Acquisition date	*Balance sheet date*	
	£000	£000	£000
Share capital	30		30
Profit and loss account	20	78	
Less: Proposed dividend		(8)	
			70
	50		100

(W3) Goodwill schedule

	£000
Shares in Christie Ltd	45
Net assets acquired [80% × 50 (W2)]	(40)
Goodwill (fully amortised)	5

(W4) Minority interest schedule

	£000
20% × 100 (W2)	20

(W5) Profit and loss account schedule

	£000	£000
Wells Ltd	280	
Add: Dividend receivable (80% × 8)	6.4	
		286.4
Share of Christie Ltd [80% × (70 – 20)(W2)]		40
Less: goodwill (fully amortised)		(5)
		321.4

8 Unrealised intra–group profit

8.1 Introduction

Where, during the period under review, goods (or any other assets) are transferred between group companies at prices other than cost, the transferring company can make a profit.

In consolidated accounts, we want to reflect only profits made by group companies trading with third parties (single entity concept).

No adjustment is necessary on consolidation if the goods (or assets) have been sold on, outside the group, within the period. However, where such goods (or assets) are still held within the group at the end of the accounting period, the consolidated accounts would not show a true and fair view of the profits of the group as a whole if the profits made on such transfers were not eliminated.

8.2 Stocks

The consolidated balance sheet should show stocks at the lower of cost and net realisable value to the group. The effects of transactions between group members should be eliminated on consolidation (single entity concept).

The adjustment for the unrealised profit on stocks is straightforward where the parent company sells goods to the subsidiary. The profit is made by the parent and recorded in its books. Hence, it is all owned by the parent.

8.3 Example

During the current accounting period P Ltd transferred goods to S Ltd for £12,000, which gave P Ltd a profit of £3,000. One third of these goods were included in the stocks of S Ltd at the balance sheet date.

What consolidation adjustment is required?

8.4 Solution

The adjustment in the consolidated balance sheet would be as follows:

		£	£
Dr	Profit and loss account ($\frac{1}{3}$ × £3,000)	1,000	
Cr	Balance sheet stocks		1,000

The stock of goods still held by S Ltd, valued at £4,000 in S's stock, is being reduced to its cost to the group of £3,000.

8.5 Sales of goods from subsidiary to parent company

On the net assets side of the balance sheet, the unrealised profit is still eliminated from stocks in full. This is because the group as a whole has bought and is holding stock, which should therefore be shown at the lower of cost and net realisable value to the group. The profit on the sale will have been recorded in the subsidiary's books. On consolidation, the adjustment to eliminate this is apportioned between the parent and minority interests according to the ownership interests in the subsidiary.

8.6 Example

During the current accounting period S Ltd sold goods to P Ltd for £18,000 which gave S Ltd a profit of £6,000. At the balance sheet date half of these goods are included in P Ltd's stock. P owns 80% of S.

What consolidation adjustment is required?

8.7 Solution

The adjustment in the consolidated balance sheet would be as follows:

		£	£
Dr	Group profit and loss account (½ × 6,000 × 80%)	2,400	
Dr	Minority interest (½ × 6,000 × 20%)	600	
Cr	Balance sheet stocks (½ × 6,000)		3,000

9 Fair values

9.1 Introduction

Goodwill is determined by comparing the value of the business as a whole with the aggregate of the fair values of its identifiable net assets. In our consolidation examples to date we have assumed that the fair value of the subsidiary's assets was equal to their book values. This approach is fine for assessment tasks where you are not given any information about the fair values.

If the fair value of the subsidiary's net assets, at the date of acquisition, is different from their book value, the book amounts should be **adjusted to fair value on consolidation.**

9.2 Example

Hardy Ltd acquired 80% of the share capital of Woolf Ltd for £54,000 on 31 December 20X7. The draft balance sheets of the two companies have been drawn up on that date.

		Hardy Ltd	Woolf Ltd
		£	£
Fixed assets			
Tangible assets		75,000	35,000
Investment in Woolf Ltd		54,000	-
Current assets		35,000	39,500
Creditors:	Amounts falling due within one year	(42,000)	(16,000)
		122,000	58,500
Share capital - £1 ordinary shares		60,000	20,000
Profit and loss account		62,000	38,500
		122,000	58,500

You are given the following additional information:

The fair value of the net assets of Woolf Ltd, on 31 December 20X7, was £66,000. This increase can be attributed to freehold land.

Required

Prepare the consolidated balance sheet of Hardy Ltd as at 31 December 20X7.

9.3 Solution

Fair value adjustment

Looking at the net assets of Woolf Ltd:

	£
Fair value at 31 December 20X7	66,000
Book value at 31 December 20X7	58,500
Revaluation	7,500

We must increase the book value of Woolf Ltd's freehold land by £7,500. The necessary journal entry is:

		£	£
Dr	Fixed assets - freehold land	7,500	
Cr	Revaluation reserve		7,500

Putting through this adjustment Woolf Ltd's balance sheet becomes:

Woolf Ltd: Balance sheet at 31 December 20X7

		£
Fixed assets at valuation		42,500
Current assets		39,500
Creditors:	Amounts falling due within one year	(16,000)
		66,000
Share capital - £1 ordinary shares		20,000
Revaluation reserve		7,500
Profit and loss account		38,500
		66,000

The increase in the value of Woolf Ltd's land occurred over time up to the date of takeover. The revaluation reserve is therefore a **pre-acquisition** reserve and is treated in the same way as pre-acquisition profits.

We will now prepare the consolidated balance sheet.

Hardy Ltd: Consolidated balance sheet at 31 December 20X7

	£
Fixed assets:	
Intangible assets: goodwill (W3)	1,200
Tangible assets (75 + 42.5)	117,500
Current assets (35 + 39.5)	74,500
Creditors: Amounts falling due within one year (42 + 16)	(58,000)
	135,200
Share capital - £1 ordinary shares	60,000
Profit and loss account (W5)	62,000
	122,000
Minority interest (W4)	13,200
	135,200

Consolidation workings

(W1) Group structure

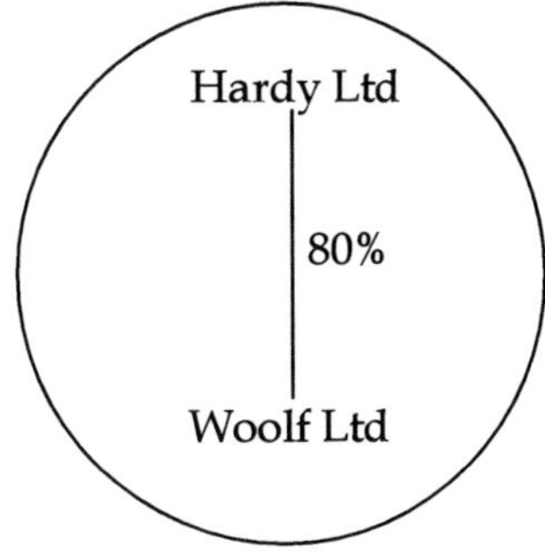

(W2) Net assets of Woolf at 31 December 20X7

	£
Share capital	20,000
Profit and loss account	38,500
	58,500
Revaluation reserve	7,500
Fair value of net assets	66,000

(W3) Goodwill schedule

	£
Cost of shares in Woolf	54,000
Net assets acquired (80% × 66,000) (W2)	52,800
	1,200

(W4) Minority interest schedule

	£
20% × 66,000 (W2)	13,200

(W5) Profit and loss account schedule

	£
Hardy Ltd	62,000

(Note that there are no post-acquisition profits for the subsidiary, and no need to amortise the goodwill since the acquisition has only just taken place.)

10 Other considerations

10.1 Other reserves

In many cases, there is only one reserve, the profit and loss account reserve, in the subsidiary's balance sheet. The pre-acquisition profit and loss reserves are taken to the goodwill computation and the parent's share of the subsidiary's post-acquisition reserves is included in the group reserves calculation.

A subsidiary may have other reserves in its balance sheet, such as a revaluation reserve. On consolidation, we treat these in exactly the same way as the profit and loss reserve. Hence, the reserves at acquisition are taken to the goodwill computation and the parent's share of any post-acquisition reserves is added to the parent's own reserves. However, it is important not to mix up the different categories of reserve. Therefore, if a subsidiary has a post-acquisition revaluation reserve, for example, the parent's share goes in the consolidated balance sheet under 'revaluation reserve' not 'profit and loss account'.

10.2 Accounting policies

All balances included in consolidated accounts should be based on the same accounting policies. If a subsidiary uses different accounting policies in preparing its own accounts from those adopted by the group as a whole (eg regarding development costs), the subsidiary's accounts should be adjusted prior to consolidation for consistency. We should make any necessary adjustment to the subsidiary's profit and loss account reserve in the net assets working prior to calculating goodwill, minority interests and group reserves.

10.3 Goodwill in a subsidiary's own books

We calculate goodwill on consolidation based on the fair value of the subsidiary's separable net assets acquired. Any goodwill recorded in the subsidiary's own balance sheet is not an asset separable from the business as a whole. Hence we need to eliminate this goodwill by adjusting the subsidiary's net assets prior to consolidating.

Note that, for uniform accounting policies, fair value adjustments and goodwill in a subsidiary's own books, we do not need to adjust in the subsidiary's own accounts as an individual company. Instead, we can make the adjustment just for the consolidated accounts.

Activity 6 *(The answer is in the final chapter of this book)*

Heavy plc

As on 31 March 20X1 the draft balance sheets of Heavy plc and its subsidiary, Side Ltd showed the following positions:

	Heavy plc		*Side Ltd*	
	£	£	£	£
Fixed assets (tangible)		180,000		40,000
Investment in Side Ltd		49,200		-
		229,200		40,000

Current assets				
Stock	40,000		32,000	
Inter–company account	-		10,500	
Cash at bank and in hand	-		3,000	
	40,000		45,500	
Creditors: Amounts falling due within one year				
Bank overdraft	6,000		-	
Trade creditors	41,000		17,000	
Inter–company account	8,000		-	
	55,000		17,000	
Net current (liabilities)/assets		(15,000)		28,500
Total assets less current liabilities		214,200		68,500
Creditors: Amounts falling due after more than one year				
Debenture loan		(50,000)		-
		164,200		68,500
Financed by:				
Share capital - £1 ordinary shares		100,000		10,000
Share premium account		20,000		10,000
Profit and loss account		44,200		48,500
		164,200		68,500

You are given the following additional information:

(1) Shortly before the year-end, Heavy plc paid £2,500 to Side Ltd. At 31 March 20X1, Side Ltd had not yet received this amount.

(2) It has been decided that Heavy plc and Side Ltd should declare dividends of 10 pence per share and 20 pence per share respectively for the year ended 31 March 20X1.

(3) Heavy plc acquired 80% of the issued share capital of Side Ltd on 1 April 20X0. Side Ltd made a profit available for distribution for the year of £10,500.

(4) It is group accounting policy to amortise any goodwill on acquisition through the profit and loss account over five years.

Required

Prepare the consolidated balance sheet of Heavy plc as on 31 March 20X1, together with your consolidation schedules.

---

11 Quick quiz *(The answers are in the final chapter of this book)*

1 P Ltd acquires 90% of S Ltd for £100,000 on a date when S Ltd's net assets total £80,000. What is the goodwill arising on consolidation?

2 P Ltd owns 80% of S Ltd. S Ltd's net assets total £100,000 on the balance sheet date. What figure for minority interests will appear in the consolidated balance sheet?

3 What accounting treatment does FRS 10 require for purchased goodwill?

4 If S Ltd has sent a cheque to its parent company, P Ltd, but the parent company has not received it on the balance sheet date, how is this accounted for?

12 Summary

In this chapter, we have met the basic principles of preparing a consolidated balance sheet. Make sure that you understand the concept of the group as a single entity and the distinction between control and ownership. This last point is summarised in the following proforma:

Consolidated balance sheet

		£
Net assets		X
P + S (100%)		
CONTROL		X
OWNERSHIP:		
Capital and reserves:		
Share capital	(P only)	X
Reserves	(P + P% × S post acq)	X
Owned by P's shareholders		X
Minority interests		X
(MI% × S's net assets consolidated)		
		X

Key

P = parent
S = subsidiary
P% = parent share of subsidiary
MI% = Minority interest share of subsidiary

A lot of detailed points have been covered in this chapter. However, if you remember the single entity concept and use the five standard workings then assessment tasks should be achievable.

CHAPTER 8

Consolidated accounts – profit and loss account

ASSESSMENT FOCUS

For this Unit you may have to draft a consolidated profit and loss account from the financial statements of a parent and a subsidiary undertaking. In this chapter therefore we will build on the consolidation principles from the previous chapter and prepare a consolidated profit and loss account.

This chapter covers the following Knowledge and Understanding of the AAT Syllabus.

Generally accepted accounting principles and concepts *(Element 11.1)*

The general principles of consolidation *(Element 11.1)*

In order to cover these the following topics are included.

Basic principles of a consolidated profit and loss account
Intra-group trading and provision for unrealised profit
Treatment of goodwill

Key definitions

Consolidated profit and loss account	Profit and loss account prepared for a group as though the group were a single economic entity.
Unrealised profit	Profit which has been reported in the individual accounts of a group member, but where the items sold remain in group stocks at the balance sheet date.

1 Basic principles

1.1 Introduction

In this chapter, we switch our attention to the consolidated profit and loss account. This is prepared on the same basis as the consolidated balance sheet and thus most of the key principles will already be familiar. In particular, the single entity concept and the distinction between control and ownership are as important to the consolidated profit and loss account as they are to the consolidated balance sheet.

The parent's own profit and loss account as an individual company will show dividend income from the subsidiary. The consolidated profit and loss account shows the incomes generated from the group's resources. Those resources are shown by the net assets in the consolidated balance sheet.

1.2 Control and ownership

When we prepared the consolidated balance sheet, we added together the net assets of the parent and subsidiary line by line to show the resources under the parent's control. We apply exactly the same principle in preparing the consolidated profit and loss account by adding together the parent's and subsidiary's income and expenses line by line. This will give us the profit after tax generated from the resources under the group's control.

In the consolidated balance sheet, we showed the ownership of the group's net assets on the capital and reserves side, where we showed the minority interests separately from the capital and reserves attributable to the parent's shareholders.

In the consolidated profit and loss account, we show the ownership of the profit after tax by deducting the minority interest share of the subsidiary's profit from the consolidated profit after tax, leaving us with the profit owned by the parent's shareholders.

1.3 Intra-group items

When we looked at the consolidated balance sheet, we saw how the single entity concept was applied by cancelling out intra-group items and unrealised profits, and how we apportioned unrealised profit adjustments according to ownership. As we shall see in more detail later in this chapter, we apply the same principles in the consolidated profit and loss account.

We shall now see in more detail how to prepare the consolidated profit and loss account.

1.4 Proforma consolidated profit and loss account

Work your way through the pro forma, referring to the tutorial notes which are referenced by letters in brackets.

Consolidated profit and loss account for the year ended....

	£
Turnover (a)	X
Cost of sales (a)	(X)
Gross profit	X
Distribution costs	(X)
Administrative expenses	(X)
Other operating income	X
Operating profit	X
Profit on the sale of fixed assets	X
Profit on ordinary activities before interest	X
Other interest receivable and similar income (b) (c)	X
Interest payable and similar charges (b)	(X)
Profit on ordinary activities before taxation (Note 1)	X
Tax on profit on ordinary activities	(X)
Profit on ordinary activities after taxation (d)	X
Minority interests (e)	(X)
Profit for the financial year attributable to parent's shareholders	X
Dividends (f)	(X)
Retained profit for the year	X

Statement of retained profits

	£
Retained profits at beginning of year (g)	X
Retained profit for the financial year	X
Retained profits at end of year	X
Earnings per share	Xp

Notes to the accounts

(1) Profit on ordinary activities before taxation is stated after charging the following:

	£
Depreciation of tangible fixed assets (h)	X
Auditors' remuneration and expenses (h)	X
Directors' emoluments (i)	
As directors	X
Remuneration as executives	X

Tutorial notes

(a) Intra-group sales must be eliminated from both the turnover of the selling company and the cost of sales of the buying company.

(b) Any intra-group interest must be eliminated from interest receivable and interest payable respectively (single entity concept).

(c) Similarly, dividends from subsidiaries must be eliminated since the whole of the profits of those subsidiaries are being consolidated and it would be double counting to include the dividends as well.

(d) Profit on ordinary activities after taxation – Up to this point, 100% of all items for the parent company and all subsidiaries have been aggregated (subject to intra-group adjustments). It is now necessary to compute the amount of the profit after taxation that is attributable to outside (minority) shareholders.

(e) Minority interests – This is calculated by taking the minority interest's share of the subsidiary's profit after taxation.

(f) Dividends paid and proposed – These will be the dividends of the *parent company only* since a subsidiary's dividends are effectively intra-group items. No dividends to minority interests are included since their share of the subsidiary's profit after tax, whether or not paid out as a dividend, has already been taken out in the minority interest line.

(g) Retained profits at beginning of year – This figure will be the retained profits brought forward of the parent company together with the parent company's share of the post-acquisition retained profits of each subsidiary, less goodwill written off to date. This is the figure which would appear in the opening consolidated balance sheet.

(h) Depreciation/auditors' remuneration – This disclosure will be the simple aggregation of the amounts in the parent company and each subsidiary.

(i) Directors' emoluments – This disclosure is an exception to the basic rule of aggregation. The statutory requirement is to show the total of all emoluments paid by companies within the group *to directors of the parent company only.*

1.5 Example

Set out below are the draft profit and loss accounts of Smiths plc and its subsidiary company Flowers Ltd for the year ended 31 December 20X7.

On 31 December 20X5 Smiths plc purchased 75,000 ordinary shares and £10,000 10% debentures in Flowers Ltd. At that date the profit and loss account of Flowers Ltd showed a credit balance of £3,000.

The issued share capital of Flowers Ltd is 100,000 £1 ordinary shares, and it had £30,000 10% debentures outstanding on 31 December 20X7. Flowers Ltd pays its debenture interest on 31 December each year.

	Smiths plc	Flowers Ltd
	£	£
Turnover	600,000	300,000
Cost of sales	(427,000)	(232,000)
Gross profit	173,000	68,000
Distribution costs	(41,000)	(14,000)
Administrative expenses	(52,000)	(31,000)
Income from shares in group undertakings	7,500	-
Income from other fixed asset investments (dividends from UK quoted companies)	3,000	1,000
Other interest receivable - from group companies	1,000	-
Interest payable	-	(3,000)
Profit on ordinary activities before taxation (Note)	91,500	21,000
Tax on profit on ordinary activities	(38,500)	(8,000)
Profit on ordinary activities after taxation	53,000	13,000
Dividends - proposed	(30,000)	(10,000)
Retained profit for the year	23,000	3,000
Retained profits brought forward	30,000	12,000
Retained profits carried forward	53,000	15,000

Note

Profit before taxation has been arrived at after charging:

	£	£
Depreciation	20,000	6,000
Auditors' remuneration and expenses	5,000	2,000
Directors' emoluments	10,000	4,000

The following additional information is relevant:

(1) During the year Smiths plc sold goods to Flowers Ltd for £20,000, making a profit of £5,000. These goods were all sold by Flowers Ltd before the end of the year.

(2) Included in the directors' emoluments of £4,000 in Flowers Ltd's accounts is £1,000 paid to a director of Smiths plc.

Required

Prepare for presentation to members the consolidated profit and loss account for the year ended 31 December 20X7.

1.6 Solution

Following through the pro forma, we will take the problems one at a time. Where you are uncertain of the treatment, refer back to the earlier tutorial notes.

Step 1

Group structure

Smiths plc

75%

Flowers Ltd

Step 2

Turnover and cost of sales

The total turnover is £900,000 but the intra-group sale has been included as part of Smiths plc's turnover. It must be eliminated, leaving £880,000.

Similarly, total cost of sales is £659,000 but the intra-group purchase has been included in cost of sales for Flowers Ltd. Therefore eliminating it leaves £639,000.

Investment income and interest payable

- **Income from shares in group companies** represents the dividend receivable from the subsidiary (75% × £10,000). It must be excluded from the consolidated profit and loss account.

- **Interest receivable from group companies** is Smiths plc's share of the debenture interest paid by Flowers Ltd (10% × £10,000). It must be cancelled against the *interest payable* in Flowers Ltd's profit and loss account to leave the net *interest payable* to people outside the group of £2,000.

Step 4

Minority interests

The minority interest is 25% of Flowers Ltd's profit after tax figure (ie 25% × £13,000 = £3,250).

Step 5

Dividends

Smiths plc's dividend only: £30,000

Step 6

Retained profits brought forward

The retained profit brought forward is calculated using the profit and loss schedule which we used for the consolidated balance sheet, except that we use the figures at the *start* of the year, not the end.

Remember we only include the parent company's share of the **post-acquisition** profits of a subsidiary:

	£
Smiths plc	30,000
Flowers Ltd [75% × £(12,000 – 3,000)]	6,750
	36,750

We are not given any information concerning goodwill, so we cannot take goodwill into account in this example.

Step 7

Disclosure of directors' emoluments

Emoluments paid to directors of Smiths plc only: (£10,000 + £1,000) £11,000

Step 8

Prepare the consolidated profit and loss account.

Smiths plc
Consolidated profit and loss account for the year ended 31 December 20X7

	£
Turnover	880,000
Cost of sales	(639,000)
Gross profit	241,000
Distribution costs	(55,000)
Administrative expenses	(83,000)
Income from other fixed asset investments	4,000
Interest payable	(2,000)
Profit on ordinary activities before taxation (Note 1)	105,000
Tax on profit on ordinary activities	(46,500)
Profit on ordinary activities after taxation	58,500
Minority interests	(3,250)
Profit for the financial year attributable to the group	55,250
Dividends – proposed	(30,000)
Retained profit for the year	25,250

Statement of retained profits

	£
Retained profits brought forward	36,750
Retained profit for the year	25,250
Retained profits carried forward	62,000

Notes to the accounts

(1) Profit before taxation has been arrived at after charging:

	£
Depreciation	26,000
Auditors' remuneration and expenses	7,000
Directors' emoluments	11,000

Activity 1 *(The answer is in the final chapter of this book)*

Pulp plc

Given below are the draft profit and loss accounts of Pulp plc and Saxon Ltd for the year ending 31 March 20X2. Pulp plc purchased 60% of the share capital of Saxon Ltd on 1 April 20X0 at which date Saxon Ltd had a balance on its profit and loss account reserve of £20,000.

	Pulp plc	*Saxon Ltd*
	£000	*£000*
Turnover	650	380
Cost of sales	320	180
Gross profit	330	200
Expenses	(190)	(90)
Proposed dividend from Saxon Ltd	24	-
Profit before tax	164	110

Tax	50	30
Profit after tax	114	80
Proposed dividend	70	40
Retained profit for the year	44	40
Retained profit brought forward	112	35
Retained profit carried forward	156	75

During the year Pulp plc sold goods costing £80,000 to Saxon Ltd and all of these had been sold outside the group by the end of the year.

You are required to prepare the consolidated profit and loss account for the Pulp plc group for the year ending 31 March 20X2. Ignore goodwill.

2 Intra–group trading and provision for unrealised profit

2.1 Introduction

We deal with **intra-group trading** and **unrealised profit** by applying the single entity concept. In the consolidated profit and loss account, we show the results of transactions which the group as a whole has made.

2.2 All goods sold

In the previous example the two group companies traded with one another, but all of the goods had been sold on, outside the group, before the year end. The journal used was:

Dr	Turnover	X	
Cr	Cost of sales		X

with the value of inter-company sales.

2.3 Goods remaining in stock

If the goods have not been sold on outside the group before the year-end, there will be two problems:

- stock in the acquiring company's balance sheet will be at cost to the acquiring company rather than to the group; and
- the profit and loss account of the selling company includes the profit on sale to the acquiring company; however this profit is not a true profit in the group accounts, since no sale has been made outside the group.

2.4 Consolidation adjustment

Therefore an additional correcting journal is necessary. Where the parent company has sold goods to its subsidiary, this will be as follows.

Dr	Cost of sales	X	
Cr	Stock (balance sheet)		X

with the element of inter-company profit in closing stock.

This is exactly the same as the consolidation adjustment made in the consolidated balance sheet where the consolidated reserves were debited and stock credited with the unrealised profit.

2.5 Example

Assume that in the previous example half of the goods sold by Smiths plc to Flowers Ltd were still in the stock of Flowers Ltd, and that the total profit made by Smiths plc on inter-company sales was £5,000. What figures would appear in the consolidated profit and loss account for turnover and cost of sales?

2.6 Solution

Journals

		£	£
Dr	Turnover	20,000	
Cr	Cost of sales		20,000
Dr	Cost of sales (½ × £5,000)	2,500	
Cr	Stock		2,500

Smiths plc - Consolidated profit and loss account for the year ended 31 December 20X7 (extract)

	£
Turnover (600,000 + 300,000 – 20,000)	880,000
Cost of sales (427,000 + 232,000 – 20,000 + 2,500)	(641,500)
Gross profit	238,500

Cost of sales is increased in order to reduce gross profit by taking out the unrealised profit.

2.7 Sales from subsidiary to parent company

Where the parent has sold goods to the subsidiary which remain in the subsidiary's stocks at the year-end, we eliminate the unrealised profit in full from closing stocks in the balance sheet and profit and loss account (where opening and closing stocks are in cost of sales).

However, where the subsidiary has made the intra-group sale, it will have recorded the unrealised profit. As you will recall from our study of the balance sheet, we reflected the ownership of this unrealised profit by apportioning the adjustment between the profit and loss reserve (owned by parent's shareholders) and the minority interests.

In the consolidated profit and loss account, we also need to reflect the ownership of the eliminated profit. We do this by charging the minority interest share in the minority interest computation, leaving us with the parent's share included in retained profit for the year.

2.8 Consolidation adjustment

The adjustment in the consolidated profit and loss account for an inter-company sale of stock will be as follows.

		£	£
Dr	Turnover	X	
Cr	Cost of sales		X
With the value of inter-company turnover			
Dr	Cost of sales	X	
Cr	Stock (balance sheet)		X
With the full unrealised profit on intra group sales			
Dr	Minority interest (balance sheet)	X	
Cr	Minority interest (profit and loss account)		X
With the minority's share of the unrealised profit on sale from subsidiary to parent only.			

2.9 Example

A subsidiary sells goods to its parent company for £10,000. These goods cost the subsidiary £8,000 and half are still in the parent's stock at the year end.

The parent and subsidiary profit and loss accounts are given below. P owns 80% of S.

	P	S
	£	£
Turnover	60,000	50,000
Cost of sales	30,000	28,000
Gross profit	30,000	22,000
Expenses	10,000	7,000
Profit before tax	20,000	15,000
Tax	6,000	4,000
Retained profit	14,000	11,000

Prepare the consolidated profit and loss account.

2.10 Solution

	£
Turnover (60,000 + 50,000 – 10,000)	100,000
Cost of sales (30,000 + 28,000 – 10,000 + 1,000)	49,000
Gross profit	51,000
Expenses (10,000 + 7,000)	17,000
	34,000
Tax (6,000 + 4,000)	10,000
	24,000
Minority interest (11,000 – 1,000) × 20%	2,000
Retained profit	22,000

3 Treatment of goodwill

3.1 Introduction

Remember that FRS 10 requires that purchased goodwill is capitalised and amortised through the profit and loss account over its useful economic life.

We will consider the effect of this on the consolidated profit and loss account using an example.

3.2 Example

A Ltd buys 90% of the shares of B Ltd on 1 January 20X9, the first day of its accounting period. Goodwill arising is £10,000, and has an estimated useful economic life of 10 years. What effects does the goodwill have on each year's consolidated profit and loss account?

3.3 Solution

- Years 1–10

  The group profit and loss account each year would include a charge of £1,000. This would be included under administrative expenses.

♦ Year 2 onwards

Note that the group retained profits brought forward would be net of the cumulative write-off of goodwill to date:

Year 2	£1,000
Year 3	£2,000
Year 4	£3,000, etc

Activity 2 (The answer is in the final chapter of this book)

Courage Ltd

The following are the draft profit and loss accounts of Courage Ltd and Brains Ltd for the year ended 31 December 20X4:

	Courage Ltd	*Brains Ltd*
	£	£
Turnover	3,000,000	900,000
Cost of sales	(1,700,000)	(600,000)
Gross profit	1,300,000	300,000
Distribution costs	(300,000)	(100,000)
Administrative expenses	(600,000)	(96,800)
Operating profit	400,000	103,200
Loss on sale of fixed asset investment	(50,000)	-
Reorganisation costs	-	(10,000)
Profit on ordinary activities before interest	350,000	93,200
Income from other fixed asset investments (dividends from UK quoted companies)	8,000	2,000
Other interest receivable - from group undertakings	1,600	-
Interest payable	-	(3,200)
Profit on ordinary activities before taxation	359,600	92,000
Tax on profit on ordinary activities	(159,600)	(40,000)
Profit on ordinary activities after taxation	200,000	52,000
Dividends: Ordinary, proposed	(20,000)	(4,000)
Retained profit for the year	180,000	48,000
Retained profits brought forward	100,000	25,000
Retained profits carried forward	280,000	73,000

You are given the following information:

(1) Issued share capital of the two companies:

Courage Ltd	£100,000	in £1 ordinary shares
Brains Ltd	£20,000	in £1 ordinary shares

(2) Courage Ltd bought an interest in Brains Ltd on 1 January 20X2, as follows:

12,000 ordinary shares
£20,000 (out of £40,000) 8% debentures

On 1 January 20X2 the balance of Brains Ltd's profit and loss account was £12,000. Goodwill of £20,000 arose on the acquisition which is to be written off over five years.

(3) During the year Brains Ltd sold goods to Courage Ltd for £10,000 which had cost £7,000. Two thirds of the goods remained in stock at the year end

(4) Brains Ltd has incurred exceptional reorganisation costs during the year.

(5) Courage Ltd does not account for dividends until they are received.

Required

Prepare the consolidated profit and loss account of Courage Ltd and its subsidiary Brains Ltd for the year ended 31 December 20X4.

4 Quick quiz *(The answers are in the final chapter of this book)*

1 P Ltd owns 80% of S Ltd. During 20X4, P Ltd reported turnover of £100,000 while S Ltd reported turnover of £50,000. What turnover will be reported in the consolidated profit and loss account?

2 What is the journal entry for the consolidation adjustment to eliminate intra-group sales, where all the items have been sold outside the group by the balance sheet date?

3 What is the annual amortisation charge if P Ltd paid £500,000 for 60% of S Ltd, whose net assets totalled £600,000, given that the goodwill has an expected life of 5 years?

5 Summary

The key thing to remember is that the consolidated profit and loss account gives the results of the group trading with third parties.

Therefore the following adjustments are necessary:

- Eliminate any intra-group sales from turnover and cost of sales.
- Eliminate intra-group profit on stock held at the year-end.
- Exclude dividends and interest received from the subsidiary.
- Include minority interest, being the minority interest's share of the subsidiary company's profit after tax.
- Only include the dividends paid and proposed by the parent company.

CHAPTER 9

Consolidated accounts – legal and professional requirements

ASSESSMENT FOCUS

For this Unit you need to have an awareness of the legal factors and FRS's that affect the preparation of consolidated accounts, namely FRS's 2, 6 and 9. In this final chapter on consolidated accounts we will cover the areas that are required knowledge.

This chapter covers the following Knowledge and Understanding of the AAT Syllabus.

> The UK regulatory framework for financial reporting and the main requirements of relevant Financial Reporting Standards *(Element 11.1)*
>
> The general principles of consolidation *(Element 11.1)*

In order to cover these the following topics are included.

> Companies Act 1985 requirements
> FRS 2: Accounting for subsidiary undertakings
> Associated undertakings
> FRS 9: Associates and joint ventures
> Acquisition accounting and merger accounting
> FRS 6: Acquisitions and mergers

Key definitions

Group accounts	Accounts prepared for a group.
Consolidated accounts	The usual form of group accounts, presenting a consolidated balance sheet and consolidated profit and loss account as though the group were a single economic entity.
Associate	Entity over which the group exerts significant influence but not control.
Equity accounting	The accounting method used to incorporate an associate into the consolidated accounts.
Acquisition	The normal type of business combination.
Merger	A rare type of business combination in which two entities pool their interests, with neither party being dominant.

1 Companies Act 1985 requirements

1.1 Definition of parent and subsidiary

The full definition is given in the Companies Act and is restated in FRS 2. The key points of the definition are summarised below:

An undertaking is the parent of another (a subsidiary) if *any* of the following apply:

- It holds a majority of voting rights.
- It is a member and can appoint/remove directors with a majority of votes.
- It is a member and controls a majority of votes via an agreement with other members.
- It has a participating interest and actually exercises dominant influence or the undertakings are managed on a unified basis.

FRS 2 defines *dominant influence*. In essence, the term means that the parent determines the financial and operating policies of the subsidiary, which effectively means that the parent has control.

FRS 2 also defines *managed on a unified basis*. This term means that the undertakings are integrated and managed as a single unit.

1.2 Requirement to prepare group accounts

A company must prepare group accounts if it is a parent company at its year-end (ie. it has one or more subsidiaries, unless it qualifies for exemption from this requirement).

1.3 Exemptions from the requirement to prepare group accounts

A company need not prepare group accounts if:

- its immediate parent is incorporated in the European Union (EU) and prepares accounts in accordance with (EU) requirements; and
- the company seeking the exemption does not have any securities listed on a stock exchange in the EU; and
- the company is a wholly owned subsidiary of its immediate parent; or
- the parent owns over 50% and notice requiring group accounts has not been served by:
  - holders of more than half of the remaining shares *not* held by the parent; or
  - holders of 5% of total shares.

1.4 Small and medium-sized groups exemptions

A small or medium-sized group, not containing a public company, a banking, authorised investment or insurance company, need not prepare group accounts if it:

- meets any two of the small/medium-size limits for two consecutive years; or
- met size criteria and was entitled to exemption last year; or
- meets size criteria this year and was entitled to exemption last year.

Size limits:

	Before consolidation adjustments		*After consolidation adjustments*
Turnover not more than	£13,440,000	or	£11,200,000
Gross assets not more than	£6,720,000	or	£5,600,000
Average number of employees not more than		250	

- The totals before consolidation adjustments are obtained by adding together the amounts in the individual company accounts.
- The totals after consolidation adjustments are obtained from the group balance sheet (and profit and loss account).

1.5 Other Companies Act requirements for group accounts

- Group accounts must be prepared as consolidated accounts.
- The parent and subsidiaries should have the same accounting period and year-end. If this is not practicable, the Act allows:
  - consolidation of a subsidiary's statutory accounts drawn up to a date within three months prior to the parent's year-end; or
  - consolidation of interim accounts for the subsidiary made up to the parent's year-end; this alternative is preferred by FRS 2.
- Uniform accounting policies should be used for amounts included in the group accounts. Different accounting policies may only be used in exceptional cases. The group accounts must disclose particulars of the different policies.
- Standard formats and disclosures must be used. These are set out in the chapters of this text on limited company accounts.

2 *FRS 2: Accounting for subsidiary undertakings*

2.1 Introduction

FRS 2 deals with the **preparation of group accounts**, including application of the Companies Act requirements.

2.2 Objective of FRS 2

The objective of FRS 2 is to require parent undertakings to provide financial information about their groups in consolidated financial statements, intended to present the parent and its subsidiaries as a single economic entity.

2.3 Definitions

- **Consolidation** is the process of adjusting and combining financial information from individual financial statements to present information for the group as a single economic entity.
- **Control** is the ability to direct the financial and operating policies of another entity.
- **Minority interests** are the interests in a subsidiary held by or on behalf of persons other than the parent and its subsidiaries.
- **Parent and subsidiary**: see section on Companies Act 1985 provisions earlier in this chapter.

2.4 Disclosures for principal subsidiary undertakings

Disclosure should be made of:

- The proportion of voting rights held by the parent and its subsidiaries
- An indication of the nature of the subsidiary's business

2.5 Minority interests

The consolidated balance sheet should show separately the minority interest share of the subsidiary's net assets or liabilities consolidated. Note that, if the subsidiary has net liabilities, we show this as a debit balance in the consolidated balance sheet.

The consolidated profit and loss account should show separately the minority interest share of the subsidiary's profit or loss after tax for the period.

2.6 Intra-group transactions

Eliminate in full any profits or losses on intra-group transactions reflected in the book value of assets included in consolidation.

Apportion the elimination of profits or losses between the parent and minority interests in proportion to their holdings in the company recording the profit or loss in its own financial statements. Hence, when the subsidiary sells goods to the parent, the subsidiary records the profit so we apportion the elimination between the parent and minority interests.

2.7 Changes in composition of a group

Changes in membership of a group occur on the date on which control passes.

3 Associated undertakings

3.1 Introduction

We have seen that, if a company has an investment in another company, the accounting treatment of that investment depends upon whether or not that investment gives *control*.

- If the investment gives control, the investment is treated as a **subsidiary** and group accounts are prepared.
- If the investment does not give control, it is treated as a simple **investment**.

3.2 Significant influence

In practice, there is a third possibility.

An **associate** is an entity (usually a company) over which the group exerts *significant influence* but *not* control. A holding of 20% to 50% usually indicates significant influence. Significant influence involves active participation in management, not simply a passive role, as would be the case with a simple trade investment.

We need to distinguish an associate from a subsidiary and from a simple trade investment because, whilst the group does not have control over the associate, it does have more than a passive interest. Hence, we need a treatment in between full consolidation and leaving the investment at cost in the group accounts.

3.3 Relationship with group

As we saw in the first chapter on group accounts, a group comprises a parent and its subsidiaries. As an associate is neither a parent nor a subsidiary, it is not part of the group. Instead, the group has an investment in the associate. When we identify the group structure, we include the associate, even though it is not part of the group, as this helps us to identify its status and the actual percentage interest which, as we shall see, is important. For example:

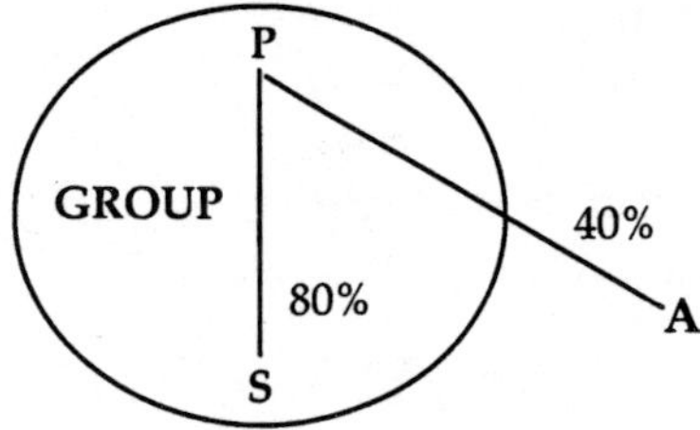

The associate is not part of the group.

3.4 *Treatment in investing company's own accounts*

In the balance sheet the investment in an associate is included in fixed asset investments, usually at cost. In the individual company, as opposed to consolidated, balance sheet, we do not use the term *associate*. Instead, we include the investment under the sub-heading 'Participating interests'. As we shall see in more detail later, this term also includes investments other than associates. As with other investments, we may revalue this investment and must write down its value if there is an impairment in value.

In the individual company profit and loss account we include dividend income from the associate under the heading 'Income from participating interests'. Again, note that the term *associate* is not used in the individual company, as opposed to group, accounts.

3.5 *Treatment in group accounts*

In the group accounts, we use a technique called *equity accounting* for an associate. We also describe the associate as an *associated undertaking*. Note that we only use this technique in group accounts (ie. where the parent also has a subsidiary), which we consolidate as normal.

Instead of bringing in all of the associate's net assets and profits and then showing a minority interest to reflect the part not actually owned, we only include the *group share* of the associate's net assets and profits from the outset.

3.6 *Balance sheet*

In fixed asset investments, we replace the investment as shown in the investing company's own individual balance sheet with the *group share* of the associate's net assets at the balance sheet date, in one line, under 'Interests in associated undertakings'.

In group reserves, we include the parent's share of the associate's post-acquisition reserves (calculated in the same way as for a subsidiary).

We cancel the investment in the associate as shown in the investing company's own individual balance sheet against the group share of the associate's net assets at the date of acquisition (at fair value). The difference is a premium or discount on acquisition (in effect, goodwill), which is included in the consolidated balance sheet carrying value for the associate, and amortised over its useful life.

3.7 *Example*

P Ltd owns 80% of S Ltd and 40% of A Ltd. Balance sheets of the three companies at 31 December 20X8 are:

	P Ltd	*S Ltd*	*A Ltd*
	£	£	£
Investment: Shares in S Ltd	800	–	–
Investment: Shares in A Ltd	600	–	–
Sundry net assets	3,600	3,800	4,400
	5,000	3,800	4,400
Share capital – £1 ordinary shares	1,000	400	800
Profit and loss account	4,000	3,400	3,600
	5,000	3,800	4,400

P Ltd acquired its shares in S Ltd when S Ltd's profit and loss reserves were £520 and P Ltd acquired its shares in A Ltd when A Ltd's profit and loss reserves were £400.

Assume that all goodwill arising on acquisition has been fully amortised through the profit and loss account.

Required

Prepare the consolidated balance sheet at 31 December 20X8.

3.8 Solution

P Ltd: Consolidated balance sheet as at 31 December 20X8

	£
Interest in associated undertakings (4,400 × 40%)	1,760
Sundry net assets (3,600 + 3,800)	7,400
	9,160
Share capital	1,000
Profit and loss account (W5)	7,400
	8,400
Minority interests (W4)	760
	9,160

Workings

(1) Group structure

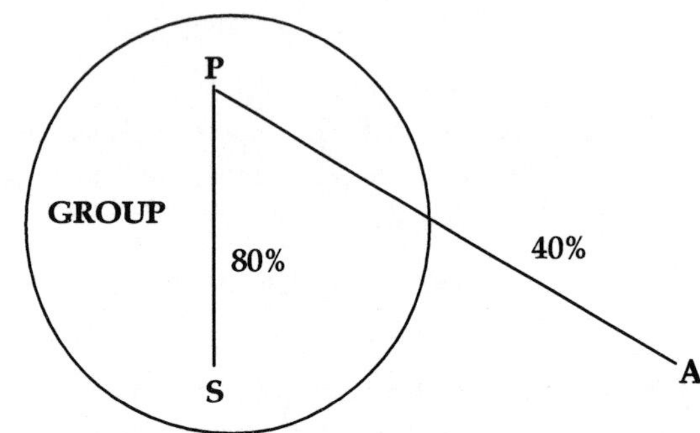

(2) Net assets working

S Ltd

	Acquisition	*Balance sheet date*
	£	£
Share capital	400	400
Profit and loss account	520	3,400
	920	3,800

A Ltd

	Acquisition	*Balance sheet date*
	£	£
Share capital	800	800
Profit and loss account	400	3,600
	1,200	4,400

(3) Goodwill

S Ltd

	£
Cost of investment	800
Net assets acquired (80% × 920 (W2))	(736)
	64

A Ltd

	£
Cost of investment	600
Net assets acquired (40% × 1,200 (W2))	(480)
	120

(4) Minority interests

	£
S Ltd only – (20% × 3,800)	760

(5) Profit and loss account

	£
P Ltd – from question	4,000
Share of S Ltd [80% × (3,400 – 520)]	2,304
Share of A Ltd [40% × (3,600 – 400)]	1,280
Less: Goodwill (64 + 120) (W3)	(184)
	7,400

Activity 1 *(The answer is in the final chapter of this book)*

A, B and C Ltd

Given below are the balance sheets of three companies at 31 March 20X2. A Ltd owns 60% of the share capital of B Ltd and 30% of the share capital of C Ltd.

	A Ltd	*B Ltd*	*C Ltd*
	£	£	£
Investment: Shares in B Ltd	1,000		
Investment: Shares in C Ltd	750		
Other net assets	5,250	4,000	3,000
	7,000	4,000	3,000
Share capital - £1 ordinary shares	3,000	1,000	1,000
Profit and loss account	4,000	3,000	2,000
	7,000	4,000	3,000

A Ltd acquired its shares in B Ltd when B Ltd's profit and loss reserves were £400 and acquired its shares in C Ltd when C Ltd's profit and loss reserves were £1,000. Assume that all goodwill has already been fully amortised through the profit and loss account.

Prepare the consolidated balance sheet at 31 March 20X2.

3.9 Profit and loss account

The treatment of an associate in the consolidated profit and loss account is consistent with its treatment in the consolidated balance sheet.

We replace the dividend income from the investment in the associate, as shown in the investing company's own profit and loss account, with the *group share* of the associate's operating profit, in one line, as 'Income from interests in associated undertakings' or 'Share of operating profit in associates'.

If there is a charge for amortisation of goodwill arising on acquiring the associate, this is included in the group's share of the associate's operating profit. It should be separately disclosed.

If the associate's profit and loss account includes exceptional items, interest payable or interest receivable, the group's share of these should be included in the consolidated profit and loss account and shown separately from the amounts for the group.

We also include the group share of the associate's tax in 'Tax on profit on ordinary activities'. The group tax and the share of the associate's tax are separately disclosed in the tax note.

Do not add in the associate's turnover or expenses line by line.

3.10 Example

P Ltd has owned 80% of S Ltd and 40% of A Ltd for several years. Profit and loss accounts for the year ended 31 December 20X8 are:

	P Ltd	*S Ltd*	*A Ltd*
	£	£	£
Turnover	14,000	12,000	10,000
Cost of sales	(9,000)	(4,000)	(3,000)
Gross profit	5,000	8,000	7,000
Administrative expenses	(2,000)	(6,000)	(3,000)
	3,000	2,000	4,000
Income from participating interests	400	–	–
Profit on ordinary activities before taxation	3,400	2,000	4,000
Tax on profit on ordinary activities	(1,000)	(1,200)	(2,000)
Profit on ordinary activities after taxation	2,400	800	2,000
Dividends (paid)	(1,000)	–	(1,000)
Retained profit	1,400	800	1,000

Required

Prepare the consolidated profit and loss account for the year ended 31 December 20X8. Assume that all goodwill arising on acquisition has been fully amortised through the profit and loss account.

3.11 Solution

P Ltd: Consolidated profit and loss account for the year ending 31 December 20X8

	£	£
Turnover (14,000 + 12,000)		26,000
Cost of sales (9,000 + 4,000)		(13,000)
Gross profit		13,000
Administrative expenses (2,000 + 6,000)		(8,000)
Operating profit		5,000
Income from interests in associated undertakings (40% × 4,000)		1,600
Profit on ordinary activities before taxation		6,600
Tax on profit on ordinary activities		
Group (1,000 + 1,200)	2,200	
Share of associated undertaking's tax (40% × 2,000)	800	
		(3,000)
Profit on ordinary activities after taxation		3,600
Minority interests (20% × 800)		(160)
Profit for the financial year attributable to the members of P Ltd		3,440
Dividends paid (P Ltd only)		(1,000)
Retained profit for the financial year		2,440

Workings

(1) Group structure

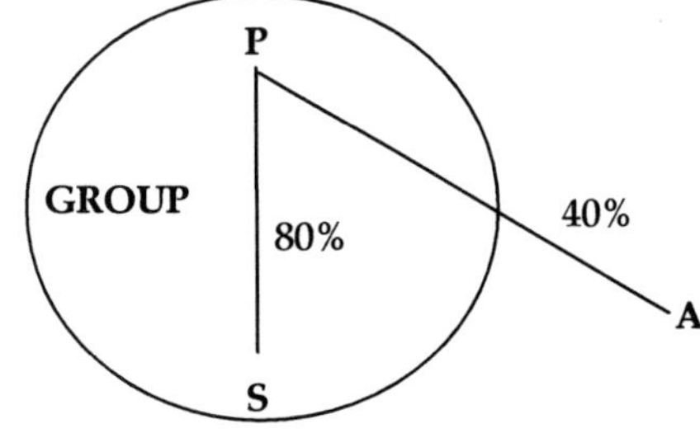

Activity 2 *(The answer is in the final chapter of this book)*

D, E and F Ltd

Given below are the profit and loss accounts for D Ltd, its 75% owned subsidiary E Ltd, and F Ltd its 30% owned associate for the year ended 30 June 20X1. Both E Ltd and F Ltd were acquired by D Ltd a number of years ago.

	D Ltd	*E Ltd*	*F Ltd*
	£	£	£
Turnover	440,000	180,000	250,000
Cost of sales	210,000	80,000	160,000
Gross profit	230,000	100,000	90,000
Administrative expenses	(80,000)	(30,000)	(25,000)
Income from participating interests	6,000	-	-
Profit before tax	156,000	70,000	65,000
Tax	46,000	20,000	18,000
Profit on ordinary activities after tax	110,000	50,000	47,000
Dividends	60,000	25,000	20,000
Retained profit	50,000	25,000	27,000

Prepare the consolidated profit and loss account for the year ended 30 June 20X1, assuming that all goodwill has already been amortised through the profit and loss account.

3.12 Companies Act 1985

The term *participating interest* is defined in the Companies Act and FRS 2 restates the definition. A participating interest is one held on a long-term basis for the purpose of securing a contribution to activities by the exercise of control or influence. This is presumed where the holding is 20% or more. Note that this does *not* automatically mean that there is significant influence as that term has a narrower meaning, given by FRS 9.

3.13 Companies Act requirements

The Act defines associated undertakings as undertakings, which are not subsidiaries, where the group:

- has a participating interest
- exercises significant influence

Significant influence is presumed, unless the contrary is shown, if the group's holding is 20% or more.

The Act requires equity accounting for an associate in the group accounts.

4 FRS 9: Associates and joint ventures

4.1 Introduction

For this Unit you need to understand the FRS 9 definition of an associate and apply equity accounting to simple examples but accounting for joint ventures is not assessed.

4.2 Definitions

An **associate** is an entity (other than a subsidiary) in which another entity (the investor) has a *participating interest* and over whose operating and financial policies the investor exercises a *significant influence.*

A **participating interest** is an interest held in the shares of another entity on a long term basis for the purpose of securing a contribution to the investor's activities by the exercise of control or influence arising from or related to that interest.

The exercise of **significant influence** means that the investor is actively involved and is influential in the direction of its investee through its participation in policy decisions covering aspects of policy relevant to the investor, including decisions on strategic issues such as:

(a) the expansion or contraction of the business, participation in other entities or changes in products, markets and activities of its investee; and

(b) determining the balance between dividend and reinvestment.

Note that the FRS 9 definition of an associate is narrower than the Companies Act definition and the emphasis is different. The Companies Act definition is based on the size of the shareholding. The FRS 9 definition is based on whether significant influence is exercised in practice (on the substance of the relationship between investor and investee, rather than on its strict legal form). For example, a holding of 25% is extremely unlikely to give rise to significant influence if the 75% remainder of the shares are owned by another single company.

4.3 Accounting treatment in the company's individual accounts

In the investing company's own accounts, the associate is included in the balance sheet as a fixed asset investment and shown at cost (or valuation) less amounts written off.

The profit and loss account includes dividends received and receivable.

4.4 Accounting treatment in the consolidated accounts

In the consolidated profit and loss account show:

Group share of associate's:

- Operating profit
- Exceptional items
- Interest payable/receivable
- Taxation

In the consolidated balance sheet show:

	£
Group share of associate's net assets	X
Goodwill arising on acquisition less amounts amortised to date	X
	X

5 Acquisition accounting and merger accounting

5.1 Acquisition accounting

You have learned to prepare consolidated accounts using the **acquisition method of accounting**. Acquisition accounting is the method used for the majority of business combinations. (*Business combination* is the generic term for transactions which result in one company becoming the subsidiary of another.)

The central idea behind acquisition accounting is that a parent *acquires* a subsidiary company. The assets and liabilities of the subsidiary company are taken over by the parent and absorbed into its operations. This scenario is typical of most business combinations.

5.2 Merger accounting

However, some business combinations arise as the result of the **uniting of interests** of two companies so that neither company can be said to have acquired the other. This type of combination is popularly known as a **merger**. A different method of consolidation, known as the *merger method*, is used to prepare consolidated accounts in this situation.

The difference between an acquisition and a merger seems to be obvious. However, the essential distinction between the two depends on future intentions and the spirit in which the combination takes place. These are subjective, rather than matters of fact. Many business combinations involve complex transactions and arrangements and in practice it can be difficult to establish whether a particular combination is an acquisition or a merger.

5.3 FRS 6: Acquisitions and mergers

The following definitions are contained in FRS 6 *Acquisitions and mergers*.

- **Merger**

  A business combination which results in the creation of a new reporting entity formed from the combining parties, in which the shareholders of the combining entities come together in a *substantially equal partnership* for the *mutual sharing* of the risks and benefits of the combined entity, and in which *no party to the combination in substance obtains control over any other, or is otherwise seen to be dominant*, whether by virtue of the proportion of its shareholders rights in the combined entity, the influence of its directors or otherwise.

- **Acquisition**

  A business combination that is *not a merger*.

Note that, in practice, merger accounting is rare.

5.4 Criteria for treating a combination as a merger

A business combination can only be treated as a merger provided that a number of specific conditions and criteria are met. These are set out in the Companies Act 1989 and in FRS 6.

5.5 Companies Act conditions

- After the combination at least 90% of equity (normally ordinary) shares are held by the group.
- The subsidiary was acquired by an arrangement providing for issue of equity shares by a parent or its subsidiaries.
- The fair value of any consideration other than equity shares does not exceed 10% of the *nominal* value of the equity shares issued.
- The adoption of merger accounting accords with generally accepted accounting principles (ie, the combination must also meet the criteria in FRS 6).

5.6 FRS 6 criteria

- No party to the combination must be portrayed as either acquirer or acquired.
- All parties to the combination must participate in the management of the combined entity.
- One party does not dominate the combined entity by virtue of its relative size.
- Non equity consideration does not represent more than an immaterial proportion of the fair value of the consideration received. (The consideration for any shares acquired in one of the combining parties by the other within the period of two years before the combination should be taken into account in determining whether this criterion has been met.)
- No equity shareholders of any of the combining entities retain any material interest in the future performance of only part of the combined entity. (This criterion would not be met if there were a substantial minority interest.)

Where all these conditions are met, FRS 6 states that the combination must be treated as a merger. If any of the conditions are not met, the combination must be treated as an acquisition.

For this Unit you do not need to prepare accounts under merger accounting only to know the criteria when merger accounting must be used.

5.7 Merger accounting method

Consolidations under acquisition accounting are based on the concept of control. This is not relevant in a merger situation where there is no control. Instead, the consolidation needs to reflect the pooling of interests of two companies.

To reflect the **pooling of interests** the following treatment is adopted:

(i) The parent records the investment in the subsidiary in its own balance sheet at *nominal* value of shares issued plus fair value of any other consideration, ie. the fair value of shares issued on combination is not recorded.

(ii) On consolidation, cancel the cost of the investment in the subsidiary against the nominal value of the subsidiary's shares obtained in exchange.

(iii) There is no need to adjust the subsidiary's net assets to fair value at combination for inclusion in the consolidated balance sheet.

(iv) Results and cash flows are consolidated as though the merger had always existed, ie. profits are included from the date of incorporation not the date of combination.

6 Quick quiz *(The answers are in the final chapter of this book)*

1 P Ltd owns 40% of S Ltd but has the power to appoint all of S Ltd's directors. Is S Ltd a subsidiary of P Ltd?

2 P Ltd and S Ltd are both very small companies. S is 100% owned by P Ltd. Do group accounts have to be prepared?

3 P Ltd owns 80% of S Ltd and 30% of A Ltd. How should A Ltd be accounted for in the group accounts prepared for P and S?

4 Are most business combinations acquisitions or mergers?

7 Summary

The main legal and professional requirements in respect of group accounts are set out in:

- the Companies Act 1985 and 1989
- FRS 2 *Accounting for subsidiary undertakings*
- FRS 6 *Acquisitions and mergers*
- FRS 9 *Associates and joint ventures*

An undertaking is the parent of another (a subsidiary) if *any* of the following apply:

- It holds a majority of voting rights.
- It is a member and can appoint/remove directors with a majority of votes.
- It is a member and controls a majority of votes via an agreement with other members.
- It has a participating interest and actually exercises dominant influence or the undertakings are managed on a unified basis.

If a parent company with subsidiaries has an associate then this must be accounted for using the equity accounting method in the consolidated financial statements.

CHAPTER 10

Reporting financial performance

ASSESSMENT FOCUS

In an earlier chapter we considered the Companies Act format for a profit and loss account. However FRS 3 *Reporting Financial Performance* has added to this format and included a number of additional statements and notes. These are relevant to Unit 11.

Also relevant to the Unit are the appreciation of the requirements of SSAP 25 and an ability to perform basic earnings per share calculations according to FRS 14.

This chapter covers the following Knowledge and Understanding of the AAT Syllabus.

> The statutory form of accounting statements and disclosure requirements *(Element 11.1)*
>
> The UK regulatory framework for financial reporting and the main requirements of relevant Financial Reporting Standards *(Element 11.1)*

In order to cover these the following topics are included.

FRS 3: Reporting Financial Performance
Statement of total recognised gains and losses
Reconciliation of movements in shareholders' funds
Prior period adjustments
Note of historical cost profits and losses
SSAP 25: Segmental Reporting
FRS 14: Earnings per share

Key definitions

Discontinued operation	Material activity that is ceased during the reporting period.
Exceptional item	Unusual material item deriving from within the ordinary activities.
Extraordinary item	Unusual material item deriving from outside the ordinary activities.
Prior period adjustment	Material adjustment applicable to prior periods arising from either changes in accounting policy or correction of fundamental errors.
Segmental reporting	Reporting of financial results split up into business segments or geographical segments.
Earnings per share	Key measure of a company's profitability, calculated by dividing the profit after tax and preference dividends by the number of ordinary shares in issue.

1 FRS 3: Reporting financial performance

1.1 Introduction

The aim of FRS 3 is to improve financial reporting by addressing a number of important issues. These include the following.

- The structure of the profit and loss account
- Extraordinary items and exceptional items
- The statement of total recognised gains and losses (STRGL)
- Other required disclosures

1.2 Structure of the profit and loss account

FRS 3 requires that all statutory profit and loss account headings from turnover to operating profit must be analysed between amounts arising from continuing operations and amounts arising from discontinued operations. In addition, turnover and operating profit must be further analysed between amounts from existing and amounts from newly acquired operations. Only the figures for turnover and operating profit need be shown on the face of the profit and loss account. All additional information may be relegated to a note.

The situation is summarised below:

Figure 1 The structure of the profit and loss account under FRS 3

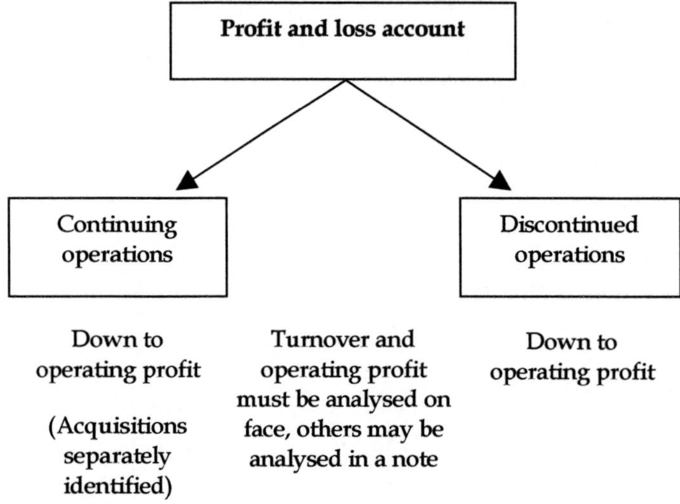

1.3 Proforma profit and loss account

A proforma profit and loss account complying with these requirements is given below.

X LIMITED
PROFIT AND LOSS ACCOUNT FOR THE YEAR ENDED 31 OCTOBER 20X4

	Continuing operations		*Discontinued*	*Total*
	Existing	*Acquisition*	*operations*	
	£000	*£000*	*£000*	*£000*
Turnover	550	50	175	775
Cost of sales	(415)	(40)	(165)	(620)
Gross profit	135	10	10	155
Distribution costs	(35)	(4)	(8)	(47)
Administrative expenses	(50)		(7)	(57)
Operating profit	50	6	(5)	51
Profit on sale of properties	22			22
Loss on sale of discontinued operations			(10)	(10)

Profit on ordinary activities before interest	72	6	(15)	63
Interest payable				(18)
Profit on ordinary activities before taxation				45
Tax on profit on ordinary activities				(16)
[Profit before extraordinary items]				29
[Extraordinary items] (to show position only)				-
Profit for the financial year				29
Dividends				(8)
Retained profit for the financial year				21

1.4 Discontinued operations

A discontinued operation is one that meets all of the following conditions.

- The sale or termination must have been completed before the earlier of three months after the year end or the date the financial statements are approved. (Terminations not completed by this date may be disclosed in the notes).
- The former activity must have ceased permanently.
- The sale or termination has a material effect on the nature and focus of the entity's operations and represents a material reduction in its operating facilities resulting either from its withdrawal from a particular market (class of business or geographical), or from a material reduction in turnover in its continuing markets.
- The assets, liabilities, results of operations and activities are clearly distinguishable, physically, operationally and for financial reporting purposes.

1.5 Further required disclosures

Three exceptional items are required to be disclosed on the face of the profit and loss account.

- Profits or losses on the sale or termination of discontinued operations
- Costs of a fundamental restructuring/reorganisation
- Profit/loss on disposal of fixed assets

FRS 3 defines an **exceptional item** as a material item deriving from within the ordinary activities of the entity, but which is unusual in size or incidence such that it must be disclosed separately in order that the financial statements will give a true and fair view.

The three categories of exceptional item listed above must be disclosed on the face of the profit and loss account. Other exceptional items would normally only be disclosed in a note to the accounts, only requiring to be shown on the face of the profit and loss account if this was necessary to give a true and fair view.

Extraordinary items are defined as material items deriving from outside the ordinary activities of the entity.

FRS 3 attempts to define "ordinary activities" so widely that it is impossible to imagine any example of an extraordinary item in practice (some commentators have suggested losses arising from alien invasion might qualify!). In effect FRS 3 virtually abolishes extraordinary items. Although the above proforma shows where extraordinary items would be shown in a profit and loss account, the ASB's clear intention is that extraordinary items should never be included in practice.

1.6 Example

A&Z PLC

PROFIT AND LOSS ACCOUNT FOR THE YEAR ENDED 31 DECEMBER 20X1

	20X1
	£
Turnover	300,000
Cost of sales	(100,000)
Gross profit	200,000
Distribution costs	(40,000)
Administrative expenses	(90,000)
Operating profit	70,000

During the year the company ran down a material business operation with all activities ceasing on 26 January 20X2. The costs attributable to the closure amounted to £3,000 charged to administrative expenses. The results of the operation for 20X1 were as follows.

	20X1
	£
Turnover	32,000
Cost of sales	(15,000)
Distribution costs	(12,000)
Administrative expenses	(10,000)
Operating loss	(5,000)

In addition, the company acquired an unincorporated business which contributed £9,000 to turnover and an operating profit of £1,500. Its distribution costs and administrative expenses were £2,900 and £1,000 respectively. Cost of sales was £3,600.

Required

Prepare the profit and loss account for the year ended 31 December 20X1 for A&Z plc complying with the provisions of FRS 3.

1.7 Solution

As soon as you see in a question that a company has closed a significant operation you must now consider whether FRS 3 applies. Remember that the question will not necessarily mention FRS 3. This means that you will need to learn the definition of a discontinued activity.

As soon as you notice a discontinuance, the easiest approach is to use a four-column layout.

Profit and loss account

Continuing			
Existing	*Acquisitions*	*Discontinued*	*Total*
£	£	£	£

Remember that all we are doing here is a simple analysis. We can therefore start by identifying, from within the question, any misclassification of costs.

We can see here that costs attributable to the closure of £3,000 have been charged into administrative expenses. Under FRS 3 this will need to be extracted and separately disclosed as an exceptional item immediately after operating profit.

We can then consider the analysis required. We need to set out our four columns. Our starting point is to do the total column as normal.

Profit and loss account

	Continuing			
	Existing	*Acquisitions*	*Discontinued*	*Total*
	£	£	£	£
Turnover				300,000
Cost of sales				(100,000)
Gross profit				200,000
Distribution costs				(40,000)
Administrative expenses				(87,000)
Operating profit				73,000
Costs of closure				(3,000)
Profit before interest				70,000

We can then add in the information given about the discontinued activity and the acquisition.

Profit and loss account

	Continuing			
	Existing	*Acquisitions*	*Discontinued*	*Total*
	£	£	£	£
Turnover		9,000	32,000	300,000
Cost of sales		(3,600)	(15,000)	(100,000)
Gross profit		5,400	17,000	200,000
Distribution costs		(2,900)	(12,000)	(40,000)
Administrative expenses		(1,000)	(7,000)	(87,000)
Operating profit/loss		1,500	(2,000)	73,000
Costs of closure		-	(3,000)	(3,000)
Profit/loss before interest		1,500	(5,000)	70,000

Remember: the £3,000 closure costs must be extracted from the discontinued column as well as from the total column.

The existing operations column will now become the balancing figure.

Profit and loss account

	Continuing			
	Existing	*Acquisitions*	*Discontinued*	*Total*
	£	£	£	£
Turnover	259,000	9,000	32,000	300,000
Cost of sales	(81,400)	(3,600)	(15,000)	(100,000)
Gross profit	177,600	5,400	17,000	200,000
Distribution costs	(25,100)	(2,900)	(12,000)	(40,000)
Administrative expenses	(79,000)	(1,000)	(7,000)	(87,000)
Operating profit/loss	73,500	1,500	(2,000)	73,000
Costs of closure	-	-	(3,000)	(3,000)
Profit/loss before interest	73,500	1,500	(5,000)	70,000

1.8 The rationale of FRS 3

FRS 3 achieves a *clarification* of what is included in the profit figure and generally adds *completeness* of information.

The profit of £70,000 in itself is quite informative, but when we look at the analysis provided by FRS 3 we can see that the £70,000 is in fact *distorted* by a loss of £5,000 on an activity which is now discontinued.

By 'stripping out' the loss on the discontinued activity we can see that the profit on continuing activities is actually £75,000, of which £1,500 was achieved by a new acquisition.

Activity 1 *(The answer is in the final chapter of this book)*

Sunshine plc

You have been given the following details about Sunshine plc for the year ending 31 December 20X4.

SUNSHINE PLC
PROFIT AND LOSS ACCOUNT FOR THE YEAR ENDED 31 DECEMBER 20X4

	£m
Turnover	2,709.0
Net operating costs	2,303.2
Operating profit	405.8
Interest receivable	8.2
Profit on ordinary activities before taxation	414.0
Taxation	148.0
Profit on ordinary activities after taxation	266.0
Dividends	95.0
Retained profit	171.0

The company ceased production of its manufacturing product line in June 20X4, having decided to concentrate on its growing distribution and aftermarket work. The turnover of this product during the year ended 31 December 20X4 was £100 million based on market prices and expenses were £51 million.

Required

Prepare the profit and loss account for Sunshine plc for the year ended 31 December 20X4, incorporating the disclosure requirements of FRS 3. Comparative figures for 20X3 are not required.

2 *Other disclosures required by FRS 3*

2.1 Statement of total recognised gains and losses (STRGL)

This is required by FRS 3 to be presented with the same prominence as the profit and loss account, balance sheet and cash flow statement as a primary statement.

A proforma is given below.

STATEMENT OF TOTAL RECOGNISED GAINS AND LOSSES FOR THE YEAR

	£
Profit for the financial year (per the profit and loss account)	X
Items taken directly to reserves	
Unrealised surplus on revaluation of fixed assets	X
Surplus/deficit on revaluation of investment properties	X
Foreign currency exchange differences	X
Total recognised gains and losses for the year	X
Prior period adjustments	(X)
Total gains and losses recognised since last annual report	X

The statement will include all gains and losses occurring during the period. FRS 3 requires that transactions with shareholders are to be excluded (ie dividends paid and proposed; share issues and redemptions). This is because these transactions do not represent either gains or losses.

Where profit or loss for the year is the only recognised gain or loss, a statement to that effect should be given immediately below the profit and loss account.

2.2 Reconciliation of movements in shareholders' funds

This is required by FRS 3 to be included in the notes to the accounts, or it may be a separate financial statement. What the statement aims to do is to pull together the financial performance of the entity as reflected in:

- the profit and loss account
- other movements in shareholders' funds as determined by the statement of total recognised gains and losses
- all other changes in shareholders' funds not recognised in either of the above, such as new share capital issued.

Once again, a proforma is given below.

RECONCILIATION OF MOVEMENTS IN SHAREHOLDERS' FUNDS FOR THE YEAR

	£
Profit for the financial year	X
Dividends	(X)
	X
Other recognised gains and losses (per STRGL)	X
New share capital	X
Net addition to shareholders' funds	X
Opening shareholders' funds	X
Closing shareholders' funds	X

2.3 Example

KENNETH LTD
PROFIT AND LOSS ACCOUNT EXTRACTS FOR THE YEAR ENDED 31 DECEMBER 20X1

	£000
Profit after tax	421
Dividend	(98)
Retained profit	323

During the year the following important events took place.

- Assets were revalued by £105,000.
- £250,000 share capital was issued at par during the year.
- Certain stock items were written down by £21,000.
- Net gains of £18,000 on foreign exchange translation were recorded in reserves.
- Opening shareholders' funds were £2,302,000.

Required

Show how the events for the year would be shown in the statement of total recognised gains and losses and the reconciliation of movements in shareholders' funds.

2.4 Solution

The key is to remember that the statement of total recognised gains and losses is a very simple statement.

The main gain or loss in the year is always the profit or loss from the profit and loss account (before dividends).

The other gains and losses from the balance sheet are limited in number.

- Asset revaluations
- Foreign exchange differences

Once you have the statement of total recognised gains and losses the only other items to include in the reconciliation of movements in shareholders' funds are:

- dividends
- changes in issued share capital.

The key is therefore to learn the formats.

STATEMENT OF TOTAL RECOGNISED GAINS AND LOSSES FOR THE YEAR ENDED 31 DECEMBER 20X1

	£000
Profit for year	421
Asset revaluation	105
Foreign exchange gains	18
Total recognised gains for the year	544

The write down of the stock items will not be included in the statement as it has already been included in the profit and loss account in determining the profit for the year.

RECONCILIATION OF MOVEMENTS IN SHAREHOLDERS' FUNDS FOR THE YEAR ENDED 31 DECEMBER 20X1

	£000
Profit for the year	421
Dividends	(98)
	323
Other recognised gains and losses (105 +18)	123
New share capital	250
	696
Opening shareholders' funds	2,302
Closing shareholders' funds	2,998

Activity 2 *(The answer is in the final chapter of this book)*

Coffee Ltd

PROFIT AND LOSS ACCOUNT EXTRACTS FOR THE YEAR ENDED 31 DECEMBER 20X1

	£000
Profit after tax	450
Dividend	(120)
Retained profit	330

During the year the following important events took place.

- Assets were revalued by £48,000.
- £140,000 share capital was issued at par during the year.
- Temporary fall in value of £20,000 on investment properties occurred during the year. This has been charged to reserves as required by SSAP 19.
- Opening shareholders' funds were £945,000.

Required

Show how the events for the year should be shown in the statement of total recognised gains and losses and the reconciliation of movements in shareholders' funds.

2.5 Prior period adjustments

Prior period adjustments (also called 'prior year adjustments') are material adjustments applicable to prior periods arising from:

- changes in accounting policy, or
- correction of fundamental errors.

They are *not* recurring adjustments or revision of estimates.

The definition is a narrow one and in practice prior period adjustments are rare.

Changes in accounting policy are permitted only if the new policy gives a fairer presentation. This usually arises when a new accounting standard is issued or where an existing standard allows a choice and the company switches from one option to the other (eg SSAP 13 in relation to capitalising development costs).

Distinguish a change in accounting policy from:

- a change in an estimate (eg useful economic life, outcome of development project)
- a refinement of accounting policy (eg if business moves into a new area).

Fundamental errors are extremely rare and are so large that they destroy the true and fair view.

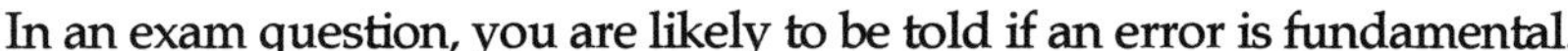

In an exam question, you are likely to be told if an error is fundamental.

2.6 Recording a prior period adjustment

To record a prior period adjustment proceed as follows.

- Restate opening balances for current year and apply new basis in preparing the current year's accounts.
- Adjust comparative figures.

Calculate what amounts would have been in the opening balance sheet for the current year on the new basis. The difference in opening net assets for the current year compared to the old basis gives the prior period adjustment to:

- opening reserves for the current year, shown in the statement of reserves and in the statement of total recognised gains and losses
- opening shareholders' funds in the reconciliation of movements in shareholders' funds, and
- balance sheet comparatives in the current year's accounts.

2.7 Example

Leonard plc incurs considerable research and development expenditure. Its accounting policy to date has been to carry forward development expenditure where the criteria for this are met. The final accounts for the year ended 30 June 20X2, and the 20X3 draft accounts, reflect this policy and show the following.

	20X3	20X2
	£000	£000
Profit after tax	4,712	3,200
Dividends	(2,500)	(1,750)
Retained profit for the financial year	2,212	1,450
Profit and loss account brought forward	23,950	22,500
	26,162	23,950

The directors have now decided to change the accounting policy to one of immediate write-off of all development expenditure as it is incurred.

The net book value of development costs included in intangible fixed assets has been as follows.

	£000
At 30 June 20X1	400
At 30 June 20X2	450
At 30 June 20X3	180

Amortisation of, and expenditure on, development has been as follows.

	Amortisation	*Expenditure*
	£000	£000
Year ended 30 June 20X2	450	500
Year ended 30 June 20X3	870	600

The issued share capital of Leonard plc is £10,000,000. Leonard plc has no other recognised gains and losses apart from its trading profits, and no other reserves apart from its profit and loss account.

Required

Show how the change in accounting policy will be reflected in the financial statements for the year ended 30 June 20X3.

2.8 Solution

LEONARD PLC

PROFIT AND LOSS ACCOUNT FOR THE YEAR ENDED 30 JUNE 20X3 (EXTRACT)

	20X3	20X2
	£000	*As restated* £000
Profit after tax (W1)	4,982	3,150
Dividends	(2,500)	(1,750)
Retained profit for the financial year	2,482	1,400

STATEMENT OF TOTAL RECOGNISED GAINS AND LOSSES FOR THE YEAR ENDED 30 JUNE 20X3

	20X3	20X2
	£000	*As restated* £000
Profit for the financial year	4,982	3,150
Prior period adjustment (note) (W2)	(450)	
Total recognised gains and losses since last annual report	4,532	3,150

RECONCILIATION OF MOVEMENTS IN SHAREHOLDERS' FUNDS FOR THE YEAR ENDED 30 JUNE 20X3

	20X3 £000	20X2 As restated £000
Profit for the financial year	4,982	3,150
Dividends	(2,500)	(1,750)
Net addition to shareholders' funds	2,482	1,400
Opening shareholders' funds (originally £33,950,000 before a prior period adjustment of £450,000)	33,500	32,100
Closing shareholders' funds	35,982	33,500

STATEMENT OF RESERVES FOR THE YEAR ENDED 30 JUNE 20X3

	Profit and loss account 20X3 £000
At 30 June 20X2	
As previously stated	23,950
Prior year adjustment (W2)	(450)
As restated	23,500
Retained profit for the financial year (2,212 + 270)	2,482
At 30 June 20X3 (26,162 - 180 (W3))	25,982

Note. The prior year adjustment arises from a change of accounting policy from capitalisation of development costs to immediate write-off of expenditure as incurred.

Workings

(W1) Profit after tax

	20X3 £000	20X2 As restated £000
As previously stated	4,712	3,200
Add back amortisation	870	450
Deduct expenditure in year	(600)	(500)
As restated	4,982	3,150

(W2) Prior year adjustment (in balance sheet at 30 June 20X2)

Adjustment is the elimination of the £450,000 asset. This gives the figure for the prior year adjustment in the statement of reserves, ie adjustment in opening balances for current year.

(W3) Balance sheet at 30 June 20X3

Adjustment is £180,000 asset to be eliminated.

Activity 3 *(The answer is in the final chapter of this book)*

Claret Ltd

Claret Ltd has an issued share capital of 2,000,000 50p ordinary shares, all of which were issued at par on incorporation.

The balance on the profit and loss account at 1 January 20X8 was £20,658,000 and the draft retained profit for the year was £1,825,000. The directors had decided to propose a dividend of £250,000 for the year.

At 1 January 20X8 the balance on the revaluation reserve was £83,000. On 31 December 20X8 a property was revalued to £430,000. It was purchased on 1 January 20X1 for £650,000 and is being depreciated over 20 years.

During the year the company issued 160,000 50p ordinary shares at a market price of 210p per share.

After the preparation of the draft accounts had been completed, it was discovered that the method of valuing closing stock had been incorrectly applied for the last three years resulting in the following overvaluations of stock which are considered fundamental.

	£000
At 31 December 20X6	40
At 31 December 20X7	55
At 31 December 20X8	62

Required

Prepare the following extracts from the financial statements of Claret Ltd as at 31 December 20X8:

(a) statement of total recognised gains and losses;
(b) note on reconciliation of shareholders' funds.

Ignore the requirement to produce comparative figures.

2.9 Note of historical cost profits and losses

Normally a company will prepare its financial statements in accordance with the historical cost convention, so that fixed assets will be shown in the balance sheet at cost less accumulated depreciation to date. However the CA 1985 also contains "alternative accounting rules" under which assets may be revalued to market values at the balance sheet date.

If a company has adopted any of the alternative accounting rules as regards revaluation of assets then the reported profit figure per the profit and loss account may differ from the historical cost profit figure. If the difference is material then the financial statements must include a reconciliation statement after the statement of recognised gains and losses or the profit and loss account. The profit figure to be reconciled is profit before tax. However, the retained profit for the year must also be restated.

The reason is that one of the key qualities of financial statements is the requirement for them to be comparable. This causes difficulties where we have a choice of accounting method (as we do, for example, with fixed assets).

The difference in profit is usually due to revaluation of fixed assets. This can be illustrated in the diagram below.

Historical cost vs revaluation

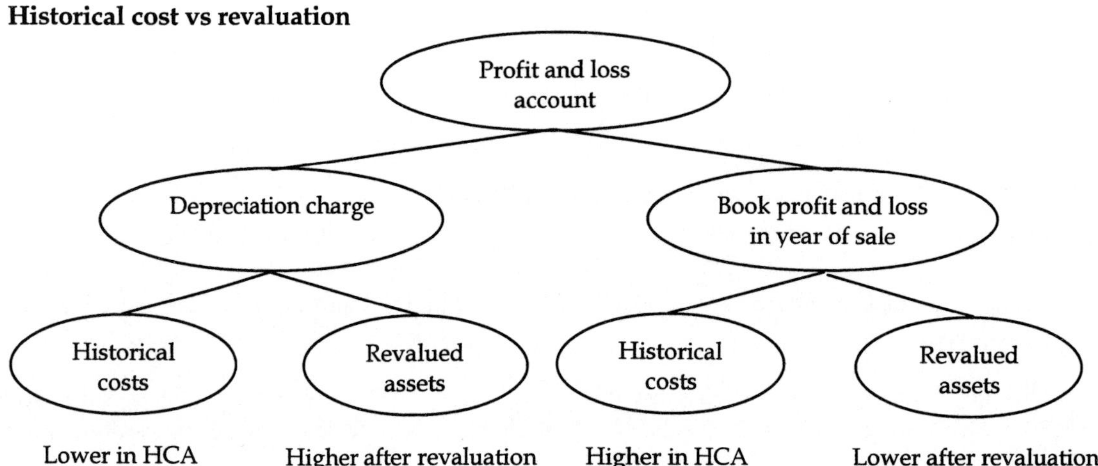

Companies who revalue their assets suffer a 'double whammy' of increased depreciation charges and reduced profit on disposals, giving them an overall lower profit figure. The impact of this distortion is highlighted for users in the note of historical cost profits and losses.

2.10 Example

Beta Ltd reported a profit before tax of £705,000 for the year ended 31 December 20X4 and a retained profit of £300,000. During the year the following transactions in fixed assets took place:

An asset with a book value of £70,000 was revalued to £110,000. The remaining useful life is estimated to be five years.

A piece of land which was revalued by £200,000 five years ago was sold to a property developer for £1,200,000, giving a profit of £340,000.

Required

Show the note of historical cost profit for the year ended 31 December 20X4.

2.11 Solution

Start with reported profit before tax.

Note of historical cost profits and losses	£000
Profit before tax per profit and loss account	705
'Excess' depreciation	8
Realisation of revaluation surplus	200
Historical cost profit on ordinary activities before tax	913
Historical cost profit retained (300 + 208)	508

The 'excess' deprecation is the difference between historical cost depreciation and depreciation on the revalued amount.

$$\frac{£110{,}000 - £70{,}000}{5} = £8{,}000 \text{ pa}$$

2.12 Recognition of gains and losses

Once an unrealised gain or loss is recognised in the statement of total recognised gains and losses, transfer for inclusion in the profit and loss account when it becomes realised at a later date is not allowed. For example, on the sale of an asset originally revalued, any remaining revaluation reserve can be credited to the profit and loss reserve and must not be reported in the profit and loss account for the year.

2.13 Example

Western Enterprise plc wholesales and distributes toys and models. The following information has been extracted from the first draft of the accounts for the year to 31 December 20X3.

	£000
Share capital (including new issue in year of £100,000)	1,300.0
Share premium account (including £200,000 on new issue in year)	2,600.0
Revaluation reserve	415.0
Profit and loss account at 1 January 20X3	8,569.0
Sales	10,750.0
Purchases and production costs	8,935.0
Stocks at 1 January 20X3	974.0

Staff costs	
Distribution	269.5
Other (administration)	351.3
Depreciation	
Vehicles	115.5
Other (administration)	171.5
General expenses	233.2
Interest receivable	25.5
Interest payable	33.8
Taxation payable	335.8
Dividends (interim paid)	100.0
Provisions for losses (at 1 January 20X3)	150.0

Additional information

During the year, the company acquired Pioneer Ltd, a distribution company. Its results since acquisition are already included in the amounts given.

In May 20X3, the company closed its manufacturing division. The closure had been announced in 20X2 and a progressive rundown of the operation had commenced. At 31 December 20X2, operating losses foreseen up to the closure of £100,000 and on the actual closure of £50,000 had been provided for. The final loss on the actual closure was £65,000.

The company revalued premises used in its continuing operations on 1 January 20X3, resulting in a surplus of £262,000. This has been credited to revaluation reserve but no other entries in this account have been made since 31 December 20X2. Depreciation charged in the year increased by £13,800 as a result of revaluations.

General expenses include a bad debt of £100,000 due to the liquidation of a major customer. This is considered material.

The company wishes to propose a final dividend of £150,000. Closing stock is valued at £1,304,000.

Acquisitions and discontinued activities represent the following proportions of the year's totals for income and expenses:

	Percentage of year's total	
	Acquisition	*Discontinued*
	%	%
Turnover	25	10
Cost of sales	20	15
Distribution costs	30	10
Administrative expenses	25	20

Required

In so far as the information given permits, prepare the following for the year ending 31 December 20X3.

(a) Profit and loss account and the note relating to exceptional items required by FRS 3 *Reporting financial performance*

(b) Statement of total recognised gains and losses

(c) Note of historical cost profits and losses

(d) Statement of reserves

(e) Reconciliation of movements in shareholders' funds

Earnings per share and the remaining notes are not required. Make all calculations to the nearest £100.

2.14 Solution

(a) *WESTERN ENTERPRISE PLC*
PROFIT AND LOSS ACCOUNT FOR THE YEAR ENDED 31 DECEMBER 20X3

	Existing operations	*Acquisitions*	*Discontinued operations*	*Total*
	£000	£000	£000	£000
Turnover (split 65:25:10)	6,987.5	2,687.5	1,075.0	10,750.0
Cost of sales (W)	(5,593.2)	(1,721.0)	(1,290.8)	(8,605.0)
Gross profit	1,394.3	966.5	(215.8)	2,145.0
Distribution costs (W)	(231.0)	(115.5)	(38.5)	(385.0)
Administrative expenses (W)	(415.8)	(189.0)	(151.2)	(756.0)
Less 20X2 provision	-	-	100.0	100.0
Operating profit (see note)	747.5	662.0	(305.5)	1,104.0
Loss on disposal of discontinued operations	-	-	(65.0)	(65.0)
Less 20X2 provision	-	-	50.0	50.0
Profit on ordinary activities before interest	747.5	662.0	(320.5)	1,089.0
Other interest receivable and similar income				25.5
Interest payable and similar charges				(33.8)
Profit on ordinary activities before taxation				1,080.7
Tax on profit on ordinary activities				(335.8)
Profit for the financial year				744.9
Dividends				(250.0)
Retained profit for the financial year				494.9

Note	£000
Operating profit is stated after charging an exceptional bad debt write-off due to liquidation of a customer	100

(b) *STATEMENT OF TOTAL RECOGNISED GAINS AND LOSSES FOR THE YEAR ENDED 31 DECEMBER 20X3*

	£000
Profit for the financial year	744.9
Unrealised surplus on revaluation of properties	262.0
Total recognised gains and losses relating to the year	1,006.9

(c) *NOTE OF HISTORICAL COST PROFITS AND LOSSES FOR THE YEAR ENDED 31 DECEMBER 20X3*

	£000
Reported profit on ordinary activities before taxation	1,080.7
Difference between historical cost depreciation charge and the actual charge for the year calculated on the revalued amount	13.8
Historical cost profit on ordinary activities before taxation	1,094.5
Historical cost profit for the year retained after taxation and dividends (494.9 + 13.8)	508.7

(d) *STATEMENT OF RESERVES FOR THE YEAR ENDED 31 DECEMBER 20X3*

	Share premium account	*Revaluation reserve*	*Profit and loss account*	*Total*
	£000	£000	£000	£000
At 1 January 20X3	2,400.0	153.0	8,569.0	11,122.0
Premium on issue of shares (nominal value of £100,000)	200.0	-	-	200.0
Transfer from profit and loss account of the year	-	-	494.9	494.9
Transfer of realised profits	-	(13.8)	13.8	-
Surplus on property revaluations	-	262.0	-	262.0
At 31 December 20X3	2,600.0	401.2	9,077.7	12,078.9

(e) *RECONCILIATION OF MOVEMENTS IN SHAREHOLDERS' FUNDS FOR THE YEAR ENDED 31 DECEMBER 20X3*

	£000
Profit for the financial year	744.9
Dividends	(250.0)
	494.9
Other recognised gains and losses relating to the year	262.0
New share capital subscribed (100 + 200)	300.0
Net addition to shareholders' funds	1,056.9
Opening shareholders' funds (1,200 + 2,400 + 153 + 8,569)	12,322.0
Closing shareholders' funds	13,378.9

Working

	£000
Cost of sales (974 + 8,935 – 1,304) split 65:20:15	8,605
Distribution costs (269.5 + 115.5) split 60:30:10	385
Administrative costs (351.3 + 171.5 + 233.2) split 55:25:20	756

Activity 4 *(The answer is in the final chapter of this book)*

Meld plc

Draft accounts for Meld plc for the year ended 30 June 20X4 include the following amounts.

	£
Turnover	472,800
Cost of sales and expenses (including interest payable of £15,000)	(376,800)
Profit before tax	96,000
Tax	(28,800)
Dividends proposed	(21,600)
Retained profit for the year	45,600

Additional information

- Meld plc acquired an unincorporated business during the year for £12,000. The fair value of the net assets acquired was £9,120 and the £2,880 difference between these two figures represents goodwill which is to be carried as a permanent intangible asset. Turnover and operating expenses (included in the figures above) for this business since acquisition were £4,800 and £3,600 respectively.
- The directors have decided to change the company's accounting policy for development costs from one of capitalisation and amortisation to immediate write-off of all expenditure as incurred. At present, development costs are included in the draft figures as follows.

	Cost	*Amortisation*
	£	£
At 1 July 20X3	34,560	20,160
Costs incurred	3,100	-
Amortisation charged	-	4,800
At 30 June 20X4	37,660	24,960

- In July 20X3, the company revalued fixed assets which had originally cost £19,200 to £28,800. Accumulated depreciation at the date of revaluation was £7,200. At the date of revaluation, the remaining useful economic life of these assets was five years and depreciation has been charged on the revalued amount for the year.
- At 1 July 20X3, capital and reserves were as follows.

	£
Ordinary share capital	240,000
Revaluation reserve (relating to freehold land)	48,000
Profit and loss account	168,000
	456,000

Required

Prepare the following for the year ended 30 June 20X4, insofar as the information given permits.

(a) Profit and loss account
(b) Statement of total recognised gains and losses
(c) Note of historical cost profits and losses
(d) Reconciliation of movements in shareholders' funds
(e) Statement of reserves.

Note. Comparatives are not required.

3 SSAP 25: Segmental reporting

3.1 The need for a Standard

Many enterprises carry on several classes of business or operate in several geographical areas, with different rates of profitability, different opportunities for growth and different degrees of risk. Segmental information will therefore provide users of financial statements with more information about the company's past performance and future prospects.

Although the CA 85 requires some basic disclosures of segmental information, SSAP 25 goes further to provide more information to users of the financial statements.

3.2 Scope

SSAP 25 *Segmental reporting* applies to all financial statements intended to give a true and fair view. However the disclosure requirements which go further than statutory requirements only apply to an entity that:

(a) is a public limited company or a holding company that has a public limited company as a subsidiary; or

(b) is a banking or insurance company; or

(c) satisfies the criteria, multiplied in each case by 10, for defining a medium-sized company under S248 CA 1985.

Where, in the opinion of the directors, the disclosure of any information required by this Accounting Standard would be seriously prejudicial to the interests of the company, that information need not be disclosed, but the fact that any such information has not been disclosed must be stated.

Before looking at its detail, we will first consider the overall impact of the standard.

3.3 Overview of SSAP 25

The additional disclosures required by SSAP 25 are designed to reveal significant information which might otherwise be hidden by the aggregation process of presenting a single profit and loss account and a single balance sheet for a business.

Consider a business with three segments as follows:

		£000	
Segment	A	B	C
Operating profits	100	200	(250)

Disclosing the three figures is obviously much more revealing than just disclosing an overall profit of £50,000.

3.4 Segmental ROCE

The standard requires turnover, result (ie operating profit or loss) and net assets to be disclosed for each class of business and geographical segment; this means that segmental return on capital employed (ROCE) can be calculated.

The analysis of this key ratio is one of the main benefits to users offered by compliance with SSAP 25.

3.5 Problems in segmental reporting

One problem is that directors can choose to opt out by claiming that disclosure is 'seriously prejudicial'.

Segment identification is also fraught with problems, being highly subjective.

Allocation of common costs between segments is another difficulty. Although these can be deducted from the total of segment results, some arbitrary allocation is likely to be necessary.

Finally, it is not the intention of SSAP 25 that it should facilitate inter-firm comparisons between similarly named segments - for example, engineering - which may in fact be quite different in nature.

The segmentation of information is more to allow comparison of one enterprise through time, rather than between enterprises.

3.6 Definitions

A **class of business** is a distinguishable component of an enterprise that provides a separate product or service or a separate group of related products or services.

A **geographical segment** is a geographical area comprising an individual country or group of countries in which a company operates, or to which it supplies products or services.

Common costs are costs that relate to more than one segment.

3.7 How segments should be identified

The directors should determine whether the company has carried on business of two or more classes or has supplied markets that differ substantially from each other. In identifying separate reportable segments, the directors should have regard to the overall purpose of presenting segmental information and the need of the user of the financial statements to be informed where a company carries on operations in different classes of business or in different geographical areas that:

(a) earn a return on investment that is out of line with the remainder of the business; or
(b) are subject to different degrees of risk; or
(c) have experienced different rates of growth; or
(d) have different potentials for future development.

The definition of the segments should be reviewed annually and re-defined when appropriate. Where a change is made, the reason for it and its nature and effect should be disclosed. The previous year's figures should be restated to reflect the change.

3.8 Disclosure required for each class of business and each geographical segment

(a) *Turnover*, distinguishing between:

(i) turnover derived from external customers; and
(ii) turnover derived from other segments.

Note that segmental information should be given in terms of the geographical origin of the turnover, rather than the destination. So we are principally showing the geographical segments *from which* the segments were supplied, rather than the segments *to which* they were supplied. Turnover split by destination need only be disclosed if this is materially different from turnover split by source.

(b) *Segment result*, before accounting for taxation and extraordinary items and normally before taking account of interest.

(c) *Segment net assets*, normally being the non-interest-bearing operating net assets.

The total of the information disclosed by segment should agree with the related figure in the financial statements. If it does not, the company should provide a reconciliation between the two figures.

Comparative figures for the previous accounting period should be provided. If, however, on the first occasion on which a company provides a segmental report the necessary information is not readily available, comparative figures need not be provided.

3.9 Illustration of SSAP 25 disclosures

Analysis by classes of business (ignoring prior year comparatives)

	Industry A	*Industry B*	*Other industries*	*Total*
	£m	*£m*	*£m*	*£m*
TURNOVER				
Total sales	33	42	26	101
Inter-segment sales	(4)	-	(12)	(16)
Sales to third parties	29	42	14	85

PROFIT BEFORE TAX				
Segment profit	3	4.5	1.8	9.3
Common costs				(0.3)
Operating profit				9.0
Net interest				(0.4)
Group profit before tax				8.6
NET ASSETS				
Segment net assets	17.6	24	19.4	61
Unallocated assets				3
Total net assets				64

Analysis by geographical areas

	United Kingdom £m	*Far East* £m	*Other* £m	*Group* £m
TURNOVER				
Total sales	67	23	12	102
Inter-segment sales	(8)	(9)	-	(17)
Sales to third parties	59	14	12	85
PROFIT BEFORE TAX				
Segment profit	6.5	1.8	1.0	9.3
Common costs				(0.3)
Operating profit				9.0
Net interest				(0.4)
Group profit before tax				8.6
NET ASSETS				
Segment net assets	41	16	4	61
Unallocated assets				3
Total net assets				64

For Unit 11 all that is required is an appreciation of the need to provide segmental information in the financial statements but no computation of the disclosures is required.

4 FRS 14: Earnings per share

4.1 Introduction

The basic earnings per share (EPS) calculation is simply $\frac{\text{Earnings for the year}}{\text{Number of shares in issue}}$.

Here 'earnings' means the profit after tax and preference dividends; and 'shares' means the weighted average number of ordinary shares outstanding during the period.

FRS 14 requires that companies with publicly traded shares must disclose the EPS for the period on the face of the profit and loss account. Other companies do not have to disclose their EPS, but where they voluntarily decide to do so, they should follow the principles in FRS 14.

4.2 Example

GERARD PLC
DRAFT PROFIT AND LOSS ACCOUNT FOR THE YEAR ENDED 31 DECEMBER 20X4

	£000	£000
Profit before tax		5,060
Taxation		(2,300)
Profit after tax		2,760
Transfer to reserves	230	
Dividends		
Paid - preference interim dividend	276	
Paid - ordinary interim dividend	368	
Proposed - preference final dividend	276	
Proposed - ordinary final dividend	460	1,610
Retained profit		1,150

On 1 January 20X4 the issued share capital of Gerard plc was 9,200,000 6% preference shares of £1 each and 8,280,000 ordinary shares of £1 each.

Required

Calculate the earnings per share (EPS) in respect of the year ended 31 December 20X4 on the basis that there was no change in the issued share capital of the company during the year.

4.3 Solution

The amount of earnings available to the ordinary shares (ie excluding the preference dividend) is divided by the number of ordinary shares.

$$\frac{£2,760,000 - £276,000 - £276,000}{8,280,000} = 26.7p$$

The EPS of 26.7p would be disclosed at the bottom of the profit and loss account for the year 20X4.

4.4 Issue of shares at full market price

In the example of Gerard plc, suppose that the company had issued 3,312,000 new ordinary shares at their full market value on 30 June 20X4. The money raised would have had an impact on the earnings. We would need to reflect this in the earnings per share working by recognising the impact on the earnings using a weighted average number of shares.

Date	*Actual number of shares*	*Fraction of year*	*Total*
1 January 20X4	8,280,000	$\frac{6}{12}$	4,140,000
30 June 20X4	11,592,000 (W1)	$\frac{6}{12}$	5,796,000
Number of shares in EPS calculation			9,936,000

(W1) New number of shares

Original number	8,280,000
New issue	3,312,000
New number	11,592,000

The earnings per share for 20X4 would now be calculated as:

$$\frac{£2,760,000 - £276,000 - £276,000}{9,936,000} = 22.2p$$

4.5 Bonus issue of shares

Suppose now that the company made no issue of shares at full price but instead made a bonus issue on 1 October 20X4 of one ordinary share for every four shares in issue at 30 September 20X4.

A bonus issue causes no impact on earnings, therefore EPS can be calculated based on the new number of shares.

8,280,000 × ¼ =	2,070,000 extra shares
Original number of shares	8,280,000
New number of shares	10,350,000

The earnings per share for 20X4 would now be calculated as:

$$\frac{£2,208,000}{10,350,000} = 21.3p$$

The comparative figure for EPS (reported as the EPS in the previous year's accounts) must be restated to reflect the greater number of shares now in issue. For example, if the EPS reported for 20X3 in the 20X3 accounts had been 24p, the 20X3 comparative EPS shown in the 20X4 accounts would be $\frac{4}{4+1} \times 24p = 19.2p$.

4.6 When a rights issue takes place

Suppose now that Gerard's only share issue in 20X4 was a rights issue of £1 ordinary shares on 1 October 20X4 in the proportion of one for every five shares held at a price of £1.20. The middle market price for the shares on the last day of quotation cum rights (ie before the rights issue) was £1.80 per share.

When a rights issue takes place shares are issued at less than full market price. We treat this as a combination of a bonus issue and an issue at full market price. We will therefore need to calculate the rights issue bonus fraction by using share prices.

$$\text{Rights issue bonus fraction} = \frac{\text{Actual cum rights price}}{\text{Theoretical ex rights price}}$$

Actual cum rights price	=	Price of share with rights attached immediately before rights issue.
Theoretical ex rights price	=	Expected share price immediately after rights issue (weighted average of actual cum rights price and exercise price of rights issue shares).

Use a table for full computation of the number of shares, as follows.

Date	*Actual number of shares*	*Fraction of year*	*Rights issue bonus fraction*	*Total*

In the present case, we have a rights issue made in the proportion of one for every five shares held, (ie for every five shares previously owned you now own six).

Rights issue bonus fraction

	£	£
5 shares at	1.80	9.00
1 share at	1.20	1.20
6 shares		10.20

Expected share price after rights issue = $\frac{£10.20}{6}$ = £1.70

Therefore rights issue bonus fraction = $\frac{£1.80}{£1.70}$

Date	*Actual number of shares*	*Fraction of year*	*Rights issue bonus fraction*	*Total*
1 January 20X4	8,280,000	$\frac{9}{12}$	$\frac{1.80}{1.70}$	6,575,294
1 October 20X4	9,936,000 (W1)	$\frac{3}{12}$		2,484,000
Number of shares to be used in EPS calculation				9,059,294

EPS = $\frac{£2,208,000}{9,059,294}$ = 24.4p.

Again, just as with the bonus issue, the comparative figure for EPS must be adjusted to reflect the bonus element of the rights issue. For example, if the 20X3 EPS had been reported in the 20X3 accounts as 24p, the 20X3 comparative EPS shown in the 20X4 accounts would now be $\frac{1.70}{1.80} \times 24p = 22.7p$.

Working

(W1) New number of shares

8,280,000 × 1 ÷ 5 = 1,656,000 extra shares

New number of shares = 8,280,000 + 1,656,000 = 9,936,000

***Activity 5** (The answer is in the final chapter of this book)*

Radar plc

Extracts from the balance sheet of Radar plc as at 1 April 20X2 are set out below.

	£000	£000
Ordinary shares of 25p		4,000
8% preference shares		1,000
Reserves		
Share premium	700	
Capital redemption reserve	1,300	
Revaluation reserve	90	
Profit and loss account	750	
		2,840
		7,840
10% debentures		2,000

Note: The above are extracts from the *opening* balance sheet for the current reporting year.

The following draft profit and loss account has been prepared for the year to 31 March 20X3, prior to the declaration of the proposed final ordinary dividend for the year.

			£000	£000
Profit before interest and tax				1,510
Debenture interest				(200)
Profit before tax				1,310
Taxation	-	provision for 20X3	300	
	-	deferred tax	100	
				(400)
				910
Dividends	-	ordinary	320	
	-	preference	80	
				(400)
				510

The following information is relevant.

(i) A bonus issue of 1 for 8 ordinary shares was made on 7 September 20X2.

(ii) A fully subscribed rights issue of 1 for 5 ordinary shares at a price of 50p each was made on 1 January 20X3. Immediately prior to the issue the market price of Radar plc's ordinary shares was £1.40 each.

(iii) The earnings per share (EPS) was correctly reported in last year's accounts at 8p.

Required

Calculate the basic EPS (including the comparative figure) for the year ended 31 March 20X3.

---

5 Quick quiz *(The answers are in the final chapter of this book)*

1 Could a temporary mothballing of a factory be a discontinued operation?

2 Distinguish between an exceptional item and an extraordinary item.

3 A business has re-assessed the remaining useful life of their machinery from 20 years to 10 years. Is this a change in accounting policy?

4 A company reports profit before tax of £10m, a tax charge of £2m, and has £20m in 50p shares. What is the EPS for the year?

6 Summary

FRS 3 is an important accounting standard and you need to know how to set out a profit and loss account if there are acquisitions or discontinued activities during the year. The definition of discontinued activities is important as it will not necessarily be the case that all activities that appear to be discontinued in an assessment actually fall into the FRS 3 category of such. You also need to be able to recognise the three exceptional items that appear on the face of the profit and loss account.

The other important areas of FRS 3 are the introduction of the Statement of Total Recognised Gains and Losses, the note for movements in shareholders' funds and the note for reconciliation of historical cost profits and losses.

For Unit 11 you also need an appreciation of the need for the segmental disclosures required by SSAP 25 although no computation of the disclosures is required. Finally the calculation of the basic earnings per share is required. The importance of this figure is considered in the chapter on interpretation of accounts.

lesson on 21-1-04

CHAPTER 11

Tangible fixed assets

ASSESSMENT FOCUS

For Unit 11 you need to be able to draft limited company year end financial statements and for that purpose you need to be aware of the main requirements of relevant accounting standards. In this chapter we will consider the detailed requirements of FRS 15: Tangible fixed assets. For this FRS all aspects are assessable but the emphasis is on discursive rather than computational tasks. We will also consider SSAP 19: Accounting for investment properties and SSAP 4: Accounting for government grants, both of which are straightforward.

This chapter covers the following Knowledge and Understanding of the AAT Syllabus.

The UK regulatory framework for financial reporting and the main requirements of relevant Financial Reporting Standards *(Element 11.1)*

Preparing financial statements in proper form *(Element 11.1)*

In order to cover these the following topics are included.

FRS 15: Tangible fixed assets
SSAP 19: Accounting for investment properties
SSAP 4: Accounting for government grants

Key definitions

Tangible fixed assets	Assets with physical substance that are held on a long-term basis in the entity's activities.
Depreciation	The measure of the consumption of a tangible fixed asset during the reporting period.
Investment property	Property held for its investment potential rather than to be consumed within the business.
Revenue-based grant	Grant received to help with the cost of revenue expenditure.
Capital-based grant	Grant received to help with the cost of capital expenditure (ie fixed assets).

1 *FRS 15: Tangible fixed assets*

1.1 Introduction

FRS 15 **Tangible fixed assets** is a largely straightforward FRS regulating the initial measurement, valuation and depreciation of all tangible fixed assets other than investment properties (to which SSAP 19 applies - see later).

Tangible fixed assets (such as buildings and machinery) have physical substance; you can touch them. They can be distinguished from **intangible** fixed assets (such as goodwill) which have no physical substance. Intangible fixed assets are covered in the next chapter.

1.2 Definitions

- Tangible fixed assets

  Assets that have physical substance and are held for use in the production or supply of goods or services, for rental to others, or for administrative purposes on a continuing basis in the reporting entity's activities.

- Depreciation

  The measure of the cost or revalued amount of the economic benefits of the tangible fixed assets that have been consumed during the period.

  Consumption includes the wearing out, using up or other reduction in the useful economic life of a tangible fixed asset whether arising from use, effluxion of time or obsolescence through either changes in technology or changes in demand for the goods and services produced by the asset.

The useful economic life of a tangible fixed asset is the period over which the entity expects to derive economic benefit from that asset.

1.3 Initial measurement

Initial measurement of a tangible fixed asset (whether acquired or self-constructed) should be at its **cost**.

Cost should include all costs directly attributable to bringing the asset into working condition for its intended use. Cost can include finance costs – see 1.4.

If the carrying amount of a tangible fixed asset exceeds its recoverable amount (defined as the higher of net realisable value and value in use) then the asset is impaired and it should be written down to its recoverable amount - see FRS 11 in the next chapter.

1.4 Capitalising finance costs

Finance costs (such as interest payable) directly attributable to the construction of a tangible fixed asset may be capitalised as part of the cost of the asset. Such capitalisation is optional.

Conditions:

- Finance costs may only be capitalised if the entity adopts a policy of capitalising them. If such a policy is adopted, all qualifying finance costs must be capitalised.
- Finance costs capitalised in a period must not exceed finance costs incurred in the period.
- Capitalisation should **begin** when:
  - finance costs are being incurred; and
  - expenditure for the asset is being incurred; and
  - work has begun on the asset or on getting it ready for use
- Capitalisation should **cease** when:
  - substantially all the activities necessary to get the asset ready for use are complete
- Capitalisation should be suspended if work on the asset is interrupted for an extended period.

Disclosures when finance costs are capitalised:

- Accounting policy adopted
- Finance costs included in the cost of the asset
- Finance costs capitalised in the period
- Finance costs recognised in the profit and loss account in the period
- Capitalisation rate used

1.5 Example

AB plc incurs the following costs in constructing a new fixed asset:

	£
Site clearance	2,000
Cost of materials used in asset	30,000
Legal fees to secure a licence	1,000
Interest at 10% pa on £40,000 loan raised to finance the asset's construction:	
3 month construction period ($10\% \times £40,000 \times \frac{3}{12}$)	1,000
Cost of materials wasted in a flood	500
Cost of labour used in asset	8,000
Cost of industrial dispute	1,500

Which of the above costs can be capitalised into the initial cost of the fixed asset?

1.6 Solution

The directly attributable costs are:

	£
Site clearance	2,000
Cost of materials in asset	30,000
Necessary legal fee	1,000
Interest during construction period	1,000
Cost of labour in asset	8,000
	42,000

The cost of the wasted materials and the industrial dispute are not direct costs and must be written off to the profit and loss account as incurred. Note that capitalisation of the interest cost (£1,000 in the example) is not compulsory, but is permitted by FRS 15.

1.7 Subsequent expenditure

Subsequent expenditure should be capitalised if it enhances the economic benefits of the asset in excess of its previously assessed standard of performance. Otherwise, subsequent expenditure that helps to maintain the asset's standard of performance (eg, routine repairs and maintenance) should be charged to the profit and loss account as it is incurred.

1.8 Valuation

Revaluation of tangible fixed assets is allowed if a policy of revaluation is adopted. Just as with the capitalisation of interest, revaluation is optional rather than mandatory.

Conditions:

- All assets of the same class must be revalued. For example, if certain land and buildings were to be revalued, this would not require the revaluation of plant and machinery, but would require the revaluation of all land and buildings held.
- Once revalued, the carrying amount in each balance sheet must be current value.

  This requirement is met for properties, according to FRS 15, by a full valuation every five years and an interim valuation in year 3. Interim valuations should be carried out in years 1, 2 and 4 if it is likely there has been a material change in value.

  Alternatively, for non-specialised properties, a rolling revaluation may be undertaken, with (say) one fifth of properties valued each year, with interim valuations of the remainder when it is likely that values have changed materially.

- A qualified valuer must be used for a full valuation. If an internal valuer is used, the valuation must be reviewed by a qualified external valuer.
- The basis of valuation should be:
    - non-specialised properties: existing use value, with open market value shown by note if materially different
    - specialised properties: depreciated replacement cost
    - assets other than landed property: open market value

1.9 Reporting valuation gains and losses

- Gains
    - Show in the statement of total recognised gains and losses (STRGL) unless they reverse previous losses recognised in the profit and loss account, when they can be taken to the profit and loss account
- Losses
    - Losses caused by consumption of economic benefits – show in profit and loss account
    - Other losses – show in STRGL until the carrying amount reaches depreciated historical cost, then the excess balance thereafter in the profit and loss account
- In reporting gains and losses, material revaluation gains and losses on individual assets in a class of assets should **not** be offset

1.10 Example

A building costing £200,000 was purchased on 1 January 20X1. It is being depreciated over its useful life of 20 years on a straight line basis down to a nil residual value. At 31 December 20X1 the building was revalued at £247,000 and at 31 December 20X2 it was revalued at £150,000.

Show how these revaluations should be dealt with in the financial statements as at 31 December 20X1 and 20X2.

1.11 Solution

In the year ended 31 December 20X1, depreciation of $\frac{£200{,}000}{20}$ = £10,000 would originally be charged, so the revaluation gain is £57,000 (from a net book value of £190,000 up to £247,000). This gain would be reported in the STRGL and would be shown in the balance sheet as a revaluation reserve.

The double entry for the revaluation is:

	£	£
DR Building (247 – 200)	47,000	
DR Accumulated depreciation	10,000	
CR Revaluation reserve		57,000

In the year ended 31 December 20X2, depreciation of $\frac{£247{,}000}{19}$ = £13,000 would originally be charged, so the revaluation loss is £84,000 (from a net book value of £234,000 down to £150,000). This loss can be charged in the STRGL until the carrying amount reaches depreciated historical cost. After 2 years, the depreciated historical cost would be £200,000 - £20,000 = £180,000, so the revaluation loss is charged £54,000 (£234,000 - £180,000) to the STRGL and the excess £30,000 to the profit and loss account.

1.12 Gains and losses on disposal

Gains and losses on disposal of tangible fixed assets are shown in the profit and loss account and are calculated as the difference between proceeds and carrying amount at the date of sale.

1.13 Depreciation

The depreciable amount (cost or valuation, less residual value) of a tangible fixed asset should be allocated on a systematic basis over its useful economic life. The depreciation method used should reflect as fairly as possible the pattern in which the asset's economic benefits are consumed.

The following factors need to be considered when determining the useful economic life, residual value and depreciation method of an asset:

- Expected usage, assessed by reference to expected capacity or physical output
- Expected physical deterioration through use or the passage of time
- Economic or technological obsolescence
- Legal or similar limits on use, such as the expiry dates of related leases

FRS 15 mentions the straight-line and reducing balance methods but does not stipulate a particular method. It is up to the directors to choose the fairest method possible.

Where the tangible fixed asset comprises two or more major components with different useful economic lives, each component should be accounted for separately for depreciation purposes and depreciated over its individual useful economic life.

1.14 Example

PQ plc buys a blast furnace for £1m, of which £100,000 is the cost of the lining of the furnace. While the furnace itself has a useful life of 40 years, the lining must be replaced at the end of every 10 years. What is the depreciation charge each year for the furnace and lining?

1.15 Solution

The furnace and lining must be recognised as separate components. The furnace will be capitalised at £0.9m with a life of 40 years, while the lining will be capitalised at £0.1m with a life of 10 years.

The annual depreciation charge is $\frac{£900,000}{40} + \frac{£100,000}{10} = £32,500$.

1.16 Change in method of depreciation

A change from one method of providing depreciation to another (for example, from machine hour rate to straight line) is only allowed if the 'new method will give a fairer presentation of the result and of the financial position'.

However, this is not treated as a change in accounting policy, meaning that there is no prior year adjustment. Instead, the carrying amount of the tangible fixed asset is depreciated using the new method over the asset's remaining useful economic life, beginning in the period in which the change is made.

1.17 Example

Ford plc makes up its accounts to 31 December each year. On 1 January 20X0, it bought a machine for £100,000, and started depreciating it at 15% per annum, on the reducing-balance basis. During 20X4, the company decided to change the basis of depreciation to straight-line, with the machine having a total useful life of 10 years.

1.18 Solution

At 31 December 20X3 the machine would be included in the accounts at:

	£
Cost	100,000
Accumulated depreciation	47,800
Net book value	52,200

In accordance with FRS 15 the unamortised cost at 1 January 20X4 of £52,200 must be written off over the six years remaining of the ten-year life.

The new annual charge will be:

$$\frac{£52,200}{6 \text{ years}} = £8,700 \text{ per annum}$$

- Balance sheet presentation would be:

	20X4	*20X3 (not restated)*
	£	£
Cost	100,000	100,000
Accumulated depreciation	56,500	47,800
Net book value	43,500	52,200

- Profit and loss account for 20X4 would show:

(i) Depreciation charge for the year £8,700

(ii) *Note.* As a result of the change in depreciation policy from 15% reducing balance to 10% straight-line, the charge for depreciation is £870 (£8,700 – 15% × £52,200) higher than it would otherwise have been.

1.19 Useful economic lives and residual values

The length of a fixed asset's life is clearly a very important number in a depreciation calculation. However, it is an estimate, as it is necessary to make predictions about the future.

Both the useful economic life and the residual value (if material) of a tangible fixed asset should be reviewed at the end of each reporting period. They should be revised 'if expectations are significantly different from previous estimates'. Reasonably expected technological changes based on prices prevailing at the date of acquisition (or revaluation) should be taken into account.

If either a useful economic life or a residual value is revised, the accounting treatment is to depreciate the net book amount over the revised remaining useful economic life.

1.20 Example

A moulding machine cost £50,000 on 1 January 20X1 and at the date of purchase had an estimated useful economic life of ten years. Its estimated residual value is nil. At 31 December 20X4 it has a remaining useful economic life of six years.

In 20X5 the management decided that the machine was wearing out more rapidly than expected and revised its remaining useful life down to three years.

1.21 Solution

Initially the annual depreciation charge is:

$$\frac{£50{,}000}{10 \text{ years}} = £5{,}000 \text{ pa}$$

At 31 December 20X4 the machine would be stated in the accounts at:

		£
Cost		50,000
Less:	Accumulated depreciation (four years @ £5,000)	(20,000)
Net book value		30,000

Therefore, the new annual depreciation charge is:

$$\frac{£30{,}000}{3 \text{ years}} = £10{,}000 \text{ pa}$$

At 31 December 20X5 the machine would be included in the accounts at:

		£
Cost		50,000
Less:	Accumulated depreciation (£20,000 + £10,000)	(30,000)
Net book value		20,000

Activity 1 *(The answer is in the final chapter of this book)*

Ford plc

The following fixed asset balances have been extracted from the books of Ford plc as at 31 December 20X7.

	£000	£000
Freehold factory cost at 1 January 20X7	1,440	
Freehold factory revaluation	760	
Freehold factory additions	500	
Freehold factory depreciation at 1 January 20X7		144
Freehold factory revaluation adjustment	144	
Freehold factory depreciation charge		60
Plant and machinery cost at 1 January 20X7	1,968	
Plant and machinery additions	75	
Plant and machinery depreciation at 1 January 20X7		257
Plant and machinery depreciation charge		233
Motor vehicles cost at 1 January 20X7	449	
Motor vehicles additions	35	
Motor vehicles depreciation at 1 January 20X7		194
Motor vehicles depreciation charge		87
Office equipment and fixtures cost at 1 January 20X7	888	
Office equipment and fixtures additions	22	
Office equipment and fixtures depreciation at 1 January 20X7		583
Office equipment and fixtures depreciation charge		182

You are given the following information for the year ended 31 December 20X7:

(1) The factory was acquired in March 20X2 and is being depreciated over 50 years.

(2) At 1 January 20X7, depreciation was provided on cost on a straight-line basis. The rates used were 20% for office equipment and fixtures, 25% for motor vehicles and 10% for plant and machinery.

(3) Early in the year the factory was revalued to an open market value of £2.2 million and an extension was built costing £500,000.

(4) During the year the directors decided to change the method of depreciating motor vehicles to 30% reducing balance to give a fairer presentation of the results and of the financial position. The effect of this change was to reduce the depreciation charge for the year by £34,000.

(5) It is the company's policy to charge a full year's depreciation in the year of acquisition.

Required

Prepare the disclosure notes for fixed assets for the year ended 31 December 20X7 required by FRS 15 and CA 1985 in so far as the information permits.

1.22 Disclosures

The following information should be disclosed separately in the financial statements for each class of tangible fixed assets:

- the depreciation methods used;
- the useful economic lives or the depreciation rates used;
- total depreciation charge for the period;
- where material, the financial effect of a change during the period in either the estimate of useful economic lives or the estimate of residual values;
- the cost or revalued amount at the beginning of the financial period and at the balance sheet date;
- the cumulative amount of provisions for depreciation or impairment at the beginning of the financial period and at the balance sheet date;
- a reconciliation of the movements, separately disclosing additions, disposals, revaluations, transfers, depreciation, impairment losses, and reversals of past impairment losses written back in the financial period;
- the net carrying amount at the beginning of the financial period and at the balance sheet date; and
- where there has been a change in the depreciation method used, the effect, if material, should be disclosed in the period of change. The reason for the change should also be disclosed.

For each class of revalued assets, the following should be disclosed:

- the name and qualifications of the valuer(s) or the valuer's organisation and a description of its nature;
- the basis or bases of valuation (including whether notional directly attributable acquisition costs have been included or expected selling costs deducted);
- the date and amounts of the valuations;

- where historical cost records are available, the carrying amount that would have been included in the financial statements had the tangible fixed assets been carried at historical cost less depreciation;
- whether the person(s) carrying out the valuation is (are) internal or external to the entity.

2 SSAP 19: Accounting for investment properties

2.1 Definition

An investment property is an interest in land and/or completed buildings which is held for its investment potential, any rental income being negotiated at arm's length.

Property owned by a company and occupied for its own purposes, or let to and occupied by another group company, is not an investment property.

2.2 Example

Which of the following are investment properties?

(a) Land which is leased out at an arm's length rental to a third party for use as a car park.
(b) A building used by the owning company as the company head office.
(c) A building leased to a subsidiary at an arm's length rental.

2.3 Solution

(a) This is an investment property.

(b) This is not an investment property, since it is occupied by the owning company for its own purposes.

(c) This is not an investment property, since it is let to a group company (ie a company in the same group of companies, a group comprising the parent company and the various subsidiaries).

2.4 Accounting treatment

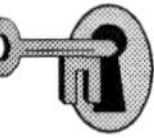

Investment properties should not be depreciated. Instead, they are revalued annually at their open market value, gains and losses being taken to an investment revaluation reserve and included in the statement of total recognised gains and losses (STRGL). If a deficit is expected to be permanent, it should be charged to the profit and loss account.

As an exception to the general rule of non-depreciation, leased investment properties with an unexpired term of twenty years or less must be depreciated over their remaining lives in the normal way.

2.5 Example

RJ plc purchased two investment properties on 31 December 20X4. The following valuations have been made at the annual balance sheet dates to 31 December 20X7:

	31 Dec 20X4	*31 Dec 20X5*	*31 Dec 20X6*	*31 Dec 20X7*
	£000	*£000*	*£000*	*£000*
Property A	100	120	130	110
Property B	120	110	110	120

For Property A, the deficit in the year ending 31 December 20X7 is expected to be permanent. For Property B, the deficit in the year ending 31 December 20X5 is expected to be temporary.

Show the balance on the investment revaluation reserve at each balance sheet date from 31 December 20X4 to 20X7.

2.6 *Solution*

	31 Dec 20X4 £000	31 Dec 20X5 £000	31 Dec 20X6 £000	31 Dec 20X7 £000
Investment revaluation reserve	-	10	20	30

The properties are acquired on 31 December 20X4, so will be shown at their cost, which equals their market value, at that date. No revaluation has taken place.

At 31 December 20X5 Property A increases in value by £20,000 while Property B falls by a temporary £10,000 (so this fall does not have to be charged to the profit and loss account). A net investment revaluation reserve of £10,000 can be recognised.

At 31 December 20X6 Property A increases in value by a further £10,000 while Property B stays at the same value. The investment revaluation reserve rises by £10,000, to £20,000.

At 31 December 20X7, Property A suffers a permanent fall of £20,000 which must be charged to profit and loss. Property B increases in value by £10,000 which can be recognised in the investment revaluation reserve.

2.7 *Commentary on SSAP 19*

SSAP 19 recognises that the economic substance of holding investment properties is different from other tangible fixed assets. Usually tangible fixed assets are owned in order to be consumed within the business, therefore FRS 15 requires them to be shown in the balance sheet at the amount of the cost/revalued amount which has not yet been consumed, since this is what users are most interested in.

However, investment properties are not held to be consumed, but instead for their investment potential. Depreciation (as a measure of consumption) is irrelevant; what users are most interested in is the market value, so this is the balance sheet valuation required by SSAP 19.

2.8 *Concern as to the legality of SSAP 19*

The CA 85 states that all fixed assets with a finite useful life must be depreciated. SSAP 19 requires that investment properties (which surely have a finite life, however well they are maintained) should not be depreciated, which appears contrary to the Act.

However the Act contains the true and fair view override, saying that the overriding requirement is for accounts to give a true and fair view. Any specific requirement of the Act or any accounting standard should be departed from to the extent necessary to give a true and fair view.

In such a situation, whenever the override is invoked, the accounts must disclose the particulars, reasons and effect of the departure.

Companies that follow SSAP 19 must therefore invoke the true and fair view override and disclose the matters required.

Activity 2 *(The answer is in the final chapter of this book)*

Hamilton

Hamilton plc owns the leasehold on a large 12-storey office block in the City area of London, which it purchased on 1 April 20X5 for £3 million. On that date the lease had a remaining life of 25 years. The building has been available for subletting, which on average over the three years since its acquisition has been 70% occupied. The building is currently classified in Hamilton plc's balance sheet as an investment property under SSAP 19 *Accounting for investment properties*, and not depreciated. Hamilton plc does not intend to sell the property.

Platonic and Company, a firm of Chartered Surveyors has revalued the office block annually since acquisition on an open market value basis. The values have been as set out below.

Year ended 31 March	*20X6*	*20X7*	*20X8*
	£3.2 million	£3.6 million	£3.6 million

Hamilton plc has adopted these values as the balance sheet carrying value of the property. Included in the report on the valuation for the current year end (31 March 20X8) the surveyors noted that over the next few years there is expected to be a surplus of rented property space in the City and sublease rentals are expected to fall. This in turn is expected to lead to a serious decline in the value of properties like Hamilton plc's.

In view of this the directors of Hamilton plc sought further advice from Platonic and Company as to the future use of the property. They were advised that the future anticipated levels of occupancy and rental income would be unlikely to cover the financing and running costs of the property. They suggested that Hamilton plc should consider using the building for the company's administration and as the registered office. They should then change the classification of the office block from an investment property to a leasehold building and this would avoid having to recognise any future revaluation movements on the property as it could then be carried at 'cost'.

During the year the audit manager has made the following notes in the working papers.

- An article in 'Accountancy Updates' reported that an important paper in the 'Journal of Valuation Surveyors' had reported dramatic falls averaging 25% in the value of office property in the City during the last six months of Hamilton plc's current accounting year.
- The Managing Director has refused a suggestion by the audit manager that another firm of surveyors should give an opinion on the value of the office block. The refusal was made on the basis that a second valuation would be an unnecessary cost as the fee would be 2% of the valuation.
- The draft profit and loss account for the year to 31 March 20X8, treating the office block as an investment property, shows only a small after tax profit of £60,000. No dividends have been paid in the year to 31 March 20X8.

Required

(a) Describe the circumstances in which companies are normally permitted to change their accounting policies, and consider whether the change in the classification of Hamilton plc's office block would represent a change in accounting policy. **(10 marks)**

(b) Explain the accounting implications of Hamilton plc using the office block as a leasehold property rather than an investment property and, assuming the proposed change of use is from 1 April 20X8, quantify the effect on the Financial Statements for the years to 31 March 20X8 and 20X9:

(i) if Platonic and Company's current valuation is correct and the value of the property will fall by 25% (to £2.7 million) in the year to 31 March 20X9, and

(ii) if the value of the property had already fallen by 25% during the year to 31 March 20X8. **(10 marks)**

(Total : 20 marks)

3 SSAP 4: Accounting for government grants

3.1 Introduction

Government grants have been made available in various forms from time to time, notably from the Industry Act 1972 and subsequent modifications.

Such grants may fall into one of the two main categories:

(a) *revenue-based grants* for specified categories of revenue expenditure;

(b) *capital-based grants* to help with the cost of capital expenditure.

However, today's complex grants are difficult to categorise (eg job creation).

No complicated accounting problem is presented by revenue-based grants, which should clearly be credited to revenue in the same period as that in which the related expenditure is charged.

SSAP 4 was introduced in April 1974 to standardise the accounting treatment of capital-based grants, for which various methods of accounting had previously been practised.

3.2 Accounting treatment

Possible methods of accounting for capital-based grants

Three main methods of accounting could be envisaged:

(a) to credit the whole grant to profit and loss account immediately on receipt;

(b) to credit the whole grant to a non-distributable reserve;

(c) to credit the grant to revenue over the useful life of the asset concerned, by one of two methods:

  (i) by reducing the cost of the asset by the amount of the grant and then charging depreciation on the net amount; or

  (ii) by treating the grant as a deferred credit, a portion of which is transferred to revenue annually, probably in step with the depreciation of the asset.

SSAP 4 rejects methods (a) and (b) on the grounds that they are both contrary to the accruals basis of accounting: in both methods there is no correlation between the accounting treatment of the grant and the accounting treatment of the asset to which it relates.

In principle SSAP 4 accepts that either method (c)(i) or (c)(ii) is acceptable, since both these methods do follow the accruals basis. However there are some differences in the effect of these two methods.

An economist would probably prefer to show the net cost of the asset, using method (c)(i), on the grounds that the net cost is the only relevant figure and without the grant the asset might never have been acquired.

Accountants, on the other hand, may well prefer the neat debits and credits of method (c)(ii), on the following grounds:

(a) assets acquired at different times and locations are recorded on a uniform basis regardless of changes in government policy (such comparability is often important to management in establishing price structures and investment policies);

(b) control over the ordering, construction and maintenance of assets is based on the gross value;

(c) as capital allowances for tax purposes are normally calculated on the cost of an asset before deduction of the grant, the tax calculations will be easier.

3.3 Example

To illustrate the two permitted methods, consider the following simple example.

Sponger Ltd purchases a fixed asset for £6,000 and receives a 20% government grant. The asset has an expected life of three years at the end of which it is expected to have nil scrap value.

3.4 Solution

Method (c) (i): Reduce the cost of the acquisition of the fixed asset by the amount of the grant.

Profit and loss account

		Year	
	1	2	3
	£	£	£
Depreciation charge $\frac{£6,000 - £1,200}{3}$	1,600	1,600	1,600

Balance sheet at end of year

		Year	
	1	2	3
	£	£	£
Fixed assets			
Cost (net of government grants)	4,800	4,800	4,800
Less: Accumulated depreciation	1,600	3,200	4,800
Net book value	3,200	1,600	-

Method (c) (ii): Treat the amount of the grant as a deferred credit, a portion of which is transferred to revenue annually.

Profit and loss account

		Year	
	1	2	3
	£	£	£
Depreciation charge	2,000	2,000	2,000
Credit related government grant	(400)	(400)	(400)

Balance sheet at end of year

		Year	
	1	2	3
	£	£	£
Fixed assets			
Cost	6,000	6,000	6,000
Less: Accumulated depreciation	2,000	4,000	6,000
Net book value	4,000	2,000	-
Net current assets	xxxx	xxxx	xxxx
Creditors: Amounts falling due after more than one year			
Deferred income: Government grants	(800)	(400)	-
	xxxx	xxxx	xxxx
Capital and reserves	xxxx	xxxx	xxxx

When using method (c)(ii), the amount of the grant shown in the balance sheet must be shown as a long-term creditor, and not within shareholders' funds (ie as a reserve).

3.5 Effect of the Companies Act

The CA 85 requires that fixed assets must be shown at cost less amounts written off. For purchased assets, cost is defined as the actual price paid plus any additional expenses. If a company were to use method (c)(i) above, the cost of the fixed asset would be shown at purchase price less grant received, which is arguably contrary to the Act.

Legal opinion has been sought on this matter, which confirmed that the problem described above is a genuine problem. The conclusion is that companies should account for capital-based grants using method (c)(ii), while unincorporated bodies (which of course do not have to comply with the Companies Act) have a choice between method (c)(i) and method (c)(ii) (both of which are capable of giving a true and fair view).

3.6 Accounting for more complex grants

Some grants are given nowadays, not to help with specific revenue costs or capital costs, but to encourage other objectives (eg job creation). Such grants should be accounted for as follows:

Objective of grant	*Accounting treatment*
To provide immediate financial help	Recognise on receipt in profit and loss account
To reimburse previously incurred costs	Recognise on receipt in profit and loss account
To provide general financial help over a period	Recognise in profit and loss account over the relevant period

In the case of a grant which is not based on the incurring of specific expenditure, but on some other criteria (for example, the creation of jobs) such grants should be recognised in the profit and loss account so as to match them as closely as possible with the costs involved in meeting the specific criteria, for example in providing the jobs.

3.7 Disclosure

Disclosure of the following matters is required by SSAP 4 (revised):

(a) the accounting policy adopted for government grants;

(b) the effects of government grants on the results for the period and the financial position of the enterprise;

(c) where material assistance has been received in the form of government assistance other than grants, details of that assistance;

(d) potential liabilities to repay grants, in accordance with FRS 12.

4 Quick quiz *(The answers are in the final chapter of this book)*

1 Is the capitalisation of finance costs into the cost of fixed assets mandatory or optional?

2 How should directors choose the depreciation method to be used?

3 At what value should investment properties be shown in the balance sheet?

4 Can capital-based grants be credited immediately to the profit and loss account on receipt?

5 Summary

FRS 15 covers the accounting for tangible fixed assets other than investment properties (to which SSAP 19 applies).

- Fixed assets should initially be shown at cost.
- Subsequently they may either be shown at cost less depreciation, or revalued to fair value. Where revalued, the revaluation must be kept up to date.
- The useful lives and residual values of fixed assets should be reviewed annually and revised if necessary.

SSAP 19 requires that investment properties should not be depreciated, but should be shown on the balance sheet at market value.

SSAP 4 requires that government grants should be recognised in the profit and loss account to be matched with the expenditure to which they contribute. Companies receiving a capital-based grant should credit the grant to a deferred income creditor, and release it to the profit and loss account over the life of the asset to which it relates.

Notes – classwork 28-1-04

CHAPTER 12

Intangible fixed assets

ASSESSMENT FOCUS

For Unit 11 you need knowledge of all aspects of FRS 10: Goodwill and intangible assets and of SSAP 13: Accounting for research and development. You also need a limited understanding of the notion of an impairment review of fixed assets and goodwill and the principles of recognition and measurement of impairment losses from FRS 11: Impairment of fixed assets and goodwill. However, only the principles of calculation of impairment losses will be assessed and there will be no assessment of the calculation of impairment losses.

This chapter covers the following Knowledge and Understanding of the AAT Syllabus:

> The UK regulatory framework for financial reporting and the main requirements of relevant Financial Reporting Standards *(Element 11.1)*
>
> Preparing financial statements in proper form *(Element 11.1)*

In order to cover these the following topics are included:

> FRS 10: Goodwill and intangible assets
> SSAP 13: Accounting for research and development
> FRS 11: Impairment of fixed assets and goodwill

Key definitions

Intangible fixed assets	Fixed assets without physical substance. Examples are purchased goodwill and deferred development costs.
Purchased goodwill	Difference between the cost of shares acquired and the fair value of net assets acquired.
Research	Investigation to seek new scientific knowledge.
Development	Use of existing scientific knowledge to produce commercial products.
Amortisation	The word used instead of 'depreciation' when writing off intangible fixed assets.
Impairment	Reduction in the recoverable amount of a fixed asset below its carrying amount.

1 *FRS 10: Goodwill and intangible assets*

1.1 Introduction

In the previous chapter you studied the accounting for tangible fixed assets such as buildings, cars and computers. Tangible assets have physical form, so you can see what the company has paid for. Sometimes a company will pay money to acquire an intangible asset which has no physical form. A common example is goodwill, where a company will pay say, £100,000 to acquire a successful going-concern business which has tangible assets of only £80,000. The acquiring company is paying the extra £20,000 to recognise the fact that the acquired business will have trained employees in place and an existing good reputation amongst its customer base. In accounting terms, the acquiring company has purchased an intangible asset of £20,000 goodwill.

1.2 Definitions

Purchased goodwill is the difference between the cost of an acquired entity and the aggregate of the fair values of that entity's identifiable assets and liabilities.

Non-purchased goodwill is any other goodwill. At any time, the value of a business is likely to be different to the aggregate of the fair values of the net assets of the business. However the value of non-purchased (or inherent) goodwill is uncertain since no purchase transaction has taken place to confirm its value.

Intangible assets are non-financial fixed assets that do not have physical substance but are identifiable and are controlled by the entity through custody or legal rights.

1.3 Example

Goodwill can be either positive or negative. Consider the following examples:

(a) A plc pays £100,000 to acquire 80% of B plc, whose net assets have a fair value of £110,000 at the acquisition date. Calculate the purchased goodwill.

(b) C plc issues 100,000 £1 shares, each with a fair value of £1.20, to acquire 70% of D plc, whose net assets have a book value of £200,000 and a fair value of £250,000. Calculate the purchased goodwill.

(c) E plc has received an offer of £100,000 for all of its equity share capital, at a time when it believes its net assets have a fair value of £80,000. Estimate the inherent goodwill.

1.4 Solution

(a)	Positive purchased goodwill	= £100,000 – (80% × £110,000) = £12,000
(b)	Negative purchased goodwill	= £120,000 – (70% × £250,000) = £55,000
(c)	Inherent goodwill	= £100,000 – £80,000 = £20,000

1.5 Accounting for goodwill

(a) *Inherent goodwill*

Inherent goodwill should not be recognised in the balance sheet, due to the subjectivity required to value it. It should be ignored.

(b) *Positive purchased goodwill*

Positive purchased goodwill should be recognised as an intangible fixed asset and amortised through the profit and loss account over its useful economic life.

There is a rebuttable presumption that the useful life does not exceed 20 years from the date of acquisition. However it is possible for goodwill to have a life greater than 20 years, or even an indefinite life.

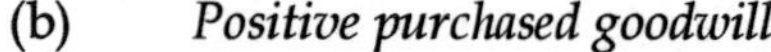

If a useful life of more than 20 years is used, annual impairment reviews must be carried out on the goodwill balance (in accordance with FRS 11 – see later) to demonstrate the durability of the acquired business.

No residual value may be placed on goodwill in calculating the annual amortisation charge. The straight line method of amortisation should normally be used.

(c) *Negative purchased goodwill*

If an acquisition appears to give rise to negative goodwill, first the fair values of the net assets acquired should be checked carefully to ensure that they have not been overstated. Negative goodwill remaining after this check should be recognised and separately disclosed on the face of the balance sheet, immediately below the goodwill heading. A subtotal should show the net total of positive and negative goodwill.

Negative goodwill should normally be recognised in the profit and loss account in the periods in which the assets acquired are consumed in the business.

1.6 Example

On 1 January 20X2 XY plc acquired 100% of the business of CD for £200,000, at which date CD owned net assets with a total fair value of £210,000. The assets acquired will be used up in the business evenly over a period of four years.

Calculate the credit to the profit and loss account of XY plc in respect of negative goodwill for the year ended 31 December 20X2.

1.7 Solution

Negative goodwill at 1 January 20X2 = £200,000 - £210,000 = £10,000.

This negative goodwill is to be released to the profit and loss account evenly over four years, so the credit to the 20X2 profit and loss account is $\frac{\text{£}10{,}000}{4}$ = £2,500.

Extracts from the financial statements at 31 December 20X2

	£
Balance sheet	
Fixed assets	
Intangible assets	
Negative goodwill	(7,500)
Profit and loss account	
Release of negative goodwill for the year	(2,500)

1.8 Accounting for other intangible assets

Examples of other intangible assets are patents, copyrights, licences, trademarks and similar rights. Development costs are not included within the scope of FRS 10. They are accounted for per SSAP 13 – see next section.

(a) *Internally generated intangible assets*

Internally developed intangible assets should be capitalised only where they have a readily ascertainable market value.

(b) *Purchased intangible assets*

An intangible asset purchased separately from a business should be capitalised at its cost.

An intangible asset acquired as part of the acquisition of a business should be capitalised separately from goodwill if its value can be measured reliably on initial recognition. Otherwise it should be subsumed into the amount of the purchase price paid for goodwill.

Once capitalised, the requirements for amortising intangible assets are the same as for goodwill: they should be amortised over their useful lives, which are assumed to be 20 years or less. If a longer, or even indefinite, life is used, then annual impairment reviews are required.

2 SSAP 13: Accounting for research and development

2.1 Introduction

FRS 10 applies to intangible assets in general (including patents, copyrights, brands, know-how, etc) but not to research and development costs, for which a specific accounting standard, SSAP 13, has been developed.

It has proved extremely difficult to standardise the accounting treatment of research and development (R and D) expenditure. This has been because this is an area where two fundamental accounting concepts, those of 'accruals' and of 'prudence' come into head-on conflict. From one point of view, R and D expenditure is incurred for the future development of business, with a view to decreasing future costs or increasing future revenue, so the 'accruals' concept would therefore have R and D expenditure which leads to reduced costs or increased sales carried forward and written off over all the accounting periods which benefit from that expenditure.

The contrary argument holds that it is effectively impossible to judge at any date which R and D expenditure will lead to future benefits, since such a large proportion of such expenditure proves totally abortive, or else turns out to have less than the anticipated future benefit. The 'prudence' concept is then invoked to justify the full write-off of all such expenditure in the year in which it is incurred. The accounting problem is then: which of the two concepts should have precedence?

SSAP 13 gives guidance regarding the appropriate accounting treatment for R and D expenditure, and sets out disclosure requirements.

2.2 Definitions

Research and development activity is distinguished from non-research based activity by the presence or absence of an appreciable element of innovation.

The SSAP classifies R and D expenditure in the following broad categories:

(a) *Pure (or basic) research*: original investigation undertaken in order to gain new scientific or technical knowledge and understanding. Basic research is not primarily directed towards any specific practical aim or application;

(b) *Applied research:* original investigation undertaken in order to gain new scientific or technical knowledge and directed towards a specific practical aim or objective;

(c) *Development:* use of scientific or technical knowledge in order to produce new or substantially improved materials, devices, products, processes, systems or services prior to the commencement of commercial production.

Research and development expenditure as defined by SSAP 13 does *not* include expenditure incurred in locating and exploiting oil, gas and mineral deposits in the extractive industries (but development of new surveying methods and techniques as an integral part of research on geological phenomena is classified as R and D).

2.3 Examples

SSAP 13 cites various examples of activities normally included and those normally excluded from R and D.

Normally included

(a) experimental, theoretical or other work aimed at the discovery of new knowledge, or the advancement of existing knowledge;

(b) searching for applications of that knowledge;

(c) formulation and design of possible applications for such work;

(d) testing in search for, or evaluation of, product, service or process alternatives;

(e) design, construction and testing of pre-production prototypes and models and development batches;

(f) design of products, services, processes or systems involving new technology or substantially improving those already produced or installed;

(g) construction and operation of pilot plants.

Normally excluded

(a) testing and analysis either of equipment or product for purposes of quality or quantity control;

(b) periodic alterations to existing products, services or processes even though these may represent some improvement;

(c) operational research not tied to a specific research and development activity;

(d) cost of corrective action in connection with break-downs during commercial production;

(e) legal and administrative work in connection with patent applications, records and litigation and the sale or licensing of patents;

(f) activity, including design and construction engineering, relating to the construction, relocation, rearrangement or start-up of facilities or equipment other than facilities or equipment whose sole use is for a particular research and development project;

(g) market research.

2.4 Accounting treatment of fixed assets used in R and D

The cost of fixed assets acquired or constructed in order to provide facilities for research and development activities over a number of accounting periods should be capitalised and written off over their useful life. Depreciation will be calculated in accordance with FRS 15 and such depreciation may itself form part of development expenditure covered below which can be carried forward to later periods.

2.5 Other R and D expenditure

Expenditure on pure and applied research (other than on fixed assets) should be written off through the profit and loss account in the year of expenditure. This is based on the premise that expenditure incurred on pure and applied research can be regarded as part of a continuing operation required to maintain a company's business and its competitive position. In general, one particular period rather than another will not be expected to benefit and therefore it is appropriate that these costs should be written off as they are incurred.

Regarding development expenditure, the Standard argues that the development of new and improved products is, however, distinguishable from pure and applied research. Expenditure on such development is normally undertaken with a reasonable expectation of specific commercial success and of future benefits arising from the work, either from increased revenue and related profits or from reduced costs. On these grounds it may be argued that such expenditure should be deferred to be matched against the future revenue.

In general, SSAP 13 requires that development expenditure should also be written off in the year of expenditure. However, it permits the deferral of such expenditure, to the extent that its recovery can reasonably be regarded as assured, if all the following circumstances apply:

(a) There is a clearly defined project.

(b) The related expenditure is separately identifiable.

(c) The outcome of such a project has been assessed with reasonable certainty as to:

   (i) its technical feasibility, and

   (ii) its ultimate commercial viability considered in the light of factors such as likely market conditions (including competing products), public opinion, consumer and environmental legislation.

(d) The aggregate of the deferred development costs, any further development costs, and related production, selling and administration costs is reasonably expected to be exceeded by related future sales or other revenues.

(e) Adequate resources exist, or are reasonably expected to be available, to enable the project to be completed and to provide any consequential increases in working capital.

2.6 Example

The Ansi Company is midway through development of a new sweet, the 'Tasstea'.

Cash expenditure on development so far has amounted to £164,000 and work has involved the use of a simulator machine for a period of 6 months. The machine cost £40,000 and has a three-year life, and a residual value of £4,000.

Although the project is both technically feasible and commercially viable, further work is required before production can commence. This work is estimated to involve cash expenditure of £27,000 and will require another three months' use of the simulator.

Once production of the new sweet starts, total variable production costs will be 6p per sweet plus 3p packaging plus annual fixed costs of £280,000 including provision for machinery costs. Sales are expected to be 2,000,000 units per month at 12p each, but in order to obtain this level, heavy television advertising of £750,000 is required in the first six months. Demand will remain at the 2 million level for two and a half years and production will then cease.

Adequate resources exist to enable completion of the programme outlined above. Advise whether the development costs to date can be capitalised under SSAP 13.

2.7 Solution

Calculation of future revenues and costs

Selling price per unit		12p
Production cost per unit	6p	
Packaging cost per unit	3p	
	—	
		9p
		—
Contribution per unit		3p

		£
Contribution per month 3p × 2m = £60,000		
Total contribution £60,000 × 30 months		1,800,000
Fixed costs £280,000 × 2½ yrs		700,000
Advertising		750,000
Future development costs	27,000	
Add: Depreciation on machine (3 months)	3,000	
		30,000
Total costs		1,480,000
Surplus of future revenues over future costs		£320,000

Development costs to date

	£
Cash expenditure	164,000
Add: Depreciation on machine	6,000
Total costs to date	170,000

As this figure of £170,000 is adequately covered by the £320,000 surplus of future revenues over future costs the £170,000 may be deferred until production commences, and then amortised over the two and a half year production period. If the total costs to date had exceeded the surplus of future revenues over future costs then that excess would be written off immediately as irrecoverable.

2.8 Amortisation

Amortisation of deferred development costs should commence with the commercial production of the product or process, and should be allocated on a systematic basis to each accounting period over which the product or process is expected to be sold or used.

Deferred development expenditure should be reviewed at the end of each accounting period and written off to the extent that it is deemed irrecoverable.

2.9 Example

In the above example, suppose that the production and sale of the Tasstea commenced in April 20X4.

2.10 Solution

The amortisation of the by then £200,000 development costs (£170,000 + £30,000) would thus begin in the accounts to 31 December 20X4. The notes to the balance sheet would show:

			£000	
		20X4	*20X5*	*20X6*
Intangible fixed assets				
Development costs				
Costs	- b/f	170	200	200
	- additions	30	-	-
	- c/f	200	200	200
Amortisation	- b/f	-	60	140
	- charge (W)	60	80	60
	- c/f	60	140	200
Net book value		140	60	-

WORKING

As sales are expected to arise evenly, amortisation will be pro-rata over 30 months, commencing in April 20X4:

20X4 charge	$= 9/30 \times$ £200,000	= £60,000
20X5 charge	$= 12/30 \times$ £200,000	= £80,000 etc

2.11 *Disclosure requirements of SSAP 13*

(a) The accounting policy on R and D expenditure should be stated and explained.

(b) The total amount of R and D expenditure charged in the profit and loss account should be disclosed, analysed between the current year's expenditure and amounts amortised from deferred expenditure (see below).

(c) Movements on deferred development expenditure and the amount carried forward at the beginning and end of the period should be disclosed.

(d) Deferred development expenditure should be disclosed under intangible fixed assets in the balance sheet.

Note

The disclosure requirement (b) outlined above applies only to companies that are:

(a) (i) public limited companies; or
(ii) special category companies (eg, banks or insurance companies); or
(iii) holding companies with a PLC or special category company as a subsidiary;

or

(b) exceed the criteria, multiplied by 10, for defining a medium-sized company (S248 CA 1985).

All the other requirements of SSAP 13 apply to all financial statements intended to give a true and fair view.

Activity 1 *(The answer is in the final chapter of this book)*

Plant

The following is an extract from the financial statements of Plant.

(1) Intangible fixed assets

	Goodwill	*Development expenditure*	*Software and brands*	*Total*
Cost	£000	£000	£000	£000
At 1 April 20X5	6,750	5,700	37,500	49,950
Amortisation				
At 1 April 20X5	(1,350)	-	(15,000)	(16,350)
Provision for year	(1,350)	(1,140)	(7,500)	(9,990)
At 31 March 20X6	(2,700)	(1,140)	(22,500)	(26,340)
Net book value				
At 1 April 20X5	5,400	5,700	22,500	33,600
At 31 March 20X6	4,050	4,560	15,000	23,610

Required

(a) Describe the difference between purchased and non-purchased goodwill, stating how each is created. **(4 marks)**

(b) How does FRS 10 require each type of goodwill to be accounted for? Suggest reasons for the different treatments. **(6 marks)**

(c) SSAP 13 *Accounting for research and development* defines certain categories of research and development expenditure. The standard also lays down rules which must be applied to the capitalisation of research and development expenditure.

(i) List and explain the categories of expenditure. **(4 marks)**

(ii) Explain the criteria applied to research and development expenditure according to SSAP 13 to determine whether the cost should be capitalised. **(6 marks)**

(Total : 20 marks)

3 FRS 11: Impairment of fixed assets and goodwill

3.1 Introduction

We have already met impairment in two places in this text:

(a) FRS 15 requires tangible fixed assets to be written down to their recoverable amount when it is known that the carrying amount exceeds the recoverable amount.

(b) FRS 10 requires annual impairment reviews to be carried out whenever a useful life of more than 20 years is selected for goodwill and intangible assets.

The purpose of FRS 11 is to standardise the accounting treatment of impairment, so that impairment losses are recognised on a consistent basis.

The syllabus requires that you need only understand the basic principles of FRS 11 for this Unit, so don't get bogged down in the intricacies of impairment calculations.

3.2 Definitions

Impairment is the reduction in the recoverable amount of a fixed asset or goodwill below its carrying amount.

Recoverable amount is the higher of net realisable value and value in use.

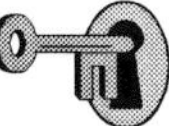

Net realisable value is the amount at which an asset could be disposed of, less any direct selling costs.

Value in use is the present value of the future cash flows arising from an asset's continued use, including those resulting from its ultimate disposal.

3.3 Example

A machine has a net book value of £5,000 in the draft balance sheet as at 31 December 20X3. It could be sold now for £4,000, or retained in the business where it is expected to earn cash inflows of £1,800 pa for each of the next three years after which it will expire worthless. Current interest rates are 10% pa.

Assess whether the machine is impaired at 31 December 20X3.

3.4 Solution

Current book value (= carrying amount) = £5,000

Compare this with the recoverable amount, ie the higher of NRV and value in use.

NRV = £4,000

$$\text{Value in use} = \frac{£1,800}{1.1} + \frac{£1,800}{(1.1)^2} + \frac{£1,800}{(1.1)^3} = £4,476$$

∴ Recoverable amount = £4,476

∴ the machine has a book value of £5,000 but a recoverable amount of only £4,476. It is impaired and should be written down to £4,476 in the balance sheet. An impairment loss of £5,000 - £4,476 = £524 must be recognised.

3.5 Accounting for impairment losses

Impairment losses must be recognised in the profit and loss account, unless they arise on a previously revalued fixed asset. Impairment losses on revalued fixed assets are recognised in the STRGL until the carrying amount of the asset falls below depreciated historical cost (unless the impairment is clearly caused by a consumption of economic benefits, in which case the loss is recognised in the profit and loss account).

Impairments below depreciated historical cost are recognised in the profit and loss account.

3.6 When an impairment review is required

It is not necessary to carry out a test for impairment of all fixed assets and goodwill every year; that would be unnecessarily expensive. Instead, FRS 11 requires that fixed assets and goodwill need only be reviewed for impairment if there is some indication that impairment has occurred.

FRS 15 and FRS 10 contain additional requirements:

- FRS 15 requires an annual impairment review whenever the useful life of a tangible fixed asset has been chosen as greater than 50 years.
- FRS 10 requires an annual impairment review whenever the useful life of goodwill or an intangible asset has been chosen as greater than 20 years.

3.7 Indicators of impairment

Examples of indications that an impairment may have occurred are as follows:

- a current period operating loss or net cash outflow from operating activities
- a significant decline in a fixed asset's market value during the period
- obsolescence or physical damage to a fixed asset
- a significant adverse change in the business or the market in which the fixed asset or goodwill is involved
- a management commitment to undertake a significant reorganisation
- a major loss of key employees, or
- a significant increase in market interest rates

3.8 Disclosure requirements

In the profit and loss account, impairment losses should be included within operating profit as part of the appropriate statutory headings.

In the notes to the balance sheet, the impairment loss should be included within accumulated historical cost depreciation; the cost of the asset should not be reduced. For revalued assets held at market value, the impairment loss should be included within the revalued carrying amount.

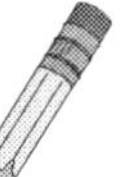

Activity 2 (The answer is in the final chapter of this book)

Newprods Ltd

During the course of a year, Newprods Ltd incurred expenditure on many research and development activities. Details of three of them are given below.

Project 3 To develop a new compound in view of the anticipated shortage of a raw material currently being used in one of the company's processes. Sufficient progress has been made to suggest that the new compound can be produced at a cost comparable to that of the existing raw material.

Project 4 To improve the yield of an important manufacturing operation of the company. At present, material input with a cost of £100,000 pa becomes contaminated in the operation and half is wasted. Sufficient progress has been made for the scientists to predict an improvement so that only 20% will be wasted.

Project 5 To carry out work, as specified by a creditworthy client, to attempt to bring a proposed aerospace product of that client into line with safety regulations.

Costs during the year

		Project	
	3	4	5
	£	£	£
Staff salaries	5,000	10,000	20,000
Overheads	6,000	12,000	24,000
Plant at cost (life of ten years)	10,000	20,000	5,000

Required

(a) State the circumstances in which it may be appropriate to carry forward research and development expenditure to future periods.

(b) Show how the expenditure on projects 3, 4 and 5 would be dealt with in the balance sheet and profit and loss account in accordance with SSAP 13.

4 Quick quiz (The answers are in the final chapter of this book)

1 What is negative goodwill?

2 What is the required accounting treatment for research costs?

3 What is the requirement if a 30 year life is used for goodwill?

4 Explain how the recoverable amount of an asset is estimated.

5 Summary

This chapter has covered three important accounting standards:

- **FRS 10: Goodwill and intangible assets**

  FRS 10 requires positive purchased goodwill to be capitalised as an intangible fixed asset, and amortised over its useful life. Typically the life of goodwill used in practice is around five years. There is a presumption in FRS 10 that the life is 20 years or less, but a longer life can be used if justified in the circumstances.

- **SSAP 13: Accounting for research and development**

  SSAP 13 requires all pure and applied research costs to be written off as incurred. If specific conditions apply, development costs may be carried forward as an intangible fixed asset.

- **FRS 11: Impairment of fixed assets and goodwill**

  FRS 11 requires impaired assets (those for which the carrying value exceeds the recoverable amount) to be written down to their recoverable amount. The impairment loss is normally recognised in the profit and loss account.

CHAPTER 13

Stocks

ASSESSMENT FOCUS

In order to prepare a set of limited company accounts you need to know how to deal with the valuation of the closing stock of a business. This is covered by SSAP 9: Stocks and long-term contracts. Although you need to have knowledge of all aspects of the SSAP that deal with stock you do not need any knowledge of the accounting for long-term contracts.

This chapter covers the following Knowledge and Understanding of the AAT Syllabus:

> The UK regulatory framework for financial reporting and the main requirements of relevant Financial Reporting Standards *(Element 11.1)*
>
> Preparing financial statements in proper form *(Element 11.1)*

In order to cover these the following topics are included:

> Valuation of stock
> Methods of costing stock
> Disclosure requirements

Key definitions

Cost of stock	That expenditure which has been incurred in the normal course of business in bringing the product or service to its present location and condition.
Net realisable value	Estimated selling price less all costs to completion and all selling costs.
First in, first out	FIFO assumes that the stocks in hand represent the latest purchases or production.
Last in, first out	LIFO assumes that the stocks in hand represent the earliest purchases or production.

1 Valuation of stock

1.1 The basic rule

Stocks should be stated at the **lower of cost and net realisable value.**

1.2 Cost

SSAP 9 defines **cost** as: 'that expenditure which has been incurred in the *normal course of business* in bringing the product or service to its *present location and condition*'.

This means that two identical items may have different costs if they are in different locations. For example, the cost of an item which has been shipped to a distribution centre in France will include the normal transport costs to France and hence will have a higher cost than a similar item held in the factory in England.

Note that only costs incurred in the *normal* course of business should be included. If the lorry taking items to France broke down, the costs of the breakdown would not be included as part of the transport costs since they are considered abnormal.

1.3 Elements of cost

Cost includes the following.

- *Cost of purchase* which comprises:
  - purchase price – including import duties, transport, handling costs and any other directly attributable costs; less
  - trade discounts, rebates and subsidies.
- *Cost of conversion* which comprises:
  - costs which are specifically attributable to units of production – direct labour, direct expenses and subcontracted work;
  - production overheads;
  - other overheads, if any, attributable in the particular circumstances of the business to bringing the product or service to its present location and condition.

1.4 Example

The Standard Company plc has stock at 31 December 20X7 and has gathered the following information together in order to determine its cost.

	£
Cost of original materials	16,000
Cost of work on material	
Labour 1,000 hours @ £2.50	2,500
Variable overhead	700
Fixed production overhead during the period 1 October to 31 December 20X7	40,000
Number of hours worked in the period 1 October to 31 December 20X7	18,000 hours

You also discovered that 2,000 hours of work were lost during December due to an industrial dispute over the holiday work programme.

Selling and distribution costs during the quarter were £10,000.

What is the value of the stock held at 31 December 20X7?

1.5 Solution

	£
Material cost	16,000
Labour cost	2,500
Variable overhead	700
Fixed overhead $\frac{£40{,}000}{20{,}000 \text{ hrs}} \times 1{,}000 \text{ hrs}$	2,000
	21,200

Fixed overheads are absorbed on the basis of the labour hours worked, 1,000 hours, as a proportion of normal working hours for the period, 20,000 hours.

The industrial dispute will not increase the value of the stock even though it reduced the number of hours actually worked in the quarter.

Selling and distribution overheads have been ignored as the goods in stock have not been sold or distributed.

1.6 Net realisable value

Net realisable value is defined as the actual or estimated selling price (net of trade but before settlement discounts) less: (Cash discount)

- all further costs to completion;
- all costs to be incurred in marketing, selling and distributing the product

Settlement discounts are those discounts which are offered as an inducement for early payment of an invoice; as such, they are more akin to an interest or finance expense than to a true discount and hence are not deducted in determining net realisable value.

1.7 Example

The Standard Mix Company plc has the following items in stock at its year-end:

	Cost	*Normal selling price*
	£	£
Item A	7,000	10,000
Item B	8,400	10,200
Item C	9,200	10,400

Item A is ready for immediate sale.

Item B is also ready for sale but, due to falling demand, a 25% special discount will be needed to encourage a buyer to come forward.

Item C requires packaging before it can be sold and this cost is estimated at £1,800.

What are the net realisable values of these items?

1.8 Solution

		£	£
Item A	NRV		10,000
Item B	Selling price	10,200	
	Discount 25%	(2,550)	
	NRV		7,650
Item C	Selling price	10,400	
	Packaging	(1,800)	
	NRV		8,600

For stock purposes, these items will be valued as follows:

Item	*Cost*	*NRV*	*Stock value*
	£	£	£
A	7,000	10,000	7,000
B	8,400	7,650	7,650
C	9,200	8,600	8,600
Stock at lower of cost and net realisable value			23,250

1.9 Separate valuation principle

The comparison of cost and net realisable value needs to be made in respect of each item of stock *separately*. If this is difficult in practice, similar groups or categories of stock should be taken together.

By comparing the total realisable value of stocks with the total cost, you could net off foreseeable losses against unrealised profits. This is not acceptable under SSAP 9 and the Companies Act.

1.10 NRV lower than cost

SSAP 9 gives a useful list of the principal situations in which net realisable value is likely to be less than cost. These instances are useful material for a written task so let us consider each in turn.

(a) *Increase in cost or fall in selling price.* These are obvious but examples can still be given. An increase in costs is very pertinent in inflationary times and price controls may make it impossible to recover the increased cost by raising selling prices. Examples of a fall in selling price in recent years would be home computers or DVD players. Any manufacturer with slow turnover of stocks may find that net realisable value is now below the historic cost of manufacture.

(b) *Physical deterioration of stocks.* Especially relevant in the food industry and in other perishable goods sectors.

(c) *Obsolescence of products.* The microprocessor/computer industry provides a good example because of the pace of technological progress.

(d) Decision as part of a company's marketing strategy to *manufacture and sell products at a loss.* This is a situation of marketing a 'loss leader'. Many car manufacturers sell their mini cars at a loss in the hope that satisfied buyers will eventually trade up to larger and more profitable models.

(e) *Errors in production or purchasing.* The production of faulty products is self-explanatory. Errors in purchasing often occur in the fashion industry where much depends on the whims of customers.

2 Methods of costing

2.1 Acceptable inventory accounting methods

When a number of identical items of stock have been purchased or made at different times, the **actual** cost of the items in stock at the year-end may not be known, so assumptions have to be made of the way in which the stock items flowed through the business. Only methods that give the fairest practicable approximation to *actual cost* are acceptable.

2.2 Acceptable methods

SSAP 9 accepts the use of any one of the following methods, consistently applied:

(i) *Unit cost* – The actual cost of purchasing or manufacturing identifiable units of stock.

(ii) *Weighted average cost* – The calculation of the cost of stocks and work in progress on the basis of the application to the units of stocks on hand of an average price computed by dividing the total cost of units by the total number of such units (this average price may be arrived at by means of a continuous calculation, a periodic calculation or a moving periodic calculation).

(iii) *FIFO (first in, first out)* – The calculation of the cost of stocks and work in progress on the basis that the quantities in hand represent the latest purchases or production.

(iv) *Standard cost* – The calculation of the cost of stocks and work in progress on the basis of periodically predetermined costs calculated from management's estimates of expected levels of costs, operations, operational efficiency, and the related expenditure.

There is a proviso. Standards must be reviewed frequently to ensure that they bear a reasonable relationship to the actual costs of the period.

(v) *Selling price less an estimated profit margin* – This is acceptable only if it can be clearly shown that it gives a reasonable approximation of the actual cost.

The Companies Act 1985 states that the following methods are acceptable:

(i) first in, first out (FIFO);
(ii) last in, first out (LIFO);
(iii) a weighted average price;
(iv) any other method similar to the methods mentioned above.

2.3 LIFO and base stock methods

The following methods are normally not acceptable according to SSAP 9:

(a) *LIFO (last in, first out)* – The calculation of the cost of stocks and work in progress on the basis that the quantities in hand represent the earliest purchases or production.

(b) *Base stock*– The calculation of the cost of stocks and work in progress on the basis that a fixed unit value is ascribed to a predetermined number of units of stock, any excess over this number being valued on the basis of some other method. If the number of units in stock is less than the predetermined minimum, the fixed unit value is applied to the number in stock.

The *base stock method* is often applied to stocks of raw materials in industry where the raw material price is extremely volatile. Its purpose is to prevent violent swings in profitability from one year to the next solely attributable to stock profits or losses as the case may be.

The principle behind the method is that a business requires a certain minimum level of stocks in order to operate. This minimum level would be required in order to avoid stock-outs and would also cover materials in the manufacturing pipeline. The view is that this minimum physical stock level or 'base stock' is more in the nature of a fixed asset than a trading asset (without it the business would cease to operate) and as such this base stock should be valued at a fixed or historic cost. Any stocks held in excess of the base stock are considered to be true trading stocks and, among other reasons, may be held for speculative purposes (ie. actually trading to make stock profits by buying raw materials in excess of immediate requirements). These excess stocks would be valued on a more normal basis such as FIFO.

The base stock method has a convincing theoretical appeal, especially in times of inflation and could be applied to any business. However, the practical application is very subjective in terms of determining base stock levels which may need continuous revision as the business expands. In addition, although it may produce a more meaningful profit figure in times of inflation, it is likely to produce a misleading balance sheet figure for stock which in the main would be stated in terms of out of date costs. The same criticism is, of course, levelled at the LIFO method.

Principally because of these reservations, SSAP 9 states that the base stock and LIFO methods are not usually acceptable bases of stock valuation since they do not normally bear a sufficiently close relationship to 'actual costs pertaining during the period'. Nevertheless, the base stock method is still used by a few companies in practice and whilst mention of the fact is usually made in the auditors' report, the auditors concurred in all cases.

2.4 Replacement cost method

Replacement cost is the cost at which an identical asset could be purchased or manufactured at the balance sheet date. SSAP 9 states that replacement cost is 'unacceptable in principle because it is not necessarily the same as actual cost, and, in times of rising prices, will result in the taking of a profit which has not been realised'.

However, the explanatory note introducing the Standard states: 'In some circumstances (eg, in the case of materials whose price has fluctuated considerably and which have not become the subject of firm sales contracts by the time the accounts are prepared) replacement cost may be the best measure of *net realisable value*'.

2.5 Example

RJ plc made the following purchases and sales of grommets in May 20X1:

1 May	Opening stock	Nil
8 May	Bought 200 units	@ £5 each
13 May	Bought 400 units	@ £5.60 each
20 May	Sold 300 units	@ £8 each

Determine the closing stock valuation at 31 May and the gross profit for the month using:

(a) FIFO
(b) LIFO
(c) Weighted average cost

2.6 Solution

(a) Closing stock = 300 units @ £5.60 = £1,680
Gross profit = £2,400 – (200 × £5 + 100 × £5.60) = £840

(b) Closing stock = (200 × £5 + 100 × £5.60) = £1,560
Gross profit = £2,400 – (300 × £5.60) = £720

(c) Average price = $\frac{200 \times £5 + 400 \times £5.60}{600\text{ units}} = £5.40$

∴ Closing stock = 300 × £5.40 = £1,620

Gross profit = £2,400 – (300 × £5.40) = £780

3 Disclosure requirements

3.1 Accounting policies

Accounting policies adopted for stocks in calculating the following must be disclosed:

- Cost
- Net realisable value

3.2 Stocks and work in progress

Total stocks and work in progress should be sub-classified in a manner appropriate to the business so as to indicate the amount held in each of the main categories. This is usually achieved by giving the analysis required in the balance sheet formats by CA 1985.

	£
Raw materials and consumables	X
Work in progress	X
Finished goods and goods for resale	X
	X

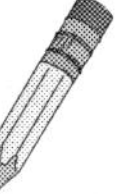

Activity 1 *(The answer is in the final chapter of this book)*

S Ltd

S Ltd is a manufacturing company. It held its annual stock count on 31 March 20X2, the company's year-end. The accounts department is currently working its way through the stock sheets placing a value on the physical stocks. The company has had a difficult year and profits are likely to be lower than in the previous year.

Raw materials

Stocks of raw materials are valued at cost. The finance director has suggested that the cost has been understated in previous years because the company has not taken the costs of delivery or insurance into account. These can be substantial in the case of imported goods. It has been proposed that these costs be taken into account in the valuation of closing stocks of raw materials.

Work in progress

The cost of work in progress includes an element of overheads. The following table of figures has been prepared in order to assist in the calculation of the overhead absorption.

	£
Fixed costs	
Factory rent, rates and insurance	150,000
Administration expenses	240,000
Factory security	110,000
Variable costs	
Factory heat, light and power	300,000
Sales commissions and selling costs	120,000
Depreciation of machinery	200,000
Depreciation of delivery vehicles	70,000

Overheads are usually absorbed on the basis of labour hours. The stock sheets suggest that 500 labour hours have been included in work in progress. A total of 70,000 hours have been worked by production staff during the year. The figure is, however, much lower than the normal figure of 95,000 hours.

Finished goods

Finished goods have already been valued at £400,000. This figure includes some obsolete stocks which cost £70,000 to produce, but which are likely to be sold at a scrap value of £500. There are also several batches of a new product which will be launched early in the new financial year. These cost £90,000 to manufacture. Independent market research suggests that it is very likely that the new product will be sold for considerably more than this. If, however, the launch is unsuccessful, the new product will have to be sold as scrap for £1,000. The finance director has said that the aggregate net realisable value of all closing stocks of finished goods is at least £500,000 and so there is no need to worry about the obsolete and new stock products.

Required

(a) Explain whether the costs of delivery and insurance should be included in the valuation of raw materials.

(b) (i) Explain how SSAP 9 requires overheads to be treated in the valuation of closing stocks.

(ii) Calculate the value of overheads to be absorbed into S Ltd's closing stock of work in progress.

(c) (i) Explain whether the valuation of closing stocks at the lower of cost and net realisable value should be done on an item-by-item basis or on the basis of the aggregate cost of all items as compared with their aggregate net realisable value.

(ii) State how you would value the obsolete items and the new product line, giving reasons for your valuation in each case.

---

4 Quick quiz *(The answers are in the final chapter of this book)*

1 A company has closing stocks of 100 items of Unit X. Each unit cost £4 but can only be sold for £3.50. What is the total closing stock valuation?

2 State two circumstances when NRV is likely to be lower than cost.

3 Does SSAP 9 favour the LIFO method?

4 What categories of stocks would typically be shown on the face of the balance sheet or in the notes?

5 Summary

SSAP 9 requires that stocks should be stated in the balance sheet at the lower of cost and net realisable value.

Cost comprises all expenditure which has been incurred in the normal course of business in bringing the product or service to its present location and condition.

NRV is the expected selling price less further costs to completion and costs to be incurred in selling the item.

If the actual costs of the items in closing stock are not known (since the items are interchangeable), an assumption has to be made of how the items physically flow through the business. The usual assumption is FIFO.

CHAPTER 14

Tax in company accounts

ASSESSMENT FOCUS

In order to prepare a set of limited company accounts you need to know how to deal with Corporation Tax in the profit and loss account and the balance sheet. This is covered by FRS 16: Current tax. You also need to know the definition of deferred tax from FRS 19: Deferred tax, and the circumstances in which it should be accounted for and where disclosed. No computations for deferred tax or detailed accounting treatment will be assessed. We will also cover the accounting treatment of VAT from SSAP 5: Accounting for value added tax.

This chapter covers the following Knowledge and Understanding of the AAT Syllabus:

The presentation of Corporation Tax in financial statements *(Element 11.1)*

The UK regulatory framework for financial reporting and the main requirements of relevant Financial Reporting Standards *(Element 11.1)*

Preparing financial statements in proper form *(Element 11.1)*

In order to cover these the following topics are included:

FRS 16: Current tax
Deferred tax
Bases for providing for deferred tax
FRS 19: Deferred tax
SSAP 5: Accounting for value added tax

Key definitions

Current tax	The corporation tax payable on a company's profits for the year, along with any adjustments made in respect of previous periods.
Deferred tax	The tax attributable to timing differences.
Full provision basis	The basis of providing for deferred tax on all timing differences, required by FRS 19.

1 FRS 16: Current tax

1.1 Introduction

The current tax for a company is the amount of corporation tax estimated to be payable in respect of the taxable profit for the year, along with adjustments to estimates in respect of previous periods.

1.2 Corporation tax

Companies pay corporation tax on their profits. The current rate of corporation tax is 30% normally but companies with 'small' profits pay corporation tax at 19% only. In principle, the amount of current corporation tax should be calculated using the tax rates that the legislation has laid down for the company's financial year. In assessment tasks you will normally be told the rate, and often the amount, of corporation tax.

It is obvious that corporation tax cannot be calculated until after the profit figure has been found. When preparing a profit and loss account, provision must be made for the corporation tax payable on those profits.

1.3 Example

A company makes an operating profit before taxation of £300,000. Corporation tax is estimated at £105,000. (The corporation tax charge is not 30% of the accounting profit before tax, since accounting profits are adjusted to calculate the taxable profit before tax.)

1.4 Solution

Profit and loss account (extract) for the year

	£
Profit on ordinary activities before taxation	300,000
Tax on profit on ordinary activities	
Corporation tax based on the profit of the year @ 30%	105,000
Profit on ordinary activities after taxation	195,000

Corporation tax account

	£		£
Balance c/f	105,000	Profit and loss	105,000
	105,000		105,000
		Balance b/f	105,000

The balance on the corporation tax account is carried forward and will appear on the balance sheet under the 'creditors within one year' heading. The full description given in the profit and loss account above is required either on the face of the profit and loss account as shown, or in the notes to the accounts.

1.5 Due dates for payment

Companies with large profits are required to pay their corporation tax due by quarterly equal instalments. For other companies, corporation tax is payable nine months after the end of the company's accounting period. In the profit and loss account above, being (say) to 31 December 20X1, the corporation tax we have identified will be payable on 1 October 20X2. In the statutory accounts the amount of £105,000 will be included in:

> 'Creditors: amounts falling due within one year'

and within that heading it will be included under the description:

> 'Other creditors, including taxation and social security'.

1.6 Adjustments relating to prior years

When the provision for corporation tax is made in the accounts, it is only an estimate of the actual liability which will eventually be agreed with HM Inspectors of Taxes. Any difference between the original estimate and the actual figure will be adjusted in the next year's provision. If material this figure will be shown separately.

1.7 Example

Continuing with the previous example, suppose that in 20X2 the company pays £99,000 corporation tax on the 20X1 profit on 1 October (not the £105,000 as estimated). The profit for the year 20X2 is £400,000 and corporation tax is estimated at £132,000.

Profit and loss account (extract) 20X2

	£	£
Profit on ordinary activities before taxation		400,000
Tax on profit on ordinary activities		
Corporation tax based on the profit of the year @ 30%	132,000	
Adjustment for overprovision in previous year	(6,000)	
		(126,000)
Profit on ordinary activities after taxation		274,000

Corporation tax account

		£			£
01.10.X2	Bank	99,000	01.01.X2	Balance b/f	105,000
31.12.X2	Profit and loss overprovision	6,000	31.12.X2	Profit and loss	132,000
31.12.X2	Balance c/f	132,000			
		237,000			237,000
			01.01.X3	Balance b/f	132,000

Activity 1 *(The answer is in the final chapter of this book)*

Rubislaw plc

Rubislaw plc was formed in 20X0. During the year to 31 December 20X3 the following payments of tax were made:

	£
Corporation tax - accounting period ended 31.12.X2	69,000

At 1.1.X3 the balance on the taxation account was £74,000.

The profit for tax purposes was estimated at £150,000.

The corporation tax rate is 30%.

Required

Disclose how the above should be presented in the profit and loss account for the year ended 31 December 20X3 and in the balance sheet as at that date, in a form suitable for presentation to the members of Rubislaw plc.

2 Deferred tax

2.1 Accounting profits and taxable profits

The amount of current taxation payable on the profits of a particular period may bear little relationship to the reported profit before tax appearing in the published accounts. The difference comes from two sources: permanent differences and timing differences.

Permanent differences arise where items taken into account for the purpose of the financial accounts are disallowable or non-taxable for tax purposes. An example might be disallowable entertaining expenses. This is a permanent difference because no tax relief will ever be received for such expenditure, even though it is quite properly deducted as an expense when computing accounting profits.

Timing differences arise when certain types of income and expenditure are recognised in different periods for the purpose of financial accounts on the one hand and taxation on the other.

2.2 An example of timing differences

An example of a timing difference is that depreciation charges appear in the financial accounts, but are not allowed as an expense for tax purposes. Instead, *capital allowances* reduce taxable profits. Over the lifetime of a fixed asset total depreciation charges will equal (roughly) total capital allowances. However, in any particular accounting period the two amounts will differ - a timing difference.

The common feature of timing differences, which distinguishes them from permanent differences, is simply this: timing differences *originate* in one period and are capable of *reversal* in later periods.

Deferred taxation is a system of dealing with the distortions caused by timing differences. It is not concerned at all with permanent differences. The objective of deferred taxation is to ensure that the tax charge shown in the profit and loss account is not out of line with the amount of profit earned.

Without deferred taxation, the tax charge in the profit and loss account would be based on the actual current liability payable to the Inland Revenue. This would have the following effects.

- In a year when tax allowances (eg capital allowances) are high compared to the expenditure shown in the accounts (eg depreciation) our tax liability will be *lower* than our reported profits would suggest.
- In a year when capital allowances fall short of depreciation charges our tax liability will be *higher* than our reported profits would suggest.

To overcome this problem, the tax charge shown in the profit and loss account is not simply the tax liability agreed with the Inland Revenue. Instead, it is this liability adjusted — up or down — by an amount reflecting the value of timing differences.

2.3 Example

A company makes a profit of £100,000 (after depreciation but before taxation) each year. The company buys an asset in Year 1 costing £40,000 and claims a 25% writing down allowance on the reducing balance basis each year.

Depreciation policy is to write off the cost of the asset over five years on a straight line basis. The rate of corporation tax is 30%.

Show the company's tax liability for each of the years from Year 1 to Year 6.

2.4 Solution

A tabular layout is needed.

	Year 1	Year 2	Year 3	Year 4	Year 5	Year 6
	£	£	£	£	£	£
Profit before tax	100,000	100,000	100,000	100,000	100,000	100,000
Add back depreciation	8,000	8,000	8,000	8,000	8,000	
	108,000	108,000	108,000	108,000	108,000	100,000
Less capital allowances	(10,000)	(7,500)	(5,625)	(4,218)	(3,164)	(2,373)
Taxable profit	98,000	100,500	102,375	103,782	104,836	97,627
Tax at 30%	29,400	30,150	30,712	31,135	31,451	29,288

We can see from this that the tax liability is not the same as 'profit before tax × corporation tax rate' (£100,000 × 30% = £30,000).

- In Year 1 the liability is less than this: we have deferred some tax by virtue of generous capital allowances exceeding the depreciation charge.
- In Years 2 to 5 the liability is greater than £30,000: the originating timing difference reverses.

This example shows the accounting problem very clearly. The company's operating performance is identical in each of the six years, and yet its tax liability differs from one year to the next. Deferred tax is designed to remove this kind of distortion.

3 Bases for providing for deferred tax

3.1 Possible approaches

Three possible approaches have been suggested to deal with the problem of timing differences: nil provision, full provision and partial provision.

Nil provision, as the name suggests, means that we simply ignore the problem. In the example above, the tax charge shown in our profit and loss account each year would simply be the liability payable to the Inland Revenue. We would resign ourselves to the distortions caused by timing differences.

Full provision means that we adjust our tax liability in respect of every timing difference we can identify. The tax charge reported in the profit and loss account is this adjusted liability.

Partial provision is the middle course. We provide for deferred tax on timing differences *only if their reversal in later years is probable*. Where a timing difference is likely to persist for some time into the future we ignore it.

Figure 1. Alternative approaches to timing differences

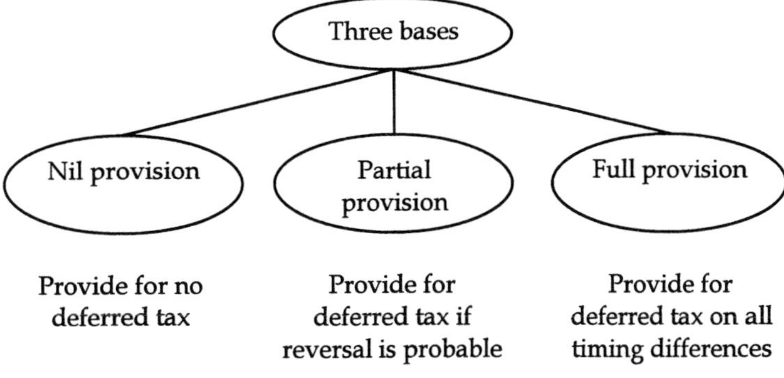

3.2 Example

Peter Ltd was incorporated on 1 April 20X1. In the year ended 31 March 20X2 the company made a profit before tax of £100,000 (after charging depreciation of £10,000) and made the following capital additions.

Plant	£48,000
Motor vehicles	£12,000

Corporation tax is chargeable at the rate of 30%, and writing down allowances are available at 25%.

Required

Compute the following

(a) The corporation tax payable for the year ended 31 March 20X2.

(b) The deferred tax charge for the year on the basis that full provision is made for all originating timing differences, showing also the relevant extracts from the financial statements.

3.3 Solution

Start with the accounting profit, then add back the depreciation and deduct the capital allowance to find the taxable profit.

	£
Reported profit	100,000
Add back depreciation	10,000
	110,000
Less capital allowance (48,000 + 12,000) × 25%	(15,000)
Taxable profit	95,000

Remember that tax payable is calculated on taxable profit not accounting profit. Tax payable is therefore £95,000 × 30% = £28,500.

To calculate the amount of tax deferred, you need first of all to identify the timing difference by comparing accumulated depreciation to cumulative capital allowances.

	£
Depreciation	10,000
Capital allowance	(15,000)
Originating timing difference	(5,000)

To calculate the amount of tax deferred simply apply the current tax rate to the timing difference. Tax deferred is therefore £5,000 × 30% = £1,500.

You will then need to make a provision for deferred tax. The double entry is as follows.

Debit Taxation charge (profit and loss)

Credit Provision for deferred tax (shown in the balance sheet under 'Provisions for liabilities and charges')

This leads to the following extracts from the accounts.

EXTRACT FROM BALANCE SHEET		£
Provisions for liabilities and charges		
Deferred tax		1,500
EXTRACT FROM PROFIT AND LOSS ACCOUNT	£	£
Profit before tax		100,000
Taxation		
UK corporation tax at 30%	28,500	
Deferred tax	1,500	
		30,000
Profit after tax		70,000

You will not be assessed on deferred tax calculations but this example illustrates how deferred tax works.

4 FRS 19: Deferred tax

4.1 Introduction

The previous accounting standard, SSAP 15, required the partial provision basis for calculating deferred tax. However this had two main disadvantages:

(a) it relies on forecasts of the future to determine which timing differences will reverse, so is subjective

(b) it is contrary to the International Accounting Standard on deferred tax which requires full provision.

In December 2000 the ASB therefore brought the UK into line with international practice by issuing FRS 19 which requires the full provision basis for calculating deferred tax.

4.2 The requirements of FRS 19

Deferred tax must be recognised in full on timing differences such as:

- accelerated capital allowances (as seen earlier, where the capital allowances granted against taxable profits exceed the depreciation charge made against accounting profits)
- accruals for pension costs that will be deductible for tax purposes only when paid
- other short-term timing differences (those that originate in one period and are expected to reverse in the following period).

4.3 Tax rate to be used

Deferred tax should be calculated using the average tax rates that are expected to apply in the periods in which the timing differences are expected to reverse, based on tax rates that have been enacted by the balance sheet date.

Usually, future tax rates will not be known, so the current rate of tax is used as the best estimate of the future rate in force when the reversal occurs.

5 Accounting for value added tax

5.1 Introduction

The accounting requirements of SSAP 5: Accounting for value added tax are very straight forward and reflect the accounting treatment of VAT that you have come across in your earlier studies.

5.2 VAT and sales

SSAP 5 requires that VAT should be excluded from sales. Therefore when a sale is made the double entry is:

Debit	Debtors control	-	including VAT
Credit	Sales	-	excluding VAT
Credit	VAT control	-	VAT

5.3 VAT and purchases

In just the same way, any purchases or expenses should also be included in the profit and loss account at their VAT exclusive amount. The double entry is:

Debit	Purchases/expenses	-	excluding VAT
Debit	VAT control	-	VAT
Credit	Creditors control	-	including VAT

5.4 VAT control account

The balance on the VAT control account (normally a credit balance) appears in the balance sheet as part of creditors: amounts falling due within one year.

6 Quick quiz *(The answers are in the final chapter of this book)*

1 On what date is a small company's corporation tax liability due to be paid?

2 Are capital allowances an example of a permanent difference or a timing difference?

3 Which basis for providing for deferred tax does FRS 19 require: nil provision, partial provision or full provision?

4 Is turnover shown in the profit and loss account inclusive or exclusive of VAT?

7 Summary

This chapter has summarised all the information regarding tax that you need for the preparation of a set of limited company financial statements. According to FRS 16 the current corporation tax provision appears as an expense in the profit and loss account and as a creditor in the balance sheet. If there is a balance on the corporation tax account already this will represent an under or over provision from the previous year. This is also included as part of the current year tax charge.

FRS 19 deals with deferred tax, which is a tax adjustment to reflect timing differences. FRS 19 requires that deferred tax is calculated using full provision on all timing differences at the balance sheet date.

SSAP 5 requires that VAT should be excluded from sales, purchases and expenses in the profit and loss account.

CHAPTER 15

Leases

ASSESSMENT FOCUS

Leases are covered by SSAP 21: Accounting for leases and hire purchase contracts. For Unit 11 you need an appreciation of the difference between finance and operating leases and an overview of the differences in accounting treatment but no detailed computations will be assessed.

This chapter covers the following Knowledge and Understanding of the AAT Syllabus:

> The UK regulatory framework for financial reporting and the main requirements of relevant Financial Reporting Standards *(Element 11.1)*
>
> Preparing financial statements in proper form *(Element 11.1)*

In order to cover these the following topics are included:

> Types of extended credit agreement
> Accounting for finance leases
> Operating leases
> Disclosure requirements of SSAP 21

Key definitions

Lease	A contract to hire an asset between the lessor (who owns the asset) and the lessee (who gains use of the asset during the period of the lease).
Finance lease	A long-term lease.
Operating lease	A short-term lease.

1 Types of extended credit agreement

1.1 Introduction

A business may acquire the use of a fixed asset by outright purchase (cash or credit) or by some form of 'extended credit' agreement – credit sale, hire purchase, a finance lease or operating lease.

If these transactions were to be recorded according to their strict legal form, the picture presented by the balance sheet and profit and loss account of the business using the asset could be quite misleading.

The purpose of SSAP 21 is to ensure that transactions that are *in substance* the same, even if not *in legal form,* are treated in the same way in the financial accounts of a business.

1.2 Types of extended credit

Credit sale – involves a contract of sale with payment by instalments. Ownership of the goods passes on delivery by the supplier, and a binding debt is created which cannot be avoided by returning the goods.

Hire purchase – goods are supplied on hire to customers until, on fulfilment of certain conditions (usually the payment of an agreed number of instalments), the customer becomes entitled to purchase the asset (usually for a nominal amount). Legal title passes to the customer at this point.

Lease – involves a contract to hire out an asset between the lessor (who owns the asset and will continue to own the asset) and the lessee (who gains the right to use the asset for an agreed period of time).

SSAP 21 distinguishes between two types of lease, finance and operating:

A *finance lease* is a lease that transfers substantially all the risks and rewards of ownership of an asset to the lessee. It should be presumed that such a transfer of risks and rewards occurs if at the inception of a lease the present value of the minimum lease payments, including any initial payment, amounts to substantially all (normally 90% or more) of the fair value of the leased asset. The present value should be calculated by using the interest rate implicit in the lease. If the fair value of the asset is not determinable, an estimate thereof should be used.

An *operating lease* is a lease other than a finance lease.

1.3 Substance over form

Although each of the above types of agreement is different in its legal form, SSAP 21 recognises that they could be very similar in substance.

1.4 Credit sale/finance leases

It can be seen that a finance lease (being for a period of time close to the life of the asset) is similar in substance to the ownership of an asset, financed by a loan repayable by instalments over the period of the lease. The lessee would normally have sole use of the asset and would be responsible for its maintenance, repair and insurance even though legal title to the asset remains with the lessor.

Thus SSAP 21 requires that finance leases (or equivalent agreements) are capitalised in the lessee's balance sheet by including both the

- value of the asset in fixed assets; and
- the outstanding lease commitment in creditors.

The profit and loss account is charged with depreciation on the asset and an appropriate share of the finance charge each year.

The lessor will account for future amounts receivable under finance leases as a debtor, which are then allocated to the profit and loss account over the term of the lease.

1.5 Operating lease

An operating lease is effectively a short-term rental agreement, with no option to purchase the goods. The supplier retains title throughout, and usually undertakes to keep them in good working order. The domestic rental of a television or video recorder would generally constitute such an agreement.

In this case, it is the lessor that records the asset as a fixed asset and depreciates it. Rental is recognised on a straight-line basis in both the lessee's and the lessor's books over the lease term.

1.6 Hire purchase

Hire purchase agreements could fall into either of these categories, depending upon the terms of the agreement, and SSAP 21 requires that they are accounted for accordingly. It is more common that they are treated as a finance lease. A difference may be that the hire purchase seller takes credit not only for finance income, but also for gross profit on the actual sale of the asset.

2 Accounting for finance leases

2.1 Capitalisation of finance leases and off balance sheet gearing

Where finance leases are not reflected in the lessee's balance sheet as described above, the economic resources and the level of future obligations of the business are understated. In this situation, the leasing of assets under finance leases becomes a form of 'off balance sheet gearing' and a good example of the dangers of this is Court Line, the holiday company which was forced into liquidation in 1974. Its 1973 accounts showed a debt/equity ratio of 59/41 but if the leased assets (comprising 11 aeroplanes together with various items of ground equipment) had been capitalised in the balance sheet, the ratio would have shown a much more precarious level of gearing, of 76/24.

Whilst it would be naïve to suggest that the group collapsed solely because of the 'off balance sheet gearing', investors and creditors might have been more reticent in putting their money at risk in the group (whether through equity purchases, loans or simply trade credit) had the extent of the 'off balance sheet gearing' been known. In that respect, the truth and fairness of the accounts must be questioned.

Without capitalisation, the profit and loss account is only charged with the lease payments. This charge does not reflect the use of the asset, especially where there is a secondary term to the lease at nominal rental. For example, if the lease term for an asset stipulated four annual rentals of £5,000 followed by six annual rentals of £1, simply charging the rental paid against income would not adequately match the revenues (which would, other things being equal, stay constant over the 10 years) with the costs associated with those revenues.

A similar problem arises in lessor accounting – how to match the lease rentals receivable over the period of the agreement to the cost of generating rentals.

2.2 Capitalisation of finance leases in the lessee's accounts

The two critical questions to be answered are:

(a) At what value should the asset be capitalised?
(b) What finance charge should be made in the profit and loss account?

2.3 The capitalised value in the balance sheet

At the start of the lease, the sum to be recorded both as an asset and as a liability should be the present value of the minimum lease payments, derived by discounting them at the interest rate implicit in the lease.

In practice in the case of a finance lease the fair value of the asset will often be a sufficiently close approximation to the present value of the minimum lease payments and may in these circumstances be substituted for it.

2.4 The finance charge

The excess of the minimum lease payments over the initial capitalised value represents the finance charge. The total finance charge should be allocated to accounting periods during the lease term so as to produce a constant periodic rate of charge on the remaining balance of the obligation for each accounting period (ie, the actuarial method), or a reasonable approximation thereto.

2.5 Example

A lessee enters into a lease on 1 January 20X1 for an item of plant with a life of five years. The following details are relevant:

Fair value of asset	£10,000
Residual value	Nil after five years
Lease terms	£2,500 pa in advance for five years, the first rental payable on 1.1.X1

The interest rate implicit in the lease is 12.6%.

Required

Show how this transaction would be recorded in the ledger accounts of the lessee for the first two years, and show also how the transaction would be reflected in the profit and loss account and balance sheet over the five years.

2.6 Solution

The finance charge will be calculated as follows for each year:

Year	*Amount outstanding*	*Interest @ 12.6%*	*Repayment on 1 January following*
	£	£	£
1	7,500	945	2,500
2	5,945	749	2,500
3	4,194	528	2,500
4	2,222	278	2,500
5	-	-	-
		2,500	

The annual depreciation charge will be:

$$\frac{£10,000}{5} = £2,000 \text{ pa}$$

The ledger entry at the beginning of the lease will be:

		£	£
Dr	Leased assets	10,000	
	Cr Obligation under finance leases		10,000

being the recording of the 'purchase' of an asset under a finance lease at its fair value and the assumption of a liability.

Thereafter the entries in the leased asset account and the depreciation account will be exactly the same as for a purchased asset. The entries in the leasing obligation account will be as follows:

Obligation under finance leases account

		£			£
1.1.X1	Cash	2,500	1.1.X1	Leased asset	10,000
31.12.X1	Balance c/f	8,445	31.12.X1	Interest expense	945
		10,945			10,945
1.1.X2	Cash	2,500	1.1.X2	Balance b/f	8,445
31.12.X2	Balance c/f	6,694	31.12.X2	Interest expense (8,445 - 2,500) × 12.6%	749
		9,194			9,194
			1.1.X3	Balance b/f	6,694

The charges to the profit and loss account over the period of the lease are:

Year	*1*	*2*	*3*	*4*	*5*	*Total*
	£	£	£	£	£	£
Depreciation	2,000	2,000	2,000	2,000	2,000	10,000
Interest	945	749	528	278	-	2,500
	2,945	2,749	2,528	2,278	2,000	12,500

The balance sheets would reflect the net book value of the asset and the outstanding principal of the loan together with the accrued interest for the year which will be paid on the first day of the next period.

Balance sheets

Year	*1*	*2*	*3*	*4*	*5*
	£	£	£	£	£
Fixed assets					
Leased plant					
Cost	10,000	10,000	10,000	10,000	10,000
Accumulated dep'n	2,000	4,000	6,000	8,000	10,000
Net book value	8,000	6,000	4,000	2,000	-

Year	*1*	*2*	*3*	*4*	*5*
	£	£	£	£	£
Creditors: amounts falling due within one year					
Obligations under finance leases:					
Principal	1,555	1,751	1,972	2,222	-
Accrued interest	945	749	528	278	-
	2,500	2,500	2,500	2,500	-
Creditors: amounts falling due after more than one year					
Obligations under finance leases (principal only)	5,945	4,194	2,222	-	-
	8,445	6,694	4,722	2,500	-

Obligations under finance leases have been split between the current portion (payable within 12 months of the balance sheet date) and the long-term portion.

The accounting treatment adopted for hire purchase contracts is very similar to the above. SSAP 21 requires that 'those hire purchase contracts which are of a financing nature should be accounted for on a basis similar to that set out for finance leases'.

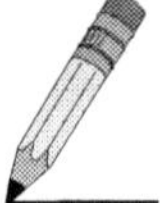

Activity 1 *(The answer is in the final chapter of this book)*

Finch

Finch Ltd entered into a leasing agreement with Tyrrell plc on 1 October 20X5. This involves a specialised piece of manufacturing machinery which was purchased by Tyrrell plc to Finch Ltd's specifications.

The contract involves an annual payment in arrears of £1,200,000 for five years.

At the start of the lease with Tyrrell plc the present value of the minimum lease payments was calculated in accordance with the rules contained in SSAP 21 and found to be £4,100,000. The fair value of the machinery at the commencement of the contract was £4,680,000.

Finch Ltd is responsible for the maintenance of the machinery and is required to insure it against accidental damage.

The machinery would normally be expected to have a useful life of approximately seven years. Finch Ltd depreciates its tangible fixed assets on the straight line basis.

The implied rate of interest is 14.2% per annum.

Required

(a) Discuss how you would classify this lease with reference to the rules in SSAP 21. **(10 marks)**

(b) Describe the impact in the accounts of Finch Ltd on the assumption you decide to classify the lease as a finance lease. **(10 marks)**

(Total : 20 marks)

---

3 Operating leases

An operating lease is a lease other than a finance lease, under which there is no suggestion that the risks and rewards of ownership are transferred from the lessor to the lessee. A business may lease a photocopier or fax machine under this type of shorter-term lease.

Thus the asset is treated as a fixed asset in the books of the lessor and the rental is treated as income for the lessor and as expense for the lessee. The treatment of operating leases in the lessee's books is that the rental should be charged on a straight-line basis over the lease term.

4 Disclosure requirements of SSAP 21

4.1 Disclosure requirements by lessees

The disclosures required by SSAP 21 are complex. The principal disclosures for lessees are in respect of:

- assets held under finance leases;
- maturity of the obligations;
- charges in the profit and loss account; and
- commitments under operating leases.

The first two can be illustrated using the earlier example at the end of Year 2:

- **Assets held under finance leases**

  The net book value of fixed assets of £X includes an amount of £6,000 in respect of assets held under finance leases.

- **Obligations under finance leases**

  The minimum lease payments to which the company is committed fall due as follows:

	£	£
Under one year		2,500
Over one year		
In the 2nd to 5th years inclusive	5,000	
Over 5 years	-	
		5,000
		7,500
Amount representing future financing charges (2,500 - 945 - 749)		806
Obligations under finance leases		6,694

The other required disclosures are illustrated below:

- **Profit is stated after charging:**

	£
Depreciation of owned assets	X
Depreciation of assets held under finance leases and hire purchase contracts	X
Interest payable - bank loans and overdrafts	X
Finance charges payable - finance leases and hire purchase contracts	X
Hire of plant and machinery - operating leases	X
Hire of other assets - operating leases	X

- **Operating lease commitments**

  At 31 December 20X7 the company had annual commitments under non-cancellable operating leases as set out below.

	20X7		*20X6*	
	Land and buildings	*Other*	*Land and buildings*	*Other*
	£000	£000	£000	£000
Operating leases which expire				
within one year	X	X	X	X
in the second to fifth years inclusive	X	X	X	X
over five years	X	X	X	X
	X	X	X	X

5 *Quick quiz* *(The answers are in the final chapter of this book)*

1. A lessor hires out an asset with a five year life to a lessee for a period of five years. Is this a finance lease or an operating lease?

2. Are assets which are the subject of operating leases shown on the lessee's balance sheet?

3. Explain briefly how SSAP 21 prevents off balance sheet finance.

6 Summary

SSAP 21 is an important contribution in the development of Accounting Standards since it represents the application of commercial substance as the solution to one form of off-balance sheet finance. The important matters which you must appreciate are:

(a) the problem of legal form accounting;

(b) the distinction between a finance lease and an operating lease;

(c) the capitalisation of finance leases in the lessee's books and the recognition of the obligation;

(d) the treatment of operating lease rentals in the lessee's books;

(e) the disclosures required by SSAP 21.

CHAPTER 16

Post balance sheet events and contingencies

ASSESSMENT FOCUS

For Unit 11 you need to know all aspects of SSAP 17: Accounting for post balance sheet events and almost all aspects of FRS 12: Provisions, contingent liabilities and contingent assets.

This chapter covers the following Knowledge and Understanding of the AAT Syllabus:

> The UK regulatory framework for financial reporting and the main requirements of relevant Financial Reporting Standards *(Element 11.1)*
>
> Preparing financial statements in proper form *(Element 11.1)*

In order to cover these the following topics are included:

> SSAP 17: Accounting for post balance sheet events
> FRS 12: Provisions, contingent liabilities and contingent assets

Key definitions

Post balance sheet events	Events occurring between the balance sheet date and the date on which the directors approve the financial statements.
Adjusting events	Concern conditions that existed at the balance sheet date.
Non-adjusting events	Concern conditions that arose after the balance sheet date.
Provision	Liability of uncertain timing or amount.
Contingency	Condition existing at the balance sheet date whose outcome depends on uncertain future events.

1 SSAP 17: Accounting for post balance sheet events

1.1 Introduction

Post balance sheet events are those events, both favourable and unfavourable, which occur between the balance sheet date and the date on which the financial statements are approved by the board of directors.

The explanatory note to SSAP 17 gives the following reasons for the standard:

(a) Events arising after the balance sheet date need to be reflected in financial statements if they provide additional evidence of conditions that existed at the balance sheet date and materially affect the amounts to be included.

(b) To prevent financial statements from being misleading, disclosure needs to be made by way of notes of other material events arising after the balance sheet date which provide evidence of conditions not existing at the balance sheet date. Disclosure is required where this information is necessary for a proper understanding of the financial position.

The standard therefore distinguishes two types of post balance sheet event:

(a) adjusting events, which require the accounts to be adjusted to reflect their impact; and

(b) non-adjusting events, which are merely noted in the accounts if material.

1.2 Adjusting events

These are defined as being 'post balance sheet events which provide additional evidence of conditions existing at the balance sheet date'. Such events are relevant because they relate to items appearing in the accounts or transactions reported in them. Examples of adjusting events are:

(a) *Fixed assets.* The subsequent determination of the purchase price or of the proceeds of sale of assets purchased or sold before the year-end.

(b) *Property.* A valuation which provides evidence of an impairment in value.

(c) *Investments.* The receipt of a copy of the financial statements or other information in respect of an unlisted company that provides evidence of an impairment in the value of a long-term investment.

(d) *Stocks and work in progress.*

  (i) The receipt of proceeds of sales after the balance sheet date or other evidence concerning the realisable value of stocks.

  (ii) The receipt of evidence that the previous estimate of accrued profit on a long-term contract was materially inaccurate.

(e) *Debtors.* The renegotiation of amounts owing by debtors, or the insolvency of a debtor.

(f) *Dividends receivable.* The declaration of dividends by subsidiaries and associated companies relating to periods prior to the balance sheet date of the holding company.

(g) *Taxation.* The receipt of information regarding rates of taxation.

(h) *Claims.* Amounts received or receivable in respect of insurance claims which were in the course of negotiation at the balance sheet date.

(i) *Discoveries.* The discovery of errors or frauds which show that the financial statements were incorrect.

1.3 Non-adjusting events

These are post balance sheet events which concern conditions which did not exist at the balance sheet date. These events therefore have no relevance in considering the profit or loss of the accounting year just ended, or the balance sheet at the end of the year. Some examples of non-adjusting events are:

(a) mergers and acquisitions;

(b) reconstructions;

(c) issues of shares and debentures;

(d) purchases and sales of fixed assets and investments;

(e) losses of fixed assets or stocks as a result of a catastrophe, such as a fire or flood;

(f) decline in the value of property and investments held as fixed assets, if it can be demonstrated that the decline occurred after the year end.

1.4 Requirements of SSAP 17

(a) Financial statements should be prepared on the basis of conditions existing at the balance sheet date.

(b) A material post balance sheet event requires changes in the amounts to be included in financial statements where:

  (i) it is an adjusting event; or

  (ii) it indicates that application of the going concern concept to the whole or a material part of the company is not appropriate.

(c) A material post balance sheet event should be disclosed where:

  (i) it is a non-adjusting event of such materiality that its non-disclosure would affect the ability of the users of financial statements to reach a proper understanding of the financial position; or

  (ii) it is the reversal or maturity after the year end of a transaction entered into before the year-end, the substance of which was primarily to alter the appearance of the company's balance sheet.

(d) In respect of each post balance sheet event which is required to be disclosed, the following information should be stated by way of notes in financial statements:

  (i) the nature of the event; and

  (ii) an estimate of the financial effect, or a statement that it is not practicable to make such an estimate.

(e) The date on which the financial statements are approved by the board of directors should be disclosed in the financial statements.

1.5 Commentary on SSAP 17 requirements

SSAP 17 is applying the accruals concept: the profit and loss account should contain all the transactions and events that occurred before the year end, whenever the directors actually became aware of these events. The balance sheet should similarly show the best understanding of the position at the year end, regardless of when that information became known.

Disclosure (c)(ii) above relates to "window dressing" of accounts, where transactions are artificially entered into before the year end and reversed soon after the year end, in order to improve the view given by the balance sheet. SSAP 17 requires that the details of such transactions should be explained in the notes to the accounts, which would defeat their whole purpose of artificially improving the look of the balance sheet.

1.6 Example

How would the following events be accounted for in the financial statements for the year to 31 December 20X2? Assume that each event is material in size in the context of the accounts as a whole.

(a) On 5 January 20X3 a large debtor went into liquidation owing £100,000 as at the balance sheet date. It is likely that this debtor balance will realise nothing.

(b) On 10 January 20X3 all the stocks in the Dudley warehouse were destroyed by fire. They had a cost at that date of £50,000 and a net realisable value of £70,000. Although this loss is serious, it is not so serious that the company is no longer able to continue as a going concern.

(c) The managing director was concerned in December 20X2 that stocks were too high, so he arranged to sell stock items with a cost of £200,000 at cost to the bank, on the arrangement that the items would be bought back at cost on 1 January 20X3. These goods were not included in the balance sheet stock figure at 31 December 20X2.

1.7 Solution

(a) This is an adjusting event giving additional information on the receivables figure at the year end. The £100,000 bad debt must be written off in the 20X2 accounts.

(b) This is a non-adjusting event, which should be described in a note to the accounts.

(c) This is window dressing. SSAP 17 requires that the details of the transaction should be disclosed in a note. It could also be argued that the substance over form principle suggests that no genuine sale occurred in 20X2, so that the sale should not be recognised in the accounts at all.

1.8 Companies Act 1985

The Companies Act requires disclosure of the particulars of any important events affecting the company or any of its subsidiaries which have occurred since the end of that year.

This disclosure is required by the Act to be in the directors' report. SSAP 17 on the other hand requires that these items be shown as a note to the accounts. Accordingly there is likely to be some duplication of disclosure, and it will not be sufficient for the directors' report merely to refer to the appropriate note in the accounts.

The Companies Act makes no distinction between adjusting and non-adjusting events.

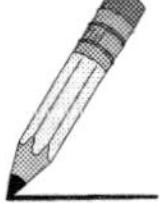

Activity 1 *(The answer is in the final chapter of this book)*

As the company accountant to Jam Limited you have started to finalise your company's accounts for the year ended 31 October 20X1. This follows a very hectic month during which, in addition to normal business, the events recorded below occurred:

October	10	Paid for a press advertising campaign due to take place during the last two weeks in October.
	14	A company warehouse was flooded during storms. Much of the company's stock was lost and a considerable quantity of returnable containers, on loan from a supplier, were severely damaged.
	25	The second week of the advertising campaign was deferred because of a strike by printers.

November	7	Letter received from company's insurers agreeing the full claim in respect of the flood on 14 October, except for the returnable containers which, they say, are not covered by the company's insurance policy.
	9	The government announced a ban on one of the company's major activities.

Required

State how the events listed above would affect the financial statements for the year ended 31 October 20X1.

2 FRS 12: Provisions, Contingent Liabilities and Contingent Assets

2.1 Introduction

FRS 12 is a far reaching standard that explores one of the basic notions of accounting: the fundamental accounting concept of prudence. This has traditionally encouraged accountants to provide early for potential liabilities and to err on the side of caution in estimating the amounts involved.

The problem is that prudence not only allows us to make sure that the bad news gets into the accounts as soon as possible; it also allows the accounts to be manipulated. By careful use of provisions, managers can smooth results from one year to another and produce year on year good results using the release of provisions to manipulate profits.

FRS 12 was issued to prevent this manipulation and force the accounts to show a true and fair view without 'fudging'.

The objective of the standard is to ensure that:

- provisions and contingencies are recognised and measured consistently
- sufficient information is disclosed to enable a user of the accounts to understand the nature, timing and amount of any provisions and contingencies included in the accounts.

2.2 Recognition of a provision

A provision is defined as a liability where there is uncertainty over either the timing or the amount of the future expenditure. It is not necessary to know the identity of the person to whom the obligation is owed. It is acceptable to recognise a provision only when the reporting entity has a legal or constructive obligation to transfer economic benefits as a result of past events, and a reasonable estimate can be made of the amount needed to settle the obligation. A legal obligation arises by operation of the law. A constructive obligation arises from the entity's past actions, for example:

- A retail store that habitually refunds purchases for dissatisfied customers and could not change its policy without damaging its reputation.
- An entity that has caused environmental damage and is obliged to rectify this because of its published policies and previous actions, even though there may be no legal obligation for it to do so.

2.3 Guidance on specific situations

Detailed guidance is given on the following specific situations.

- Future operating losses – no provisions should be recognised for such losses, since there is no liability at the balance sheet date. However the assets relating to the loss-making operation may need to be reviewed for impairment under the requirements of FRS 11.
- Reorganisation costs – provision should only be made where the entity is demonstrably committed to the reorganisation. In the past provisions have been made on the basis of a board decision taken before the financial year end, but under FRS 12, provisions for reorganisation costs are only justifiable when a specific announcement has been made and/or the reorganisation is under way.
- Onerous contracts – these are contracts where the unavoidable costs of meeting the terms of the contract exceed the expected revenues (for instance, where an entity is committed to continuing the lease on a vacant property). Provision should be made for the net loss that is expected to arise.
- Environmental liabilities – provision should be made when the entity becomes legally or constructively obliged to rectify the damage it has caused, but the creation of environmental contamination does not in itself give rise to such an obligation.
- Major refurbishment programmes – a business may have to undertake a major refurbishment programme every few years in order to continue its operations, but it does not have an obligation to transfer economic benefits until each refurbishment has been completed and the related payment is due. It is therefore not acceptable to recognise a provision for such costs in the years between actual refurbishments.

2.4 Measurement of a provision

The amount recognised as a provision should be the best estimate of the expenditure needed to settle the obligation existing at the balance sheet date, and provisions should be discounted whenever the effect of this is material. FRS 12 sets out guidance on appropriate methods of estimation, establishing appropriate discount rates and accounting for the amortisation of the discount in subsequent years.

Prudence can never be used to justify the creation of excessive reserves or provisions and care should be taken to avoid any effective double counting. For instance, if an estimate is based on prudent assumptions, it should not be necessary to make a further adjustment for prudence when carrying out the calculation.

In some cases, part or all of the expenditure covered by a provision may be recoverable from a third party. In these circumstances, FRS 12 requires the provision and the anticipated recovery to be accounted for as separate items unless the reporting entity no longer has any obligation for the element to be met by the third party, in which case the amounts should be offset.

2.5 Disclosure of provisions

For each class of provision, an entity should disclose:

- A brief description of the nature of the obligation and the timing of the payment.
- The amount provided and the basis of any estimates.
- Details of movements during the year, showing separately additions and adjustments, amounts used in the year, amounts released unused, the amortisation of any discount and the effect of any exchange differences.
- Where relevant, the discount rate used.

2.6 *Accounting for contingencies*

FRS 12 deals with contingencies as well as provisions.

The objective of FRS 12 in relation to contingencies is to ensure that:

- contingencies are recognised and measured consistently
- sufficient information is disclosed to enable a user of the accounts to understand the nature, amount and uncertainties relating to any contingent assets and liabilities.

A contingency is defined as a condition that exists at the balance sheet date whose outcome will be confirmed only on the occurrence of one or more uncertain future events.

Contingent liabilities should be recognised as an actual liability in the balance sheet when there is sufficient evidence of an obligation to transfer economic benefits as a result of past events, and a reasonable estimate of the obligation can be made. This mirrors the requirements in respect of provisions. Where a contingent liability may be partly reduced or avoided by a matching claim or counter-claim, the two aspects should be accounted for separately.

Contingent assets should only be recognised as actual assets in the balance sheet when they are virtually certain to generate economic benefits. In fact, if this is the case, then the asset was not a contingent asset in the first place.

The accounts should give the following disclosures for each material class of contingent liability and asset that are not recognised in the balance sheet, unless the possibility of transfer of economic benefits is remote:

- The nature of the contingency
- The uncertainties expected to affect the ultimate outcome.
- An estimate of the potential financial effect.

2.7 *Criticisms of the standard*

As in FRS 18, it can be argued that the ASB is in danger of going beyond the elimination of a bias towards prudence and actively encouraging imprudence.

Possible losses that were known about but didn't meet FRS 12's definitions can be excluded from accounts. It is debatable whether this is in the best interests of the users of accounts.

Activity 2 *(The answer is in the final chapter of this book)*

Hill plc

The year end of Hill plc is 31 March 20X0. Hill plc is a very diverse group. One of its consistent features is that it has a reputation as an ethical organisation. Much is made of the company's policies with regard to recycling, controls over emission of noxious substances and making use only of renewable resources.

Many of its goods in its beauty and cosmetic range (Sophie Beauty Products) use ingredients that are sourced overseas and the company publishes full details of its environmental policies as part of its annual report.

You are the chief accountant of the group and your assistant has prepared draft accounts for the year ended 31 March 20X0. Your assistant, however, is uncertain as to the application of FRS 12 *Provisions, Contingent Liabilities and Contingent Assets* to three material items described below and has requested your advice.

Required

(a) (i) Explain why there was a need for FRS 12 to be issued on accounting for provisions in the UK. **(7 marks)**

(ii) Explain the circumstances under which a provision should be recognised in the financial statements according to FRS 12. **(6 marks)**

(b) Explain how each of the following issues should be treated in the consolidated financial statements for the year ended 31 March 20X0.

(i) On 12 February 20X0 the board of Hill plc decided to close down a large factory in Aylesbury. The board expects that production will be transferred to other factories. No formal plan has yet been drawn up but it is expected the closure will occur on 31 August 20X0. As at the balance sheet date this decision has not been announced to the employees or to any other interested parties. The overall costs of this closure are foreseen as £79 million. **(3 marks)**

(ii) During the year to 31 March 20X0, a customer started legal proceedings claiming one of the products from the 'Sophie Beauty' range had caused a skin complaint. The group's lawyers have advised that the chances of this action succeeding are remote. **(3 marks)**

(iii) The group has an overseas subsidiary 'Melinat' that is involved in mining certain minerals. These activities cause significant damage to the environment, including deforestation. The company expects to abandon the mine in eight years time. The country where the subsidiary is based has no environmental legislation obligating companies to rectify environmental damage and it is unlikely that such legislation will be enacted within the next eight years. It has been estimated that the cost of putting right the site will be £10 million if the tree re-planting were successful at the first attempt, but it will probably be necessary to have a further attempt costing an additional £5 million. **(3 marks)**

---

3 Quick quiz *(The answers are in the final chapter of this book)*

1 A debtor goes into liquidation on 12 January 20X8, owing £300,000 to the company on its balance sheet date of 31 December 20X7. Is this an adjusting or a non-adjusting event?

2 A company issues new shares soon after its balance sheet date. Is this an adjusting or a non-adjusting event?

3 What is an onerous contract?

4 Should contingent assets be shown on the balance sheet?

4 Summary

You need to be able to recognise both adjusting and non-adjusting post balance sheet events. You should also ensure that you understand what is meant by a provision and when provisions should be shown as a creditor in the balance sheet. Distinguish a provision from a contingent liability and make sure that you understand the different treatment of contingent liabilities and contingent assets.

CHAPTER 17

Other accounting standards

ASSESSMENT FOCUS

In this chapter we will briefly consider the few remaining accounting standards that have not been covered earlier in this text. In each case the knowledge that will be assessed for each of these standards is very limited and we will only cover what is required for the assessment.

This chapter covers the following Knowledge and Understanding of the AAT Syllabus:

> The UK regulatory framework for financial reporting and the main requirements of relevant Financial Reporting Standards *(Element 11.1)*
>
> Preparing financial statements in proper form *(Element 11.1)*

In order to cover these the following topics are included:

> FRS 4: Capital instruments
> FRS 5: Reporting the substance of transactions
> FRS 8: Related party disclosures
> FRS 17: Retirement benefits
> SSAP 20: Foreign currency translation
> Financial Reporting Standard for Smaller Entities

Key definitions

Capital instrument	Shares, loans, etc issued as a means of raising finance.
Related party transaction	Transaction with a party who is not in an arm's length relationship.
Defined contribution scheme	Pension scheme where the employer pays regular amounts into the scheme, and the size of the fund on retirement depends on the investment performance achieved.
Defined benefit scheme	Pension scheme where the employer agrees to pay stated benefits on retirement.

1 FRS 4: Capital instruments

1.1 Introduction

All that is required for Unit 11 is the definition of capital instruments.

1.2 Definition

The FRS 4 definition of a capital instrument is as follows:

'All instruments that are issued by reporting entities as a means of raising finance, including shares, debentures, loans and debt instruments, options and warrants that give the holder the right to subscribe for or obtain capital instruments'.

2 FRS 5: Reporting the substance of transactions

2.1 Introduction

We have already seen in the chapter on accounting for leases how SSAP 21 was concerned about the reporting of the economic substance of transactions rather than their strict legal form. FRS 5 *Reporting the substance of transactions* was issued not to consider a particular area of accounting but to provide general guidance on this area.

2.2 Off balance sheet finance

In recent years as transactions and operations undertaken by businesses have become more and more complex, there have been many opportunities for assets and liabilities to be accounted for according to their strict legal form rather than their true commercial substance. This has resulted in the manipulation of the balance sheet and results in order to improve the picture shown by the balance sheet and to reduce significant ratios such as the gearing ratio.

2.3 Objective of FRS 5

The objective of FRS 5 is to ensure that the substance of an entity's transactions is reported in its financial statements.

2.4 Types of transactions

For the vast majority of transactions their commercial substance and their legal form will be one and the same thing. However, the FRS indicates three general types of transactions where care should be taken that the true commercial substance is recognised:

- where the person benefiting from an asset is not the legal owner;
- where the transaction is linked to others in such a way that the true commercial effect can only be understood by considering the whole series of transactions;
- an option is included in the transaction where its terms make it highly likely that it will be exercised.

2.5 Recognition of assets and liabilities

The key to determining the substance of a transaction is to identify whether it has given rise to new assets or liabilities or increased or decreased the existing assets and liabilities.

For Unit 11 you only need an appreciation of the importance of recognising the substance of transactions and you will not be assessed on determining the substance of transactions or the disclosures required. However, a short, simple example may illustrate the type of problem that FRS 5 is trying to overcome.

2.6 Example

A business has surplus stock that it sells to a bank on 31 December for £1,000,000. There is an agreement that the business will repurchase this stock for £1,200,000 in six months time. How should this be treated in the financial statements on 31 December?

2.7 Solution

The strict legal form is that a sale has been made to the bank for £1,000,000. However, the substance of the transaction is that the bank has loaned the business £1,000,000, with the stock as security. The additional £200,000 that the business will pay for the stock in six months time represents the interest on this loan.

Therefore, instead of the financial statements showing a sale of goods, the balance sheet will show a loan of £1,000,000 together with stocks of the same value.

3 FRS 8: Related party disclosures

3.1 Introduction

You already know that the overriding requirement of financial statements is that they present a true and fair view. When examining a set of accounts, the assumption is that all sales have been made to third parties at arm's length prices, and that all goods and services have also been acquired from third parties at arm's length prices. The profit and loss account therefore shows the true profitability of the company's operations.

But what if some purchases and sales are carried out deliberately at other than arm's length prices? For example, a holding company might insist that a subsidiary sells goods to it at cost price. Or the chairman and largest shareholder of a company might sell a building to a company at a price greater than market value. FRS 8 is based on the premise that, where related party relationships and transactions exist, the accounts will only give a true and fair view if those relationships and transactions are disclosed in notes to the accounts.

3.2 Definitions

(a) Two or more parties are **related parties** if:

- (i) one party controls the other party; or
- (ii) the parties are subject to common control from the same source; or
- (iii) one party has significant influence over the other party; or
- (iv) the parties are subject to significant influence from the same source.

(b) A **related party transaction** is the transfer of assets or liabilities or the performance of services by, to or for a related party irrespective of whether a price is charged.

3.3 Examples of related parties

The following are related parties:

(a) companies in the same group (eg holding company and subsidiary)

(b) associates and joint ventures of the reporting entity (where the reporting entity has influence but not control over an investment, for example the reporting company might own 40% of the shares of another company)

(c) directors of the reporting entity

(d) pension funds for the benefit of employees of the reporting entity

The following are assumed to be related parties unless the contrary can be demonstrated:

(a) the key management of the reporting entity (those in senior positions, even if they are not directors)

(b) a person owning more than 20% of the voting rights of the reporting entity

(c) persons acting together in such a way as to be able to control or significantly influence the reporting entity

(d) an entity managing or managed by the reporting entity under a management contract.

If an individual is a related party of the reporting entity, then all members of his close family are also presumed to be related parties.

3.4 Disclosures required of related party transactions

FRS 8 states that material transactions with a related party must be disclosed.

For Unit 11 the only knowledge that is required is the definition of a related party and the fact that transactions with related parties should be disclosed.

Important

4 FRS 17: Retirement benefits

4.1 Introduction

Over the past 40 years there has been a huge increase in the number and importance of pension schemes in the UK:

- very many employers offer pension scheme membership to their employees as part of the remuneration package offered
- the Government is keen to encourage individuals to have their own pension arrangements rather than rely on the State scheme, therefore tax benefits are offered
- as a category, pension schemes own a large proportion of the issued share capital of all public companies

The cost of pension provision to companies has increased accordingly. In November 2000 the ASB issued FRS 17 *Retirement benefits* to regulate accounting in this area.

4.2 Two sorts of scheme

There are two sorts of pension scheme available:

(a) In a **defined contribution scheme**, an employer pays regular contributions into the scheme which are fixed as an amount or as a percentage of pay. On retirement, the size of the member's benefits depends on the size of the fund which has accumulated to that date. This will depend on the size of the amounts paid in, and the investment returns achieved by the scheme managers.

(b) In a **defined benefit scheme**, the scheme rules define the benefits payable, independently of the contributions paid in. The size of the benefits payable is not directly related to the investment performance of the scheme assets.

4.3 Example

(a) H plc operates a pension scheme where 5% of an employee's gross pay is deducted and paid to the scheme, along with an 8% contribution paid by the company. No promise is made as to the size of pension to be paid; this depends on the size of the fund of assets accumulated at the date of retirement.

(b) I plc operates a pension scheme where the same 5% and 8% of gross pay are currently paid to the scheme respectively by the employee and employer. On retirement, the scheme promises to pay a pension calculated as

$$\frac{\text{Number of years worked}}{60} \times \text{Salary at retirement date}$$

For example, an employee who has worked 20 years for the company and retires when earning £45,000 pa would receive an annual pension of $\frac{20}{60} \times$ £45,000 = £15,000 pa from the scheme.

What type of pension scheme are (a) and (b) above?

4.4 Solution

(a) H plc has a defined contribution scheme.
(b) I plc has a defined benefit scheme.

4.5 Funded and unfunded schemes

In a **funded scheme**, the employer pays the contributions to an external pension fund which is legally separate from the employer. If the employer company is wound up, the pension scheme assets are still secure for the employees.

In an **unfunded scheme**, there is no separate fund of assets. The employer pays the pensions due, directly out of the company's assets. This is much less secure for the employees; if the company is wound up, the employees' pension rights are just one of many liabilities to be settled out of the available assets.

4.6 Funding and accounting

A final distinction to be made is between funding a scheme and the accounting cost of contributing to a scheme. Funding relates to the actual transfer of assets from the employer company to the scheme. For example, a company might pay £1m cash to a scheme every other year. Each year in the profit and loss account must be shown the expense of pension provision; this accounting charge must comply with the accruals concept, so a regular amount must be charged each year. For example, the company paying £1m every second year might decide on an appropriate accounting cost of £0.5m pa.

5 Accounting for defined contribution schemes

5.1 Introduction

Accounting for a defined contribution scheme is simple, since the employer company has no further liability after paying the agreed contributions payable to the scheme.

5.2 Profit and loss account

The pension cost for a period is equal to the contributions payable to the scheme for the period.

5.3 Balance sheet

A prepayment or accrual might arise if the employer company has made too large or too small payments to the scheme. These will be shown in current assets or current liabilities in the normal way.

6 Accounting for defined benefit schemes

6.1 Introduction

This is more complicated, since estimates of the future will be required, concerning future investment returns, future salary increases, deaths before retirement etc. The professional advice of an actuary is required to advise on such matters. The actuary will recommend a contribution rate to be applied now to build up sufficient assets to meet the future liabilities of the scheme.

In practice, an actuary usually carries out a full actuarial valuation every three years to ensure that the scheme's assets are sufficient and to identify any shortfall or surplus of assets.

6.2 Measuring the assets of defined benefit schemes

Defined benefit scheme assets should be measured at fair value, so that:

- quoted securities should be at mid-market value
- unquoted securities should be at estimated fair value
- property should be at open market value

6.3 Measuring the liabilities of defined benefit schemes

The scheme liabilities comprise the benefits promised under the formal terms of the scheme, plus any constructive obligations for further benefits that the employer cannot avoid.

The scheme liabilities should be measured using an actuarial basis, ie estimating the future cash flows arising under the actuarial assumptions and then discounting these cash flows at an appropriate discount rate.

6.4 Accounting for the surplus or shortfall

The excess/shortfall in the value of the assets over the present value of the liabilities is the actuarial surplus/deficit in the scheme. The employer and actuary will consult on whether and how to clear the surplus or deficit.

The employer should recognise a surplus as an asset in his balance sheet to the extent that he will benefit from reduced contributions in the future or refunds from the scheme.

The employer should recognise a deficit as a liability in his balance sheet to the extent that it reflects a legal or constructive obligation.

The asset or liability arising should be shown on the face of the balance sheet separately from any sundry prepayments or accruals arising from the timing of the payments of contributions to the scheme.

For Unit 11 you need an appreciation of the general principles of accounting for pension costs and the difference between defined contribution and defined benefit schemes. Also, you must have an appreciation of the general problems of accounting for defined benefit schemes.

7 SSAP 20: Foreign currency translation

7.1 Introduction

A business can have dealings in foreign currencies in one of two ways:

- by directly buying or selling goods in a foreign currency;
- by investing in a foreign subsidiary company.

7.2 Individual company transactions

If a company buys or sells goods which are denominated in a foreign currency then the sale or purchase must be included in the financial statements in sterling. Therefore the foreign currency amount of the transaction must be translated into sterling using an appropriate exchange rate.

When the transaction takes place the foreign currency amount will normally be translated at the actual rate of exchange on the date of the transaction. When the amount is paid or received, if the exchange rate has changed, then this will give rise to an exchange gain or loss.

A further problem arises if the goods have not been paid for by the end of the accounting period as there will be a debtor or creditor in the balance sheet for the amount due. According to SSAP 20 this should be translated at the exchange rate on the balance sheet date in order to give the fairest estimate of the actual amount due. This again may give rise to an exchange gain or loss.

These exchange gains or losses should be recognised in the profit and loss account for the year.

7.3 Example

On 1 October 20X2 a UK business had the following transactions:

Sale	\$500,000
Purchase	\$200,000

The exchange rate on 1 October was \$2 to the pound.

On 1 December 20X2 the purchase was paid for when the exchange rate was \$1.80 to the pound. At 31 December 20X2, the business' year end, the exchange rate was \$1.60 and the debtor for the sale had still not paid.

Calculate any exchange gains or losses on these transactions.

7.4 Solution

Initial translation @ \$2.

Sale and debtor	=	$\frac{\$500,000}{2}$	=	£250,000
Purchase and creditor	=	$\frac{\$200,000}{2}$	=	£100,000
Payment of creditor @ \$1.80	=	$\frac{\$200,000}{1.80}$	=	£111,111
Exchange loss (£111,111 - £100,000)			=	£11,111
Retranslation of debtor at year end @ \$1.60	=	$\frac{\$500,000}{1.6}$	=	£312,500
Exchange gain (£312,500 - £250,000)			=	£62,500

7.5 Foreign subsidiary companies

If a company buys a foreign subsidiary then at the year end the subsidiary's financial statements must be consolidated with those of the parent company. However, the subsidiary's own individual financial statements will be expressed in its own currency.

Therefore, before consolidation takes place, the subsidiary's financial statements must be translated into sterling. SSAP 20 lays down distinct rules as to how this translation is to be carried out.

For the purposes of Unit 11 all the knowledge that you require of SSAP 20 is an appreciation of the need to account for foreign currency transactions for both individual companies and for foreign enterprises in consolidated financial statements.

8 Financial Reporting Standard for Smaller Entities

8.1 Introduction

The Financial Reporting Standard for Smaller Entities (the FRSSE) was first issued in 1996 and has subsequently been updated with the latest version issued in December 2001.

8.2 Scope

The FRSSE is aimed at the financial statements of companies that fall within the Companies Act definition of small companies.

8.3 Objective

The objective of the FRSSE is to ensure that these small companies provide in their financial statements information that is useful to the users of those statements in assessing the stewardship of management and for making economic decisions. The FRSSE recognises that the needs of users in small companies are different from those of users in other entities.

8.4 Content

The FRSSE is a summary of all of the measurement and disclosure requirements that a small company must follow when preparing their financial statements. It contains in simplified form the requirements from existing accounting standards that are relevant to these smaller entities. Therefore if a company complies with the FRSSE then they are exempt from the requirements of all other accounting standards.

For Unit 11 all that is required is an awareness of the objective of the FRSSE and its scope.

9 Quick quiz *(The answers are in the final chapter of this book)*

1 A company issues some preference shares. Are these capital instruments?

2 A parent company has two subsidiaries. Which of the three companies are related to others in the group?

3 Which are more complicated to account for: defined contribution schemes or defined benefit schemes?

10 Summary

In this chapter we have included the required knowledge of the remaining accounting standards not covered in other chapters.

For FRS 4 you are required to know the definition of capital instruments.

For FRS 5 you need an appreciation of the importance of recognising the substance of transactions but no detailed tasks requiring determination of the substance of a transaction will be set.

For FRS 8 what is required is a knowledge of the definition of a related party and the fact that transactions between related parties must be disclosed.

For FRS 17 an appreciation is required of the need for companies to make a charge in the accounts for pension costs, the difference between defined contribution and defined benefit schemes and a general appreciation of the problems in accounting for defined benefit schemes.

For SSAP 20 an appreciation is required of the need to account for foreign currency transactions for individual companies and for foreign enterprises in consolidated financial statements.

Finally an awareness of the objective and scope of the FRSSE is required although there will be no assessment of the detailed accounting requirements of the standard or of the differences or similarities between the requirements of the FRSSE and those of other accounting standards applicable to entities that do not fall within the scope of the FRSSE.

CHAPTER 18

Interpretation of accounts

ASSESSMENT FOCUS

Element 2 of this Unit is entitled "Interpret Limited Company Financial Statements" therefore it is likely that every assessment will include some task which asks you to apply ratio analysis to company financial statements and analyse and interpret the results.

This chapter covers the following Knowledge and Understanding of the AAT Syllabus.

Analysing and interpreting the information contained in financial statements *(Element 11.2)*

Computing and interpreting accounting ratios *(Element 11.2)*

In order to cover these the following topics are included.

Profitability ratios
Liquidity ratios and asset utilisation
Investor ratios
Risk
Interpretation
General points about financial ratios

Key definitions

Profitability ratios	Ratios that measure profitability
Liquidity ratios	Ratios that measure short term solvency
Gearing ratios	Ratios that measure the dependence on non-equity funds
Risk	In this context, risk is the danger that a business will be unable to meet its financial objectives (in particular dividends to shareholders) because of excessive interest payments on debt.

1 *Profitability ratios*

1.1 Introduction

Ratios calculated from financial statements help to interpret the information they present. Various users may use these ratios to analyse financial statements.

We can break down the ratios into categories to make our discussion more structured. To begin with we look at ratios relating to profitability.

1.2 Return on capital employed (ROCE)

Capital employed is normally measured as fixed assets plus current assets less current liabilities and represents the long-term investment in the business, or owners' capital plus long-term liabilities. Return on capital employed is frequently regarded as the best measure of profitability, indicating how successful a business is in utilising its assets. The ratio is only meaningful when the true values of assets are known and used in the formula.

$$\text{Return on capital employed} = \frac{\text{Profit before interest and taxation (PBIT)}}{\text{Average capital employed}} \times 100\%$$

Note that the profit *before* interest is used, because the loan capital rewarded by that interest is included in capital employed.

A low return on capital employed (assets used) is caused by either a low profit margin or a low asset turnover or both. This can be seen by breaking down the primary ROCE ratio into its two components: profit margin and asset turnover.

$$\text{ROCE} = \frac{\text{PBIT}}{\text{Capital employed}}$$

$$= \frac{\text{PBIT}}{\text{Sales}} \times \frac{\text{Sales}}{\text{Capital employed}}$$

$$= \text{Profit margin} \times \text{Asset turnover}$$

1.3 Profit margin (on sales)

$$\text{Operating profit margin} = \frac{\text{Profit before interest and taxation}}{\text{Sales}} \times 100\%$$

A low margin indicates low selling prices or high costs or both. Comparative analysis will reveal the level of prices and costs in relation to competitors.

1.4 Asset turnover

This will show how fully a company is utilising its assets.

$$\text{Asset turnover} = \frac{\text{Sales}}{\text{Capital employed}}$$

A low turnover shows that a company is not generating a sufficient volume of business for the size of the asset base. This may be remedied by increasing sales or by disposing of some of the assets or both.

1.5 Gross profit margin

$$\text{Gross profit margin} = \frac{\text{Gross profit}}{\text{Sales}} \times 100\%$$

The gross profit margin focuses on the trading account. A low margin could indicate selling prices too low or cost of sales too high.

1.6 Return on owners' equity

$$\text{Return on owners' equity} = \frac{\text{Profit after interest and preference dividends but before tax}}{\text{Ordinary share capital and reserves}} \times 100\%$$

This looks at the return earned for ordinary shareholders. We use the profit after preference dividends and interest (ie the amounts that have to be paid before ordinary shareholders can be rewarded).

2 Liquidity ratios and asset utilisation

2.1 Current ratio

This is a common method of analysing working capital (net current assets) and is generally accepted as a good measure of short-term solvency. It indicates the extent to which the claims of short-term creditors are covered by assets that are expected to be converted to cash in a period roughly corresponding to the maturity of the claims.

$$\text{Current ratio} = \frac{\text{Current assets}}{\text{Current liabilities}}$$

The current ratio should ideally fall between 1:1 and 2:1.

2.2 Acid test ratio (quick ratio)

This is calculated in the same way as the current ratio except that stocks are excluded from current assets.

$$\text{Acid test ratio} = \frac{\text{Current assets - Stock}}{\text{Current liabilities}}$$

This ratio is a much better test of the immediate solvency of a business because of the length of time necessary to convert stocks into cash (via sales and debtors).

Contrary to what might be expected, this ratio may fall in a time of prosperity since increased activity may lead to larger stocks but less cash; conversely, when trade slows down stocks may be disposed of without renewal and the ratio will rise.

Although increased liquid resources more usually indicate favourable trading, it could be that funds are not being used to their best advantage (eg a large cash balance).

2.3 Debtors ratio

This is computed by dividing the debtors by the average daily sales to determine the number of days sales held in debtors.

$$\text{Average collection period} = \frac{\text{Trade debtors}}{\text{Credit sales}} \times 365 \text{ days}$$

A long average collection period probably indicates poor credit control.

2.4 Creditors ratio

This is computed by dividing the creditors by the average daily purchases to determine the number of days purchases held in creditors.

$$\text{Average payment period} = \frac{\text{Trade creditors}}{\text{Credit purchases}} \times 365 \text{ days}$$

If only cost of sales rather than purchases is available in the information given this can be used as an approximation to purchases.

2.5 Stock turnover

This ratio indicates whether stock levels are justified in relation to cost of sales. The higher the ratio, the healthier the cash flow position, but with the qualification that the profit margin must also be acceptable.

$$\text{Stock turnover} = \frac{\text{Cost of sales}}{\text{Stocks}}$$

It is usual to calculate this ratio using the closing stock. A limitation on this ratio is that in a seasonal business stock levels may fluctuate considerably during the year.

2.6 Stock turnover in days

Stock turnover can also be calculated in days like debtors and creditors.

$$\text{Stock turnover period} = \frac{\text{Stocks}}{\text{Cost of sales}} \times 365 \text{ days}$$

3 Investor ratios

3.1 Earnings per share

This ratio has no connection with the other profitability ratios and is used primarily by potential investors. It is, however, a very important ratio and it is required that listed companies actually disclose the figure for earnings per share at the foot of the profit and loss account. It is calculated as follows.

$$\text{Earnings per share} = \frac{\text{Earnings available for ordinary shareholders}}{\text{Number of ordinary shares in issue}}$$

The calculation can be complicated in some instances but, for the purposes of this chapter, it is enough to be aware that 'earnings available for ordinary shareholders' means profits after interest, taxation and preference dividends.

3.2 Price earnings ratio

Earnings per share is used by investors in calculating the price–earnings ratio or PE ratio. This is simply calculated as follows.

$$\text{PE ratio} = \frac{\text{Market price of share}}{\text{Earnings per share}}$$

A high PE ratio means that the shares are seen as an attractive investment. For example, if the PE ratio is 20, it means that investors are prepared to pay 20 times the annual level of earnings in order to acquire the shares.

3.3 Dividend cover

$$\text{Dividend cover} = \frac{\text{Earnings available to ordinary shareholders}}{\text{Dividend paid}}$$

This gives an indication of the security of future dividends. A high dividend cover ratio means that available profits comfortably cover the amount being paid out in dividends.

4 Risk

4.1 Gearing

Gearing measures the extent to which a business is dependent on non-equity funds, as opposed to equity funding. A high gearing ratio means that the business has a high proportion of borrowed funds in its total capital.

Gearing gives an indication of long-term liquidity and the financial risk inherent within the business. Highly geared companies have to meet large interest commitments before paying dividends and may have problems raising further finance if expansion is necessary.

$$\text{Gearing} = \frac{\text{Long - term debt and preference share capital}}{\text{Shareholder funds and long - term debt and preference share capital}} \times 100\%$$

4.2 Interest cover

$$\text{Interest cover} = \frac{\text{Profit before interest}}{\text{Interest paid}}$$

Interest on debt has to be paid before shareholders can receive dividends. Therefore a good measure of risk is to compare available profit with the amount of interest to be paid.

4.3 Example

We will now calculate all of the above ratios on the following profit and loss account and balance sheet for JG Ltd.

SUMMARISED BALANCE SHEET AT 31 DECEMBER 20X8

	£000	£000
Fixed assets		2,600
Current assets		
Stocks	600	
Debtors	900	
Balance at bank	100	
	1,600	
Trade creditors	800	
		800
		3,400
Debenture stock		1,400
		2,000
Capital and reserves		
Ordinary share capital (£1 shares)		1,000
Preference share capital		200
Profit and loss account		800
		2,000

SUMMARISED PROFIT AND LOSS ACCOUNT FOR THE YEAR ENDED 31 DECEMBER 20X8

	£000
Sales	6,000
Cost of sales (including purchases £4.3m)	4,500
Gross profit	1,500
Administrative and distribution costs	1,160
Operating profit	340
Debenture interest	74
Profit before tax	266
Taxation	106
Profit after tax	160
Preference dividend	10
Profit available for ordinary shareholders	150
Ordinary dividend	10
Retained profit	140

4.4 Solution

Return on capital employed	=	10%	$340/3{,}400 \times 100$
Profit margin	=	5.7%	$340/6{,}000 \times 100$
Asset turnover	=	1.8 times	$6{,}000/3{,}400$
Gross profit margin	=	25%	$1{,}500/6{,}000 \times 100$
Return on owners' equity	=	14.2%	$(266 - 10)/(1{,}000 + 800) \times 100$
Current ratio	=	2 times	$1{,}600/800$
Acid test ratio	=	1.25 times	$(900 + 100)/800$
Debtors ratio	=	55 days	$900/6{,}000 \times 365$
Creditors ratio	=	68 days	$800/4{,}300 \times 365$
Stock turnover period	=	7.5 times	$4{,}500/600$
or			
Stock turnover period	=	49 days	$600/4{,}500 \times 365$
Earnings per share	=	15p	$150/1{,}000$
Dividend cover	=	15 times	$150/10$
Gearing	=	47%	$(1{,}400 + 200)/3{,}400 \times 100$
Interest cover	=	4.6 times	$340/74$

We can now use these figures to interpret the financial statements.

5 Interpretation

5.1 Introduction

The first stage of answering questions on interpretation is to calculate the ratios; the second is to draw conclusions about the company based on those ratios. It is important to remember that there are limitations to the use of ratios, not the least of which is that a study of the trend of ratios for several years is desirable before drawing firm conclusions about many aspects of a company's position.

Let us consider what conclusions we may draw from the illustrative accounts of J G Ltd above and the ratios derived from them. It will be useful to consider five aspects: profitability, liquidity, asset utilisation, investor ratios and risk.

5.2 Profitability

Return on capital employed - The company shows a return on total capital employed of 10%: not dramatically good, but satisfactory. Note that it exceeds the rate of interest being paid on the debentures (5.3%). If this were not so, the company would be borrowing money by way of the debenture and investing it so that the income derived was less than the interest payable on it: not a good deal.

Net profit as percentage of sales - This is fairly low at 5.7%. The net profit as a percentage of sales varies greatly from industry to industry: more information is needed about the performance of other companies to draw useful conclusions about the level of this ratio.

Asset turnover ratio - The overall efficiency may be judged by asset turnover. This is 1.8 times for J G Ltd. (See asset utilisation for further details.)

Gross profit margin - This is a more respectable 25% but again comparison to the industry average would indicate whether it is acceptable.

Return on owners' equity - The level of acceptability of 14.2% will depend on four things.

- The investors' anticipated return and whether income or capital growth is more important.
- The industry average or that of competitors.
- The return available in other forms of investment, eg building society.
- The level of capital growth, ie the increase in the value of the shares.

5.3 Liquidity

We measure liquidity by the use of two main ratios - the current ratio (current assets/current liabilities, here 2:1) and the quick ratio or acid test ratio (current assets - stock/current liabilities, here 1.25:1)

A quick ratio of about 1:1 is normally regarded as indicating a reasonable level of liquidity. The current ratio is often more variable, because of variations in a company's need to hold stocks. For example a retailer will normally hold less stock than a manufacturer, because no stocks of raw materials or work in progress will be required. A ratio of perhaps 1.5:1 could be acceptable for the average manufacturing business.

We may deduce either that the nature of J G Ltd's business is such that above-average stock levels are needed, or that its stock control procedures leave something to be desired. More information is clearly needed. The stock turnover ratio may throw more light on this aspect: see 'asset utilisation' below.

5.4 Asset utilisation

Several ratios give some idea of asset utilisation and management efficiency.

Asset turnover ratio - Unfortunately we can draw no conclusions whatsoever about the company and the efficiency of its management without more information to compare it with (the ratios for J G Ltd in past years and the ratios for other similar companies in the current year). An increasing ratio compared with previous years for the same company or a ratio above that of other comparable companies may indicate better overall efficiency of operation.

Debtors ratio - J G Ltd's figure of 55 days is probably acceptable, since 60 days is often regarded as 'par' for a company offering normal credit terms of monthly settlement for all its sales. Ideally we need to know whether there are substantial cash sales, or whether the business is seasonal, before making any firm statements about the efficiency of the company's credit control.

Creditors ratio - J G Ltd is paying its creditors on average in 68 days. This is after the period from which it collects its debtors (55 days) so it will help cash flow overall. However, J G Ltd must be careful not to antagonise suppliers especially if they are fundamental to the business.

Ideally both debtors and creditors ratios would be compared to the industry average to see if credit terms for customers/suppliers are too harsh or too generous.

Stock turnover ratio – This comes to 7.5 times for J G Ltd or 49 days. It is again difficult to draw conclusions about this figure in isolation. It needs to be compared with other years for J G Ltd and with other companies.

5.5 Investor ratios

Earnings per share – J G Ltd's earnings per share is 15p. There are two issues here.

- Shareholders' expectation of the level of return on their investment as evidenced by previous year EPS figures and by the PE ratio.
- Industry average and competitors' PE ratios.

Dividend cover – This is fifteen times, a very secure profit to dividend ratio. If J G Ltd continues to trade in the same way then it should have no problems paying future dividends.

5.6 Risk

The gearing ratio tells us what proportion of the company's long-term capital is provided by loans and preference shares. The figure for J G Ltd is 47%. Anything over 50% would probably be regarded as fairly high. A useful basic principle is that a business with a high operational risk attaching to it should be low-geared: that is, it should have the majority of the capital in the form of equity provided by ordinary shareholders.

Interest cover – For J G Ltd this is 4.6 times. This may be considered reasonable until you compare it to other companies within the industry.

5.7 Summary

Ratios can be useful in analysing and interpreting the financial statements of a company.

However, interpretation is difficult unless there is a benchmark against which to compare the ratios. Comparable ratios from other businesses, or from the same business in earlier periods, can provide such a benchmark.

In an assessment task you may get two years of a company's figures to compare or two companies in the same business or one year of figures and industry averages for comparison.

Activity 1 *(The answer is in the final chapter of this book)*

Falcon Ltd

The draft accounts of Falcon Ltd for the years ended 30 June 20X8 and 30 June 20X7 are as follows.

BALANCE SHEETS

	20X8		*20X7*	
	£	£	£	£
Freehold premises at cost		125,000		75,000
Plant at cost	210,000		125,000	
Less: Depreciation	80,000		55,000	
		130,000		70,000
Debtors		80,000		60,000
Stock		120,000		100,000
		455,000		305,000

£1 ordinary shares	100,000	50,000
Trade creditors	45,000	30,000
7% debentures	50,000	50,000
Bank overdraft	15,000	5,000
Revenue reserves	135,000	120,000
Share premium account	90,000	35,000
Current taxation	20,000	15,000
	455,000	305,000

PROFIT AND LOSS ACCOUNTS

	20X8		20X7	
	£	£	£	£
Sales		525,000		425,000
Trading profit		78,500		61,000
Depreciation	25,000		20,000	
Debenture interest	3,500		3,500	
Corporation tax	20,000		15,000	
Dividends paid	15,000		10,000	
		63,500		48,500
Added to reserves		15,000		12,500

Required

Draw as many conclusions as you can from these accounts using ratio analysis. **(15 marks)**

6 General points about financial ratios

There are some more points on ratio analysis which should be particularly noted.

6.1 Caution in interpretation

Dogmatic conclusions should be avoided. For example, a reduction in the stockholding period may be a good thing, but if it is likely to cause loss of customer goodwill or production dislocations due to stock shortages, it may not be such an advantage. Ratios rarely answer questions but they can highlight areas where questions might usefully be asked.

6.2 Balance sheet figures

Many of the ratios considered in this chapter involve the use of balance sheet figures. These ratios should be interpreted with caution since the balance sheet shows the position at a specific moment only and this may not be typical of the general position. This point is particularly important where the ratio is derived from a balance sheet figure in conjunction with a figure from the trading or profit and loss account. This is because the first figure relates to a moment in time whereas the second is a total for a period. A sensible way to try to avoid possible distortions here is to use the average figure for the balance sheet figure. So, for example, the debtor collection period would relate credit sales to the average of the trade debtor figures at the beginning and at the end of the year. But in many industries the existence of recurrent seasonal factors may mean that averaging beginning and end of year figures will not solve the problem. It may, for example, be that the date up to which a business draws up its final accounts has been selected because it is a time when stock levels are always low, so that stock is relatively easy to value. In such cases, averaging the stock figures for two consecutive year end dates would simply be averaging two figures which were totally untypical of stock levels throughout the rest of the year. Averaging monthly figures would usually be the solution to this problem. However, outsiders would not typically have access to such information.

6.3 Other financial ratios

There are an almost infinite number of ratios which can be calculated from a set of final accounts. The ones shown above are those most commonly used in practice and include those which have been specifically asked about in examination questions. It should be noted, however, that there are many other ratios which could be useful in particular contexts.

6.4 Partial sightedness of ratios

It is usually unwise to limit analysis and interpretation only to information revealed by ratios. For example, sales for a business could double from one year to the next. This would be a dramatic and important development, yet none of the ratios whose use is advocated in most textbooks would reveal this, at least not directly. However, this significant increase in turnover would be fairly obvious from even a superficial glance at the final accounts. There is the danger that excessive reliance on ratios in interpretation and analysis can lead to a 'blinkered' approach.

7 The working capital cycle

7.1 Introduction

The working capital cycle can be illustrated by the following set of activities which underpin the process of manufacture and trade:

- a company acquires stock on credit;
- the stock is held until sold (or used in production);
- the sale is usually made on credit;
- creditors need to be paid and cash needs to be collected from debtors;
- more stock is then acquired and the cycle starts again.

The working capital cycle

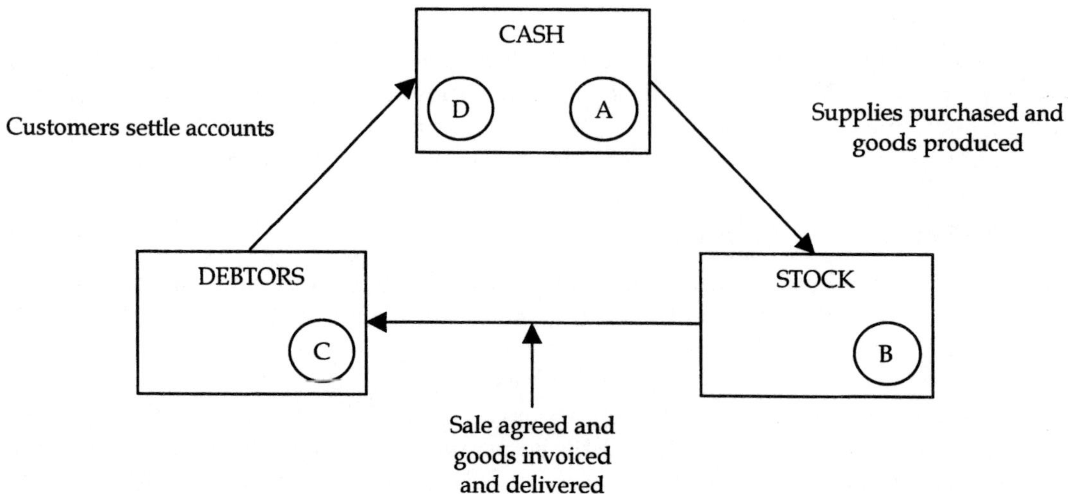

7.2 Effect on cash flows

All of these activities affect cash flows:

- acquisition of stock on credit helps cash flow temporarily;
- when creditors are paid cash flows out;
- while stocks are held, and until customers settle, cash is 'tied up', ie cash inflow is deferred;
- when customers settle, cash flows in.

The longer the period over which cash is tied up, the greater is the exposure of the firm to exceptional demands for cash. In terms of cash management:

- a working cash balance must be retained at the bank to avoid the bank imposing bank interest and charges;
- any surplus cash in excess of the working balance could be invested in higher interest earning accounts.

The longer the period of time that cash is tied up in working capital the more cost that is incurred by companies either directly, by virtue of bank interest, or indirectly, as a result of the inability to invest cash surpluses into higher interest yielding accounts.

7.3 Working capital management

The company must therefore ensure that stock levels are watched very carefully and that debtors' cash is collected on a timely basis whilst simultaneously monitoring the cash balance to ensure that sufficient funds are held for short-term requirements. Any genuinely surplus funds in excess of a working cash balance should be reinvested in higher interest accounts.

Activity 2 *(The answer is in the final chapter of this book)*

C plc

You are the accountant of C plc. F plc is a competitor in the same industry and it has been operating for many years. You have the following information relating to F plc.

(1) *Summarised profit and loss accounts for the year ended 31 December*

	20X6		20X7		20X8	
	£m	£m	£m	£m	£m	£m
Turnover		3,120		2,700		3,000
Materials	630		480		600	
Labour	480		480		600	
Overhead	390		420		450	
		(1,500)		(1,380)		(1,650)
Gross profit		1,620		1,320		1,350
Administrative expenses	780		690		720	
Distribution costs	750		570		690	
		(1,530)		(1,260)		(1,410)
Profit on ordinary activities before taxation		90		60		(60)

(2) *Extracts from the balance sheets at 31 December*

	20X6		20X7		20X8	
	£m	£m	£m	£m	£m	£m
Fixed assets at net book value		1,170		1,110		1,050
Raw material	300		300		300	
Work in progress and finished goods	480		450		480	
Debtors	390		420		450	
		1,170		1,170		1,230
		2,340		2,280		2,280
Creditors: amounts falling due within one year (including bank overdraft)		(810)		(810)		(870)
Capital employed		1,530		1,470		1,410

(3) You may assume that the index of retail prices has remained constant between 20X6 and 20X8.

(4) No fixed assets were purchased or sold by F plc between 20X6 and 20X8.

Required

Write a report for the board of directors of C plc:

(a) analysing the profitability and liquidity of F plc and showing any calculations in an appendix to this report.

(b) explaining the limitations of your analysis of the performance of F plc.

Activity 3 *(The answer is in the final chapter of this book)*

Big Brother plc

Big Brother plc serves the growing market for electronic security systems and equipment. The accounts for the year ended 31 December 20X8 are summarised below.

Profit and loss accounts	*20X8*	*20X7*
	£000	£000
Turnover	51,882	43,217
Cost of sales	(21,705)	(18,221)
Gross profit	30,177	24,996
Expenses	(17,020)	(14,235)
Operating profit	13,157	10,761
Interest payable	(4,695)	(3,574)
Profit before tax	8,462	7,187
Taxation	(3,071)	(2,694)
Profit after tax	5,391	4,493
Dividends	(700)	(600)
Retained profit	4,691	3,893
Reserves brought forward	4,669	776
Reserves carried forward	9,360	4,669

Balance sheets	*20X8*		*20X7*	
	£000	£000	£000	£000
Tangible fixed assets		62,247		51,457
Current assets				
Stocks	8,159		7,181	
Debtors	10,021		8,715	
Cash	3,609		1,924	
	21,789		17,820	
Creditors: amounts falling due within one year	(15,215)		(12,615)	
Net current assets		6,574		5,205
Total assets less current liabilities		68,821		56,662
Creditors: amounts falling due after more than one year				
Loans		(30,105)		(27,419)
Accruals and deferred income				
Rentals in advance		(8,261)		(4,357)
		30,455		24,886

Capital and reserves		
Called up share capital (see note)	10,000	10,000
Share premium account	11,095	10,217
Profit and loss account	9,360	4,669
	30,455	24,886

Note *Called up share capital*

Authorised	£000
40,000,000 Ordinary shares of 50p each	20,000
10,000,000 6% Preference shares of £1 each	10,000
	30,000
Issued (all fully paid)	
10,000,000 Ordinary shares of 50p each	5,000
5,000,000 6% Preference shares of £1 each	5,000
	10,000

The directors have asked for your comments about the profitability, liquidity and solvency of the group and have provided you with the following typical industry statistics which have been independently assimilated from the statutory accounts of companies in the security systems and equipment sector. The industry statistics have been calculated on the basis that accruals and deferred income are included within 'creditors: amounts falling due within one year' and that preference shares are treated as debt.

Gross profit margin	50%
Net profit margin (based on operating profit)	25%
Current ratio	1.20
Quick ratio	0.90
Gearing (debt divided by total capital employed)	50%
Stock turnover (based on year end stocks and cost of sales)	3.5
Debtors turnover (based on year end debtors and net sales)	5.0
Return on capital employed (profit before interest and tax divided by total capital employed)	17%

Required

In your capacity as a financial advisor write a report for submission to the directors of Big Brother plc.

8 Quick quiz *(The answers are in the final chapter of this book)*

1. What is the numerator of the formula for return on capital employed?
2. What is the numerator for return on owners' equity?
3. What is the difference between the current ratio and the acid test ratio?
4. What does the PE ratio measure?
5. What does interest cover measure?

9 Summary

Many ratios can be calculated from a set of financial statements. By comparison with the ratios of other businesses, or of the same business in previous years, it is possible to interpret the messages conveyed by the accounts.

To give structure to your solutions in an assessment it is helpful to analyse ratios under a number of categories. In this chapter we have used the following categories.

- Profitability
- Liquidity and asset utilisation
- Investor ratios
- Ratios relating to risk

CHAPTER 19

Answers to chapter activities

Chapter 1 answers

Quick quiz

1 The Companies Act 1985.

2 Going concern, consistency, prudence, accruals and separate valuation.

3 SSAPs and FRSs.

4 Accounting Standards Board.

5 No. From 2005 listed companies must prepare their consolidated accounts in compliance with IASs.

Chapter 2 answers

1

Going concern	-	Fixed assets are shown in the balance sheet at cost or valuation less accumulated depreciation.
Accruals	-	Closing stock is carried forward at the end of the accounting period to be matched against the revenue from the stock when it is sold in the next accounting period.
Consistency	-	The same depreciation method should be used for all fixed assets of the same class.
Prudence	-	A provision for doubtful debts is set up if there is doubt about the eventual receipt of cash from a debtor.
Non-aggregation	-	When valuing closing stock at the lower of cost and net realisable value, each item or line of stock should be considered separately.

2

Accruals concept and realisation concept.

3

The seven elements of financial statements according to the Statement of Principles are:

- Assets
- Liabilities
- Ownership interest
- Gains
- Losses
- Contributions from owners
- Distributions to owners

Quick quiz

1 The enterprise is assumed to continue in operational existence for the foreseeable future.

2 Items acquired under hire purchase are shown in the purchaser's balance sheet immediately, even though legal title does not pass until the final instalment has been paid.

3 To provide information to a wide range of users.

4 Assets – Liabilities = Ownership interest.

5 Profit and loss account, statement of total recognised gains and losses, balance sheet, cash flow statement.

6 Going concern concept, accruals concept.

Chapter 3 answers

1 Sandro Venus

Task 1

			£	£
1)	DR	Increase in provision for doubtful debts	937	
	CR	Provision for doubtful debts (5% × £18,740)		937
2)	DR	Drawings	500	
	CR	Purchases		500
3)	DR	Motor vehicles - accumulated depreciation	2,400	
	DR	Sundry debtors	3,500	
	CR	Motor vehicles - cost		5,500
	CR	Profit on sale of motor vehicle		400

Task 2

Sandro Venus
Profit and loss account for the year ended 31 March 20X7

		£	£
Sales		187,325	
Less	Returns inwards	1,437	
			185,888
Less	Cost of sales		
	Opening stock	27,931	
	Purchases (103,742 - 500)	103,242	
	Carriage inwards	923	
Less	Returns outwards	(1,014)	
		131,082	
Less	Closing stock	30,229	
			100,853
Gross profit			85,035
Plus	Profit on the sale of motor vehicle		400
	Interest on bank deposit		972
Less	Expenses		
	Wages and NIC	29,344	
	Rent, rates and insurance	7,721	
	Depreciation - Motor vehicles	6,094	
	- Office equipment	1,375	
	- Fixtures and fittings	2,780	
	Bad debts	830	
	Increase in provision for doubtful debts	937	
	Motor expenses	4,762	
	Bank charges	693	
	Lighting and heating	3,755	
	Postage and stationery	524	
	Telephone	4,307	
	Carriage outwards	657	
	Discounts allowed	373	
			(64,152)
Net profit			22,255

Task 3

Notes

(i) A sole trader is liable for all of the debts of the business and his personal possessions can be used to meet the debts of the business. A company normally has limited liability and hence the owners of the business, once they have paid the full value of their shares, cannot be forced to contribute more money to pay for the liabilities of the business.

(ii) In law, there is no distinction between the owner of the business and the business itself for a sole trader. However, a company is a separate legal entity and can sue and be sued in its own right.

(iii) The production of financial statements of a company is regulated by the Companies Act. By law, a company must prepare financial statements in accordance with the requirements of the Companies Acts, send them to members and file them with the Registrar of Companies who makes them available to members of the public. Sole traders are not regulated as to production of financial statements, although they may be required to be produced for taxation and other purposes.

2

Profit and loss account for the year ended 31 March 20X5

		£	£
Sales			106,080
Less:	Cost of sales		
	Opening stock	5,460	
	Purchases (58,760 – 400)	58,360	
	Carriage inwards	570	
		64,390	
Less:	Closing stock	6,100	
			58,290
Gross profit			47,790
Discount received			130
			47,920
Less:	Expenses		
	Motor van depreciation (25,700 × 15%)	3,855	
	Bad debt write off	240	
	Doubtful debts provision ((8,840 – 240) × 3%)	258	
	Discount allowed	160	
	Carriage outwards	800	
	Rent (1,250 × 12/15)	1,000	
	Heat, light and power (1,400 + 200)	1,600	
	Telephone	1,670	
	Wages	25,220	
	Motor expenses	1,700	
			36,503
Net profit			11,417

Note that carriage inwards is treated as part of cost of sales as it is a cost of getting the stock to its current location and condition. Carriage outwards, however, is treated as an expense.

Balance sheet as at 31 March 20X5

	£	£
Fixed assets:		
Motor vans at cost		25,700
Less: Accumulated depreciation (6,460 + 3,855)		10,315
Net book value		15,385
Current assets:		
Stock	6,100	
Debtors (8,840 – 240 – 258)	8,342	
Prepayment – rent (1,250 × 3/15)	250	
Bank	1,420	
	16,112	
Current liabilities:		
Creditors	4,940	
Accruals – electricity	200	
	5,140	
Net current assets		10,972
		26,357
Loan		(5,000)
		21,357
Capital at 1 April 20X4		20,740
Profit for the year		11,417
		32,157
Less: Drawings (10,400 + 400)		10,800
		21,357

3

Profit and loss account for the year ended 30 June 20X4

	£	£
Sales		272,800
Less: Cost of sales		
Opening stock	14,880	
Purchases	175,150	
Carriage inwards	990	
	191,020	
Less: Closing stock	19,800	
		171,220
Gross profit		101,580
Discount received		1,730
		103,310

		£	£
Less:	Expenses		
	Motor vehicle depreciation (20% × (75,000 – 26,000))	9,800	
	Fixtures and fittings depreciation (10% × 18,400)	1,840	
	Electricity	1,490	
	Loan interest (550 + 50)	600	
	Carriage outwards	500	
	Bad debt	1,800	
	Increase in provision for doubtful debts (W1)	60	
	Wages	64,400	
	Discount allowed	2,720	
	Rent (12 × 250)	3,000	
	Insurance (1,980 – 280)	1,700	
			87,910
Net profit			15,400

Balance sheet as at 30 June 20X4

	£	£	£
Fixed assets:			
Motor vehicles	75,000	35,800	39,200
Fixtures and fittings	18,400	6,000	12,400
	93,400	41,800	51,600
Current assets:			
Stock		19,800	
Debtors (24,800 – 1,800)	23,000		
Less: Provision for doubtful debts	460		
		22,540	
Prepayment - insurance		280	
- rent (3,750 – 3,000)		750	
Bank		4,960	
		48,330	
Current liabilities:			
Creditors		14,880	
Accruals - loan interest		50	
		14,930	
Net current assets			33,400
			85,000
Loan			12,500
			72,500
Capital at 1 July 20X3			79,100
Net profit for the year			15,400
			94,500
Less: Drawings			22,000
			72,500

Workings

(W1)

	£
Provision for doubtful debts required (£24,800 – 1,800) × 2%	460
Opening provision	400
Increase in provision	60

Quick quiz

1 Yes.

2 The shareholders are only liable for the company's debts to the amounts unpaid on their shares.

3 Trading account.

4 Stocks, debtors, prepayments, bank balance.

5 The balance sheet of the business.

Chapter 4 answers

1 Pirbright

(a)

Suspense account

	£		£
Incorrect stock in trial balance (£9,880 – £8,220)	1,660	Commission not posted	1,385
		Difference, to be added back to administrative expenses	275
	1,660		1,660

(b)

Profit and loss account for the year ended 31 March 20X8

	£	£
Sales		102,142
Cost of sales (W1)		65,091
		37,051
Selling and distribution expenses (£2,610 + £1,385 + £230)	4,225	
Administrative expenses (W4)	30,621	
		34,846
Net profit before tax		2,205
Less: Taxation (W6)		10,560
Net loss after tax		(8,355)
Profit and loss account balance at 1 April 20X7		7,613
Retained loss carried forward at 31 March 20X8		(742)

Balance sheet at 31 March 20X8

	£	£
Fixed assets (W3) at net book value		
Fixtures and fittings		294
Motor vehicles		7,554
Plant and machinery		5,537
Premises		10,560
		23,945
Current assets		
Stock (£9,880 – £500)	9,380	
Debtors and prepayments	12,390	
Bank (£715 – £187)	528	
	22,298	
Creditors: amounts falling due within one year		
Creditors and accruals (W5)	7,585	
Taxation (due on 1 January 20X9)	10,400	
	17,985	
		4,313
		28,258
Creditors: amounts due after one year		
Debentures		(4,000)
		24,258

Capital and reserves	
Share capital	20,000
Share premium account	5,000
Profit and loss account	(742)
	24,258

Workings

(1) *Cost of sales*

	£
Opening stock (as adjusted)	8,220
Purchases (£66,751 - £500)	66,251
	74,471
Closing stock (£9,880 - £500)	(9,380)
	65,091

(2) *Disposals of fixtures and fittings*

	£
Cost	1,000
Less: Accumulated depreciation (20% × 1 year)	200
Net book value	800
Sales proceeds	400
Loss on disposal	400

(3) *Fixed assets and depreciation*

	F & F	*MV*	*P & M*	*Premises*
Cost	£	£	£	£
Balance b/f	2,280	17,284	16,327	12,000
Add back: Sale proceeds	400			
Less: Disposal (W2)	(1,000)			
	1,680	17,284	16,327	12,000
Depreciation				
Balance b/f	1,250	7,212	9,557	1,200
Disposals (W2)	(200)			
Charge for year				
20% × £1,680	336			
25% × (£17,284 - £7,212)		2,518		
10% × (£16,327 - £4,000)			1,233	
2% × £12,000				240
	1,386	9,730	10,790	1,440
Net book value	294	7,554	5,537	10,560

(4) *Administrative expenses*

		£
Per question		8,474
Trial balance difference		275
		8,749
Loss on disposal (W2)		400
Depreciation (W3)	- Fixtures	336
	- Motor vehicles	2,518
	- Plant	1,233
	- Premises	240
Wages and salaries		18,518
Bank charges		187
		32,181
Less: Taxation paid		1,560
		30,621

(5) *Creditors and accruals*

	£
Per question	7,855
Commission due	230
	8,085
Sale or return	(500)
	7,585

(6) *Taxation charge*

	£
Current year	10,400
Under provision in previous year (1,560 – 1,400)	160
	10,560

2 Collins

Trading and profit and loss account for the year ended 31 December 20X8

	£	£
Turnover		142,770
Cost of sales (W1)		107,770
Gross profit		35,000
Administrative expenses (W1)	23,797	
Distribution costs (W1)	7,507	
		31,304
Profit before and after corporation tax		3,696
Proposed dividend (5% × 80,000)		4,000
Retained loss for the year		(304)
Retained profit brought forward		2,430
Retained profit carried forward		2,126

Balance sheet at 31 December 20X8

	Cost	Depn	
	£	£	£
Fixed assets			
Freehold property (59,000 + 380)	59,380		59,380
Motor vans (W3, W4)	15,095	9,294	5,801
	74,475	9,294	65,181
Current assets			
Stock		14,600	
Debtors and prepayments, less provision for doubtful debts (12,395 – 1,075 – 350 + 140)		11,110	
Cash at bank		6,615	
		32,325	
Current liabilities			
Creditors		11,380	
Proposed dividend		4,000	
		15,380	
			16,945
			82,126
Capital and reserves			
Ordinary shares of £1 each			80,000
Profit and loss account			2,126
			82,126

Workings

(1)

	Cost of sales	Admin expenses	Distribution costs
	£	£	£
Opening stock	13,930		
Purchases	108,440		
Directors' remuneration		4,000	
Wages and salaries		13,127	
Rates (700 – 140)		560	
Legal expenses (644 – 380)		264	
General		5,846	
Bad debts (W2)			1,150
Motor and delivery			3,258
Loss on sale (W5)			80
Depreciation (W4)			3,019
Closing stock	(14,600)		
	107,770	23,797	7,507

(2)

Bad debts

	£		£
Debtors (written off)	1,075	Provision b/f	275
Provision c/f	350	Profit and loss account (bal fig)	1,150
	1,425		1,425

(3)

Motor vans - cost

	£		£
Balance b/f	15,000	Disposals	680
Additions (650 + 125)	775	Balance c/f	15,095
	15,775		15,775

(4)

Provision for depreciation

	£		£
Disposals	475	Balance b/f	6,750
Balance c/f	9,294	Profit and loss account	3,019
		(15,095 × 20%)	
	9,769		9,769

(5)

Disposals

	£		£
Motor vans	680	Provision for depreciation	475
		Proceeds	125
		Loss on disposal	80
	680		680

Quick quiz

1 Public companies can offer their shares to the public.

2 Debit cash, Credit share capital.

3 Debit cash £3,000
Credit share capital £1,000
Credit share premium £2,000

4 Debit cash £18,000
Credit share capital £10,000
Credit share premium £8,000

Chapter 5 answers

1 Suzanne

Balance sheet as at 31 March 20X5

	Notes	£	£
Fixed assets			
Tangible assets	2		315,520
Current assets			
Stocks		320,000	
Debtors	3	360,000	
Cash at bank and in hand		180,000	
		860,000	
Creditors: amounts falling due within one year	4	420,000	
Net current assets			440,000
Total assets less current liabilities			755,520
Creditors: amounts falling due after more than one year	5		(120,000)
			635,520
Capital and reserves			
Called up share capital	6		400,000
Profit and loss account	7		235,520
			635,520

Notes to the accounts

1 *Statement of accounting policies*

(a) The accounts have been prepared in accordance with the historical cost convention and applicable accounting standards.

(b) Depreciation is charged at the following rates.

1 Leasehold factory

Depreciation is calculated at 2% per annum on cost.

2 Plant and machinery

Depreciation is calculated on the reducing balance method at 20% per annum. Assets acquired in the year are charged a full year's depreciation.

(c) Stock has been valued at the lower of cost and net realisable value.

2 *Tangible assets*

	Long leasehold property	*Plant and machinery*	*Total*
	£	£	£
Cost			
At 1 April 20X4	400,000	160,000	560,000
Additions	-	20,000	20,000
Disposals	-	(32,000)	(32,000)
At 31 March 20X5	400,000	148,000	548,000
Accumulated depreciation			
At 1 April 20X4	152,000	60,000	212,000
Eliminated on disposal	-	(6,400)	(6,400)
Charge for year	8,000	18,880	26,880
At 31 March 20X5	160,000	72,480	232,480
Net book value at 31 March 20X4	248,000	100,000	348,000
Net book value at 31 March 20X5	240,000	75,520	315,520

3 *Debtors*

	£
Trade debtors	200,000
Prepayments and accrued income	160,000
	360,000

4 *Creditors: amounts falling due within one year*

	£
Trade creditors	340,000
Proposed dividend (400 × 20%)	80,000
	420,000

5 *Creditors: amounts falling due after more than one year*

This consists of 6% debenture stock. The debenture stock is secured on the leasehold factory.

6 *Called up share capital*

	Authorised	*Allotted and fully paid*
Ordinary shares of £1 each	£500,000	£400,000

7 *Profit and loss account*

	£
Retained profit as at 1 April 20X4	122,000
Add: retained profit for the year (W3)	113,520
Retained profit as at 31 March 20X5	235,520

Workings

(W1) *Depreciation*

Leasehold factory £400,000 × 2%	£8,000
Plant and machinery	
Net book value brought forward	100,000
Additions	20,000
Disposals at net book value	(25,600)
	94,400
At 20%	£18,880

(W2) *Disposal of plant*

Disposal account

	£		£
Cost	32,000	Proceeds	24,000
		Depreciation	6,400
		Loss on disposal	1,600
	32,000		32,000

(W3) *Retained profit for the year*

	£
Per trial balance	(98,000)
Add back closing stock	320,000
Less depreciation (£8,000 + £18,880) (W1)	(26,880)
Loss on sale (W2)	(1,600)
Proposed dividend £400,000 × 20%	(80,000)
	113,520

2 Prescriptive

Advantages and disadvantages of prescriptive formats

Advantages

(i) Aid comparability both between companies and between successive sets of accounts for the same company by

(1) prescribing classifications which are understandable as common to all accounts rather than allowing each company to choose its own terms

(2) ensuring same emphasis is given to certain items in the accounts (eg dividends must always be shown on the face of the profit and loss account).

(ii) Ensure companies must disclose key information which they may have wished to overlook eg directors' emoluments.

(iii) Reduce time and cost of producing accounts year on year due to staff expertise.

Disadvantages

(i) The format may be too inflexible and could fail to reflect the specific nature of a company's accounts.

(ii) Potentially too arduous and worthless for small owner managed companies.

---

3 Readycut

Profit and loss account for the year ended 30 September 20X2

	Notes	*£000*
Turnover	1	318,000
Cost of sales (W1)		(267,428)
Gross profit		50,572
Distribution costs (W1)		(29,381)
Administrative expenses (W1)		(8,065)
Operating profit	2	13,126
Interest payable and similar charges (W3)	4	(540)
Profit on ordinary activities before taxation		12,586
Tax on profit on ordinary activities	5	(4,340)
Profit on ordinary activities after taxation		8,246
Dividends paid and proposed	6	(1,690)
Retained profit for the financial year		6,556

Notes to the accounts

(1) *Accounting policies*

(a) Depreciation is charged on a straight line basis to write off the cost of each asset over its expected useful life.

The following rates are used.

Buildings	2% pa
Plant and machinery	20% pa
Fixtures and fittings	10% pa

(b) Turnover represents sales for the year.

(c) Stock is valued at the lower of cost and net realisable value.

(2) *Operating profit is stated after charging the following*

	£000
Directors' emoluments	
Fees	34
Other emoluments	366
Auditors' remuneration	93
Depreciation (W2)	666

(3) *Directors' emoluments*

Highest paid director	£156,000

(*Tutorial note:* This disclosure is required since the aggregate emoluments exceed £200,000.)

(4) *Interest payable*

	£000
Loan interest (6,000 × 9%)	540

(5) *Taxation*

	£000
Estimated tax charge for the year	4,360
Over provision for corporation tax in prior period	(20)
	4,340

(6) *Dividends paid and proposed*

	£000	£000
8% preference shares		
Paid	120	
Proposed	120	
Total (£3,000,000 × 8%)		240
Ordinary shares		
Paid	370	
Proposed (4,500 × 24%)	1,080	
		1,450
		1,690

Workings

(W1) *Cost of sales, distribution costs and administrative expenses*

	Direct cost of sales £000	*Selling and distribution costs* £000	*General and admin expenses* £000
Provision for bad debts		131	
Auditors' remuneration			93
Depreciation (W2)			
Buildings	78		
Plant and machinery	516		
Fixtures and fittings			72
Directors' emoluments			400
Admin expenses			7,500
Distribution costs		29,250	
Opening stock	9,000		
Purchases	267,662		
Closing stock	(9,828)		
	267,428	29,381	8,065

(W2) *Depreciation*

	£000
Buildings 3,900 × 2%	78
Plant and machinery 2,580 × 20%	516
Fixtures and fittings 720 × 10%	72
Total depreciation	666

(W3) *Loan interest*

	£000
6,000 × 9%	540

---

4 KL

(a)

KL plc
Profit and loss account for the year ended 31 December 20X4

	Note	£000	£000
Turnover			7,000
Cost of sales (W1)			(3,354)
Gross profit			3,646
Distribution costs (W1)			(866)
Administrative expenses (W1)			(870)
Operating profit	1		1,910
Loss on discontinued operations	2		(350)
Income from current asset investments			6
Interest payable	3		(34)
Profit on ordinary activities before tax			1,532
Tax on profit on ordinary activities	4		(961)
Profit for the financial year			571
Dividends			
Ordinary – Paid		(36)	
Ordinary – Proposed		(72)	
			(108)
Retained profit for the financial year			463
Retained profit brought forward			416
Retained profit carried forward			879

KL plc
Balance sheet as at 31 December 20X4

	Note	£000	£000	£000
Fixed assets				
Tangible assets	5			2,376
Current assets				
Stocks - Raw materials		390		
- Work in progress		255		
- Finished goods		615		
			1,260	
Debtors (580 - 22)			558	
Investments			28	
			1,846	
Creditors: amounts falling due within one year	6		(1,642)	
Net current assets				204
Total assets less current liabilities				2,580
Provisions for liabilities and charges				
Deferred taxation	7			(137)
				2,443
Capital and reserves				
Called up share capital				600
Share premium account				200
Revaluation reserve	8			764
Profit and loss account				879
				2,443

Notes to the accounts

(1) *Operating profit*

Operating profit is stated after accounting for:

	£000	£000
Depreciation		378
Audit fee		14
Staff costs		1,560
Directors' emoluments		
- Fees	36	
- Other emoluments	101	
		137

(2) Loss on discontinued operations

This loss arose on the sale of a subsidiary company UJ Ltd.

(3) Interest payable

Interest is payable on a bank overdraft.

(4) Tax on profit on ordinary activities

	£000
Corporation tax based on the profit on ordinary activities for the year	920
Under provision in previous year	14
Transfer to deferred taxation	27
	961

(5) Tangible fixed assets

	Property £000	*Plant* £000	*Total* £000
Cost at 1 January 20X4	1,200	1,820	3,020
Revaluation	300	-	300
Disposals	-	(50)	(50)
Cost or valuation at 31 Dec 20X4	1,500	1,770	3,270
Depreciation at 1 January 20X4	440	570	1,010
Revaluation	(464)	-	(464)
Disposals		(30)	(30)
Charge for the year	24	354	378
	-	894	894
Net book value at 31 December 20X4	1,500	876	2,376
Net book value at 1 January 20X4	760	1,250	2,010

The freehold property was revalued at 31 December 20X4 by S and J, Chartered Surveyors. Their valuation amounted to £1,500,000.

(6) Creditors: amounts falling due within one year

	£000
Bank overdraft	280
Trade creditors	320
Corporation tax	920
Proposed dividends	72
Accruals	50
	1,642

(7) Deferred taxation

	£000
Deferred taxation	137

(8) Revaluation reserve

	£000
Balance 1 January 20X4	-
Surplus on revaluation of freehold property	764
Balance 31 December 20X4	764

Workings

(W1) Expenses in profit and loss account

	Cost of sales £000	*Distribution costs* £000	*Administrative expenses* £000
Purchases	1,280		
Wages	800	340	420
Administration costs			400
Selling and advertising		480	
Manufacturing overhead	740		
Opening stocks			
Raw materials	370		
Work in progress	410		
Finished goods	640		
Bad debts		44	
Closing stocks			
Raw materials	(390)		
Work in progress	(255)		
Finished goods	(615)		
Depreciation			
Buildings (2% × 1,200)	24		
Plant (20% × (1,820 – 50))	354		
Profit on disposal (W2)	(4)		
Audit fees			14
Directors' fees			36
Increase in provision for doubtful debts		2	
	3,354	866	870

(W2)

Plant and machinery disposal account

	£000		£000
Cost	50	Sale proceeds (per TB)	24
Profit (bal figure)	4	Depreciation (20% × 50 × 3)	30
	54		54

Quick quiz

1 Format 1, the vertical format.

2 Format 1, the vertical format.

3 Yes.

4 Yes. It satisfies the criteria for assets and employees.

Chapter 6 answers

1 Fallen

Cash flow statement for the year ended 31 December 20X8

	£000	£000
Net cash inflow from operating activities (note 1)		5,271
Returns on investments and servicing of finance		
Interest paid		(152)
Taxation (W5)		(1,775)
Capital expenditure		
Payments to acquire plant	(2,500)	
Payments to acquire leasehold premises	(1,300)	
Receipts from sales of plant	168	
		(3,632)
Equity dividends paid (W4)		(544)
Management of liquid resources		
Payments to acquire investments		(198)
Financing		
Issue of ordinary share capital (480 + 312)	792	
Redemption of debenture loan	(560)	
		232
Decrease in cash		(798)

Notes to the cash flow statement

(1) Reconciliation of operating profit to net cash inflow from operating activities

	£000
Operating profit (4,625 + 152)	4,777
Depreciation (400 + 964) (W1/W2)	1,364
Loss on disposal (W3)	108
Increase in deferred repairs provision	186
Increase in stock	(894)
Increase in debtors	(594)
Increase in creditors	324
Net cash inflow from operating activities	5,271

(2) Reconciliation of net cash flow to movement in net funds (note 3)

	£000	£000
Decrease in cash in the period	(798)	
Cash to redeem debenture	560	
Cash used to increase liquid resources	198	
Change in net funds		(40)
Net funds at 1 January 20X8		984
Net funds at 31 December 20X8		944

(3) **Analysis of changes in net funds**

	At 1 January 20X8	Cash flows	At 31 December 20X8
	£000	£000	£000
Cash in hand, at bank	576	(576)	-
Overdrafts	-	(222)	(222)
		(798)	
Debt	(1,800)	560	(1,240)
Current asset investments	2,208	198	2,406
Total	984	(40)	944

Workings

(1)

Leasehold premises (NBV)

	£000		£000
Brought forward	5,700	Depreciation (balance)	400
Additions	1,300	Carried forward	6,600
	7,000		7,000

(2)

Plant (NBV)

	£000		£000
Brought forward	3,780	Disposals	276
Additions	2,500	Depreciation (balance)	964
		Carried forward	5,040
	6,280		6,280

(3)

Disposals

	£000		£000
Plant	276	Cash	168
		Loss on sale (balance)	108
	276		276

(4)

Dividends

	£000		£000
Cash (balance)	544	Balance brought forward	234
Carried forward	390	Profit and loss account	700
	934		934

(5)

Taxation

	£000		£000
Cash (balance)	1,775	Balance brought forward	2,176
Carried forward	1,932	Profit and loss account	1,531
	3,707		3,707

2 Oxford

Cash flow statement for the year ended 30 June 20X8

	£	£
Net cash inflow from operating activities (note)		44,100
Returns on investments and servicing of finance		
Interest paid		(3,200)
Taxation (W4)		(1,100)
Capital expenditure		
Payments to acquire tangible fixed assets (W5)	(36,800)	
Receipts from sales of fixed assets	4,200	
		(32,600)
Equity dividends paid (W3)		(9,200)
Management of liquid resources		
Purchase of bank deposit		(13,000)
Financing		
Issue of ordinary share capital (W6)		20,000
Increase in cash (£7,100 - £2,100)		5,000

Note Reconciliation of operating profit to net cash inflow from operating activities

	£
Operating profit	38,900
Depreciation charges (W1)	11,800
Profit on sale of fixed assets (W2)	(2,800)
(Increase) in stocks (£11,100 – £10,000)	(1,100)
(Increase) in debtors (£11,000 – £7,500)	(3,500)
Increase in creditors (£13,400 – £12,600)	800
Net cash inflow	44,100

Workings

(1)

Accumulated depreciation

	£		£
Depreciation on disposals	12,600	b/d	48,300
c/d	47,500	Depreciation charge for the year (balancing figure)	11,800
	60,100		60,100

(2)

Disposal account

	£		£
Plant and machinery (cost)	14,000	Provision for depreciation	12,600
Profit on disposal (balancing fig)	2,800	Cash proceeds	4,200
	16,800		16,800

(3)

Proposed dividends

	£		£
Dividends paid (balancing figure)	9,200	b/d	6,000
c/d	7,700	Dividends in P/L a/c	10,900
	16,900		16,900

(4)

Tax liability

	£		£
Tax paid (balancing figure)	1,100	b/d	700
c/d	900	Charge for year	1,300
	2,000		2,000

(5)

Plant and machinery (cost)

	£		£
Brought forward	99,000	Disposal (cost)	14,000
Additions (balancing figure)	36,800	Carried forward	121,800
	135,800		135,800

(6) *Issue of shares for cash*

	£
Nominal value of shares issued	15,000
Increase in share premium	5,000
Proceeds of share issue	20,000

Quick quiz

1 No. Small companies are excused.

2 Non-equity dividend.

3 Added.

4 Net debt = £10m + £2m - £1m = £11m.

Chapter 7 answers

1 Puffin (I)

Consolidated balance sheet as at 31 December 20X1

	£000
Fixed assets	
Intangible assets (W3)	50
Tangible assets (146 + 35)	181
Current assets (24 + 15)	39
	270
Creditors: amounts falling due within one year (30 + 10)	(40)
	230
Capital and reserves	
Share capital	100
Profit and loss account	130
	230

Workings

(W1) *Group structure*

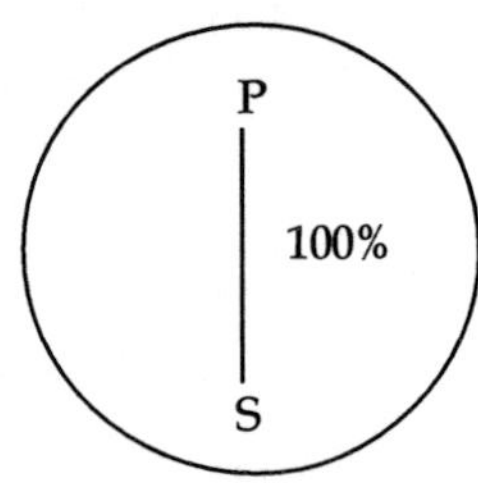

(W2) *Net assets of Seagull Ltd*

	At date of acquisition £000	*At balance sheet date* £000
Share capital	40	40
Reserves	-	-
	40	40

(W3) *Goodwill*

	£000
Purchase consideration	90
For 100% of net assets acquired	(40)
Goodwill	50

2 Puffin (II)

Consolidated balance sheet as at 31 December 20X1

	£000
Fixed assets	
Intangible assets (W3)	54
Tangible assets (146 + 35)	181
Current assets (24 + 15)	39
	274
Creditors: amounts falling due within one year (30 + 10)	(40)
	234
Capital and reserves	
Share capital	100
Profit and loss account	130
	230
Minority interest (W4)	4
	234

Workings

(W1) *Group structure*

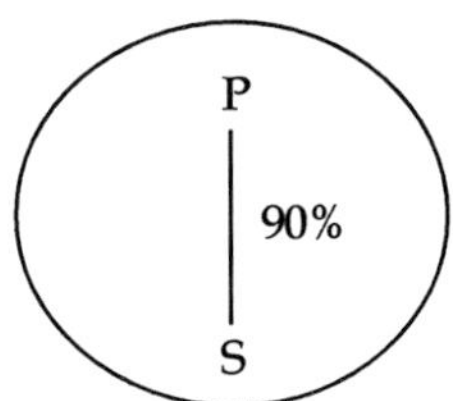

(W2) *Net assets of Seagull Ltd*

	At date of acquisition £000	*At balance sheet date* £000
Share capital	40	40
Reserves	-	-
	40	40

(W3) *Goodwill*

	£000
Purchase consideration	90
For 90% of net assets acquired [40] (W2)	(36)
Goodwill	54

(W4) *Minority interests*

10% of net assets at balance sheet date [40] (W2)	4

3 Pluto

Consolidated balance sheet as at 31 December 20X8

	£000
Fixed assets	
Intangible assets (W3)	35
Tangible assets (120 + 150)	270
Current assets (40 + 50)	90
	395
Creditors: amounts due within one year (40 + 30)	(70)
	325
Capital and reserves	
Share capital	100
Profit and loss account (W5)	182.5
	282.5
Minority interest (W4)	42.5
	325

Workings

(W1) *Group structure*

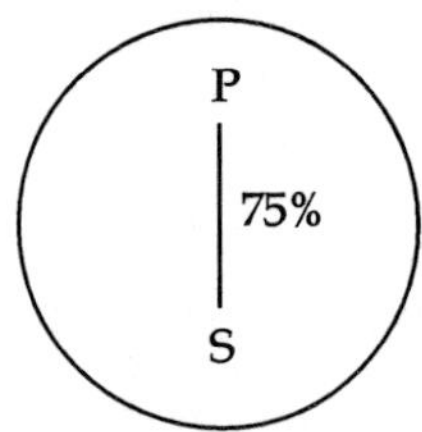

(W2) *Net assets – Snoopy Ltd*

	At date of acquisition £000	*At balance sheet date* £000
£1 shares	100	100
Profit and loss	40	70
	140	170

(W3) *Goodwill*

	£000
Purchase consideration	140
For 75% of net assets acquired (140)	(105)
Goodwill	35

(W4) *Minority interest*

	£000
25% of net assets at balance sheet date (170)	42.5

(W5) *Group profit and loss account*

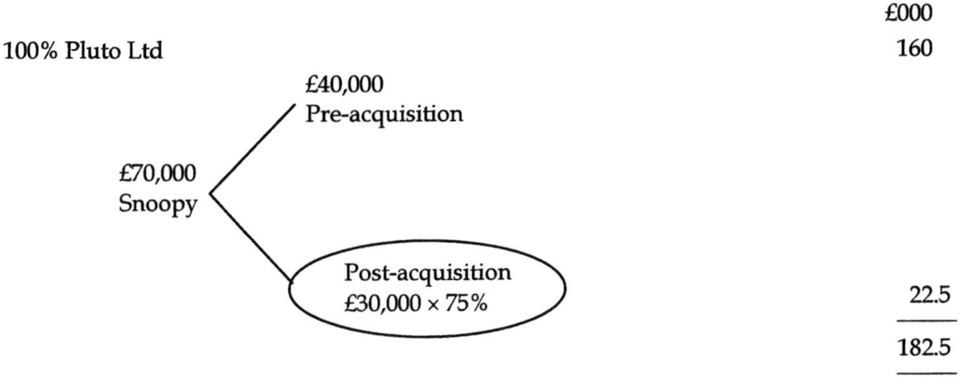

	£000
100% Pluto Ltd	160
Post-acquisition £30,000 × 75%	22.5
	182.5

4 Dublin

Consolidated balance sheet as at 31 December 20X9

	£
Fixed assets	
Intangible (W3)	1,600
Tangible (100,000 + 60,000)	160,000
	161,600
Current assets (215,000 + 50,000)	265,000
Creditors: amounts due under one year (150,000 + 20,000)	(170,000)
	256,600
Capital and reserves	
Called up share capital	190,000
Profit and loss account (W5)	30,600
	220,600
Minority interest (W4)	36,000
	256,600

Workings

(W1) *Group structure*

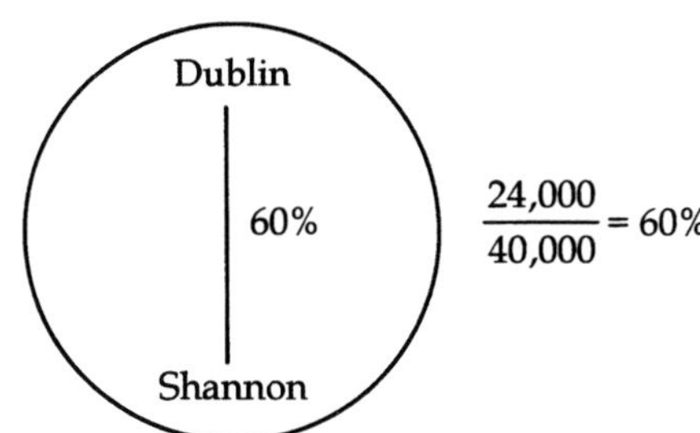

$\frac{24,000}{40,000} = 60\%$

(W2) *Net assets – Shannon*

	At the date of acquisition	At the balance sheet date
	£	£
Share capital	40,000	40,000
Profit and loss account	40,000	50,000
	80,000	90,000

(W3) *Goodwill*

	£
Purchase consideration	50,000
For 60% net assets acquired (80,000)	(48,000)
Goodwill	2,000

In consolidated balance sheet: £2,000 × 4/5 = £1,600

(W4) *Minority interest*

40% (90,000)	£36,000

(W5) *Group reserves*

	£
100% Dublin	25,000
£50,000 Shannon: £40,000 Pre-acquisition; Post-acquisition £10,000 × 60%	6,000
Less goodwill amortised $\frac{2,000}{5}$	(400)
	30,600

5 Prince plc

Consolidated balance sheet at 31 December 20X4

	£	£
Fixed assets		
Intangible assets: Goodwill (W3)		10,000
Tangible assets (60 + 40 + 32)		132,000
		142,000
Current assets (90 + 86 + 52)	228,000	
Creditors: Amounts falling due within one year (50 + 41 + 40)	(131,000)	
Net current assets		97,000
Total assets less current liabilities		239,000
Creditors: Amounts falling due after more than one year (18 + 30 + 10)		(58,000)
		181,000
Capital and reserves		
Called-up share capital		60,000
Profit and loss account (W4)		121,000
		181,000

Workings

(1) Group structure

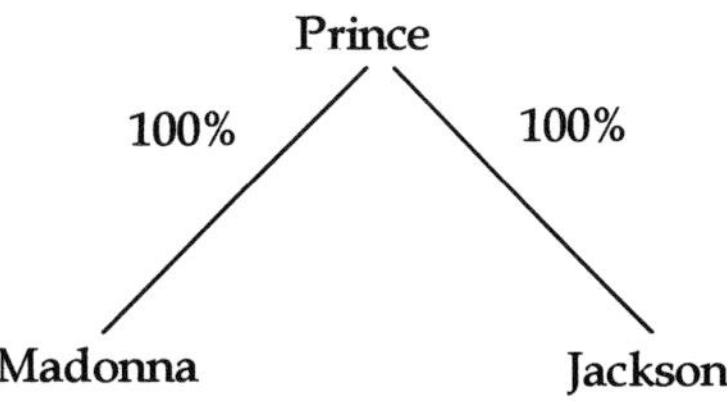

(2) Net assets at acquisition

	Madonna £	*Jackson* £
Share capital	50,000	30,000
Profit and loss account (5 – 1, 4 – 3)	4,000	1,000
	54,000	31,000

(3) Goodwill schedule

	Madonna £	*Jackson* £
Cost of investment	60,000	40,000
Net assets acquired (W2)	(54,000)	(31,000)
Goodwill	6,000	9,000
Less: amortisation ($\frac{1}{3}$)	(2,000)	(3,000)
	4,000	6,000

Total at balance sheet date = 4,000 + 6,000 = 10,000.

(4) Profit and loss account schedule

		£
P		122,000
M's post-acquisition profit		1,000
J's post-acquisition profit		3,000
		126,000
Less:	Goodwill (W3)	(5,000)
		121,000

---

6 Heavy plc

Consolidated balance sheet as on 31 March 20X1

		£	£
Fixed assets:			
Intangible assets: Goodwill (W3)			2,240
Tangible assets (180 + 40)			220,000
			222,240
Current assets			
Stocks (40 + 32)		72,000	
Cash at bank and in hand (3 + 2.5) (W6)		5,500	
		77,500	
Creditors: Amounts falling due within one year			
Bank loans and overdrafts		6,000	
Trade creditors (41 + 17)		58,000	
Proposed dividends	– parent company	10,000	
	– minority interests	400	
		74,400	
Net current assets			3,100
Total assets less current liabilities			225,340
Creditors: Amounts falling due after more than one year			
Debenture loans			(50,000)
			175,340
Capital and reserves			
Called-up share capital – £1 ordinary shares			100,000
Share premium account			20,000
Profit and loss account (W5)			42,040
			162,040
Minority interests (W4)			13,300
			175,340

Workings

(1) Group structure

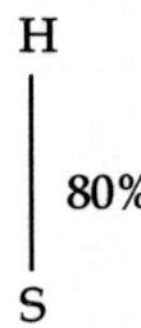

(2) Net assets of Side Ltd

	Acquisition	*Balance sheet date*	
	£	£	£
Share capital	10,000		10,000
Share premium	10,000		10,000
Profit and loss			
Per question		48,500	
Dividend proposed		(2,000)	
	38,000		46,500
	58,000		66,500

Reserves at acquisition = £48,500 – £10,500 = £38,000

(3) Goodwill

		£
Cost of acquisition		49,200
Share of net assets acquired	80% × 58,000 (W2)	(46,400)
		2,800
Less: amortisation ($\frac{1}{5}$)		(560)
		2,240

(4) Minority interest

20% × 66,500 (W2)	13,300

(5) Profit and loss

	£
Heavy plc	44,200
Dividend proposed	(10,000)
Dividend receivable (80% × 2,000)	1,600
Side Ltd post-acquisition [80% × (46,500 – 38,000) (W2)]	6,800
Goodwill (W3)	(560)
	42,040

(6) Cash in transit

	£	£
Dr Cash at bank	2,500	
Cr Inter-company account		2,500

Quick quiz

1 Goodwill = £100,000 – 90% × £80,000 = £28,000.

2 Minority interests = 20% × £100,000 = £20,000.

3 Purchased goodwill should be capitalised as a fixed asset and amortised over its life.

4 This is cash in transit, which must be included in group cash in the consolidated balance sheet.

Chapter 8 answers

1 Pulp plc

Consolidated profit and loss account for the year ending 31 March 20X2

	£000
Turnover (650 + 380 – 80)	950
Cost of sales (320 + 180 - 80)	420
Gross profit	530
Expenses (190 + 90)	280
Profit before tax	250
Tax (50 + 30)	80
Profit after tax	170
Minority interest (40% × 80)	32
	138
Proposed dividend (P only)	70
Retained profit for the year	68
Retained profit brought forward 112 + ((35 – 20) × 60%)	121
Retained profit carried forward	189

2 Courage Ltd

Consolidated profit and loss account for the year ended 31 December 20X4

	£
Turnover (3,000 + 900 – 10)	3,890,000
Cost of sales (1,700 + 600 – 10 + 2)	(2,292,000)
Gross profit	1,598,000
Distribution costs (300 + 100)	(400,000)
Administrative expenses (600 + 96.8 + 4 (W2))	(700,800)
Operating profit	497,200
Loss on sale of fixed asset investment	(50,000)
Reorganisation costs	(10,000)
Profit on ordinary activities before interest	437,200
Income from other fixed asset investments (8 + 2)	10,000
Interest payable and similar charges (3.2 – 1.6)	(1,600)
Profit on ordinary activities before taxation	445,600
Tax on profit on ordinary activities (159.6 + 40)	(199,600)
Profit on ordinary activities after taxation	246,000
Minority interests (W3)	(20,000)
Profit for the financial year attributable to members of Courage Ltd	226,000
Dividends – proposed	(20,000)
Retained profit for the financial year	206,000
Retained profits brought forward (W4)	99,800
Retained profits carried forward	305,800

Workings

(1) Group structure

Courage Ltd

| 60%

Brains Ltd

(2) Goodwill

Goodwill of £20,000 is being written off over five years, so the annual amortisation charge is £20,000 ÷ 5 = £4,000.

(3) Minority interest

	£
Share of subsidiary's profit after tax (40% × 52)	20,800
Share of unrealised profit (40% × 2)	(800)
	20,000

(4) Retained profits brought forward

	£
Courage Ltd	100,000
Brains Ltd [60% × (25,000 – 12,000)]	7,800
Less goodwill amortised (2 × 4,000)	(8,000)
	99,800

Quick quiz

1 £100,000 + £50,000 = £150,000.

2 Debit group turnover, Credit group cost of sales.

3 Goodwill = £500,000 - 60% × £600,000
= £140,000

Annual amortisation charge = $\frac{1}{5}$ × £140,000 = £28,000.

Chapter 9 answers

1 A, B and C Ltd

Consolidated balance sheet as at 31 March 20X2

	£
Interest in associated undertakings (3,000 × 30%)	900
Other net assets (5,250 + 4,000)	9,250
	10,150
Share capital	3,000
Profit and loss account (W5)	5,550
	8,550
Minority interest (W4)	1,600
	10,150

Workings

(W1) *Group structure*

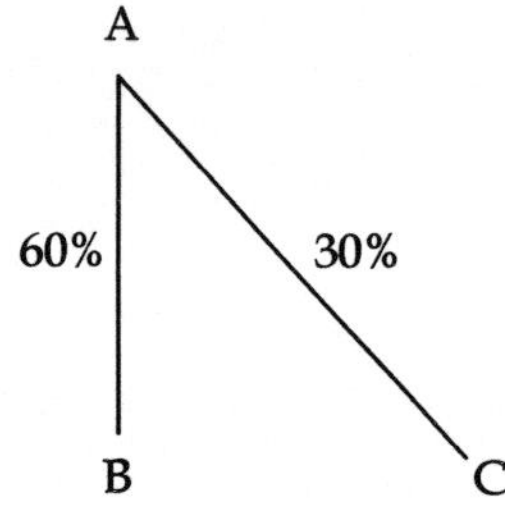

(W2) *Net assets working*

B Ltd

	At acquisition	*At balance sheet date*
	£	£
Share capital	1,000	1,000
Profit and loss account	400	3,000
	1,400	4,000

C Ltd

	£	£
Share capital	1,000	1,000
Profit and loss account	1,000	2,000
	2,000	3,000

(W3) *Goodwill*

		£
B Ltd	Cost	1,000
	Net assets acquired 60% × 1,400 (W2)	840
		160

		£
C Ltd	Cost	750
	Net assets acquired 30% × 2,000 (W2)	600
		150

(W4) *Minority interest*

	£
B Ltd only – 40% × 4,000 (W2)	1,600

(W5) *Profit and loss account*

	£
A Ltd	4,000
B Ltd 60% × (3,000 – 400)	1,560
C Ltd 30% × (2,000 – 1,000)	300
Less: Goodwill (160 + 150) (W3)	(310)
	5,550

---

2 **D, E and F Ltd**

Consolidated profit and loss account for the year ended 30 June 20X1

	£	£
Turnover (440,000 + 180,000)		620,000
Cost of sales (210,000 + 80,000)		290,000
Gross profit		330,000
Administrative expenses (80,000 + 30,000)		110,000
		220,000
Income from interests in associated undertakings (30% × 65,000)		19,500
		239,500
Tax on profit on ordinary activities		
Group (46,000 + 20,000)	66,000	
Share of associated undertakings (30% × 18,000)	5,400	
		71,400
Profit on ordinary activities after tax		168,100
Minority interest (25% × 50,000)		12,500
		155,600
Dividends		60,000
Retained profit for the year		95,600

Quick quiz

1 Yes. P controls S.

2 No. Small groups are excused.

3 A is an associate, so should be included in the group's accounts using equity accounting.

4 Acquisitions.

Chapter 10 answers

1 Sunshine

(When approaching an assessment test on FRS 3 do make sure you consider whether the discontinuation or sale of an operation fulfils the strict definition of the standard. In this case it does, but do not assume it should. If you feel it does not then write down that it has been included in continuing operations and justify your classification. Even if you are incorrect and it should be treated as discontinued, you will gain some credit for having applied your knowledge.)

Profit and loss account for the year ended 31 December 20X4

	Continuing operations £m	*Discontinued operations* £m	*Total* £m
Turnover	2,609.0	100	2,709.0
Net operating costs	2,252.2	51	2,303.2
Operating profit	356.8	49	405.8
Interest receivable			8.2
Profit on ordinary activities before taxation			414.0
Taxation			148.0
Profit on ordinary activities after taxation			266.0
Dividends			95.0
Retained profit			171.0

2 Coffee Ltd

Statement of total recognised gains and losses for the year ended 31 December 20X1

	£000
Profit for the year	450
Asset revaluation	48
Investment property devaluation	(20)
Total gains for the year	478

Reconciliation of movements in shareholders' funds for the year ended 31 December 20X1

	£000
Profit for the year	450
Dividend	(120)
	330
Other recognised gains and losses (48 + (20))	28
New shares issued	140
Net addition to shareholders' funds	498
Opening shareholders' funds	945
Closing shareholders' funds	1,443

3 Claret

Statement of total recognised gains and losses for the year ended 31 December 20X8

	£000
Profit for the financial year (1,825 + 250 - 62 + 55)	2,068
Unrealised surplus on revaluation (W1)	40
	2,108
Prior period adjustment (note 2)	(55)
Total gains and losses recognised since last annual report	2,053

Notes to the accounts

(1) Reconciliation of shareholders' funds

	£000
Profit for the financial year (W3)	2,068
Dividends	(250)
Surplus on revaluation	40
Shares issued (160 × £2.10)	336
Net addition to shareholders' funds	2,194
Opening shareholders' funds (W2)	21,741
Prior period adjustment	(55)
Closing shareholders' funds	23,880

(2) Prior period adjustment

The prior period adjustment is in respect of a fundamental error in the valuation of stock. Closing stock and, hence, reserves at 31 December 20X7 were overstated by £55,000.

Workings

(1) Unrealised surplus on revaluation

	£000	£000
Revalued amount		430
Original cost	650	
Accumulated depreciation to 31 December 20X8 (650 × 8/20)	(260)	
Net book value at revaluation		(390)
		40

(2) Opening total shareholders' funds

	£000
Share capital (2,000 × 50p)	1,000
Profit and loss account	20,658
Revaluation reserve	83
	21,741

(3) Profit for the financial year

	£000	£000
Retained profit		1,825
Add back dividend		250
Profit for financial year		2,075
Less overstatement of stock		
Opening stock	55	
Less closing stock	(62)	
		(7)
		2,068

---

4 Meld

(a) Profit and loss account for the year ended 30 June 20X4

	Continuing operations	*Acquisitions*	*Total*
	£	£	£
Turnover	468,000	4,800	472,800
Cost of sales and expenses (W)	(356,500)	(3,600)	(360,100)
Operating profit	111,500	1,200	112,700
Interest payable and similar charges			(15,000)
Profit on ordinary activities before taxation			97,700
Tax on profit on ordinary activities			(28,800)
Profit for the financial year			68,900
Dividends			(21,600)
Retained profit for the financial year			47,300

(b) Statement of total recognised gains and losses for the year

	£
Profit for the financial year	68,900
Unrealised surplus on revaluation of fixed assets (28,800 – (19,200 – 7,200))	16,800
Total recognised gains and losses relating to the year	85,700
Prior year adjustment (34,560 – 20,160)	(14,400)
Total gains and losses recognised since last annual report	71,300

(c) Note of historical cost profits and losses for the year

	£
Reported profit on ordinary activities before taxation	97,700
Difference between a historical cost depreciation charge and the actual depreciation charge for the year calculated on the revalued amount	3,360
Historical cost profit on ordinary activities before taxation	101,060
Historical cost profit for the year retained after taxation and dividends (47,300 + 3,360)	50,660

(d) **Reconciliation of movements in shareholders' funds for the year**

	£
Profit for the financial year	68,900
Dividends	(21,600)
	47,300
Other recognised gains and losses relating to the year	16,800
Net addition to shareholders' funds	64,100
Opening shareholders' funds (£456,000 before the prior-year adjustment of £14,400)	441,600
Closing shareholders' funds	505,700

(e) **Statement of reserves**

	Revaluation reserve £	*Profit and loss account* £	*Total* £
At 1 July 20X3			
As previously stated	48,000	168,000	216,000
Prior year adjustment	-	(14,400)	(14,400)
As restated	48,000	153,600	201,600
Retained profit for the year	-	47,300	47,300
Surplus on property revaluations	16,800	-	16,800
Transfer of realised profits	(3,360)	3,360	-
At 30 June 20X4	61,440	204,260	265,700

Working

Cost of sales and expenses

	£
Per question	376,800
Interest	(15,000)
Acquisition element	(3,600)
Change of accounting policy regarding development costs	
Amortisation	(4,800)
Expenditure incurred	3,100
	356,500

---

5 Radar

Basic earnings per share

Actual number of shares (thousands)	×	*Fraction of year*	×	*Rights issue bonus fraction*	*Total*
18,000 (W1)	×	$\frac{9}{12}$	×	$\frac{140}{125}$ (W2)	15,120
21,600 (W3)	×	$\frac{3}{12}$			5,400
Weighted average number of shares to be used in earnings per share					20,520

$$\text{Earnings per share} = \frac{\text{£830,000(W4)}}{20{,}520{,}000} = \text{4p per share for 20X3.}$$

The 20X2 restated comparative EPS is 6.3p per share (W5).

Workings

(W1) **Original shares**

4,000 × 4	16,000
Bonus issue	2,000
	18,000

(W2) **Rights issue bonus fraction**

	£
5 shares at £1.40	7.00
1 share at £0.50	0.50
6 shares	7.50

$$\frac{7.50}{6} = \text{£1.25 = Price after rights issue}$$

$$\text{Therefore rights issue bonus fraction} = \frac{\text{£1.40}}{\text{£1.25}}$$

(W3) **Shares after rights issue**

New shares 18,000 × $\frac{1}{5}$ =	3,600
Original shares	18,000
	21,600

(W4) **Earnings**

	£000
Profit after tax	910
Less preference dividend	(80)
	830

(W5) **Restate comparative**

To restate the comparative when there has been a bonus issue and a rights issue, multiply by reciprocal of bonus fraction and rights fraction.

$$8p \times \frac{8}{9} \text{ (bonus)} \times \frac{1.25}{1.40} \text{ (rights)} = \text{6.3p restated}$$

Quick quiz

1 No. Discontinued operations must have ceased permanently.

2 Exceptional items derive from within the ordinary activities, while extraordinary items derive from outside the ordinary activities.

3 No. It is a change in an accounting estimate.

4 $$\text{EPS} = \frac{\text{Profit after tax}}{\text{Number of ordinary shares}} = \frac{\text{£8m}}{\text{40m}} = \text{20p}$$

Chapter 11 answers

1 Ford plc

Accounting policy note

(1) *Tangible fixed assets*

Interests in buildings are stated at a valuation.

Other tangible fixed assets are stated at cost, together with any incidental expenses of acquisition.

Depreciation is calculated so as to write off the net cost or valuation of tangible fixed assets over their expected useful economic lives. A full year's charge is provided in the year of acquisition. The rates and bases used are as follows:

Buildings - on the straight-line basis	2% pa
Plant and machinery - on the straight-line basis	10% pa
Office equipment and fixtures - on the straight-line basis	20% pa
Motor vehicles - on the reducing-balance method	30% pa

(2) *Operating profit*

Operating profit is stated after charging:

	£000
Depreciation of tangible fixed assets	562

(3) *Tangible fixed assets*

	Freehold land and buildings £000	*Plant and machinery* £000	*Motor vehicles* £000	*Fixtures, fittings, tools and equipment* £000	*Total* £000
Cost or valuation					
At 1 January 20X7	1,440	1,968	449	888	4,745
Additions	500	75	35	22	632
Revaluations	760	-	-	-	760
At 31 December 20X7	2,700	2,043	484	910	6,137
Depreciation					
At 1 January 20X7	144	257	194	583	1,178
Revaluation adjustment	(144)				(144)
Charge for year	60	233	87	182	562
At 31 December 20X7	60	490	281	765	1,596
Net book value					
At 31 December 20X7	2,640	1,553	203	145	4,541
At 1 January 20X7	1,296	1,711	255	305	3,567

(a) Buildings were valued for the purposes of the 20X7 accounts at existing use value. This valuation was made by a firm of independent chartered surveyors. The historical cost of the factory is £1,940,000 and the related historical cost accumulated depreciation is £183,000 (W).

(b) The company's depreciation policy on motor vehicles has been changed from a rate of 25% pa on cost to a rate of 30% pa on reducing balance in order to give a fairer presentation of the results and of the financial position. The effect of this change is to reduce the depreciation charge for the year by £34,000.

Working

Historical cost depreciation of factory

	£000
Factory $6/50 \times 1{,}440$	173
Extension $1/50 \times 500$	10
	183

2 Hamilton

(a) There are circumstances in which companies are permitted to change their accounting policies, as follows.

- When changing the accounting policies will result in a fairer presentation of the financial statements of a company.
- A change may be required by statute. For example the Companies Act 1985 changed the definition of a subsidiary. This could mean that an entity which was not previously a subsidiary, and therefore not included in the group accounts, now falls within the definition of a subsidiary and so must be included in the group accounts.
- A new accounting standard may be different from the previous approach, which is then no longer acceptable. For example FRS 3 changed the presentation of exceptional items on the face of the profit and loss account and any other presentation is no longer acceptable.

The term 'change in accounting policy' can be confusing – for example a change in a depreciation policy (eg straight line to reducing balance) is not a change in accounting policy whereas to begin to depreciate an asset not previously depreciated is classed as a change in accounting policy.

Hamilton plc has proposed a change in accounting policy to change the balance sheet classification of the property to a leasehold building. This would require a different accounting treatment. The property must be shown at cost or revalued amount and depreciated over its useful life. In this case 'cost' would be the carrying value at the date of the change of use, not the property's original cost. As an investment property it would have been revalued each year and not depreciated. The property now has a different accounting treatment but this is not a change in accounting policy for the purposes of FRS 3.

(b) (i) On the assumption that the surveyor's valuation is correct the financial statements for the year ended 31 March 20X8 would show the property at a value of £3.6 million. The profit and loss account would show any rental income received and would have no other changes.

From 1 April 20X8 the property would be leasehold property at the same value and depreciation of £163,636 would be charged annually to the profit and loss account. The fall in value that will occur during the year to 31 March 20X9 need not be reflected in the financial statements unless it is considered to be an impairment.

(ii) If the value of the property had fallen in the year to 31 March 20X8 the effect on the financial statements for that year would be the fall in value of the property to £2.7 million being the revalued amount in the current year. This should be reflected as the new balance sheet value and the deficit would be applied to reverse the previous revaluation surplus of £600,000 (£3.6 million – £3 million) through the Statement of Total Recognised Gains and Losses and the additional fall of £300,000 should either also be charged to the Statement of Total Recognised Gains and Losses thus creating a negative 'investment property revaluation' reserve, or be charged to the profit and loss account.

The effect on the financial statements for the year to 31 March 20X9 would be that depreciation of £122,727 (£2.7 million/22 years – remaining life) would be charged annually.

Quick quiz

1 Optional.

2 The depreciation method should reflect the pattern in which the asset's economic benefits are consumed.

3 Open market value.

4 No. The grant must be credited to revenue over the useful life of the asset concerned.

Chapter 12 answers

1 Plant

(a) Purchased goodwill is goodwill which is established as a result of a purchase of a business. Under these circumstances goodwill is measured as the difference between the value of the business as a whole and the aggregate value of the separable tangible and intangible assets. This represents a valuation of goodwill at the time of acquisition but does not attempt to identify how such goodwill has been created.

All other forms of goodwill are considered to be non-purchased goodwill. Whilst it is possible to speculate about how such goodwill has come into existence, (eg from the reputation of the business as a supplier of quality goods, good customer and/or staff relations, advantageous location etc) any list such as the foregoing cannot be considered either complete or definitive. Any expenditure incurred in creating circumstances where goodwill may arise cannot be directly related to the value of the resulting goodwill, and indeed may be completely unrelated to any goodwill in the business.

(b) FRS 10 requires that purchased positive goodwill should be capitalised as an intangible fixed asset. Where goodwill has a limited useful economic life it should be amortised over its expected life through the profit and loss account. The straight-line method should normally be used. Where goodwill is regarded as having an indefinite useful economic life, it should not be amortised.

There is a rebuttable presumption that the useful economic life of goodwill does not exceed 20 years. However, FRS 10 allows that the useful economic life of goodwill can be more than 20 years or even indefinite provided that the durability of the goodwill can be demonstrated and that the goodwill is capable of continued measurement. Where the useful economic life of goodwill is more than 20 years annual impairment reviews must be performed in order to identify any fall in value. The value of the goodwill should then be written down if necessary.

FRS 10 requires capitalisation of purchased goodwill for the following reasons.

- Including goodwill in the balance sheet means that users of the financial statements recognise that it is part of the cost of an investment, a cost for which management remains accountable.
- There is consistency between the treatment of goodwill and other assets.

Non-purchased goodwill should not be capitalised.

It can be argued that goodwill meets the definition of an asset in the ASB's Statement of Principles. However, only where the historical costs of creating or acquiring an asset are known is it capable of being measured with sufficient reliability to be recognised in the financial statements.

Where goodwill has been purchased, the cost of the goodwill has been established by an actual transaction, and is a matter of fact. Where goodwill has been generated internally any valuation can only be subjective. For this reason non-purchased goodwill cannot be included in the balance sheet.

(c) (i) SSAP 13 *Accounting for Research and Development* defines three categories of research and development expenditure as follows.

Pure research: experimental or theoretical work undertaken primarily to acquire new scientific or technical knowledge for its own sake rather than directed towards any specific aim or application.

Applied research: original or critical investigation undertaken in order to gain new scientific or technical knowledge and directed towards a specific practical aim or objective.

Development: use of scientific or technical knowledge in order to produce new or substantially improved materials, devices, products or services; to install new processes or systems prior to the commencement of commercial production or commercial applications; or to improving substantially those already produced or installed.

(ii) Apart from the cost of fixed assets acquired or constructed in order to provide facilities for research and development activities over a number of accounting periods, SSAP 13 permits only development expenditure to be capitalised provided it meets the following criteria.

- There is a clearly defined project; and
- The related expenditure is separately identifiable; and
- The outcome of such a project has been assessed with reasonable certainty as to its technical feasibility and commercial viability.
- The total of the deferred development costs, any further costs, and related production, selling and administration costs is reasonably expected to be exceeded by future sales and other revenues.
- Resources are available to enable completion of the project.

---

2 Newprods Ltd

(a) Expenditure on pure and applied research should be written off in the year of expenditure. However, the cost of fixed assets acquired or constructed in order to provide facilities for research and development activities over a number of years should be capitalised and written off over their useful life.

Expenditure on development should be written off in the year of expenditure except in the following circumstances when it may be carried forward:

(i) there is a clearly defined project;

(ii) the related expenditure is separately identifiable;

(iii) the outcome of such a project has been assessed with reasonable certainty as to:

- its technical feasibility; and
- its ultimate commercial viability considered in the light of factors such as likely market conditions (including competing products), public opinion, consumer and environmental legislation;

(iv) the aggregate of the deferred development costs, further development costs and related production, selling and administration costs is reasonably expected to be exceeded by related future sales or other revenues; and

(v) adequate resources exist, or are reasonably expected to be available, to enable the project to be completed and to provide any consequential increases in working capital.

The principle behind the above rules is that development expenditure should only be carried forward if the recovery of that expenditure can reasonably be regarded as assured.

(b) *Project 3*

Project 3 may be regarded as development (as defined in SSAP 13) and therefore it may be correct to carry forward a certain amount of the expenditure. However, the cost of producing the new compound is comparable to that of the existing raw material and therefore unless selling prices are increased the expenditure which has been incurred in developing the new compound will not be recovered in future periods.

Assuming that selling prices cannot be increased the expenditure should be shown as follows.

Balance sheet

	£
Fixed assets	
Tangible assets (at cost less depreciation)	9,000

Profit and loss account

	£
Development expenditure written off	11,000
Depreciation	1,000

Project 4

This is also development expenditure. As the yield of the operation is being greatly improved the material costs will obviously decrease and greater profits will be made. Thus the expenditure incurred in development may be recovered in future years. To determine how much of the expenditure may be carried forward it is necessary to calculate whether the aggregate of costs already incurred and future costs will be covered by the saving of material costs which is predicted.

The saving of material costs per annum is £30,000 and the life of the plant is ten years. Therefore, assuming no increases in the costs of the materials the new process will produce a saving of £30,000 per annum for some years. As the costs to date are only £22,000 plus fixed assets cost of £20,000 it seems highly probable that the expenditure will be recovered in future years. It is necessary to assume that the market for the product and its selling price will remain unchanged.

The treatment of the expenditure on Project 4 will therefore be as follows.

Balance sheet

	£
Fixed assets	
Intangible asset: development costs (22,000 + 2,000)	24,000
Tangible assets (20,000 – 2,000)	18,000

A note to the balance sheet should state:

(i) the reasons for capitalising the expenditure; and
(ii) the period over which the costs are being written off.

Note: No charge for development expenditure has been made this year as the commercial production has not yet commenced. The development costs should be amortised over a period coincident with the commercial use of the process.

Project 5

This project should be regarded as development work which is being carried out on behalf of a third party. If there is a firm contract which states that the expenditure is to be fully reimbursed then any such expenditure which has not been reimbursed at the balance sheet date should be included in work in progress.

The treatment would therefore be as follows.

Balance sheet

	£
Fixed assets	
Tangible assets	4,500
Current assets	
Stocks: Work in progress	44,500

Quick quiz

1 Negative goodwill arises when the value of a company is less than the aggregate of the fair values of the net assets.

2 Research costs must be written off as incurred.

3 If a life greater than 20 years is used, then annual impairment reviews must be carried out.

4 Recoverable amount is the higher of net realisable value and value in use.

Chapter 13 answers

1 S Ltd

(a) Raw materials should be valued at the lower of cost and net realisable value where cost includes all costs in bringing the items to their balance sheet location and conditions.

Both delivery and insurance costs could be included in this definition and so legitimately be added to the valuation, as long as they have been incurred in bringing the stock items to their present location and condition.

(b) (i) SSAP 9 suggests that where overheads are absorbed into production it should be on the basis of a normal level of activity. The costs to be included would be all production overheads, and, at management's discretion, a portion of administrative overheads. Selling overheads should never be included in stock valuation.

(ii) WIP valuation

		£000
Overheads	– variable (300 + 200)	500
	– fixed (150 + 240 + 110)	500
		1,000

Normal level of activity = 95,000 hours

Absorbed into WIP $£1,000,000 \times \frac{500}{95,000} = £5,263$

Notes

(1) It is assumed that delivery vehicles are used in selling and so depreciation is not absorbed into stock.

(2) Alternatively, only some or possibly none of the administrative expenses might be absorbed. If none, this would give:

$£(1,000,000 - 240,000) \times \frac{500}{95,000} = £4,000$

(c) (i) Valuation at cost or net realisable value should be carried out on a product line-by-line basis in accordance with SSAP 9 and the Companies Act 1985. The latter also specifies that the value of assets and liabilities should be determined for individual items not in aggregate. The finance director's statement is therefore incorrect.

(ii) *Obsolete items* must be valued at £500, their net realisable value since this is lower than cost.

New product line. It seems likely from the initial market research that net realisable value will be considerably greater than the cost of £90,000. These items should thus be included at £90,000. If in a later period the launch proves unsuccessful the stock will need to be written down to £1,000 and, if material, may be shown as an exceptional item.

Quick quiz

1 100 × £3.50 = £350.
2 Physical deterioration, obsolescence.
3 No.
4 Raw materials, work in progress and finished goods.

Chapter 14 answers

1 Rubislaw plc

Profit and loss account (extract) for the year ended 31 December 20X3

	£
Tax on profit on ordinary activities (**Note 1**) (W1)	(40,000)

Balance sheet (extract) at 31 December 20X3

	£
Creditors: Amounts falling due within one year	
Other creditors including taxation and social security (**Note 2**)	45,000

Notes to the accounts

		£
(1)	*Tax on ordinary activities*	
	Corporation tax on ordinary activities (W1)	45,000
	Overprovision for previous year (W1)	(5,000)
		40,000

		£
(2)	*Taxation (balance sheet)*	
	Corporation tax due on 1.10.X4 (W1)	45,000

Workings

		£
(1)	*CT for accounting period ended 31.12.X3*	
	Profits	150,000
	Corporation tax at 30%	45,000
	Tax charge for the year	£
	CT for year ended 31.12.X3	45,000
	Overprovision for 31.12.X2 (£74,000 – £69,000)	(5,000)
		40,000

Quick quiz

1 Nine months after the balance sheet date.

2 Timing difference.

3 Full provision.

4 Exclusive.

Chapter 15 answers

1 Finch

(a) SSAP 21 states that a finance lease is a lease that transfers substantially all the risks and rewards of ownership to the lessee. It should be presumed that such a transfer of risks and rewards occurs if, at the inception of a lease, the present value of the minimum lease payments, including any initial payment, amounts to substantially all (normally 90% or more) of the fair value of the leased asset.

In this case the present value of the minimum lease payments is £4,100,000 and the fair value of the machinery was £4,680,000. This amounts to

$$\frac{4{,}100{,}000}{4{,}680{,}000} \times 100 = 88\% \text{ of the fair value of the machinery}$$

We can see therefore that we are outside the 90% rule. However the 90% rule is only a rule of thumb. The rule is 'is there a transfer of the risks and rewards of ownership to the lessee?'. Whilst the 90% rule of thumb is an indicator of whether such a transfer has occurred, it is not conclusive.

In this case other factors outweigh the 90% guideline and indicate that the lease should be classified as a finance lease. Firstly, the machinery was purchased by Tyrrell plc to Finch Ltd's specifications and it is therefore unlikely that Tyrrell plc would be able to lease it to any other organisation. Secondly, the lease period covers five years of the seven-year useful life of the machinery, which provides further evidence that it would be difficult to lease the asset to another organisation as it will effectively be obsolete at the end of the current lease. Thirdly, Finch Ltd is responsible for the maintenance and insurance of the machinery.

The lease should therefore be classified as a finance lease.

(b) If we treat the lease as a finance lease we capitalise based on the present value of the minimum lease payments. This means we will include it in the balance sheet as an asset and as an obligation to pay future rentals, ie a creditor. The asset will then be depreciated over the shorter of the lease term and its useful life.

The profit and loss account will be charged with a finance charge calculated by one of the following methods.

- The actuarial method – recommended by SSAP 21 but requiring complicated calculations.
- The sum of digits – a good approximation to the actuarial method and much simpler to calculate.
- The straight line method – suitable for small leases only since its apportionment of the finance charge can be quite inaccurate.

The accounting treatment required for the balance sheet is to debit fixed assets and credit creditors with £4,100,000. In the profit and loss account, if we use the actuarial method, we would calculate the interest charge based on the implied rate of interest of 14.2%. This produces a finance charge of £4,100,000 × 14.2% = £582,200.

	£000
At the end of year 1 the amount outstanding in creditors will be the original capital sum	4,100
Plus finance charge at 14.2%	582
Less lease payment	(1,200)
Creditor at end of year 1	3,482

Quick quiz

1 Finance lease. The term of the lease is for the entire useful life of the leased asset.

2 No.

3 SSAP 21 requires lessees to show assets acquired under finance leases, and the related obligation, on the balance sheet.

Chapter 16 answers

1 Jam Limited

Post balance sheet events are those events, both favourable and unfavourable, which occur between the date of the balance sheet and the date on which the financial statements are approved by the board of directors. There are two types of post balance sheet event: an adjusting event provides additional evidence of conditions existing at the balance sheet date which thus need to be reflected in the financial statements, whereas a non-adjusting event concerns conditions which did not exist at the balance sheet date but which need to be disclosed by way of notes in the financial statements to ensure a true and fair view is shown.

(i) **Stock loss by flood:** the loss occurred before the year end. The agreement of the company's insurers to the full claim is an adjusting event within the meaning of SSAP 17 and thus the amount of the full claim should be accrued in current assets. Separate disclosure may be necessary as an exceptional item.

The financial consequences of the flood (eg non-availability of stock) is a non-adjusting event and thus (in the accounts) full disclosure should be made of:

- details of the flood; and
- an estimate of the financial effect, or a statement that an estimate cannot be made.

(ii) **Returnable containers:** the company should enquire about the supplier's insurance and review the conditions on which the containers were received on loan. If liability is admitted then this is an adjusting event and a suitable accrual should be made. If liability is not admitted then the company should consider disclosure as a contingent liability after taking appropriate legal advice (ie where the ultimate outcome will be confirmed only on the occurrence or non-occurrence of one or more uncertain future events (eg a pending or possible lawsuit)).

(iii) **Payment for advertising:** advertising expenses are charged against the income of the period in which the advertising or clearly definable services took place (accruals concept). Thus the first week's advertising will be charged to the year ended 31 October 20X1. The amount of pre-payment of the second week carried forward depends on the value of the work already done. For instance if printing has been completed before the year end then this cost should be charged in 20X1, but any subsequent distribution and advertising costs not incurred until after the year end should be charged in the 20X2 accounts.

(iv) **Ban on company's activities:** the ban may involve both adjusting and non-adjusting events. Since the ban will probably result in the closing of a significant part of the company's trading activities and is thus a non-adjusting event, a note to the accounts stating a description and estimate of the financial effect will be required.

The ban may also affect estimates of amounts in the financial statements for the year ended 20X1, eg realisable value of stock, value of patents, and is thus an adjusting event.

Additionally, a review of the application of the going concern principle may be necessary, depending on the effect of the ban, eg are adequate alternative markets available? Is adequate finance available to enable the company to expand into these alternative markets?

2 Hill plc

(a) (i) *Problems of lack of guidance*

The ASB felt it was necessary to introduce a standard on provisions because the lack of guidance in this area had led to the following problems.

Inconsistency of treatment. Where a diverse range of accounting treatments is possible this will lead to a lack of comparability between the financial statements of companies.

Consistency and comparability are key principles to be applied if financial statements are to give a true and fair view.

Growth of creative accounting. Provisions had been used more and more as a method of profit smoothing in an attempt to mislead equity investors.

Risk. Equity investors are in general perceived to be risk averse. They react unfavourably to large fluctuations in reported profit. A gently increasing pattern of profits over time gives the impression of quality earnings.

Big bath provisions. This in turn has led companies to make large one-off provisions in years where a high level of underlying profits is generated. These general provisions, often known as 'big bath' provisions, smooth profits in future years as the provision is released, producing years of apparent good news.

Economic reality. Financial statements should reflect the substance (commercial reality) and if profits fluctuate then the equity investors should be informed through the annual report.

(ii) FRS 12 states that provisions should be recognised when, and only when:

1 an enterprise has a present legal or constructive obligation as a result of past events

2 it is probable that a transfer of economic benefits will be required to settle the obligation

3 a reliable estimate of the amount required to settle the obligation can be made. A reliable estimate can be made even if there is a range of possible outcomes.

An obligation exists when the entity has no realistic alternative to making a transfer of economic benefits. This is the case only where the obligation can be enforced by law or in the case of constructive obligation (see below). No provision is recognised for costs that need to be incurred to operate in the future. The only liabilities recognised are those that exist at the balance sheet date. The obligations must have arisen from past events and must exist independently from the company's future actions. If the company can avoid the expenditure by its future actions then no provision is recognised. These rules are designed to allow a provision to escape recognition only in rare cases. In these rare cases there is an obligation if, having taken into account all available evidence, it is more likely than not that a present obligation exists at the balance sheet date.

It is not necessary to know the identity of the party to whom the obligation is owed in order for an obligation to exist but in principle there must be another party. The mere intention or necessity to incur expenditure is not enough to create an obligation. Where there are a number of similar obligations the whole class of obligations must be considered when determining whether economic benefits will be transferred.

There is a need to provide for legal obligations although there is the important issue of timing and the identification of the past event which triggers the recognition. However FRS 12 also deals with the concept of 'constructive obligation', for example where a retail store gives refunds to dissatisfied customers even though there is no legal obligation to do so in order to preserve its reputation. Therefore, an entity may be committed to certain expenditure because any alternative would be too onerous to contemplate. The determination of a constructive obligation is extremely difficult; it is a somewhat subjective concept.

(b) (i) *Factory closure*

The key issue is whether or not a provision should be made for the £79 million cost of restructuring. This will depend per FRS 12 on whether the group has an obligation to incur this expenditure.

There is clearly no legal obligation to close this factory but there may be a constructive obligation. FRS 12 states that a constructive obligation only exists if the group has created valid expectations in other parties such as customers, employees and suppliers, that the restructuring will be carried out.

As no formal plan exists and no announcements have been made to any of the affected parties, no constructive obligation exists. A board decision alone is not sufficient – no provision should be made.

(ii) *Legal proceedings*

It is unlikely the group has a present obligation to compensate the customer and therefore no provision should be recognised.

There may be a contingent liability but as the possibility of a transfer of economic benefit is remote we can ignore this in the accounts.

(iii) *Environmental damage*

The company has no legal obligation to rectify this damage, but through its published policies it has created expectation on the part of those affected that it will take action to do so. There is therefore a constructive obligation to rectify the damage. It is probable that a transfer of economic benefits will take place and an estimate of the amount involved can be made.

A provision should be made of the best estimate of the cost involved, ie the full amount of £15 million should be provided for.

Quick quiz

1 Adjusting event.
2 Non-adjusting event.
3 A contract whose unavoidable costs exceed the expected revenues.
4 No. Contingent assets should be disclosed in a note to the accounts.

Chapter 17 answers

Quick quiz

1 Yes. The shares have been issued to raise finance.

2 All three companies are related to each other.

3 Defined benefit schemes.

Chapter 18 answers

1 Falcon

As a first step, you could rehash the draft accounts into a presentable form to throw out the figures you need.

Balance sheets

	20X8		20X7	
	£	£	£	£
Fixed assets				
Premises		125,000		75,000
Plant		130,000		70,000
		255,000		145,000
Current assets				
Stock	120,000		100,000	
Debtors	80,000		60,000	
	200,000		160,000	
Creditors: amounts falling due within one year				
Trade creditors	45,000		30,000	
Overdraft	15,000		5,000	
Taxation	20,000		15,000	
	80,000		50,000	
		120,000		110,000
		375,000		255,000
Creditors: amounts falling due more than one year				
7% Debentures		50,000		50,000
		325,000		205,000
Capital and reserves				
£1 ordinary shares		100,000		50,000
Share premium account		90,000		35,000
Profit and loss account		135,000		120,000
		325,000		205,000

Profit and loss accounts

	20X8	20X7
	£	£
Sales	525,000	425,000
Trading profit	53,500	41,000
Debenture interest	3,500	3,500
Profit before tax	50,000	37,500
Taxation	20,000	15,000
Profit after tax	30,000	22,500
Dividends	15,000	10,000
	15,000	12,500

(a) **Return on capital employed**

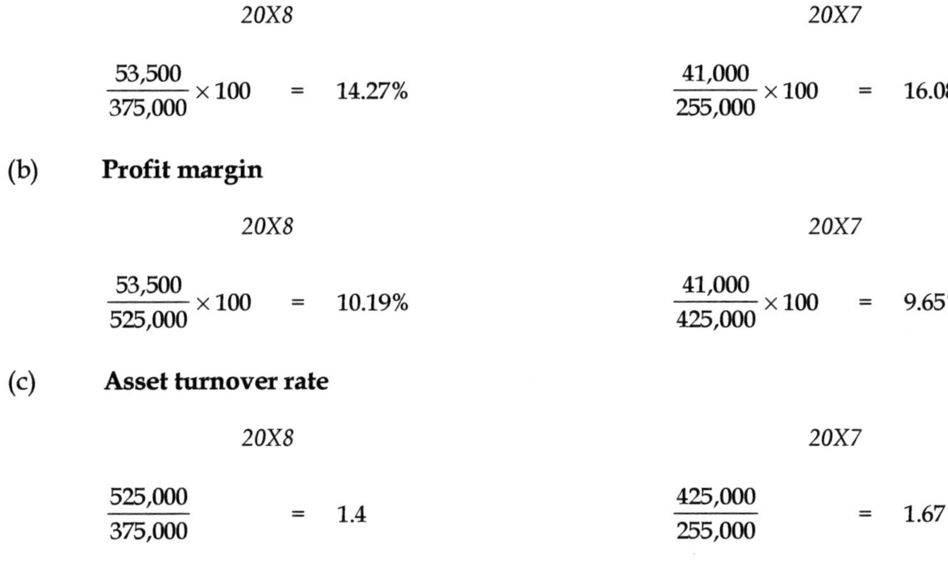

20X8	*20X7*
$\frac{53,500}{375,000}\times 100 = 14.27\%$	$\frac{41,000}{255,000}\times 100 = 16.08\%$

(b) **Profit margin**

20X8	*20X7*
$\frac{53,500}{525,000}\times 100 = 10.19\%$	$\frac{41,000}{425,000}\times 100 = 9.65\%$

(c) **Asset turnover rate**

20X8	*20X7*
$\frac{525,000}{375,000} = 1.4$	$\frac{425,000}{255,000} = 1.67$

(d) **Stock turnover rate**

20X8	*20X7*
$\frac{525,000}{120,000} = 4.37$	$\frac{425,000}{100,000} = 4.25$

Note: As there is no figure for cost of sales, the sales figure has been used instead.

(e) **Current ratio**

20X8	*20X7*
$\frac{200,000}{80,000} = 2.5$	$\frac{160,000}{50,000} = 3.2$

(f) **Acid test ratio**

20X8	*20X7*
$\frac{80,000}{80,000} = 1.0$	$\frac{60,000}{50,000} = 1.2$

(g) **Debt collection period**

20X8	*20X7*
$\frac{80,000}{525,000}\times 365 = 56$ days	$\frac{60,000}{425,000}\times 365 = 52$ days

Comments

Profitability

The return on capital employed has worsened and this is as a result of less efficient use of assets. (The asset turnover has deteriorated whereas the profit margin has improved). If we look at the assets individually the stock turnover and the debtors turnover should not have caused any substantial reduction of the asset turnover; the major change appears to have occurred in the fixed assets where at some point during the year, extra capital has been raised for a major investment in fixed assets. If these assets were purchased towards the end of the year then this would have made the figure for assets at the year end unrepresentative of the assets used throughout the year. If we take the average of the beginning and year end assets, the return on capital employed is 16.98%. Therefore, before we can draw any firm conclusions about the performance of the company, we need further information about the purchase of the fixed assets.

Liquidity

The ratios used to measure liquidity have also worsened during the year. This is mostly due to a large increase in the overdraft, perhaps to part-finance the purchase of the fixed assets. Once again, it is necessary to establish whether the year end picture is really representative of the year as a whole before coming to any firm conclusions.

Finance

The gearing ratio has been reduced over the year owing entirely to the large amount of share capital raised to finance the purchase of the fixed assets.

---

2 C and F

(a) **REPORT**

To	The Board of Directors of C plc
From	The Accountant
Subject	Analysis of F plc
Date	X.X.20XX

This report analyses the profitability and liquidity of our competitor F plc over the period 20X6 to 20X8. I draw attention to the Appendix to the report which gives a statistical analysis of key ratios.

Profitability

In absolute terms, the net profit of the company has fallen in recent years, from £90 million in 20X6, through £60 million in 20X7, to a net loss of £60 million in 20X8. This deterioration in performance has arisen for a number of reasons.

Turnover slumped in 20X7, falling 13% from the 20X6 level, and only partially recovered in 20X8.

While material costs and overheads have been reasonably constant as a proportion of turnover, labour costs have increased. The direct costs have reached a point, therefore, such that in 20X8 the indirect expenses exceeded the gross profit.

The levels of both administrative expenses and distribution costs are high, each consuming 20 to 25% of turnover. Though the proportions of turnover that these represent have remained reasonably level over the period under review, the absolute levels nevertheless are high.

Liquidity

The current ratio is constant at a level of about 1.4 to 1, which may be satisfactory for companies in certain sectors, but the low quick ratio of around 0.5 is almost certainly a cause for significant concern. The difference between the two arises from the high stock levels held: for example, around 200 days' supply of raw materials. A lack of control over stock levels is indicated, as indeed a lack of control over debtors is indicated by the high debtor days figure. If the company is offering the traditional one month's credit for goods supplied, the debtor days figure should be able to be substantially below the current 50 days.

No fixed assets were purchased or sold in the period, so the net book value has fallen only through the effects of depreciation of £60 million per year. Such a low depreciation charge suggests that the fixed assets have a long average remaining life of around 20 years.

In each of 20X7 and 20X8, the absolute level of capital employed fell by £60 million during the year. This has arisen due to a combination of tax and dividend payments and losses incurred. Unless a net increase in capital employed is forecast in the future, new funds will have to be raised to support the net operating assets of the business.

Conclusion

The profitability of the company has fallen over the period 20X6 to 20X8, due to falling turnover, high labour costs and high indirect costs.

The liquidity of the company is low but seems stable. There appears to be poor control over working capital, with high stock levels, high debtors and no cash in hand.

APPENDIX TO THE REPORT

Profitability ratios

	20X6	*20X7*	*20X8*
Percentage of turnover			
Materials	20.2	17.8	20.0
Labour	15.4	17.8	20.0
Overhead	12.5	15.5	15.0
Administrative expenses	25.0	25.6	24.0
Distribution costs	24.0	21.1	23.0
Net profit	2.9	2.2	(2.0)
	100.0	100.0	100.0
Gross profit	51.9%	48.9%	45.0%
ROCE	5.9%	4.1%	(4.3%)

Liquidity ratios

Current ratio	1.44	1.44	1.41
Quick ratio	0.48	0.52	0.52
Debtor days	46 days	57 days	55 days
Fixed asset turnover	2.67	2.43	2.86
Working capital turnover	8.67	7.5	8.33
Raw materials purchases	174 days	228 days	182 days

(b) The limitations of my analysis above of the performance of F plc are as follows.

The accounts have presumably been drawn up under the historical cost convention. Many accountants would argue that a current value for non-monetary assets such as fixed assets would give more meaningful information for ratio analysis.

We are not told the split between cash sales and credit sales, but even assuming that all sales are on credit, the debtor days ratio looks unhealthy.

A breakdown of the current liabilities would be useful, to determine for example just how big the bank overdraft is.

The most recent figures given are for 20X8; by now it might be possible to include figures for later years.

It would be useful to know the sector in which F plc operates so that the ratios we have calculated could be compared with sector norms. Only then would it be possible to draw firmer conclusions about the performance of the company.

---

3 Big Brother

REPORT

To	The Directors, Big Brother plc
From	AN Accountant
Date	20 July 20X9
Subject	Big Brother plc — Profitability, liquidity and solvency of the group

(a) **Terms of reference**

This report examines the profitability, liquidity and solvency of Big Brother in 20X7 and 20X8, and recommends necessary action. It is based on financial statements and industry statistics provided. Ratios calculated from the statutory accounts are included in Appendix 1.

(b) **Executive summary**

The group is under capitalised, highly geared, and approaching a liquidity crisis. It is, however, profitable and the ordinary dividend was covered 12 times in 20X8 (20X7 14 times).

(c) **Profitability**

The gross margin has exceeded the industry norm at the same time as the net margin remained at industry levels. This discrepancy is probably due to non-standard cost allocations between cost of sales and other categories. This would also explain the low stock turnover ratio.

It is possible that the gross margins are genuinely high, in which case overheads are also high, and savings may be available. A comparison of Big Brother's and the industry's usual cost allocation methods would allow more conclusive analysis.

Return on capital has improved in the year, and is well above industry levels. The apparent improvement is due mainly to the lack of extra long-term finance referred to below, and is not an underlying strength.

(d) **Liquidity**

Liquidity has deteriorated in the period, and the company is exhibiting signs of overtrading, its expansion not being financed by long-term methods.

The company is financing its increased working capital requirements out of rentals in advance. The low industry quick ratio indicates that some reliance on short-term finance is usual, but Big Brother's is excessive.

Unless further long-term finance (eg by a rights issue) is raised soon, the company will have liquidity problems.

(e) **Solvency**

The company is highly geared compared to the industry average, although a slight improvement occurred in the year. The gearing ratios referred to in the Appendix exclude any overdrafts and loans included within current liabilities, and it is likely that underlying gearing is substantially higher.

The high level of gearing, allied to poor liquidity, casts doubt over the company's continued stability.

Appendix 1: Ratios

	Big Brother plc		*Industry average*
	20X8	*20X7*	
Gross profit margin	58.2%	57.8%	50%
Net profit margin	25.4%	24.9%	25%
Current ratio (including rentals in advance)	0.93	1.05	1.20
Quick ratio (including rentals in advance)	0.58	0.63	0.90

Gearing

$\frac{5{,}000 + 30{,}105}{30{,}455 + 30{,}105} = 58\%$ $\quad$ $\frac{5{,}000 + 27{,}419}{24{,}886 + 27{,}419} = 62\%$ $\quad$ 50%

Stock turnover

$\frac{21{,}705}{8{,}159} = 2.66$ $\quad$ $\frac{18{,}221}{7{,}181} = 2.54$ $\quad$ 3.5

Debtors turnover

$\frac{51{,}882}{10{,}021} = 5.2$ $\quad$ $\frac{43{,}217}{8{,}715} = 5.0$ $\quad$ 5.0

ROCE

$\frac{13{,}157}{30{,}455 + 30{,}105} = 21.7\%$ $\quad$ $\frac{10{,}761}{24{,}886 + 27{,}419} = 20.6\%$ $\quad$ 17%

Dividend cover

$\frac{5{,}391 - 300}{400} = 12.73$ $\quad$ $\frac{4{,}493 - 300}{300} = 13.98$

Appendix 2

A rights issue could bring in fresh long-term funds and bring the company's gearing down to the industry average level.

Assuming that £10 million is raised from a rights issue

Gearing $\quad \frac{5{,}000 + 30{,}105}{30{,}455 + 30{,}105 + 10{,}000} = 49.8\%$

Quick ratio $\quad \frac{10{,}021 + 3{,}609 + 10{,}000}{15{,}215 + 8{,}261} = 1.01$

(including rentals in advance)

Quick quiz

1 Profit before interest and tax.

2 Profit after interest and preference dividends but (usually) before tax.

3 The current ratio includes stocks in the numerator, while the acid test ratio excludes stocks.

4 The market's expectations for future growth in earnings.

5 The risk that profits might be insufficient to pay the interest payments due.

WORKBOOK

KEY TECHNIQUES

QUESTION BANK

Key Techniques Question Bank - Questions

Chapters 1 and 2

The regulatory and conceptual framework of accounting

QUESTION 1

The Accounting Standards Board's Statement of Principles for Financial Reporting identifies a number of user groups to which financial statements should be appropriate.

(a) List these groups referred to in the Statement of Principles.

(b) Choose any three of the user groups and, with reference to the accounts of a limited company, consider the type of decisions that they are likely to wish to make in using the published accounting information.

QUESTION 2

A major objective of published financial statements is 'to provide information about the financial position, performance and financial adaptability of an enterprise that is useful to a wide range of users for assessing the stewardship of management and for making economic decisions'.

What characteristics contribute to making financial information useful in terms of both content and presentation, and how do these characteristics fulfil their objective?

QUESTION 3

The elements of financial statements comprise:

- Assets
- Liabilities
- Ownership interest
- Gains
- Losses
- Contributions from owners
- Distributions to owners

Define these terms and state which of these terms comprise the 'accounting equation'.

Answer 4 – P.432

QUESTION 4 (DECEMBER 2000) (Task 1.1)

Data

The accounting equation of a business is as follows:

Assets £1,200 – Liabilities £800 = Ownership interest £400

The business subsequently makes two transactions:

(1) it purchases on credit stock costing £120; and

(2) it sells the stock purchased in (1) for £180 cash.

Task

(a) Explain what is meant by 'assets', 'liabilities' and 'ownership interest'.

(b) Explain the effect of each transaction on the elements in the balance sheet.

(c) State the accounting equation for the business after the two transactions have taken place.

(d) Draft a simple profit and loss account for the two transactions.

(e) Give an example of a user who might be interested in a profit and loss account. Explain how the user you have chosen might find the statement useful.

QUESTION 5 (DECEMBER 1999)

The Accounting Standards Board's Statement of Principles for Financial Reporting (issued December 1999) states that:

'The objective of financial statements is to provide information about the reporting entity's financial performance and financial position that is useful to a wide range of users for assessing the stewardship of the entity's management and for making economic decisions.'

Illustrate this objective by:

(a) Selecting one external user of financial statements from profit-making organisations and showing how it uses financial statements to assess the stewardship of management.

(b) Selecting one external user of financial statements from profit-making organisations and showing how it uses financial statements to make economic decisions.

QUESTION 6 (JUNE 2002, amended)

Data

The Statement of Principles for Financial Reporting says that:

'The elements of the financial statements are:

(a) Assets
(b) Liabilities
(c) Ownership interest
(d) Gains
(e) Losses
(f) Contributions from owners
(g) Distributions to owners.'

Task

(a) (i) In which primary financial statement are 'assets', 'liabilities' and 'ownership interest' shown?

(ii) How are they related to each other in that statement?

(b) What is meant by 'gains' and 'losses' and in which primary financial statements are they shown?

QUESTION 7 (DECEMBER 2002)

(a) What sort of information in the financial statements does the ASB's Statement of Principles for Financial Reporting say that potential investors are interested in and for what purpose?

(b) How does stock meet the definition of an asset in the ASB's Statement of Principles for Financial Reporting?

Chapter 3

Drafting financial statements for a sole trader

QUESTION 8

G Hick is a retailer of sports equipment.

The following is the trial balance as at 31 December 20X3.

	Dr £	*Cr* £
Motor vehicle at cost	12,500	
Depreciation provision 1/1/X3		5,000
Fixtures and fittings at cost	7,500	
Depreciation provision 1/1/X3		2,500
Premises at cost	40,000	
Depreciation provision 1/1/X3		8,000
Capital account		43,450
Stocks 1/1/X3	17,500	
Debtors	12,500	
Bad debts provision		1,000
Cash in hand	1,250	
Cash at bank	1,700	
Creditors		21,000
Drawings	13,100	
Purchases	120,000	
Sales		170,000
Wages	14,100	
Advertising	2,100	
Insurance	1,400	
Heat and light	2,300	
Business rates	3,200	
Maintenance	150	
Motor vehicle running costs	1,650	
	£250,950	£250,950

The following additional information is available.

(1) Depreciation is to be provided as follows:

Premises	4% on cost
Fixtures	20% on cost
Motor vehicle	20% on cost

(2) A debt of £500 is irrecoverable and is to be written off, and the bad debts provision is to be revised to £1,500.

(3) Advertising includes £350 which was incurred on a private advert for sale of Hick's wife's car.

(4) £650 of the motor vehicle running costs are for private motoring.

(5) Wages are accrued due £270.

(6) The stock at 31 December 20X3 had been valued at £19,500.

(7) The business rates include a pre-payment of £800 to 31 March 20X4.

Required

Prepare a trading and profit and loss account for the year ended 31 December 20X3 and a balance sheet at that date.

QUESTION 9

Michael Jay is a retailer of antiques. He also supplies goods to trade customers. The trial balance of the business at 31 December 20X3 was:

	Dr	*Cr*
	£	£
Capital account		50,405
Freehold premises	50,000	
Fixtures and fittings at cost	13,100	
Motor vehicle	14,350	
Provisions for depreciation		
- Premises		5,000
- Fittings		7,860
- Motor vehicle		5,740
Stocks 1/1/X3	23,150	
Drawings	11,000	
Debtors	15,200	
Creditors		19,100
Provision for bad debts		500
Purchases	131,100	
Sales		193,000
Wages	13,150	
Rates	3,250	
Insurances	1,850	
Heat and light	1,260	
Motor vehicle running costs	1,050	
Maintenance	780	
Cash in hand	970	
Cash at bank	1,395	
	£281,605	£281,605

The following information is also available.

(1) Stock at 31 December 20X3 is valued at £25,600.

(2) Depreciation is to be provided as:

- Premises 5% on cost.
- Fixtures 20% on cost.
- Motor vehicles 20% on cost.

(3) The provision for bad debts is to be revised to 6% of debtors.

(4) Rates are prepaid by £250.

(5) Wages are accrued due £720.

(6) An amount of £260 for insurance has been wrongly analysed as heat and light.

(7) Some fixtures and fittings which had cost £2,100, with a net book value of £840 had been sold for £1,000 on credit terms to a dealer, but no entries had been made in the books.

(8) An amount of £280 analysed as maintenance was for some private decorating at Michael's home.

(9) An irrecoverable debt of £200 is to be written off.

Required

Prepare a trading and profit and loss account for the year ended 31 December 20X3 and a balance sheet at that date.

QUESTION 10

You work as an accounting technician for a firm of chartered accountants. Karl Hayes, a self-employed builder, is one of your clients and the following issues relate to his year end accounts.

(1) The debtors balance is £19,100, a debt of £400 is considered to be irrecoverable and is to be written off. The balance on the provision for bad debts account is currently £735 and the provision is to be revised to 5% of debtors.

The amount to be charged to the profit and loss account for the change in the bad debts provision is:

(A) £935
(B) £735
(C) £200
(D) £220

(2) During the year a fixed asset had been disposed of, the profit on sale was £750. The cost of the asset had been £3,400 and the proceeds on sale were £2,150.

The accumulated depreciation to date was:

(A) £2,150
(B) £2,650
(C) £2,000
(D) £1,250

(3) The balance on the rent and rates account as shown on the trial balance was £2,850 Dr.

At the year end, rates had been prepaid by £720 and the rent was accrued due £500.

The amount to be charged to the profit and loss account for the year was:

(A) £2,630
(B) £3,070
(C) £1,630
(D) £4,070

(4) The following information relates to items in the purchase ledger control account:

Opening balance	£15,100 Cr
Payments to suppliers	£83,200
Returns to suppliers	£1,100
Discounts received	£4,100
Amounts offset against items in the sales ledger	£1,560
Purchases on credit from suppliers	£96,000

(NB: A supplier was also a customer.)

The closing balance on the purchase ledger control account would be:

(A) £34,660
(B) £23,340
(C) £21,140
(D) None of these

(5) The trial balance included the following information.

Sales £131,700, returns outward £1,100, returns inward £1,700, purchases £96,000, opening stock valuation £16,200 and a note to the information showed that the closing stock valuation was £17,220 and that goods which had cost £1,500 had been used by Karl for his own use.

(a) The cost of goods sold for the period was:

(A) £91,780
(B) £94,420
(C) £95,380
(D) £92,380

(b) The gross profit for the period was:

(A) £32,080
(B) £37,620
(C) £38,220
(D) None of these

QUESTION 11 (DECEMBER 1999) – Section 2

Data

Elizabeth Ogier has asked you to assist in the preparation of the year end financial statements of her business. She operates a wholesale perfume business. The trial balance as at 30 September 1999 is set out below:

Elizabeth Ogier – Trial balance as at 30 September 1999

	Debit £	*Credit* £
Purchases	113,565	
Rent, rates and insurance	8,291	
Motor expenses	5,813	
Bad debts	1,420	
Drawings	24,000	
Trade debtors	38,410	
Trade creditors		18,928
Capital as at 1 October 1998		83,707

Sales		230,461
Returns outwards		2,911
Carriage inwards	1,256	
Returns inwards	3,053	
Carriage outwards	1,571	
Salesperson's commission	2,561	
Bank charges	710	
Depreciation - office equipment	2,312	
Depreciation - fixtures and fittings	602	
Stock as at 1 October 1998	46,092	
Motor vehicles at cost	36,000	
Office equipment at cost	11,560	
Fixtures and fittings at cost	6,019	
Accumulated depreciation - motor vehicles		18,360
Accumulated depreciation - office equipment		3,825
Accumulated depreciation - fixtures and fittings		1,352
Wages, salaries and National Insurance contributions	47,564	
Lighting and heating	3,056	
Postage and stationery	1,037	
Telephone	3,571	
Cash at bank	2,131	
Cash in hand	102	
Accruals		1,562
Discounts allowed	410	
	361,106	361,106

Further information:

- The stock at the close of business on 30 September 1999 was valued at cost at £49,477. However, included in this balance were some goods which had cost £8,200 but it is estimated that they could not be sold for any more than £4,800.
- Included in the rent, rates and insurance balance is a payment of £1,200 which relates to rent for the period from 1 October 1999 to 31 December 1999.
- The purchases figure includes goods to the value of £2,000 which Elizabeth took from the business for personal use and for gifts to friends.
- Although depreciation for office equipment and fixtures and fittings has been calculated and charged for the year, no depreciation has been calculated or charged for motor vehicles. Motor vehicles are depreciated using the reducing balance method at a rate of 30% per annum.

Task 11.1

Make any additional adjustments you feel necessary to the balances in the trial balance as a result of the matters set out in the further information above. Set out your adjustments in the form of journal entries.

Note: Narratives are not required.

Task 11.2

Draft a profit and loss account for the year ended 30 September 1999.

Task 11.3 Answer - P. 439

Draft a letter to Elizabeth justifying any adjustment you have made to:

- the stock valuation on 30 September 1999.
- the balances in the trial balance as a result of Elizabeth taking goods out of the business for her personal use or for gifts to friends.

Your explanations should make reference, where relevant, to accounting concepts, accounting standards or generally accepted accounting principles.

Chapter 4

Preparing limited company accounts: for internal purposes

QUESTION 12

The trial balance of Ayres Ltd at 30 September 20X8 was as follows:

	£	£
Freehold land: cost	121,500	
Freehold buildings: cost	431,000	
Freehold buildings: accumulated depreciation		68,960
Plant and machinery: cost	64,172	
Plant and machinery: accumulated depreciation		16,074
Sales		1,312,567
Purchases	839,004	
Cash in hand	1,268	
Creditors' ledger control account		21,172
Heat and light	6,917	
Share capital - 200,000 25p shares		50,000
Bank balance	1,210	
Debtors' ledger control account	61,074	
Suspense account	4,300	
Stock at 1 October 20X7	41,912	
Profit and loss account		296,057
Motor expenses	4,174	
Sundry expenses	2,002	
Wages and salaries	121,600	
Directors' remuneration	48,888	
Bank interest and charges	1,621	
Motor vehicles: cost	28,900	
Motor vehicles: accumulated depreciation		14,712
	1,779,542	1,779,542

You are provided with the following information.

(1) Bad debts should be provided as to 2% of the debtors' ledger balances after writing off irrecoverable debts of £1,370.

(2) The suspense account is analysed as follows.

	£	£
Bad debts written off during the year		512
Motor vehicles purchased on 1 April 20X8		7,400
		7,912
Motor vehicle sold on 1 April 20X8	3,000	
Amount received in respect of a bad debt written off in 20X5	612	
		3,612
		4,300

(3) The directors wish to declare a dividend of 10%.

(4) The motor vehicle sold during the year had been purchased on 1 February 20X5 for £6,500.

(5) The bank statement on 30 September 20X8 showed bank charges and interest of £533. This amount was not recorded in the cash book until October 20X8.

(6) The debtors' ledger control account did not agree with the list of balances. You ascertain that certain October 20X8 invoices had been posted in the personal accounts as September 20X8. The list of balances was overstated by £4,300.

(7) Depreciation should be provided as follows on fixed assets other than land.

(a) On buildings - 2% on cost
(b) On plant and machinery - 20% on reducing balance
(c) On motor vehicles - 25% on cost

Charge a full year's depreciation in the year of purchase and none in the year of sale.

(8) Estimated taxation charge for the year is £131,700.

(9) Closing stock is valued at £62,047.

(10) The petty cash book has not been written up for September. During that time the amounts spent were as follows:

	£
Motor vehicles	412
Sundry expenses	91
Casual labour	36

Required

Prepare a draft trading account, profit and loss account and balance sheet in a form suitable to discuss with the directors.

The accounts are for internal use only.

Chapter 5

Preparing limited company accounts: statutory formats

QUESTION 13 (JUNE 1999)

Data

You have been assigned to assist in the preparation of the financial statements of Typeset Ltd for the year ended 31 March 1999. The company is a wholesale distributor of desktop publishing equipment. You have been provided with the extended trial balance of Typeset Ltd as at 31 March 1999 which is set out below.

Typeset Ltd - Extended trial balance as at 31 March 1999

Description	*Trial balance*		*Adjustments*		*Profit and loss*		*Balance sheet*	
	Debit	*Credit*	*Debit*	*Credit*	*Debit*	*Credit*	*Debit*	*Credit*
	£000	*£000*	*£000*	*£000*	*£000*	*£000*	*£000*	*£000*
Trade debtors	3,136						3,136	
Cash at bank	216						216	
Interest	125				125			
Profit and loss account		3,533						3,533
Provision for doubtful debts		37						37
Distribution costs	3,549		59	36	3,572			
Administration expenses	3,061		63	61	3,063			
Revaluation reserve		500						500
Sales		18,757				18,757		
Land - cost	2,075						2,075	
Buildings - cost	2,077						2,077	
Fixtures and fittings - cost	1,058						1,058	
Motor vehicles - cost	2,344						2,344	
Office equipment - cost	533						533	
Stock	3,921		4,187	4,187	3,921	4,187	4,187	
Purchases	10,582				10,582			
Interim dividend	250				250			
Trade creditors		1,763						1,763
Buildings - accumulated depreciation		383						383
Fixtures and fittings - accumulated depreciation		495						495
Motor vehicles - accumulated depreciation		1,237						1,237
Office equipment - accumulated depreciation		152						152
Pre-payments			97				97	
Ordinary share capital		5,000						5,000
Share premium		1,200						1,200
Accruals				122				122
Investments	1,580						1,580	
Long-term loan		1,450						1,450
Profit					1,431			1,431
TOTAL	34,507	34,507	4,406	4,406	22,944	22,944	17,303	17,303

You have been given the following further information:

- The authorised share capital of the business, all of which has been issued, consists of ordinary shares with a nominal value of £1.
- Depreciation has been calculated on a monthly basis on all of the fixed assets of the business and has already been entered into the distribution costs and administration expenses ledger balances as shown on the extended trial balance.
- The corporation tax charge for the year has been calculated as £493,000.
- The company has paid an interim dividend of 5p per share during the year but has not provided for the proposed final dividend of 7p per share.
- One of the customers who owed the company £36,000 at the end of the year is in financial difficulties. The directors have estimated that only half of this amount is likely to be paid. No adjustment for the required provision has been made for this matter in the extended trial balance. The general provision for doubtful debts is to be maintained at 2% of the remaining debtors excluding the £36,000 balance.

Task

Using the proforma which follows, and making any adjustments required as a result of the further information provided, draft a balance sheet for Typeset Ltd as at 31 March 1999.

Note:

- You are **not** required to produce notes to the accounts.
- You must show any **workings** relevant to understanding your calculation of figures appearing in the balance sheet.
- You are **not** required to produce journal entries for any adjustments to the figures in the extended trial balance that are required.
- You should ignore any effect of these adjustments on the tax charge for the year as given above.

Proforma balance sheet (format 1)

	£000	£000
Fixed assets		
Intangible assets		
Tangible assets		
Investments		
	———	
Current assets		
Stocks		
Debtors		
Investments		
Cash at bank and in hand		
	———	
Creditors: amounts falling due within one year		
	———	
Net current assets (liabilities)		
		———
Total assets less current liabilities		
Creditors: amounts falling due after more than one year		
Provisions for liabilities and charges		
		———
		———
Capital and reserves		
		———
		———

QUESTION 14 (JUNE 2002)

Data

You have been asked to help prepare the financial statements of Hightink Ltd for the year ended 31 March 2002. The trial balance of the company as at 31 March 2002 is set out below.

Hightink Ltd
Trial balance as at 31 March 2002

	Debit *£000*	*Credit* *£000*
Interest	240	
Distribution costs	6,852	
Administrative expenses	3,378	
Trade debtors	5,455	
Trade creditors		2,363
Interim dividend	400	
Ordinary share capital		4,000
Sales		31,710
Long term loan		6,000
Land - cost	5,000	
Buildings - cost	3,832	
Fixtures and fittings - cost	2,057	
Motor vehicles - cost	3,524	
Office equipment - cost	2,228	
Purchases	15,525	
Cash at bank	304	
Profit and loss account		6,217
Stock as at 1 April 2001	6,531	
Share premium		2,000
Buildings - accumulated depreciation		564
Fixtures and fittings - accumulated depreciation		726
Motor vehicles - accumulated depreciation		1,283
Office equipment - accumulated depreciation		463
	55,326	55,326

Further information:

- The authorised share capital of the company, all of which has been issued, consists of ordinary shares with a nominal value of £1.
- The company paid an interim dividend of 10p per share during the year but has not provided for the proposed final dividend of 15p per share.
- The stock at the close of business on 31 March 2002 was valued at cost at £7,878,000.
- The corporation tax charge for the year has been calculated as £1,920,000.
- Credit sales relating to April 2002 amounting to £204,000 had been entered incorrectly into the accounts in March 2002.
- Interest on the long term loan has been paid for six months of the year. No adjustment has been made for the interest due for the final six months of the year. Interest is charged on the loan at a rate of 8% per annum.
- The land has been revalued by professional valuers at £5,500,000. The revaluation is to be included in the financial statements for the year ended 31 March 2002.

- On 21 April 2002 there was a fire at the company's premises that destroyed fixed assets and stock. The losses from the fire amounted to £487,000 and they were not covered by the company's insurance. This amount is considered by the directors to constitute a material loss to the company.
- All of the operations are continuing operations.

Task 14.1

Using the proforma provided, make the journal entries required as a result of the further information given above. Dates and narratives are not required.

Note:

(1) You must show any workings relevant to these adjustments.
(2) Ignore any effect of these adjustments on the tax charge for the year given above.

JOURNAL			
Date	*Narration*	*Debit* £	*Credit* £

Task 14.2

Using the proforma provided, and making any adjustments required as a result of the further information given above, draft a profit and loss account for the year ended 31 March 2002, and a balance sheet for Hightink as at that date.

Note: You are NOT required to produce notes to the accounts.

Hightink Ltd
Profit and loss account for the year ended 31 March 2002

	£000	£000
Turnover		
Continuing operations		
Acquisitions		
Discontinued operations		
Cost of sales		
Gross profit (or loss)		
Distribution costs		
Administrative expenses		
Operating profit		
Continuing operations		
Acquisitions		
Discontinued operations		
Profit (or loss) on disposal of discontinued operations		
Profit (or loss) on ordinary activities before interest		
Interest payable and similar charges		
Profit (or loss) on ordinary activities before taxation		
Tax on profit on ordinary activities		
Profit (or loss) on ordinary activities after taxation		
Extraordinary items		
Profit (or loss) for the financial year		
Dividends		
Retained profit for the financial year		

Hightink Ltd
Balance sheet as at 31 March 2002

	£000	£000
Fixed assets		
Intangible assets		
Tangible assets		
Investments		
Current assets		
Stocks		
Debtors		
Investments		
Cash at bank and in hand		
Creditors: amounts falling due within one year		
Net current assets (liabilities)		
Total assets less current liabilities		
Creditors: amounts falling due after more than one year		
Provisions for liabilities and charges		
Capital and reserves		

Task 14.3

(a) Explain what is meant by a 'post balance sheet event'.

(b) Explain the difference between a post balance sheet event that is an 'adjusting event' and one that is a 'non-adjusting event'.

(c) Explain the appropriate treatment in the financial statements for the year ended 31 March 2002 of the losses that arose from the fire on the company's premises on 21 April 2002.

QUESTION 15 (DECEMBER 2002)

Data

The Chief Accountant of Quine Ltd has asked you to help prepare the financial statements for the year ended 30 September 2002. The trial balance of the company as at 30 September 2002 is set out below.

Quine Ltd
Trial balance as at 30 September 2002

	Debit *£000*	*Credit* *£000*
Ordinary share capital		3,000
Interest	200	
Trade debtors	1,802	
Interim dividend	600	
Long term loan		2,500
Distribution costs	980	
Administrative expenses	461	
Sales		10,884
Profit and loss account		1,457
Cash at bank	103	
Accruals		105
Prepayments	84	
Share premium		500
Land - cost	2,800	
Buildings - cost	1,480	
Fixtures and fittings - cost	645	
Motor vehicles - cost	1,632	
Office equipment - cost	447	
Buildings - accumulated depreciation		702
Fixtures and fittings - accumulated depreciation		317
Motor vehicles - accumulated depreciation		903
Office equipment - accumulated depreciation		182
Stock as at 1 October 2001	2,003	
Trade creditors		1,309
Purchases	7,854	
Provision for doubtful debts		72
Capitalised development expenditure	840	
	21,931	21,931

Further information:

- The authorised share capital of the company, all of which has been issued, consists of ordinary shares with a nominal value of £1.
- The company paid an interim dividend of 20p per share during the year but has not provided for the proposed final dividend of 10p per share.
- The stock at the close of business on 30 September 2002 was valued at cost at £2,382,000.
- The corporation tax charge for the year has been calculated as £548,000.
- The land has been revalued by professional valuers at £3,200,000. The revaluation is to be included in the financial statements for the year ended 30 September 2002.

Task

Using the proforma provided, make any adjustments required as a result of the further information provided, and draft a balance sheet for Quine Ltd as at 30 September 2002.

Note

(1) You are not required to produce notes to the accounts.

(2) You must show any workings relevant to understanding your calculation of figures appearing in the balance sheet.

(3) You are not required to produce journal entries for any adjustments required to the figures in the trial balance.

Quine Ltd
Balance sheet as at 30 September 2002

	£000	*£000*
Fixed assets		
Intangible assets		
Tangible assets		
Investments		
	———	
Current assets		
Stocks		
Debtors		
Investments		
Cash at bank and in hand		
	———	
Creditors: amounts falling due within one year		
	———	
Net current assets (liabilities)		
		———
Total assets less current liabilities		
Creditors: amounts falling due after more than one year		
Provisions for liabilities and charges		
		———
		———

Capital and reserves

Chapter 6

Cash flow statements

QUESTION 16

FRS 1 *Cash Flow Statements* requires organisations to report their cash flows under standard headings to show 'cash generation and absorption'.

Required

Outline these standard headings and explain briefly what each category aims to show.

QUESTION 17

The financial statements of Fylingdales Ltd for the year ended 31 March 20X1 include:

Profit and loss account

	£000s
Turnover	205,000
Cost of sales	191,250
Operating profit	13,750
Interest	2,150
Profit before taxation	11,600
Taxation	2,850
	8,750
Dividends	2,250
Profit for year	6,500

NB: The depreciation charge for the year was £6.5m. There had been no disposals of fixed assets in the year.

Balance sheet as at 31 March 20X1

	20X1	*20X0*
	£000s	*£000s*
Fixed assets	73,000	70,500
Current assets		
Stocks	27,500	25,500
Debtors	37,500	33,000
Cash	2,250	1,250
	67,250	59,750
Less current liabilities		
Trade creditors	31,500	31,950
Taxation	2,850	2,260
Dividends	2,250	2,000
	36,600	36,210
Net current assets	30,650	23,540
Total assets less current liabilities	103,650	94,040
Less creditors: amounts falling due after one year		
10% debenture	21,500	20,000
	82,150	74,040
Share capital and reserves	82,150	74,040

Required

Prepare a cash flow statement for Fylingdales Ltd for the year ended 31 March 20X1 in accordance with FRS 1, including the notes required by the standard.

QUESTION 18 (DECEMBER 2000)

Data

You have been asked to assist in the preparation of financial statements for Paton Ltd for the year ended 30 September 2000. The draft profit and loss account and balance sheets of Paton Ltd are set out below.

Paton Ltd – Profit and loss account for the year ended 30 September 2000

	£000
Turnover	24,732
Cost of sales	11,129
Gross profit	13,603
Profit on the sale of fixed assets	131
Distribution costs	4,921
Administrative expenses	2,875
Profit on ordinary activities before interest	5,938
Interest paid and similar charges	392
Profit on ordinary activities before taxation	5,546
Tax on profit on ordinary activities	1,821
Profit for the financial year	3,725
Dividends	1,500
Retained profit for the financial year	2,225

Paton Ltd – Balance sheet as at 30 September

	2000		*1999*	
	£000	*£000*	*£000*	*£000*
Fixed assets		13,383		9,923
Investment in MacNeal Ltd		5,000		
Current assets				
Stocks	7,420		6,823	
Trade debtors	4,122		3,902	
Cash	102		1,037	
	11,644		11,762	
Current liabilities				
Trade creditors	1,855		1,432	
Dividends payable	900		700	
Taxation	1,821		1,327	
	4,576		3,459	
Net current assets		7,068		8,303
Long-term loan		(5,000)		(1,500)
		20,451		16,726
Capital and reserves				
Called up share capital		10,000		9,000
Share premium		3,500		3,000
Profit and loss account		6,951		4,726
		20,451		16,726

You have been given the following further information:

- A fixed asset costing £895,000 with accumulated depreciation of £372,000 was sold in the year. The total depreciation charge for the year was £2,007,000.
- All sales and purchases were on credit. Other expenses were paid for in cash.

Task

Provide a reconciliation of operating profit to net cash flow from operating activities for Paton Ltd for the year ended 30 September 2000.

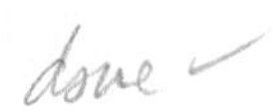

QUESTION 19 (JUNE 2000)

Data

You have been asked to assist in the preparation of financial statements for Angle Ltd for the year ended 31 March 2000. The profit and loss account and balance sheets of the company are set out below.

Angle Ltd - Profit and loss account for the year ended 31 March 2000

	£000
Turnover	
Continuing operations	8,975
Cost of sales	5,013
Gross profit	3,962
Distribution costs	1,172
Administration expenses	953
Operating profit	
Continuing operations	1,837
Interest paid and similar charges	202
Profit on ordinary activities before taxation	1,635
Tax on profit on ordinary activities	490
Profit for the financial year	1,145
Dividends	450
Retained profit for the financial year	695

Angle Ltd - Balance sheet as at 31 March 2000

	2000		1999	
	£000	£000	£000	£000
Fixed assets		7,287		4,009
Current assets				
Stocks	1,982		1,346	
Trade debtors	812		1,086	
Cash	433		82	
	3,227		2,514	
Current liabilities				
Trade creditors	423		397	
Dividends payable	450		400	
Taxation	490		370	
	1,363		1,167	
Net current assets		1,864		1,347
Long-term loan		(2,500)		(1,500)
		6,651		3,856
Capital and reserves				
Called up share capital		3,000		2,200
Share premium		1,200		400
Revaluation reserve		500		-
Profit and loss account		1,951		1,256
		6,651		3,856

Further information:

- Land included in the fixed assets was valued at market value at the end of the year by a professional valuer. The valuation has been incorporated into the financial statements of the company as at 31 March 2000.
- No fixed assets were sold during the year to 31 March 2000. Depreciation has been calculated on the fixed assets of the business and has already been entered in the profit and loss account. The charge for the year was £875,000.
- All sales and purchases were on credit. Other expenses were paid for in cash.
- Net cash inflow from operating activities for the year was £2,376,000.
- There was no over/under-provision of corporation tax for 1999.

Task 19.1

Using the proforma provided, prepare a cash flow statement for Angle Ltd for the year ended 31 March 2000 in accordance with the requirements of FRS 1 (Revised).

Notes:

You are not required to provide a reconciliation between cash flows from operating activities and operating profit.

You are not required to produce any of the notes required by FRS 1.

Task 19.2

Prepare a statement of total recognised gains and losses for the year ended 31 March 2000 for Angle Ltd as required by FRS 3.

Data

FRS 3 requires separate disclosure of the results of continuing operations, acquisitions (as a component of continuing operations) and discontinued operations.

Task 19.3

Prepare notes to explain:

(a) what is meant, in FRS 3, by 'acquisitions' and 'discontinued operations'.

(b) why it is useful to distinguish between the three types of operations for the purposes of financial reporting.

Proforma cash flow statement (in accordance with FRS 1 (Revised))

	£000
Net cash inflow from operating activities	
Returns on investments and servicing of finance	
Taxation	
Capital expenditure	
	———
Equity dividends paid	
	———
Management of liquid resources	
Financing	
	———
Increase/(decrease) in cash	
	———

QUESTION 20 (DECEMBER 1999) - Section 2 - Task 2.3

Data

A colleague has asked you to take over the drafting of a cash flow statement for Diewelt Ltd for the year ended 30 September 1999. Your colleague has already drafted a reconciliation between cash flows from operating activities and operating profit for the period. The financial statements of the company, drafted for internal purposes, along with the reconciliation are set out below, along with some further information relating to the reporting year.

Diewelt Ltd – Profit and loss account for the year ended 30 September 1999

	£000
Turnover	9,804
Cost of sales	5,784
Gross profit	4,020
Profit on sale of fixed asset	57
Depreciation	985
Other expenses	819
Operating profit for the year	2,273
Interest paid	365
Profit before tax	1,908
Taxation on profit	583
Profit after tax	1,325
Ordinary dividend	440
Retained profit	885

Diewelt Ltd – Balance sheet as at 30 September 1999

	1999		*1998*	
	£000	*£000*	*£000*	*£000*
Fixed assets		6,490		5,620
Current assets				
Stocks	3,151		2,106	
Trade debtors	2,314		1,470	
Cash	103		383	
	5,568		3,959	
Current liabilities				
Trade creditors	964		1,034	
Dividends payable	264		192	
Taxation	583		491	
	1,811		1,717	
Net current assets		3,757		2,242
Long-term loan		(3,300)		(2,900)
		6,947		4,962
Capital and reserves				
Called up share capital		2,200		1,600
Share premium		800		300
Profit and loss account		3,947		3,062
		6,947		4,962

Further information:

- A fixed asset which had cost £136,000 and had accumulated depreciation of £85,000 was sold during the year.
- All sales and purchases were on credit. Other expenses were paid for in cash.

Reconciliation of operating profit to net cash inflow from operating activities

	£000
Operating profit	2,273
Depreciation charges	985
Profit on sale of tangible fixed assets	(57)
Increase in stock	(1,045)
Increase in debtors	(844)
Decrease in creditors	(70)
Net cash inflow from operating activities	1,242

Task

Using the proforma which follows, prepare a cash flow statement for Diewelt Ltd for the year ended 30 September 1999 in accordance with the requirements of FRS 1 (Revised). No notes to the cash flow statement are required.

Proforma cash flow statement (in accordance with FRS 1 (Revised))

	£000
Net cash inflow from operating activities	
Returns on investments and servicing of finance	
Taxation	
Capital expenditure	
	–––
Equity dividends paid	
	–––
Management of liquid resources	
Financing	
	–––
Increase/(decrease) in cash	
	–––

QUESTION 21 (JUNE 1999)

Data

The directors of Machier Ltd have asked you to assist them in producing a cash flow statement for the year ended 31 March 1999 using the information in the balance sheet and profit and loss account which follows.

The following further information is provided:

- fixed assets costing £28,000 with accumulated depreciation of £19,000 were sold in the year.
- all sales and purchases were on credit. Other expenses were paid for in cash.

Machier Ltd - Profit and loss account for the year ended 31 March 1999

	1999	*1998*
	£000	*£000*
Turnover	2,636	1,687
Cost of sales	923	590
Gross profit	1,713	1,097
Depreciation	856	475
Other expenses	126	101
Profit on the sale of fixed assets	7	2
Operating profit for the year	738	523
Interest paid	252	120
Profit before tax	486	403
Taxation on profit	165	137
Profit after tax	321	266
Ordinary dividend	40	20
Retained profit	281	246
Retained profit brought forward	1,127	881
Retained profit carried forward	1,408	1,127

Machier Ltd – Balance sheet as at 31 March 1999

	1999	1998
	£000	£000
Fixed assets	4,282	2,376
Current assets		
Stocks	448	287
Debtors	527	337
Cash	-	86
	975	710
Current liabilities		
Trade creditors	381	212
Dividends payable	20	10
Taxation	165	137
Bank overdraft	183	-
	749	359
Net current assets	226	351
Long-term loan	2,800	1,500
	1,708	1,227
Capital and reserves		
Called up share capital	200	100
Share premium	100	-
Profit and loss account	1,408	1,127
	1,708	1,227

Task 21.1

Provide a reconciliation between cash flow from operating activities and operating profit of Machier Ltd for the year ended 31 March 1999.

Task 21.2

Using the proforma which follows, prepare a cash flow statement for Machier Ltd for the year ended 31 March 1999 in accordance with the requirements of FRS 1 (Revised). Notes to the cash flow statement are not required.

Proforma cash flow statement (in accordance with FRS 1 (Revised))

	£000
Net cash inflow from operating activities	
Returns on investments and servicing of finance	
Taxation	
Capital expenditure	
Equity dividends paid	
Management of liquid resources	
Financing	
Increase/(decrease) in cash	

QUESTION 22 (DECEMBER 1998)

Data

The directors of Fun Ltd have a number of questions relating to the financial statements of their recently acquired subsidiary undertaking, Games Ltd. The directors have provided you with the balance sheet of Games Ltd as at 30 September 1998 along with some further information.

Games Ltd – Balance sheet as at 30 September 1998

	1998	*1997*
	£000	*£000*
Fixed assets	1,845	1,615
Current assets		
Stocks	918	873
Trade debtors	751	607
Cash	23	87
	1,692	1,567
Current liabilities		
Trade creditors	583	512
Dividends payable	52	48
Taxation	62	54
	697	614
Net current assets	995	953
Long-term loan	560	420
	2,280	2,148
Capital and reserves		
Called up share capital	1,000	1,000
Share premium	100	100
Profit and loss account	1,180	1,048
	2,280	2,148

Further information:

- No fixed assets were sold during the year. The depreciation charge for the year amounted to £277,000.
- All sales and purchases were on credit. Other expenses were paid for in cash.
- The profit on ordinary activities before taxation was £246,000. Interest of £56,000 was charged in the year.

Task

Prepare a reconciliation between cash flow from operating activities and operating profit for the year ended 30 September 1998.

QUESTION 23 (JUNE 2002)

Data

You have been asked to prepare a reconciliation of operating profit to net cash flows from operating activities for Sholti Ltd for the year ended 31 March 2002. The profit and loss account and balance sheets of Sholti Ltd are set out below.

Sholti Ltd
Profit and loss account for the year ended 31 March 2002

	£000
Turnover	32,347
Cost of sales	14,243
Gross profit	18,104
Profit on the sale of tangible fixed assets	378
Distribution costs	6,157
Administrative expenses	4,892
Profit on ordinary activities before interest	7,433
Interest paid and similar charges	625
Profit on ordinary activities before taxation	6,808
Tax on profit on ordinary activities	1,967
Profit for the financial year	4,841
Dividends	1,800
Retained profit for the financial year	3,041

Sholti Ltd
Balance sheets as at 31 March

	2002		2001	
	£000	£000	£000	£000
Fixed assets		22,972		10,080
Current assets				
Stocks	8,632		9,013	
Trade debtors	5,391		4,728	
Cash	-		987	
	14,023		14,728	
Current liabilities				
Trade creditors	2,382		2,081	
Dividends payable	1,800		1,400	
Taxation	1,967		1,522	
	6,149		5,003	
Net current assets		7,874		9,725
Long term loan		(8,000)		(6,000)
		22,846		13,805
Capital and reserves				
Called up share capital		12,000		8,000
Share premium		4,000		2,000
Profit and loss account		6,846		3,805
		22,846		13,805

Further information:

- The total depreciation charge for the year was £1,850,000.
- All sales and purchases were on credit. Other expenses were paid for in cash.

Task

Prepare a reconciliation of operating profit to net cash flows from operating activities for Sholti Ltd for the year ended 31 March 2002.

QUESTION 24 (DECEMBER 2002)

Data

The Financial Controller of Duhem Ltd has asked you to take over the drafting of a cash flow statement for the year ended 30 September 2002. A reconciliation between cash flows from operating activities and operating profit for the period has already been prepared. The financial statements of the company - drafted for internal purposes - and the reconciliation, are set out below, along with some further information relating to the reporting year.

Duhem Ltd
Profit and loss account for the year ended 30 September 2002

	£000
Turnover	8,742
Cost of sales	4,458
Gross profit	4,284
Profit on the sale of fixed assets	106
Distribution costs	931
Administrative expenses	615
Profit on ordinary activities before interest	2,844
Interest payable and similar charges	513
Profit on ordinary activities before taxation	2,331
Tax on profit on ordinary activities	720
Profit for the financial year	1,611
Dividends	800
Retained profit for the financial year	811

Duhem Ltd
Balance sheets as at 30 September

	2002		2001	
	£000	£000	£000	£000
Fixed assets		17,144		12,710
Current assets				
Stocks	1,115		1,002	
Trade debtors	1,457		1,213	
Cash	107		324	
	2,679		2,539	
Current liabilities				
Trade creditors	1,042		671	
Dividends payable	590		500	
Taxation	720		618	
	2,352		1,789	
Net current assets		327		750
Long term loan		(6,400)		(4,800)
		11,071		8,660
Capital and reserves				
Called up share capital		4,000		2,500
Share premium		200		100
Profit and loss account		6,871		6,060
		11,071		8,660

Duhem Ltd
Reconciliation of operating profit to net cash inflow from operating activities

	£000
Operating profit	2,844
Depreciation charges	1,906
Profit on sale of tangible fixed assets	(106)
Increase in stock	(113)
Increase in debtors	(244)
Increase in creditors	371
Net cash inflow from operating activities	4,658

Further information:

- Fixed assets costing £980,000 with accumulated depreciation of £420,000 were sold during the year.
- All sales and purchases were on credit. Other expenses were paid for in cash.

Task

Using the proforma provided, prepare a cash flow statement for Duhem Ltd for the year ended 30 September 2002 in accordance with the requirements of FRS 1 (Revised).

Duhem Ltd
Cash flow statement for the year ended 30 September 2002

	£000	£000
Net cash inflow from operating activities		
Returns on investments and servicing of finance		
Taxation		
Capital expenditure		
Equity dividends paid		
Management of liquid resources		
Financing		
Increase/decrease in cash		

Chapters 7, 8 and 9

Consolidated accounts

QUESTION 25

The following are the balance sheets of Dunsley Ltd and its subsidiary undertaking Ravenscar Ltd as at 31 December 20X1.

	Dunsley Ltd		Ravenscar Ltd	
	£000s	£000s	£000s	£000s
Fixed assets		5,210		1,250
Investment in Ravenscar Ltd		1,800		
Current assets				
Stocks	1,520		610	
Debtors	1,120		520	
Cash	120		85	
	2,760		1,215	
Current liabilities	1,610		710	
Net current assets		1,150		505
		8,160		1,755
Capital and reserves				
Share capital		3,000		500
Share premium		1,000		100
Profit and loss account		4,160		1,155
		8,160		1,755

Additional information

- The share capital of both companies consists of ordinary shares of £1 each.
- Dunsley Ltd acquired 300,000 shares in Ravenscar Ltd on 31 December 20X1.
- The fair value of the fixed assets of Ravenscar Ltd at 31 December 20X1 was £1,750,000.

Required

Prepare a consolidated balance sheet for Dunsley Ltd and its subsidiary undertaking as at 31 December 20X1.

QUESTION 26

Shireoaks Ltd acquired a 60% holding in Harkhill Ltd on 1 January 20X1.

The balance sheets as at 31 December 20X1 showed the following:

	Shireoaks Ltd		*Harkhill Ltd*	
	£000s	*£000s*	*£000s*	*£000s*
Tangible fixed assets		17,500		5,750
Investment in Harkhill		5,100		
Current assets	4,750		1,520	
Current liabilities	2,250		940	
Net current assets		2,500		580
Total assets less current liabilities		25,100		6,330
Less creditors due after one year:				
Debentures		4,100		1,000
		21,000		5,330
Share capital and reserves				
Share capital		8,000		1,000
Share premium		1,500		500
Profit and loss account		11,500		3,830
		21,000		5,330

Additional information

- The share capital of both companies comprises ordinary shares of £1 each and there have been no changes during the year.
- Shireoaks acquired 600,000 shares in Harkhill Ltd.
- At 1 January 20X1 the balance on the profit and loss account of Harkhill Ltd was £3m.
- The fair value of the fixed assets of Harkhill Ltd as at 1 January 20X1 was £3.5m as compared with their book value of £3.1m. This revaluation has not been reflected in the books.
- Goodwill arising on consolidation is to be amortised using the straight line method over a period of 10 years.

Required

Prepare a consolidated balance sheet as at 31 December 20X1.

QUESTION 27 (DECEMBER 2000)

Data

Paton Ltd, the company, has one subsidiary undertaking, MacNeal Ltd, which it acquired on 30 September 2000. The balance sheet of MacNeal Ltd as at 30 September 2000 is set out below.

MacNeal Ltd – Balance sheet as at 30 September 2000

	£000	£000
Fixed assets		4,844
Current assets	3,562	
Current liabilities	1,706	
Net current assets		1,856
Long-term loan		(1,900)
		4,800
Capital and reserves		
Called up share capital		1,200
Share premium		800
Profit and loss account		2,800
		4,800

You have been given the following further information:

(i) The share capital of MacNeal Ltd consists of ordinary shares of £1 each.

(ii) Paton Ltd acquired 900,000 shares in MacNeal Ltd on 30 September 2000 at a cost of £5,000,000.

(iii) The fair value of the fixed assets of MacNeal Ltd at 30 September 2000 was £5,844,000. The revaluation has not been reflected in the books of MacNeal Ltd.

Task

Calculate the goodwill on consolidation that arose on the acquisition of MacNeal Ltd on 30 September 2000.

QUESTION 28 (JUNE 2000)

Data

You have been asked to assist in the preparation of the consolidated accounts of the Norman Group. Set out below are the balance sheets of Norman Ltd and Saxon Ltd for the year ended 31 March 2000.

Balance sheets as at 31 March 2000

	Norman Ltd		*Saxon Ltd*	
	£000	*£000*	*£000*	*£000*
Tangible fixed assets		12,995		1,755
Investment in Saxon Ltd		1,978		-
Current assets				
Stocks	3,586		512	
Debtors	2,193		382	
Cash	84		104	
	5,863		998	
Current liabilities				
Trade creditors	1,920		273	
Proposed dividend	160		-	
Taxation	667		196	
	2,747		469	
Net current assets		3,116		529
Long-term loan		-		(400)
		18,089		1,884
Share capital		2,000		1,000
Share premium		-		200
Profit and loss account		16,089		684
		18,089		1,884

Further information:

- The share capital of both Norman Ltd and Saxon Ltd consists of ordinary shares of £1 each. There have been no changes to the balances of share capital and share premium during the year. No dividends were paid by Saxon Ltd during the year.
- Norman Ltd acquired 750,000 shares in Saxon Ltd on 31 March 1999.
- At 31 March 1999 the balance on the profit and loss account of Saxon Ltd was £424,000.
- The fair value of the fixed assets of Saxon Ltd at 31 March 1999 was £2,047,000 as compared with their book value of £1,647,000. The revaluation has not been reflected in the books of Saxon Ltd. (Ignore any depreciation implications.)
- Goodwill arising on consolidation is to be amortised using the straight-line method over a period of 10 years.

Task

Using the proforma which follows, prepare the consolidated balance sheet of Norman Ltd and its subsidiary undertaking as at 31 March 2000.

Proforma consolidated balance sheet (format 1)

	£000	£000
Fixed assets		
Intangible assets		
Tangible assets		
Investments		
	——	
Current assets		
Stocks		
Debtors		
Investments		
Cash at bank and in hand		
	——	
Creditors: amounts falling due within one year		
	——	
Net current assets (liabilities)		
		——
Total assets *less* current liabilities		
Creditors: amounts falling due after more than one year		
Provisions for liabilities and charges		
		——
		——
Capital and reserves		
		——
Minority interest		
		——
		——

QUESTION 29 (DECEMBER 1999)

Data

You have been asked to assist in the preparation of the consolidated accounts of the Shopan Group. Set out below are the balance sheets of Shopan Ltd and its subsidiary undertaking, Hower Ltd, as at 30 September 1999.

Balance sheets as at 30 September 1999

	Shopan Ltd		*Hower Ltd*	
	£000	*£000*	*£000*	*£000*
Fixed assets		6,273		1,633
Investment in Hower Ltd		2,100		
Current assets				
Stocks	1,901		865	
Debtors	1,555		547	
Cash	184		104	
	3,640		1,516	
Current liabilities				
Trade creditors	1,516		457	
Taxation	431		188	
	1,947		645	
Net current assets		1,693		871
Long-term loan		(2,870)		(400)
		7,196		2,104
Capital and reserves				
Called up share capital		2,000		500
Share premium		950		120
Profit and loss account		4,246		1,484
		7,196		2,104

Further information:

- The share capital of both Shopan Ltd and Hower Ltd consists of ordinary shares of £1 each.
- Shopan Ltd acquired 375,000 shares in Hower Ltd on 30 September 1999.
- The fair value of the fixed assets of Hower Ltd at 30 September 1999 was £2,033,000.

Task 29.1

Using the proforma which follows, prepare a consolidated balance sheet for Shopan Ltd and its subsidiary undertaking as at 30 September 1999.

Task 29.2

FRS 2 states that 'a parent undertaking should prepare consolidated financial statements for its group'. Give two of the criteria that, according to FRS 2, determine whether an undertaking is the parent undertaking of another undertaking.

Proforma consolidated balance sheet (format 1)

	£000	£000
Fixed assets		
Intangible assets		
Tangible assets		
Investments		
	———	
Current assets		
Stocks		
Debtors		
Investments		
Cash at bank and in hand		
	———	
Creditors: amounts falling due within one year		
	———	
Net current assets (liabilities)		
		———
Total assets *less* current liabilities		
Creditors: amounts falling due after more than one year		
Provisions for liabilities and charges		
		———
		———
Capital and reserves		
		———
Minority interest		
		———
		———

QUESTION 30 (DECEMBER 1998)

Data

The directors of Fun Ltd have a number of questions relating to the financial statements of their recently acquired subsidiary undertaking, Games Ltd. Fun Ltd acquired 75% of the ordinary share capital of Games Ltd on 30 September 1998 for £2,244,000. The fair value of the fixed assets in Games Ltd as at 30 September 1998 was £2,045,000. The directors have provided you with the balance sheet of Games Ltd as at 30 September 1998 along with some further information.

Games Ltd – Balance sheet as at 30 September 1998

	1998	*1997*
	£000	*£000*
Fixed assets	1,845	1,615
Current assets		
Stocks	918	873
Trade debtors	751	607
Cash	23	87
	1,692	1,567
Current liabilities		
Trade creditors	583	512
Dividends payable	52	48
Taxation	62	54
	697	614
Net current assets	995	953
Long-term loan	560	420
	2,280	2,148
Capital and reserves		
Called up share capital	1,000	1,000
Share premium	100	100
Profit and loss account	1,180	1,048
	2,280	2,148

Further information:

- No fixed assets were sold during the year. The depreciation charge for the year amounted to £277,000.
- All sales and purchases were on credit. Other expenses were paid for in cash.
- The profit on ordinary activities before taxation was £246,000. Interest of £56,000 was charged in the year.

Task

Prepare notes to take to the Board meeting to answer the following questions of the directors:

- What figure for minority interest would appear in the consolidated balance sheet of Fun Ltd as at 30 September 1998?
- Where in the consolidated balance sheet would minority interest be disclosed?
- What is a minority interest?

QUESTION 31 (JUNE 1999)

Data

The directors of Machier Ltd have been in negotiation with the directors of another company, Papier Ltd, regarding the possibility of Papier Ltd buying 75% of the share capital of Machier Ltd.

The share capital and reserves of Machier Ltd showed:

	£
Share capital 200,000 ordinary shares £1 each	200,000
Share premium	100,000
Profit and loss account	1,408,000
	£1,708,000

If the acquisition goes ahead Papier Ltd will pay £1,716,000 for the shares based on the value of the company on 31 March 1999. The fair value of the fixed assets in Machier Ltd at 31 March 1999, the agreed date of acquisition, is £4,682,000. The NBV of the fixed assets is £4,282,000 on that date. All the other assets and liabilities are stated at fair value.

The directors of Machier ask you to attend a meeting to explain some of the accounting issues involved in the acquisition of Machier Ltd by Papier Ltd.

Task 31.1

Calculate the goodwill on consolidation that would arise on acquisition if Papier Ltd had purchased 75% of the shares in Machier Ltd on 31 March 1999.

Note:

You are *not* required to produce a consolidated balance sheet for the group.

Task 31.2

In a note to the directors, explain the options that are available for the accounting treatment of goodwill arising on acquisition in group accounts.

QUESTION 32 (JUNE 2002)

Data

Fertwrangler Ltd has one subsidiary undertaking, Voncarryon Ltd, which it acquired on 1 April 2001. The balance sheet of Voncarryon Ltd as at 31 March 2002 is set out below.

Voncarryon Ltd
Balance sheet as at 31 March 2002

	£000	*£000*
Fixed assets		3,855
Current assets	4,961	
Current liabilities	2,546	
Net current assets		2,415
Long term loan		(1,500)
		4,770

Capital and reserves

Called up share capital	2,000
Share premium	1,000
Profit and loss account	1,770
	4,770

Further information:

- The share capital of Voncarryon Ltd consists of ordinary shares of £1 each. There have been no changes to the balances of share capital and share premium during the year. No dividends were paid by Voncarryon Ltd during the year.
- Fertwrangler Ltd acquired 1,200,000 shares in Voncarryon Ltd on 1 April 2001 at a cost of £3,510,000.
- At 1 April 2001 the balance on the profit and loss account of Voncarryon Ltd was £1,350,000.
- The fair value of the fixed assets of Voncarryon Ltd at 1 April 2001 was £4,455,000. The book value of the fixed assets at 1 April 2001 was £4,055,000. The revaluation has not been reflected in the books of Voncarryon Ltd.
- Goodwill arising on consolidation is to be amortised using the straight-line method over a period of 10 years.

Task

Calculate the goodwill figure relating to the acquisition of Voncarryon Ltd that will appear in the consolidated balance sheet of Fertwrangler Ltd as at 31 March 2002.

QUESTION 33

You work as an accounting technician for Malton Ltd which has a single subsidiary, Whitby Ltd.

The profit and loss accounts for the two companies for the year ended 31 December 20X1 were:

	Malton Ltd *£000s*	*Whitby Ltd* *£000s*
Turnover	14,100	5,100
Cost of sales	7,150	2,750
Gross profit	6,950	2,350
Distribution costs	1,600	450
Admin costs	1,450	375
Dividends received from Whitby Ltd	360	
Profit on ordinary activities before interest	4,260	1,525
Interest paid	760	125
Profit on ordinary activities before tax	3,500	1,400
Taxation	1,200	400
Profit on ordinary activities after tax	2,300	1,000
Dividends	800	450
Retained profit	1,500	550

Additional information

- Malton Ltd acquired 80% of the ordinary share capital of Whitby Ltd on 1 January 20X1.
- During the year Whitby Ltd sold stock which had cost £500,000 to Malton Ltd for £800,000. All the stock had been sold outside the group by the end of the year.

Required

Draft a consolidated profit and loss account for Malton Ltd and its subsidiary for the year ended 31 December 20X1. Ignore goodwill.

QUESTION 34 (DECEMBER 2002)

Data

The Managing Director of Skuhn plc has asked you to prepare the draft consolidated profit and loss account for the group. The company has one subsidiary undertaking, e-Lakatos Ltd. The profit and loss accounts for the two companies prepared for internal purposes for the year ended 30 September 2002 are set out below.

Profit and loss accounts for the year ended 30 September 2002

	Skuhn plc	*e-Lakatos Ltd*
	£000	*£000*
Turnover	25,300	8,600
Cost of sales	11,385	3,870
Gross profit	13,915	4,730
Distribution costs	3,655	985
Administrative expenses	2,730	320
Operating profit	7,530	3,425
Dividends received from e-Lakatos Ltd	600	-
Profit on ordinary activities before interest	8,130	3,425
Interest payable and similar charges	2,100	400
Profit on ordinary activities before taxation	6,030	3,025
Tax on profit on ordinary activities	1,870	695
Profit on ordinary activities after taxation	4,160	2,330
Dividends	2,100	1,000
Retained profit for the financial year	2,060	1,330

Further information:

- Skuhn plc acquired 60% of the ordinary share capital of e-Lakatos Ltd on 1 October 2001.
- During the year e-Lakatos Ltd sold stock which had cost £800,000 to Skuhn plc for £1,200,000. All of the stock had been sold by Skuhn plc by the end of the year.
- Ignore any write-off of goodwill for the period.

Task

Using the proforma provided, draft a consolidated profit and loss account for Skuhn plc and its subsidiary undertaking for the year ended 30 September 2002.

Skuhn plc
Consolidated profit and loss account for the year ended 30 September 2002

	£000
Turnover	
Cost of sales	
Gross profit	
Distribution costs	
Administrative expenses	
Profit on ordinary activities before interest	
Interest payable	
Profit on ordinary activities before taxation	
Tax on profit on ordinary activities	
Profit on ordinary activities after taxation	
Minority interests	
Profit for the financial year	
Dividends	
Retained profit for the financial year	

Chapter 10-17

Reporting financial performance

QUESTION 35

The draft profit and loss account for Whitby and Sandsend Ltd for the year ended 31 December 20X1 showed the following:

	£000s	*£000s*
Turnover		45,000
Cost of sales		19,500
Gross profit		25,500
Distribution costs	5,950	
Admin costs	3,469	
		9,419
		16,081
Loss on disposal of discontinued operations		480
Profit on ordinary activities before interest		15,601

During the year the company acquired a business and also discontinued part of its operations. The loss on the disposal of discontinued operations is £480,000 (see above).

The results of the acquired and terminated businesses include:

	Business acquired £000s	*Discontinued operations £000s*
Turnover	2,850	1,240
Cost of sales	950	790
Gross profit	1,900	450
Distribution costs	720	280
Admin costs	470	160
Net profit	710	10

Required

Prepare the profit and loss account using format 1 in accordance with the 1985 Companies Act as supplemented by FRS 3 *Reporting Financial Performance.*

QUESTION 36

An extract from the accounts of Bay Ltd for the year ended 31 March 20X1 showed:

	£000s
Turnover	
Continuing operations	9,320
Cost of sales	5,120
Gross profit	4,200
Distribution costs	1,230
Admin expenses	940
Operating profit	
Continuing operations	2,030
Interest paid and similar charges	230
Profit on ordinary activities before taxation	1,800
Taxation	480
Profit for the financial year	1,320
Dividends	420
Profit retained	900

Extract from the balance sheet

	£000s
Capital and reserves:	
Share capital	3,500
Share premium	1,400
Revaluation reserve	600
Profit and loss account	1,850
	7,350

The revaluation reserve arose in the year ended 31 March 20X1 as a result of land being revalued by a professional valuer. The revaluation is also reflected in the value of the tangible assets.

Required

Prepare a statement of total recognised gains and losses for the year ended 31 March 20X1, as required by FRS 3.

QUESTION 37 (DECEMBER 2000)

Data

The directors of Mattesich Limited are to hold a board meeting next week to consider the performance of the company in the past year. They will also discuss the accounting policy for valuing fixed assets. The company accountant, who would normally prepare the documents for the meeting, is ill. He has completed the extended trial balance for the year ended 30 September 2000 which is set out below.

Mattesich Limited – Extended trial balance as at 30 September 2000

Description	*Trial balance*		*Adjustments*		*Profit and loss*		*Balance sheet*	
	Debit	*Credit*	*Debit*	*Credit*	*Debit*	*Credit*	*Debit*	*Credit*
	£000	*£000*	*£000*	*£000*	*£000*	*£000*	*£000*	*£000*
Buildings - accumulated depreciation		2,731						2,731
Office equipment - accumulated depreciation		2,456						2,456
Motor vehicles - accumulated depreciation		5,502						5,502
Fixtures and fittings - accumulated depreciation		2,698						2,698
Loss on disposal of discontinued operation	473				473			
Trade creditors		2,727						2,727
Debtors	6,654						6,654	
Distribution costs	5,695		206	38	5,863			
Administrative expenses	3,337		181	49	3,469			
Land - cost	8,721						8,721	
Buildings - cost	12,873						12,873	
Office equipment - cost	6,182						6,182	
Motor vehicles - cost	11,522						11,522	
Fixtures and fittings - cost	6,913						6,913	
Interest	544				544			
Sales		40,448				40,448		
Loan		6,800						6,800
Ordinary share capital		14,000						14,000
Stock	12,973		13,482	13,482	12,973	13,482	13,482	
Profit and loss account		12,214						12,214
Accruals				387				387
Share premium		7,200						7,200
Interim dividend	2,100				2,100			
Pre-payments			87				87	
Cash at bank and in hand	107						107	
Purchases	18,682				18,682			
Profit					9,826			9,826
	96,776	96,776	13,956	13,956	53,930	53,930	66,541	66,541

You have been given the following further information:

- The share capital of the business consists of ordinary shares with a nominal value of £1.
- The company paid an interim dividend of 15 pence per share this year and is proposing a final dividend of 20p per share.
- Depreciation has been calculated on all the fixed assets of the business and has already been entered into the distribution expenses and administrative expenses ledger balances as shown on the extended trial balance.
- The corporation tax charge for the year has been estimated at £3,813,000.

During the year the company acquired a business and also discontinued part of its operations. The results of the acquired business and the discontinued operation for the year have already been analysed by the company accountant. All of these results are included in the figures in the extended trial balance. The analysed results are set out below:

	Business acquired £000	*Discontinued operations* £000
Turnover	2,714	1,213
Cost of sales	950	788
Gross profit	1,764	425
Distribution costs	692	234
Administration expenses	469	178
Net profit	603	13

Task 37.1

Using the proforma profit and loss account which follows, draft a profit and loss account for the year ended 30 September 2000 using format 1 in accordance with the Companies Act 1985 as supplemented by FRS 3 *Reporting Financial Performance*.

Note:

You do NOT need to prepare any of the notes to the financial statements that are required by FRS 3.

You do NOT need to prepare journal entries for any additional adjustments that may be necessary as a result of the further information given above.

You do NOT need to do an analysis of distribution costs and administrative expenses.

Mattesich Ltd – Profit and loss account for the year ended 30 September 2000

	£000	£000
Turnover		
Continuing operations		
Acquisitions		
Discontinued operations		
Cost of sales		
Gross profit		
Distribution costs		
Administrative expenses		

Operating profit

Continuing operations

Acquisitions

Discontinued operations

Loss on disposal of discontinued operations

Profit on ordinary activities before interest

Interest payable

Profit on ordinary activities before taxation

Tax on profit on ordinary activities

Profit on ordinary activities after taxation

Dividends

Retained profit for the financial year

Task 37.2

Prepare brief notes to take to the board meeting covering the following questions of the directors:

(a) If we decide to adopt a policy of revaluation of land and buildings, do we need to revalue all the land and buildings that we own or can some continue to be shown at historical cost?

(b) If we do revalue land and buildings:

(i) what should be the carrying value at the balance sheet date?

(ii) what valuation basis should we adopt for our land and buildings given that they are non-specialised properties?

(iii) where should we recognise any gain that is made on revaluation?

Explain your answers by reference to relevant accounting standards.

QUESTION 38 (DECEMBER 1998)

Data

You have been asked to assist in the preparation of the financial statements of Fun Ltd for the year ended 30 September 1998. The company is a distributor of children's games. You have been provided with the extended trial balance of Fun Ltd as at 30 September 1998 which follows.

Fun Ltd - Extended trial balance as at 30 September 1998

Description	*Trial balance*		*Adjustments*		*Profit and loss*		*Balance sheet*	
	Debit	*Credit*	*Debit*	*Credit*	*Debit*	*Credit*	*Debit*	*Credit*
	£000	*£000*	*£000*	*£000*	*£000*	*£000*	*£000*	*£000*
Trade debtors	2,863						2,863	
Bank overdraft		316						316
Interest	300				300			
Profit and loss account		3,811						3,811
Provision for doubtful debts		114						114
Distribution costs	2,055		614		2,669			

Administration expenses	1,684		358		2,042			
Returns inwards	232				232			
Sales		14,595				14,595		
Land - cost	2,293						2,293	
Buildings - cost	2,857						2,857	
Fixtures and fittings - cost	1,245						1,245	
Motor vehicles - cost	2,524						2,524	
Office equipment - cost	872						872	
Stock	1,893		2,041	2,041	1,893	2,041	2,041	
Purchases	6,671				6,671			
Interim dividend	480				480			
Trade creditors		804						804
Buildings - accumulated depreciation		261		51				312
Fixtures and fittings - accumulated depreciation		309		124				433
Motor vehicles - accumulated depreciation		573		603				1,176
Office equipment - accumulated depreciation		184		81				265
Pre-payments	63						63	
Carriage inwards	87				87			
Returns outwards		146				146		
Accruals				113				113
Investments	2,244						2,244	
Loan		3,600						3,600
Ordinary share capital		2,000						2,000
Share premium		1,300						1,300
Revaluation reserve		350						350
Profit					2,408			2,408
TOTAL	28,363	28,363	3,013	3,013	16,782	16,782	17,002	17,002

You have been given the following further information:

- The share capital of the business consists of ordinary shares with a nominal value of 25 pence.
- The company has paid an interim dividend of 6 pence per share this year and is proposing a final dividend of 10 pence per share.
- Depreciation has been calculated on all of the fixed assets of the business and has already been entered into the distribution costs and administrative expenses ledger balances as shown on the extended trial balance.
- The corporation tax charge for the year has been calculated as £972,000.
- Interest on the loan has been paid for the first eleven months of the year only, but no interest has been paid or charged for the final month of the year. The loan carries a rate of interest of 8% per annum of the balance outstanding on the loan.

Task 38.1

Make any additional adjustments you feel to be necessary to the balances in the extended trial balance as a result of the matters set out in the further information above. Set out your adjustments in the form of journal entries.

Note:

- Narratives and dates are not required.
- Ignore any effect of these adjustments on the tax charge for the year as given above.

Task 38.2

Using the proforma profit and loss account provided below, and taking account of any adjustments made in Task 38.1, draft a profit and loss account for the year ended 30 September 1998 using format 1 in accordance with the Companies Act 1985 as supplemented by FRS 3 *Reporting Financial Performance.*

Note:

- You are NOT required to produce notes to the accounts.

Data

The directors are interested in expanding operations next year. They wish to be clear about the constituents of the equity on the balance sheet and on the impact that leasing equipment, rather than purchasing equipment, might have on the company's balance sheet. They would like you to attend the next meeting of the Board.

Task 38.3

Prepare notes to bring to the Board meeting dealing with the following matters.

(a) How the balances on the share premium and the revaluation reserve arose.

(b) The recommendation of one of the directors is to lease the assets as he says that this means that the asset can be kept off the balance sheet. Comment on this recommendation.

Proforma profit and loss account (format 1 as supplemented by FRS 3)

	£000	£000
Turnover		
Continuing operations		
Acquisitions		
	——	
Discontinued operations		
	——	
Cost of sales		
		——
Gross profit (or loss)		
Distribution costs		
Administrative expenses		
		——
Operating profit (or loss)		
Continuing operations		
Acquisitions		
	——	
Discontinued operations		
	——	
Profit (or loss) on disposal of discontinued operations		
		——

Other operating income
Income from shares in group undertakings
Income from participating interests
Income from other fixed asset investments
Other interest receivable and similar income
Amounts written off investments

Profit (or loss) on ordinary activities before interest
Interest payable and similar charges

Profit (or loss) on ordinary activities before taxation
Tax on profit (or loss) on ordinary activities

Profit (or loss) on ordinary activities after taxation
Extraordinary items

Profit (or loss) for the financial year
Dividends

Retained profit for the financial year

QUESTION 39 (DECEMBER 2002)

Data

The Chief Accountant of Quine Ltd has heard that SSAP 2 has been superseded by FRS 18. He knows that FRS 18 requires that an entity should adopt accounting policies that enable its financial statements to give a true and fair view. However, he is not sure how this will affect the year end financial statements and has asked you to clarify certain aspects of the accounting standard. He has arranged a meeting with you to discuss these matters.

Task

Prepare notes for the meeting covering the following matters:

(a) What accounting requirements should Quine Ltd have in selecting accounting policies according to FRS 18? Are there any circumstances where departure from these requirements is necessary?

(b) What four objectives should be used to assess the appropriateness of any particular accounting policies?

(c) What two concepts are said to play a pervasive role in financial statements and hence in the selection of accounting policies?

Chapter 18

Interpretation of accounts

QUESTION 40

Fylingdales Quarries Ltd is a medium sized business which supplies a variety of products to the civil engineering sector of industry.

The following is an extract from its accounts for the year ended 31 December 20X1. The company contributes to an inter-firm comparison scheme through the Quarrying Trade Association and a summary of performance indicators are also shown below.

Profit statement

	£m
Turnover	6.90
Cost of sales	6.08
Operating profit before tax	0.82
Taxation	0.24
Profit after tax	0.58
Dividends	0.18
Retained profits	0.40

Balance sheet

	£m	*£m*
Tangible fixed assets		2.90
Current assets		
Stocks	0.60	
Debtors	1.84	
Bank	0.05	
	2.49	
Less current liabilities	1.90	
Net current assets		0.59
Total assets less current liabilities		3.49
Financed by:		
Capital and reserves		3.49

NB: The finished goods valuation included in stocks was £0.40m.

Distribution and admin cost included in cost of sales was £0.88m and labour cost was £1.26m.

Quarrying Trade Association performance indicators – year ended 31 December 20X1

Return on capital employed	25.60%
Asset turnover	1.80
Net profit before tax to sales	14.22%
Current ratio	1.50 : 1
Liquidity ratio (acid test)	1.02 : 1
Debtors collection period	82 days
Cost of sales to finished goods	8.10
Labour cost % of sales	18.10%
Operating costs % of sales	72.1%
Distribution and admin costs as % of sales	14.12%

NB: Operating costs are defined as cost of sales less distribution and administration.

Required

(a) Calculate for Fylingdales Quarries Ltd the ratios listed in the Trade Association data based on the accounts for the year ended 31 December 20X1.

(b) Compare the performance of Fylingdales Quarries with the performance for the sector as a whole based on the data from the Trade Association.

QUESTION 41

Ocean Motors

Balance sheets

	20X8		*20X7*	
	£000	*£000*	*£000*	*£000*
Fixed assets				
Land and buildings				
Cost	600		450	
Depreciation	200		150	
		400		300
Plant and machinery				
Cost	600		400	
Depreciation	120		100	
		480		300
		880		600
Current assets				
Stock	500		200	
Debtors	600		300	
	1,100		500	
Creditors: amounts falling due within one year				
Bank overdraft	390		110	
Trade creditors	970		470	
Proposed dividend	110		100	
	1,470		680	
		(370)		(180)
		510		420
Capital and reserves				
Share capital - £1 ordinary shares		200		200
Profit and loss account		310		220
		510		420

Profit and loss accounts

	20X8	*20X7*
	£000	*£000*
Sales	1,500	1,000
Cost of sales	700	300
Gross profit	800	700
Administration and distribution expenses	400	360
Net profit before tax	400	340
Corporation tax	200	170
Net profit after tax	200	170
Dividends	110	100
Retained profit for the year	90	70
Retained profit brought forward	220	150
Retained profit carried forward	310	220

Required

Calculate the following ratios:

(i) Return on capital employed.
(ii) Asset turnover.
(iii) Net profit margin.
(iv) Gross profit margin.
(v) Stock turnover.
(vi) Current ratio.
(vii) Acid test ratio.
(viii) Stocks to (gross) current assets.
(ix) Average debtors' collection period.
(x) Debt to equity ratio, assuming that the bank overdraft is a long-term borrowing.

QUESTION 42

Wodehouse

Your firm has been asked by Wodehouse plc, a company owning a chain of hardware shops, to carry out a preliminary investigation with a view to the possible acquisition of two smaller companies in the same trade, Pelham Ltd and Grenville Ltd.

You are not yet able to visit either of the companies' premises, but have obtained copies of their latest accounts, both for the year ended 31 March 20X8. The profit and loss accounts and balance sheets are set out below.

Profit and loss accounts

	Pelham Ltd		*Grenville Ltd*	
	£000	*£000*	*£000*	*£000*
Turnover		840		762
Cost of sales		610		505
Gross profit		230		257
Distribution costs	115		56	
Administrative expenses	30		57	
		145		113

Operating profit	85	144
Interest payable	10	6
Net profit before taxation	75	138
Taxation	30	40
Net profit after taxation	45	98
Proposed dividend	10	33
Retained profit for the year	35	65
Retained profit brought forward	137	51
Retained profit carried forward	172	116

Balance sheets

	Pelham Ltd		*Grenville Ltd*	
	£000	*£000*	*£000*	*£000*
Fixed assets		216		268
Current assets				
Stocks	104		80	
Debtors	38		86	
Cash at bank	205		3	
	347		169	
Creditors: amounts falling due within one year				
Trade creditors and accruals	101		92	
Taxation payable	30		40	
Proposed dividends	10		33	
	141		165	
Net current assets		206		4
Total assets less current liabilities		422		272
Creditors: amounts falling due after more than one year				
10% debentures		150		
Bank loan (secured)				56
		272		216
Capital and reserves				
Share capital - £1 ordinary shares		100		100
Profit and loss account		172		116
		272		216

Required

Write notes for a meeting with the directors of Wodehouse plc to discuss your findings.

Include in your notes the following:

(a) Appropriate accounting ratios indicating the profitability and liquidity of the two companies.

(b) Brief comments on these ratios.

(c) An indication of the reasons for which one company might be preferable to the other as an investment.

QUESTION 43 (DECEMBER 2000)

Data

Duncan Tweedy wishes to invest some money in one of two private companies. He has obtained the latest financial statements for Byrne Ltd and May Ltd prepared for internal purposes. As part of his decision making process he has asked you to assess the relative profitability of the two companies. The financial statements of the companies are set out below.

Summary profit and loss account for the year ended 30 September 2000

	Byrne Ltd	*May Ltd*
	£000	*£000*
Turnover	5,761	2,927
Cost of sales	2,362	966
Gross profit	3,399	1,961
Distribution costs	922	468
Administrative expenses	1,037	439
Operating profit	1,440	1,054
Interest paid and similar charges	152	40
Profit on ordinary activities before taxation	1,288	1,014
Tax on profit on ordinary activities	309	243
Profit for the financial year	979	771
Dividends	312	141
Retained profit for the financial year	667	630

Balance sheets as at 30 September 2000

	Byrne Ltd		*May Ltd*	
	£000	*£000*	*£000*	*£000*
Fixed assets		6,188		2,725
Current assets	1,522		1,102	
Current liabilities	1,015		545	
Net current assets		507		557
Long-term loan		(1,900)		(500)
		4,795		2,782
Capital and reserves				
Called up share capital: ordinary shares of £1 each		2,083		939
Profit and loss account		2,712		1,843
		4,795		2,782

You have also been given the following ratios:

	Byrne Ltd	*May Ltd*
Return on capital employed	21.5%	32.1%
Gross profit percentage	59.0%	67.0%
Net profit percentage	25.0%	36.0%
Earnings per share	47p	82p

Task

Prepare a report for Duncan Tweedy that:

(a) explains the meaning of each ratio.

(b) uses each ratio to comment on the relative profitability of the companies.

(c) concludes, with reasons, which company is the more profitable.

QUESTION 44 (JUNE 2000)

Data

Magnus Carter has recently inherited a majority shareholding in a company, Baron Ltd. The company supplies camping equipment to retail outlets. Magnus wishes to get involved in the management of the business, but until now he has only worked in not-for-profit organisations. He would like to understand how the company has performed over the past two years and how efficient it is in using its resources. He has asked you to help him to interpret the financial statements of the company which are set out below.

Baron Ltd – Summary profit and loss account for the year ended 31 March

	2000	*1999*
	£000	*£000*
Turnover	1,852	1,691
Cost of sales	648	575
Gross profit	1,204	1,116
Expenses	685	524
Profit before tax	519	592
Tax	125	147
Profit after tax	394	445
Dividends	250	325
Retained profit	144	120

Baron Ltd – Summary balance sheets as at 31 March

	2000		*1999*	
	£000	*£000*	*£000*	*£000*
Fixed assets		1,431		1,393
Current assets				
Stocks	217		159	
Debtors	319		236	
Cash	36		147	
	572		542	
Current liabilities				
Trade creditors	48		44	
Proposed dividend	250		325	
Taxation	125		130	
	423		499	
Net current assets		149		43
		1,580		1,436
Share capital		500		500
Profit and loss account		1,080		936
		1,580		1,436

Task 44.1

Prepare a report for Magnus Carter that includes:

(a) A calculation of the following ratios for the two years:

(i) gross profit percentage.
(ii) net profit percentage.
(iii) debtor turnover in days (debtor payment period).
(iv) creditor turnover in days (creditor payment period based on cost of sales).
(v) stock turnover in days (stock turnover period based on cost of sales).

(b) For each ratio calculated:

(i) a brief explanation in general terms of the meaning of the ratio.

(ii) comments on how the performance or efficiency in the use of resources has changed over the two years.

Task 44.2

Prepare brief notes to answer the following questions asked by Magnus:

(a) How can the accounting equation in a company balance when, unlike a not-for-profit organisation, there are no funds to balance with net assets on its balance sheet?

(b) Can you give me two examples of users outside of the company, other than myself and the other shareholders, who may be interested in the financial statements of Baron Ltd. For each user can you tell me for what purpose they would use them?

(c) A statement, with reasons, identifying the areas that could be improved over the next year as indicated by the ratios and analysis performed.

QUESTION 45 (DECEMBER 1999) – Section 1

Data

Jonathan Fisher is intending to invest a substantial sum of money in a company. A colleague has suggested to him that he might want to invest in a private company called Carp Ltd which supplies pond equipment to retail outlets. You have been asked to assist him in interpreting the financial statements of the company which are set out below.

Carp Ltd - Summary profit and loss account for the year ended 30 September 1999

	1999	*1998*
	£000	*£000*
Turnover	3,183	2,756
Cost of sales	1,337	1,020
Gross profit	1,846	1,736
Expenses	1,178	1,047
Net profit before interest and tax	668	689
Interest	225	92
Profit before tax	443	597
Taxation	87	126
Profit after tax	356	471
Dividends	42	50
Retained profit	314	421

Carp Ltd – Summary balance sheets as at 30 September 1999

	1999		*1998*	
	£000	*£000*	*£000*	*£000*
Fixed assets		4,214		2,030
Current assets				
Stocks	795		689	
Debtors	531		459	
Cash	15		136	
	1,341		1,284	
Current liabilities				
Trade creditors	709		435	
Proposed dividend	42		50	
Taxation	87		126	
	838		611	
Net current assets		503		673
Long-term loan		(2,500)		(1,000)
		2,217		1,703
Share capital		700		500
Profit and loss account		1,517		1,203
		2,217		1,703

Task

Prepare notes for Jonathan Fisher covering the following points:

(a) Explain what a 'balance sheet' is and what a 'profit and loss account' is and identify the elements that appear in each statement.

(b) Explain the 'accounting equation' and demonstrate that the balance sheet of Carp Ltd as at 30 September 1999 confirms to it.

(c) Calculate the following ratios for the two years:

(i) gearing.
(ii) net profit percentage.
(iii) current ratio.
(iv) return on equity (after tax).

(d) Using the ratios calculated, comment on the company's profitability, liquidity and financial position and consider how these have changed over the two years.

(e) Using only the calculation of the ratios and the analysis of the changes over the two years, state whether the company is a better prospect for investment in 1999 than it was in 1998. Give reasons for your answer.

QUESTION 46 (JUNE 1999)

Data

Machier Ltd is a company that supplies stationery for business and domestic purposes. You have been asked to assist the directors in the interpretation of the financial statements of the company. They are intending to apply to the bank for a substantial loan. The bank has asked them for their financial statements for the last two years. The directors wish to know how the bank will view their profitability, liquidity and financial position on the evidence of these financial statements.

The directors are also concerned that they do not fully understand the financial statements of customers to whom they supply stationery. The customers include public sector and other not-for-profit organisations.

You have been supplied with the profit and loss account and the balance sheet of Machier Ltd for two years, prepared for internal purposes. These are set out below.

Machier Ltd - Profit and loss account for the year ended 31 March 1999

	1999	*1998*
	£000	*£000*
Turnover	2,636	1,687
Cost of sales	923	590
Gross profit	1,713	1,097
Depreciation	856	475
Other expenses	126	101
Profit on the sale of fixed assets	7	2
Operating profit for the year	738	523
Interest paid	252	120
Profit before tax	486	403
Taxation on profit	165	137
Profit after tax	321	266
Ordinary dividend	40	20
Retained profit	281	246
Retained profit brought forward	1,127	881
Retained profit carried forward	1,408	1,127

Machier Ltd - Balance sheet as at 31 March 1999

	1999	*1998*
	£000	*£000*
Fixed assets	4,282	2,376
Current assets		
Stocks	448	287
Debtors	527	337
Cash	-	86
	975	710
Current liabilities		
Trade creditors	381	212
Dividends payable	20	10
Taxation	165	137
Bank overdraft	183	-
	749	359
Net current assets	226	351
Long-term loan	2,800	1,500
	1,708	1,227

Capital and reserves		
Called up share capital	200	100
Share premium	100	-
Profit and loss account	1,408	1,127
	1,708	1,227

Task 46.1

Prepare a report for the directors which includes the following:

(a) A calculation of the following ratios of Machier Ltd for the two years:

(i) return on equity (after tax).
(ii) net profit percentage.
(iii) quick ratio/acid test.
(iv) gearing ratio.
(v) interest cover.

(b) Comments on the profitability, liquidity and the financial position of the company as revealed by the ratios and a statement of how this has changed over the two years covered by the financial statements.

(c) An opinion as to whether the bank would be likely to give the company a substantial loan based solely on the information in the financial statements.

Task 46.2

Prepare notes for the directors answering the following questions:

(a) What are the elements in a balance sheet of a company? State which of the balances in the balance sheet of Machier Ltd fall under each element.

(b) How are the elements related in the accounting equation? Show numerically that the accounting equation is maintained in the balance sheet of Machier Ltd.

QUESTION 47 (DECEMBER 1998)

Data

Bimbridge Hospitals Trust has just lost its supplier of bandages. The company that has been supplying it for the last five years has gone into liquidation. The Trust is concerned to select a new supplier which it can rely on to supply it with its needs for the foreseeable future. You have been asked by the Trust managers to analyse the financial statements of a potential supplier of bandages. You have obtained the latest financial statements of the company, in summary form, which are set out below.

Patch Ltd – Summary profit and loss account for the year ended 30 September 1998

	1998	*1997*
	£000	*£000*
Turnover	2,300	2,100
Cost of sales	1,035	945
Gross profit	1,265	1,155
Expenses	713	693
Net profit before interest and tax	552	462

Patch Ltd - Summary balance sheet as at 30 September 1998

	1998		*1997*	
	£000	*£000*	*£000*	*£000*
Fixed assets		4,764		5,418
Current assets				
Stocks	522		419	
Debtors	406		356	
Cash	117		62	
	1,045		837	
Current liabilities				
Trade creditors	305		254	
Taxation	170		211	
	475		465	
Net current assets		570		372
Long-term loan		(1,654)		(2,490)
		3,680		3,300
Share capital		1,100		1,000
Share premium		282		227
Profit and loss account		2,298		2,073
		3,680		3,300

You have also obtained the relevant industry average ratios which are as follows:

	1998	*1997*
Return on capital employed	9.6%	9.4%
Net profit percentage	21.4%	21.3%
Quick ratio/acid test	1.0 : 1	0.9 : 1
Gearing (debt/capital employed)	36%	37%

Task

Prepare a report for the managers of Bimbridge Hospitals Trust recommending whether or not to use Patch Ltd as a supplier of bandages. Use the information contained in the financial statements of Patch Ltd and the industry averages supplied.

Your answer should:

- Comment on the company's profitability, liquidity and financial position.
- Consider how the company has changed over the two years.
- Include a comparison with the industry as a whole.

The report should include calculation of the following ratios for the two years:

(i) Return on capital employed.
(ii) Net profit percentage.
(iii) Quick ratio/acid test.
(iv) Gearing.

QUESTION 48 (JUNE 2002)

Data

Michael Beacham has been asked to lend money to Goodall Ltd for a period of three years. He employed a financial adviser to advise him whether to make a loan to the company. The financial adviser has obtained the financial statements of the company for the past two years, calculated some ratios and found the industry averages. However, she was unable to complete her report. Michael has asked you to analyse the ratios and to advise him on whether he should make a loan to Goodall Ltd. The ratios are set out below.

	2002	*2001*	*Industry average*
Gearing ratio	67%	58%	41%
Interest cover	1.2	2.3	4.6
Quick ratio/acid test	0.5	0.8	1.1
Return on equity	9%	13%	19%

Task

Write a report for Michael Beacham that includes the following:

(a) an explanation of the meaning of each ratio.

(b) a comment on Goodall Ltd's financial position and the performance of the company as shown by the ratios.

(c) a statement of how the financial position and performance have changed over the two years, and how they compare with the industry average.

(d) a conclusion on whether Michael should lend money to Goodall Ltd. Base your conclusion only on the ratios calculated and the analysis performed.

QUESTION 49 (DECEMBER 2002)

Data

Karel Popper is the Managing Director of Zipps Ltd, a company that distributes clothing accessories. The company wishes to raise a loan to finance the expansion of activities. The bank has asked for information about the company including a copy of the financial statements for the past two years. Karel wants to know how likely it is that the bank would be willing to lend the company money on the basis of the financial position revealed in the financial statements alone. He has asked you to advise him on this matter. He also has some questions about financial accounting and reporting. He has given you the profit and loss accounts of Zipps Ltd and the summarised balance sheets for the past two years. These are set out below.

Zipps Ltd
Profit and loss account for the year ended 30 September

	2002 £000	*2001* £000
Turnover	2,412	2,496
Cost of sales	1,158	1,123
Gross profit	1,254	1,373
Distribution costs	814	651
Administrative expenses	486	452
Operating profit/(loss)	(46)	270
Interest payable and similar charges	104	77

Profit/(loss) on ordinary activities before taxation	(150)	193
Tax on profit on ordinary activities	-	42
Profit for the financial year	(150)	151
Dividends	50	50
Retained profit/(loss) for the financial year	(200)	101

Zipps Ltd
Balance sheet as at 30 September

	2002		*2001*	
	£000	*£000*	*£000*	*£000*
Fixed assets		1,220		1,118
Current assets				
Stocks	845		620	
Debtors	402		416	
Cash	183		266	
	1,430		1,302	
Current liabilities				
Trade creditors	650		620	
Net current assets		780		682
		2,000		1,800
Called up share capital:				
Ordinary shares of £1 each		200		200
Profit and loss account		500		700
Long term loan		1,300		900
		2,000		1,800

Task

Prepare a letter for Karel Popper that includes the following:

(a) A calculation of the following ratios of Zipps Ltd for each of the two years:

- Current ratio
- Quick ratio/acid test
- Gearing ratio
- Interest cover

(b) An explanation of the meaning of each ratio.

(c) A comment on how each ratio has changed over the two years and how this has affected the liquidity and the financial position of Zipps Ltd.

(d) A brief indication of other ratios that the bank may wish to calculate and why (you do not need to calculate them or comment on them in any way).

(e) A conclusion, with reasons, as to whether it is likely that the bank will lend the company money based solely on the ratios calculated and their analysis.

MOCK EXAMINATION

Mock Examination Questions

This examination is in TWO sections.

You have to show competence in both sections, so attempt and aim to complete EVERY task in BOTH sections.

Use the answer booklet provided. All workings should be shown in the answer booklet.

The answer booklet includes:

- a proforma Companies Act 1985 consolidated balance sheet (format 1).
- a proforma profit and loss account (format 1 as supplemented by FRS 3).
- a proforma for journal entries.

You should spend about 55 minutes on section 1 and 125 minutes on section 2.

SECTION 1

You should spend about 55 minutes on this section.

Data

Georgina Grieg is deciding whether to lend some money to Gint Ltd. She has asked you to comment on the financial position of the company and to explain certain aspects of the financial statements of the company. She has given you the financial statements of Gint Ltd. They are set out below.

Gint Ltd – Profit and loss accounts for the year ended 31 March

	2001	*2000*
	£000	*£000*
Turnover	3,851	3,413
Cost of sales	2,002	1,775
Gross profit	1,849	1,638
Distribution costs	782	737
Administrative expenses	515	491
Operating profit	552	410
Interest paid and similar charges	46	41
Profit on ordinary activities before taxation	506	369
Tax on profit on ordinary activities	126	92
Profit for the financial year	380	277
Dividends	160	140
Retained profit for the financial year	220	137

Gint Ltd - Balance sheets as at 31 March

	2001		2000	
	£000	£000	£000	£000
Fixed assets		4,372		4,341
Current assets				
Stocks	1,157		716	
Debtors	446		509	
Prepayments	23		19	
Cash at bank	37		57	
	1,663		1,301	
Current liabilities				
Trade creditors	406		392	
Accruals	31		26	
Dividends payable	160		140	
Taxation	126		92	
	723		650	
Net current assets		940		651
Long-term loan		(600)		(500)
		4,712		4,492
Capital and reserves				
Called up share capital: ordinary shares of £1 each		1,000		1,000
Profit and loss account		3,712		3,492
		4,712		4,492

TASK 1.1

Write a letter to Georgina Grieg that includes the following:

(a) A calculation of the following ratios of Gint Ltd for each of the two years:

- (i) Current ratio
- (ii) Quick ratio/acid test
- (iii) Gearing ratio
- (iv) Interest cover

(b) An explanation of the meaning of each ratio.

(c) Comments on the financial position of Gint Ltd as shown by the ratios.

(d) A statement on how the financial position has changed over the two years covered by the financial statements.

(e) A conclusion on whether Georgina Grieg should lend money to Gint Ltd. Base your conclusion only on the ratios calculated and analysis performed.

TASK 1.2

Prepare notes for a meeting with Georgina that answers the following questions relating to the financial statements of Gint Ltd:

(a) Why is the plant and machinery included in the fixed assets of the company classified as an 'asset' of the business?

(b) Why is the bank loan classified as a 'liability' of the business?

(c) (i) Why is the final figure of 'retained profit for the year' in the profit and loss account not the same figure that appears in the balance for the profit and loss account on the balance sheet of the company?

(ii) Is there any connection between the two figures?

SECTION 2

You should spend about 125 minutes on this section.

This section is in four parts.

PART A

You should spend about 45 minutes on this part.

Data

You have been asked to assist in the preparation of the consolidated accounts of the Jake Group. Set out below are the balance sheets of Jake Ltd and Dinos Ltd for the year ended 30 September 2001.

	Jake Ltd		*Dinos Ltd*	
	£000	*£000*	*£000*	*£000*
Tangible fixed assets		18,104		6,802
Investment in Dinos Ltd		5,000		
Current assets	4,852		2,395	
Current liabilities	2,376		547	
Net current assets		2,476		1,848
Long-term loan		(4,500)		(1,000)
		21,080		7,650
Share capital		5,000		1,000
Share premium		3,000		400
Profit and loss account		13,080		6,250
		21,080		7,650

You are given the following further information:

- The share capital of both Jake Ltd and Dinos Ltd consists of ordinary shares of £1 each. There have been no changes to the balances of share capital and share premium during the year. No dividends were paid or proposed by Dinos Ltd during the year.
- Jake Ltd acquired 600,000 shares in Dinos Ltd on 30 September 2000.

- At 30 September 2000 the balance on the profit and loss account of Dinos Ltd was £5,450,000.
- The fair value of the fixed assets of Dinos Ltd at 30 September 2000 was £3,652,000 as compared with their book value of £3,052,000. The revaluation has not been reflected in the books of Dinos Ltd. (Ignore any depreciation implications.)
- Goodwill arising on consolidation is to be amortised using the straight-line method over a period of 10 years.

TASK 2.1

Using the proforma provided in the answer booklet, prepare the consolidated balance sheet of Jake Ltd and its subsidiary undertaking as at 30 September 2001.

TASK 2.2

Prepare notes for the directors of Jake Ltd to answer the following question.

What would be the accounting treatment of the goodwill if, instead of having a useful life of 10 years, the goodwill was regarded as having an indefinite useful economic life?

Your answer should make reference, where relevant, to accounting standards.

PART B

You should spend about 20 minutes on this part.

Data

You have been asked to comment on the decline in the cash balance of Roth Co Ltd in 2001. The cash flow statement of Roth Co Ltd is set out below to assist you in your analysis.

Roth Co Ltd - Cash flow statement for the year ended 30 September 2001

	£000	£000
Net cash inflow from operating activities		5,959
Returns on investments and servicing of finance		
Interest paid		(542)
Taxation		(2,017)
Capital expenditure		
Payments to acquire tangible fixed assets	(1,432)	
Receipts from sale of tangible fixed assets	373	
		(1,059)
Equity dividends paid		(5,000)
		(2,659)
Financing		
Loan		1,050
Decrease in cash		(1,609)

Roth Co Ltd – Reconciliation of operating profit to net cash inflow from operating activities

	£000
Operating profit	8,763
Depreciation charges	1,847
Increase in stock	(36)
Increase in debtors	(3,584)
Decrease in creditors	(1,031)
Net cash inflow from operating activities	5,959

Further information:

- Sales and purchases for the company were similar in each of the two years.
- The cash balance at 30 September 2001 was £234,000.

TASK 2.3

Using the cash flow statement and the further information provided, prepare notes to explain why the cash balance has fallen in 2001.

PART C

You should spend about 45 minutes on this part.

Data

You have been asked to help prepare the financial statements of Leger Ltd for the year ended 30 September 2001 and to advise the directors on the regulatory framework for financial reporting. The trial balance of the company as at 30 September 2001 is shown below.

Leger Ltd – Trial balance as at 30 September 2001

	Debit	*Credit*
	£000	*£000*
Trade creditors		1,042
Interest	180	
Trade debtors	3,665	
Stock as at 1 October 2000	3,127	
Purchases	11,581	
Interim dividend	300	
Ordinary share capital		2,500
Accruals		92
9% debentures		4,000
Distribution costs	3,415	
Administrative expenses	2,607	
Land – cost	5,637	
Buildings – cost	3,615	
Fixtures and fittings – cost	2,871	
Motor vehicles – cost	1,526	
Office equipment – cost	1,651	
Profit and loss account		6,620
Revaluation reserve		1,000
Sales		21,324
Cash at bank	344	
Prepayments	84	
Share premium		1,000
Buildings – accumulated depreciation		1,147
Fixtures and fittings – accumulated depreciation		963
Motor vehicles – accumulated depreciation		784
Office equipment – accumulated depreciation		214
Carriage inwards	83	
	40,686	40,686

Further information:

- The authorised share capital of the company, all of which has been issued, consists of ordinary shares with a nominal value of £1.
- The company paid an interim dividend of 12p per share during the year but has not provided for the proposed final dividend of 15p per share.
- The stock at the close of business on 30 September 2001 was valued at cost at £5,408,000.
- The corporation tax charge for the year has been calculated as £1,567,000.
- Interest on the debentures has not been paid or charged in the accounts for the last six months of the year.
- Land and buildings were revalued during the year. The depreciation charge of £72,000 relating to the buildings has been calculated on the revalued amount and entered in the accounts in the trial balance. The depreciation charge calculated on the original historical cost of the buildings would have been £62,000.
- All of the operations of the business are continuing operations. There were no acquisitions in the year.

TASK 2.4

Using the proforma profit and loss account provided in the answer booklet, draft a profit and loss account for the year ended 30 September 2001.

TASK 2.5

Prepare a note on historical cost profits and losses as required by FRS 3.

TASK 2.6

Draft a letter to the directors of Leger Ltd telling them which regulatory bodies are involved in the process of setting and enforcing accounting standards in the United Kingdom and give a brief description of their roles.

PART D

You should spend about 15 minutes on this part.

Data

You have been asked to help prepare the financial statements of Brecked plc for the year ended 31 March 2001. The trial balance of the company as at 31 March 2001 is set out below.

Brecked plc - Trial balance as at 31 March 2001

	Debit *£000*	*Credit* *£000*
Trade creditors		2,307
Sales		21,383
Cash at bank	185	
Interest	400	
Trade debtors	3,564	
Land - cost	5,150	
Buildings - cost	3,073	
Fixtures and fittings - cost	2,169	
Motor vehicles - cost	4,609	

Office equipment - cost	927	
Interim dividend	450	
Ordinary share capital		3,000
Accruals		135
Long-term loan		5,000
Distribution costs	2,017	
Administrative expenses	1,351	
Profit and loss account		5,340
Prepayments	92	
Share premium		1,500
Buildings - accumulated depreciation		420
Fixtures and fittings - accumulated depreciation		756
Motor vehicles - accumulated depreciation		2,014
Office equipment - accumulated depreciation		382
Stock as at 1 April 2000	4,516	
Purchases	13,841	
Provision for doubtful debts		107
	42,344	42,344

Further information:

- The authorised share capital of the company, all of which has been issued, consists of ordinary shares with a nominal value of £1.
- The company paid an interim dividend of 15p per share during the year but has not provided for the proposed final dividend of 10p per share.
- The stock at the close of business on 31 March 2001 was valued at cost at £5,346,000.
- The corporation tax charge for the year has been calculated as £1,473,000.
- No depreciation charges for the year have been entered into the accounts as at 31 March 2001. The depreciation charges for the year are as follows:

	£000
Buildings	65
Fixtures and fittings	217
Motor vehicles	648
Office equipment	185

- The land has been revalued by professional valuers at £6,000,000. The revaluation is to be included in the financial statements for the year ended 31 March 2001.
- Legal proceedings have been started against Brecked Ltd because of faulty products supplied to a customer. The company's lawyers advise that it is probable that the entity will be found liable for damages of £250,000.

TASK 2.7

Using the proforma in your answer booklet, make the necessary journal entries as a result of the further information given above. Dates and narratives are not required.

Notes:

(1) You must show any workings relevant to these adjustments.

(2) Ignore any effect of these adjustments on the tax charge for the year given above.

Mock Examination Answer Booklet

SECTION 1

TASK 1.1

LETTER

TASK 1.2

NOTES

SECTION 2

TASK 2.1

Jake Ltd – Consolidated balance sheet as at 30 September 2001

	£000	£000
Fixed assets		
Intangible assets		
Tangible assets		
Investments		
		———
Current assets		
Current liabilities		
	———	
Net current assets		
		———
Total assets less current liabilities		
Less creditors: amounts falling due after more than one year		
Long-term loan		
		———
		———
Capital and reserves		
Called up share capital		
Share premium		
Profit and loss account		
		———
Minority interest		
		———
		———

WORKINGS

TASK 2.2

NOTES

TASK 2.3

NOTES

TASK 2.4

Leger Ltd – Profit and loss account for the year ended 30 September 2001

	£000	£000
Turnover		
Continuing operations		
Acquisitions		
Discontinued operations		
	——	
Cost of sales		
		——
Gross profit		
Distribution costs		
Administrative expenses		
	——	
		——
Operating profit		
Continuing operations		
Acquisitions		
Discontinued operations		
	——	
Profit on ordinary activities before interest		
Interest payable		
		——
Profit on ordinary activities before taxation		
Tax on profit on ordinary activities		
		——
Profit on ordinary activities after taxation		
Dividends		
		——
Retained profit for the financial year		
		——

WORKINGS

TASK 2.5

Note on historical cost profits and losses per FRS 3

£000

TASK 2.6

LETTER

TASK 2.7

JOURNAL		
	Dr £	*Cr* £

ANSWERS

Key Techniques Question Bank - Answers

Chapters 1 and 2

The regulatory and conceptual framework of accounting

ANSWER 1

(a) The user groups identified in the Statement of Principles are:

- Present and potential investors
- Lenders
- Suppliers and other trade creditors
- Employees
- Customers
- Government
- The public

(b) **Present and potential investors**

This group would consider whether to invest or disinvest in the entity. Equity investors consider two elements to their investment, income and capital gain. Income is received in the form of dividends, and capital gain in the upward movement of share price.

If the investor takes a short-term view then current dividends are the focus, whereas a longer term view would concern future earnings.

A guide to the future can to some extent be seen in a company report with the chairman's statement. Although it is largely based on current performance, the company's forward strategy is often reviewed.

The investor group would also be interested in profitability and its trend over a period of time, with particular emphasis on its effect on earnings per share.

Employees

Some companies produce a separate employees' report together with their annual report. Employees and their representatives require information on business performance for two principal reasons:

- Wage and salary negotiation.
- Assessment of current and forward opportunity in terms of employment.

They would be interested in both the current financial stability and the longer term financial viability of the business.

They need information in a clear, simple and understandable form.

Lenders

This group is often referred to as the loan creditor group. It would include the long, medium and short-term lenders of money. The principal concern of the existing and/or potential loan creditor is 'will we get our money back?'.

A short-term loan creditor will immediately focus on cash flow and the cash flow statement based on FRS 1 will be of particular interest here. The banks make up much of this group and they would have an interest in the net realisable value of the assets.

Medium and long-term loan creditor groups will be concerned with the future and long-term cash flow potential of the business.

The priority of claims on the business' resources would also be of concern to this group. They would be interested in the current and future profitability and growth prospects of the entity.

ANSWER 2

The ASB in the Statement of Principles for Financial Reporting identified four key characteristics which make financial information useful:

- Relevance
- Reliability
- Comparability
- Understandability

Relevance and reliability relate to the content of information, whereas comparability and understandability concern the presentation of information.

Relevance

For information to be relevant, it must have the ability to influence economic decisions. It can possess either predictive or confirmatory value.

Reliability

For information to be reliable, it must be a complete and faithful representation of the financial position. It must be neutral, free from material error, complete and possess the attribute of prudence.

Comparability

This enables a comparison of a number of previous statements with the current performance to be made. From such comparison trends may be identified. The characteristic incorporates both consistency and disclosure. Consistency in accounting technique from period to period and clear disclosure of accounting policies will assist trends to be identified fairly.

Understandability

This involves ensuring that the significance of the information can be clearly perceived by the user. Much of this depends on the users' abilities but also on aggregation and classification within the presentation of the financial statements.

ANSWER 3

- *Assets* are rights or other access to future economic benefits controlled by an entity as a result of past transactions or events.
- *Liabilities* are an entity's obligations to transfer economic benefits as a result of past transactions or events.
- *Ownership interest* is calculated as total assets less total liabilities.
- *Gains* are increases in ownership interest, other than those relating to contributions from owners.
- *Losses* are decreases in ownership interest, other than those relating to distributions to owners.
- *Contributions from owners* are increases in ownership interest resulting from investments made by owners in their capacity as owners.
- *Distribution to owners* are decreases in ownership interest resulting from transfers made to owners in their capacity as owners.

Accounting equation

Assets less liabilities = ownership interest

Question 4 – P.346 (Task 1.1)

ANSWER 4

(a) 'Assets' are rights or other access to future economic benefits controlled by an entity as a result of past transactions or events.

'Liabilities' are obligations of an entity to transfer economic benefits as a result of past transactions or events.

'Ownership interest' is the residual amount found by deducting all of the entity's liabilities from all of the entity's assets.

(b) The first transaction would increase the asset (stocks) by £120 and increase the liabilities (creditors) by £120.

The second transaction would decrease the asset (stock), ie stock at cost, by £120, but increase the asset cash by £180. This would increase net assets by £60 and ownership interest, ie capital, by £60 (the profit on the transaction).

(c) The accounting equation would then appear as:

Assets £1,380 – Liabilities £920 = Ownership interest £460

(d) A simple profit and loss account would show:

	£
Turnover	180
Cost of sales	120
Profit	60

(e) Users identified in the ASB Statement of Principles would include shareholders, customers, suppliers, loan creditor group, employees, public, government. For example, existing or potential shareholders would be interested in the business' profitability and its earning potential. They may compare current performance with the previous year's performance. Using such information they may decide to invest or disinvest in the business.

ANSWER 5

(a) **Assessing the stewardship of management**

Examples may include:

Organisation	*User*	*Use*
Limited company	Shareholders both potential and existing	Assess return on capital, return on equity and EPS
Limited company	Employees	Trade unions could campaign for failing managers to be replaced, in order to secure their members' employment.

(b) **Economic decisions**

Organisation	*User*	*Use*
Limited company	Potential investor	Decision whether or not to invest
Partnership/sole trader	Loan creditor group	Whether to grant additional loan funding

---

ANSWER 6

(a) The elements of assets, liabilities and ownership interest are shown in the balance sheet. The relationship between these elements is shown by the accounting equation as:

Assets - Liabilities = Ownership interest

(b) 'Gains', according to the Statement of Principles for Financial Reporting are 'increases in ownership interest not resulting from contributions from owners'. 'Losses' are defined by the same Statement as 'decreases in ownership interest not resulting from distributions to owners'. Both are shown either in the profit and loss account or in the statement of total recognised gains and losses.

ANSWER 7

(a) Potential investors are interested in information that is useful to them in taking decisions about potential investment in the company. They need information about the entity's potential return to investors and the risk inherent in those returns. Information about the entity's past financial performance helps them to assess its anticipated performance and cash-generation abilities. Information about its financial position and structure can be useful in assessing how future cash flows will be distributed and whether the company can meets its commitments as they fall due and raise finance in the future. Information about its financial adaptability is useful in assessing risk or benefit from unexpected changes.

(b) Assets are defined by the Statement of Principles for Financial Reporting as 'rights or other access to future economic benefits controlled by an entity as a result of past transactions or events'. Stock is an asset because it gives rise to future economic benefits controlled by the company in the form of cash that will be received from the sale of the goods. The benefits came about as a result of the past transaction of purchasing the stock for resale.

Chapter 3

Drafting financial statements for a sole trader

ANSWER 8

G Hick – Trading and profit and loss account for the year ended 31 December 20X3

	£	£
Sales		170,000
Stock 1/1/X3	17,500	
Purchases	120,000	
	137,500	
Less stock 31/12/X3	19,500	
Cost of goods sold		118,000
Gross profit		52,000
Expenses		
Wages	14,370	
Advertising	1,750	
Insurance	1,400	
Heat and light	2,300	
Business rates	2,400	
Maintenance	150	
Motor vehicle running costs	1,000	
Bad debts written off	500	
Bad debts provision	500	
Depreciation:		
Fixtures	1,500	
Premises	1,600	
Motor vehicles	2,500	
		29,970
Net profit for the year		£22,030

Balance sheet as at 31 December 20X3

	Cost	*Depreciation*	*NBV*
	£	£	£
Fixed assets			
Premises	40,000	9,600	30,400
Fixtures and fittings	7,500	4,000	3,500
Motor vehicle	12,500	7,500	5,000
	60,000	21,100	38,900
Current assets			
Stock		19,500	
Debtors	12,000		
Less provision for bad debts	1,500		
		10,500	
Pre-payments		800	
Cash in hand		1,250	
Cash at bank		1,700	
		33,750	
Less current liabilities			
Creditors		21,000	
Accruals		270	
		21,270	
Net current assets			12,480
Total assets less current liabilities			£51,380
Financed by			
Capital		43,450	
Add profit for the year		22,030	
		65,480	
Less drawings		14,100	
			£51,380

ANSWER 9

Michael Jay - Trading and profit and loss account for the year ended 31 December 20X3

	£	£
Sales		193,000
Stock 1/1/X3	23,150	
Purchases	131,100	
	154,250	
Less stock 31/12/X3	25,600	
Cost of goods sold		128,650
Gross profit		64,350

Expenses		
Wages	13,870	
Rates	3,000	
Insurances	2,110	
Heat and light	1,000	
Motor vehicle running costs	1,050	
Maintenance	500	
Bad debts written off	200	
Bad debts provision	460	
Profit on disposal of asset	(160)	
Depreciation:		
Premises	2,500	
Fixtures	2,200	
Motor vehicle	2,870	
		29,600
Net profit for the year		£34,750

Balance sheet as at 31 December 20X3

	Cost £	*Depreciation* £	*NBV* £
Fixed assets			
Premises	50,000	7,500	42,500
Fixtures	11,000	8,800	2,200
Motor vehicles	14,350	8,610	5,740
	75,350	24,910	50,440
Current assets			
Stock		25,600	
Debtors	16,000		
Less provision for bad debts	960	15,040	
Pre-payments		250	
Cash in hand		970	
Cash at bank		1,395	
		43,255	
Less current liabilities			
Creditors		19,100	
Accruals		720	
		19,820	
Net current assets			23,435
			£73,875
Financed by			
Capital		50,405	
Add profit for the year		34,750	
		85,155	
Less drawings		11,280	
			£73,875

ANSWER 10

(1) (C)

	£
Debtors	19,100
Less bad debt	400
	18,700
5% provision	935
Existing provision	735
Increase in provision	200

(2) (C)

Disposal of asset

	£		£
Asset at cost	3,400	Proceeds	2,150
Profit on sale	750	Accumulated depreciation (bal)	2,000
	£4,150		£4,150

(3) (A)

Rent and rates account

	£		£
Balance b/d	2,850	Pre-payment balance c/d	720
Accrual balance c/d	500	Profit and loss (bal)	2,630
	£3,350		£3,350
Balance b/d	720	Balance b/d	500

(4) (C)

Purchase ledger control account

	£		£
Returns	1,100	Balance b/d	15,100
Discounts	4,100	Purchases	96,000
Payments to suppliers	83,200		
Contra offset against sales ledger	1,560		
Balance c/d	21,140		
	£111,100		£111,100
		Balance b/d	21,140

(5) (a) (D)

Cost of goods sold:

	£	
Stock at start	16,200	
Add purchases	94,500	(net of drawings £1,500)
Less returns	(1,100)	
Less closing stock	(17,220)	
	92,380	

(b) (B)

	£	
Net sales	130,000	ie sales less returns inward
Cost of goods sold	92,380	
	37,620	

ANSWER 11 (Dec. 1999 Exam paper)

(Task 2.4) **Task 11.1**

			£	£
1	DR	Stock (balance sheet)	46,077	
	CR	Stock (profit and loss account)		46,077
2	DR	Prepayments	1,200	
	CR	Rent, rates and insurance		1,200
3	DR	Drawings	2,000	
	CR	Purchases		2,000
4	DR	Depreciation – motor vehicles	5,292	
	CR	Motor vehicles – accumulated depreciation		5,292

Workings

Stock:	£49,477 - £3,400	=	£46,077
Depreciation:	30% × (£36,000 - £18,360)	=	£5,292

(Task 2.5) **Task 11.2**

Elizabeth Ogier
Profit and loss account for the year ended 30 September 1999

	£	£
Sales	230,461	
Less Returns inwards	(3,053)	
		227,408
Less Cost of sales		
Opening stock	46,092	
Purchases	111,565	
Carriage inwards	1,256	
Less Returns outwards	(2,911)	
	156,002	
Less Closing stock	(46,077)	109,925
Gross profit		117,483

Less Expenses		
Rent, rates and insurance	7,091	
Motor expenses	5,813	
Bad debts	1,420	
Carriage outwards	1,571	
Salesperson's commission	2,561	
Bank charges	710	
Depreciation - Motor vehicles	5,292	
- Office equipment	2,312	
- Fixtures and fittings	602	
Wages, salaries and NIC	47,564	
Lighting and heating	3,056	
Postage and stationery	1,037	
Telephone	3,571	
Discounts allowed	410	
		83,010
Net profit		34,473

Task 11.3

(Task 2.6)

LETTER TO MS OGIER

AAT Student
Address
Date

Dear Ms Ogier

I write to explain the purpose of a number of adjustments I have made to your accounts at 30 September 1999.

The stock valuation has been adjusted to account for goods which had previously cost £8,200, which now have a net realisable value, ie can only realise on sale £4,800. This is required to comply with SSAP 9 which states that stock should be valued at the lower of cost or net realisable value. The final stock valuation is therefore £46,077.

A second adjustment is one regarding the purchases figure. The affairs of the business need to be separate from the affairs of the owner and, because some of the purchases were for personal use, they need to be deducted from the cost of purchases and charged to your drawings account.

If you have any questions relating to these adjustments, please do not hesitate to contact me.

Yours sincerely

AAT Student

Chapter 4

Preparing limited company accounts: for internal purposes

ANSWER 12

Trading and profit and loss account for the year ended 30 September 20X8

	£	£
Sales		1,312,567
Opening stock	41,912	
Purchases	839,004	
	880,916	
Closing stock	62,047	
Cost of sales		818,869
Gross profit		493,698
Heat and light	6,917	
Motor expenses (£4,174 + £412)	4,586	
Sundry expenses (£2,002 + £91)	2,093	
Wages and salaries (£121,600 + £36)	121,636	
Directors' remuneration	48,888	
Bank interest and charges (£1,621 + £533)	2,154	
Depreciation (W1)	24,315	
Bad debts (£1,370 + £1,194 + £512 - £612)	2,464	
		213,053
Net profit before tax		280,645
Corporation tax		131,700
Profit after tax		148,945
Proposed dividend		5,000
Retained profit for the year		143,945

Balance sheet at 30 September 20X8

	Cost £	*Depreciation* £	£
Fixed assets (W1)			
Freehold land	121,500	-	121,500
Freehold buildings	431,000	77,580	353,420
Plant and machinery	64,172	25,694	38,478
Motor vehicles	29,800	17,287	12,513
	646,472	120,561	525,911
Current assets			
Stock		62,047	
Debtors (W3)		58,510	
Cash in hand (£1,268 - £412 - £91 - £36)		729	
Cash at bank (£1,210 - £533)		677	
		121,963	
Creditors: amounts falling due within one year			
Trade creditors		21,172	
Dividend payable		5,000	
Taxation payable		131,700	
		157,872	
Net current liabilities			(35,909)
			490,002

Capital and reserves	
Ordinary share capital	50,000
Profit and loss account	440,002
	490,002

Workings

(1) Fixed assets

Depreciation on freehold buildings				
2% × £431,000	=	8,620 + 68,960	=	£77,580
Depreciation on plant and machinery				
20% × (£64,172 - £16,074)	=	9,620 + 16,074	=	£25,694
Depreciation on motor vehicles				
25% × (£28,900 - 6,500 + 7,400)	=	7,450 + 14,712 – 4,875	=	£17,287
		25,690		
Less profit on disposal (W2)		1,375		
Profit and loss charge for year		24,315		

(2) Profit on disposal of motor vehicle

	£
Original cost in 20X5	6,500
Three years' depreciation (20X5 – 20X7): 75%	4,875
Net book value at 30 September 20X7	1,625
Proceeds on disposal	3,000
Profit on disposal	1,375

(3) Debtors

	£
Control account balance	61,074
Less bad debts written off	1,370
	59,704
Less provision (2% × £59,704)	1,194
Per balance sheet	58,510

Chapter 5

Preparing limited company accounts: statutory formats

ANSWER 13

Typeset Ltd
Balance sheet as at 31 March 1999

	£000	£000
Fixed assets		
Tangible assets (W1)		5,820
Investments		1,580
		7,400
Current assets		
Stocks	4,187	
Debtors (W2)	3,153	
Cash at bank and in hand	216	
	7,556	
Creditors: amounts falling due within one year (W3)	2,728	
Net current assets		4,828
Total assets less current liabilities		12,228
Creditors: amounts falling due after more than one year		1,450
		10,778
Capital and reserves		
Called up share capital		5,000
Share premium account		1,200
Revaluation reserve		500
Profit and loss account (W4)		4,078
		10,778

[Note: It is also acceptable to include the investments under current assets.]

Workings (all figures £000)

W1 Fixed assets

	Cost	*Acc Dep'n*	*NBV*
Land	2,075	-	2,075
Buildings	2,077	383	1,694
Fixtures and fittings	1,058	495	563
Motor vehicles	2,344	1,237	1,107
Office equipment	533	152	381
	8,087	2,267	5,820

W2 Debtors

Trade debtors	3,136	
Less provision for doubtful debts	80	
		3,056
Prepayments		97
		3,153

Workings

$(\frac{1}{2} \times 36) + 2\% \times (3{,}136 - 36) = 80$

W3 *Creditors: amounts falling due within one year*

Trade creditors	1,763
Corporation tax payable	493
Dividends payable	350
Accruals	122
	2,728

W4 *Profit and loss account*

At 1/4/98	3,533
Retained profit for the year	545
At 31/3/99	4,078

Workings

Retained profit: 1,431 - 350 - 493 - 43 = 545
ie: (retained profit – final dividend – corporation tax – increase in provision for doubtful debts)

ANSWER 14

Task 14.1

			£000	£000
1	DR	Dividend	600	
	CR	Dividend payable		600
2	DR	Stock (balance sheet)	7,878	
	CR	Stock (trading account)		7,878
3	DR	Taxation	1,920	
	CR	Taxation payable		1,920
4	DR	Sales	204	
	CR	Trade debtors		204
5	DR	Interest	240	
	CR	Interest payable		240
6	DR	Land	500	
	CR	Revaluation reserve		500

Workings

Proposed final dividend:	4,000,000 × 15p	=	£600,000
Interest accrual:	£6,000,000 × 8% × ½	=	£240,000
Revaluation surplus:	£5,500,000 - £5,000,000	=	£500,000

Task 14.2

Hightink Ltd
Profit and loss account for the year ended 31 March 2002

	£000	*£000*
Turnover (W1)		
Continuing operations	31,506	
		31,506
Cost of sales (W2)		14,178
Gross profit		17,328
Distribution costs		6,852
Administrative expenses		3,378
Operating profit		
Continuing operations	7,098	
Profit on ordinary activities before interest		7,098
Interest payable and similar charges (W3)		480
Profit on ordinary activities before taxation		6,618
Tax on profit on ordinary activities		1,920
Profit on ordinary activities after taxation		4,698
Dividends (W4)		1,000
Retained profit for the financial year		3,698

Workings

All figures in £000

W1 Turnover

Sales per TB	31,710
Less: Credit sales recorded in wrong period	204
	31,506

W2 Cost of sales

Opening stock	6,531
Purchases	15,525
Closing stock	(7,878)
	14,178

W3 Interest paid

Interest per TB	240
Accrued interest	240
	480

W4 Dividends

Final dividend	600
Interim dividend	400
Total dividends	1,000

Hightink Ltd
Balance sheet as at 31 March 2002

	£000	£000
Fixed assets (W1)		14,105
Current assets		
Stocks	7,878	
Debtors (5,455 – 204)	5,251	
Cash	304	
	13,433	
Current liabilities		
Trade creditors	2,363	
Accruals	240	
Dividends	600	
Taxation	1,920	
	5,123	
Net current assets		8,310
Long term loan		(6,000)
		16,415
Capital and reserves		
Called up share capital		4,000
Share premium		2,000
Revaluation reserve		500
Profit and loss account (6,217 + 3,698)		9,915
		16,415

Workings

All figures in £000

W1 Fixed assets

	Cost	*Accumulated depreciation*	*NBV*
Land	5,500	-	5,500*
Buildings	3,832	564	3,268
Fixtures and fittings	2,057	726	1,331
Motor vehicles	3,524	1,283	2,241
Office equipment	2,228	463	1,765
	17,141	3,036	14,105

*Land: 5,000 + 500 = £5,500

Task 14.3

(a) A 'post balance sheet event' is an event, either favourable or unfavourable, that occurs between the balance sheet date and the date on which the Board of Directors approves the financial statements.

(b) An 'adjusting event' is an event that provides additional evidence of conditions existing at the date of the balance sheet. A 'non-adjusting event' is an event that arises after the balance sheet date that relates to conditions that did not exist at the date of the balance sheet.

(c) The losses that arose from the fire on the company's premises on 21 April 2002 constitute a 'non-adjusting' post balance sheet event. The condition did not exist at the balance sheet date, but came into existence after that date. No adjustment is required for the event as the conditions did not exist at the balance sheet date and thus do not constitute an adjusting event. However, the event is so material that failure to disclose may render the financial statements misleading. Hence, this non-adjusting event is to be disclosed by way of notes to the accounts.

ANSWER 15

Quine Ltd
Balance sheet as at 30 September 2002

	£000	*£000*
Fixed assets		
Intangible assets	840	
Tangible assets (W1)	5,300	
		6,140
Current assets		
Stocks	2,382	
Debtors (W2)	1,814	
Cash at bank and in hand	103	
	4,299	
Creditors: amounts falling due within one year (W3)	2,262	
Net current assets		2,037
Total assets *less* current liabilities		8,177
Creditors: amounts falling due after more than one year		2,500
		5,677
Capital and reserves		
Called up share capital		3,000
Share premium		500
Revaluation reserve (3,200 – 2,800)		400
Profit and loss account (bal fig)		1,777
		5,677

Workings (all £000)

1 **Fixed assets**

	Cost	Accumulated depreciation	NBV
Land (at valuation)	3,200	-	3,200
Buildings	1,480	702	778
Fixtures and fittings	645	317	328
Motor vehicles	1,632	903	729
Office equipment	447	182	265
	7,404	2,104	5,300

2 **Debtors**

Trade debtors	1,802
Less provision for doubtful debts	(72)
Prepayments	84
	1,814

3 **Creditors: amounts falling due within one year**

Trade creditors	1,309
Corporation tax payable	548
Dividends payable (3,000 × 10p)	300
Accruals	105
	2,262

Chapter 6

Cash flow statements

ANSWER 16

FRS 1 requires organisations to report their cash flows under standard headings which include:

- Operating activities.
- Returns on investments and servicing of finance.
- Taxation.
- Capital expenditure and financial investment.
- Equity dividends paid.
- Management of liquid resources.
- Financing.

Operating activities

This comprises the cash flow generated from trading. It includes profit before interest, depreciation - a non cash item added back; and the movement of cash tied up in debtors, creditors and stocks.

Returns on investments and servicing of finance

This shows any interest or dividends received, and the interest paid on long-term borrowings, eg debentures.

Taxation

Details the amount of corporation tax paid during the year.

Capital expenditure and financial investment

Outlines the investment in the acquisition of tangible fixed assets. Also shows the proceeds of any disposals of tangible fixed assets during the year.

Equity dividends paid

Shows the amount of dividends paid to ordinary shareholders in recognition of the risk inherent in equity investment.

Management of liquid resources

Shows any movement in cash tied up in short-term liquid investments.

Financing

Details cash raised from share issues, together with cash movements arising from the issue or redemption of debentures.

ANSWER 17

Cash flow statement for the year ended 31 March 20X1

	£000s
Net cash flow from operating activities (Note 1)	13,300
Returns on investments and servicing of finance: interest paid	(2,150)
Taxation	(2,260)
Capital expenditure: payment to acquire fixed assets (W1)	(9,000)
Equity dividends paid	(2,000)
Management of liquid resources	-
Financing:	
Issue of shares (W2)	1,610
Issue of debentures	1,500
Increase in cash	1,000

Note 1

Net cash flow from operating activities

	£000s
Operating profit	13,750
Depreciation	6,500
Increase in stocks	(2,000)
Increase in debtors	(4,500)
Decrease in creditors	(450)
	13,300

Note 2

Reconciliation of net cash flow to movement in net debt

	£000s
Increase in cash for the period	1,000
Cash from issue of debentures	(1,500)
Change in net debt	(500)
Net debt at 1 April 20X0	(18,750)
Net debt at 31 March 20X1	(19,250)

Note 3

Analysis of changes in net debt

	Net debt 1 April X0 £000s	*Cash flow in year £000s*	*Net debt 31 March X1 £000s*
Cash at bank	1,250	1,000	2,250
Debt	(20,000)	(1,500)	(21,500)
	(18,750)	(500)	(19,250)

Workings

(W1) Purchase of fixed assets:

	£000s
NBV 20X0	70,500
Less depreciation 20X1	6,500
	64,000
NBV 20X1	73,000
Purchases	9,000

(W2) Issue of shares:

	£000s
Share capital and reserves 31 March 20X0	74,040
Retained profit for year	6,500
	80,540
Share capital and reserves 31 March 20X1	82,150
Share issue	1,610

Question - P. 365 (Task 2.1)

ANSWER 18

Paton Ltd

Reconciliation of operating profit to net cash inflow from operating activities

	£000
Operating profit	5,938
Depreciation charges	2,007
Profit on sale of tangible fixed assets	(131)
Increase in stocks	(597)
Increase in debtors	(220)
Increase in creditors	423
Net cash inflow from operating activities	7,420

done ✓

ANSWER 19

Task 19.1

Angle Ltd
Cash flow statement for the year ended 31 March 2000

	£000	£000
Net cash inflow from operating activities		2,376
Returns on investments and servicing of finance		
Interest paid		(202)
Taxation		(370)
Capital expenditure		
Payments to acquire tangible fixed assets (W)		(3,653)
Equity dividends paid		(400)
		(2,249)
Financing		
Loan	1,000	
Issue of ordinary share capital	1,600	
		2,600
Increase in cash		351

Working

Tangible fixed assets

	£000		£000
Balance b/f	4,009	Depreciation charge	875
Revaluation	500	Balance c/f	7,287
Additions (bal fig)	3,653		
	8,162		8,162

Task 19.2

Angle Ltd
Statement of total recognised gains and losses for the year ended 31 March 2000

	£000
Profit for the financial year	1,145
Unrealised surplus on revaluation of properties	500
Total gains and losses recognised since last annual report	1,645

Task 19.3

(a) **Terms covered in FRS 3**

Acquisitions are operations the reporting entity have acquired in the trading period.

Discontinued operations are those sold or terminated which satisfy all the following conditions:

- The sale or termination is completed either in the period or before the earlier of three months after the commencement of the subsequent period and the date on which the financial statements are approved.

- If a termination, the former activities must have ceased permanently.
- The sale or termination should have a material effect on the business operations.
- The assets, liabilities, results and activities are clearly distinguishable.

(b) **Importance of distinctions**

The three categories of operation help in assessing current business activity and in forming a view of future activity.

The distinction assists with analysing the contribution of both discontinued operations and acquisitions to business performance.

ANSWER 20 (Dec. 1999 Exam paper – Task 2.3)

Diewelt Ltd
Cash flow statement for the year ended 30 September 1999

	£000	£000
Net cash inflow from operating activities		1,242
Returns on investments and servicing of finance		
Interest paid		(365)
Taxation		(491)
Capital expenditure		
Payments to acquire tangible fixed assets (W1)	(1,906)	
Proceeds of sale of asset (W2)	108	
		(1,798)
Equity dividends paid (W3)		(368)
		(1,780)
Financing		
Loan	400	
Issue of ordinary share capital	1,100	
		1,500
Decrease in cash		(280)

Workings

(W1) Fixed asset additions:

Tangible fixed assets

	£000		£000
Balance b/f	5,620	Depreciation charge	985
Additions (bal fig)	1,906	Disposal (136 – 85)	51
		Balance c/f	6,490
	7,526		7,526

(W2) Disposal proceeds:

Disposal

	£000		£000
Cost	136	Accumulated depreciation	85
Profit on disposal	57	Proceeds (bal fig)	108
	193		193

(W3) Dividends paid:

Dividends

	£000		£000
Paid (bal fig)	368	Balance b/f	192
Balance c/f	264	Profit and loss	440
	632		632

ANSWER 21

Task 21.1

Reconciliation of operating profit to net cash inflow from operating activities

	£000
Operating profit	738
Depreciation charges	856
Profit on sale of tangible fixed assets	(7)
Increase in stocks	(161)
Increase in debtors	(190)
Increase in creditors	169
Net cash inflow from operating activities	1,405

Task 21.2

Cash flow statement of Machier Ltd for the year ended 31 March 1999

	£000
Net cash inflow from operating activities	1,405
Returns on investments and servicing of finance	
Interest paid	(252)
Taxation	(137)
Capital expenditure	
Payments to acquire tangible fixed assets (W1)	(2,771)
Proceeds on sale of asset (9 + 7)	16
	(1,739)
Equity dividends paid (W2)	(30)
	(1,769)
Financing	
Loan	1,300
Issue of ordinary share capital	200
Decrease in cash	(269)

Workings

(W1) Fixed asset additions:

Tangible fixed assets

	£000		£000
Balance b/f	2,376	Depreciation charge	856
Additions (bal fig)	2,771	Disposal (28 - 19)	9
		Balance c/f	4,282
	5,147		5,147

(W2) Dividends paid:

Dividends

	£000		£000
Paid (bal fig)	30	Balance b/f	10
Balance c/f	20	Profit and loss	40
	50		50

ANSWER 22

Games Ltd
Reconciliation of operating profit to net cash flow from operating activities

	£
Operating profit (246 + 56)	302,000
Depreciation	277,000
Increase in stocks	(45,000)
Increase in debtors	(144,000)
Increase in creditors	71,000
Net cash inflow from operating activities	£461,000

ANSWER 23

Sholti Ltd
Reconciliation of operating profit to net cash inflow from operating activities

	£000
Operating profit	7,433
Depreciation charges	1,850
Profit on sale of tangible fixed assets	(378)
Decrease in stocks (8,632 - 9,013)	381
Increase in debtors (5,391 - 4,728)	(663)
Increase in creditors (2,382 - 2,081)	301
Net cash inflow from operating activities	8,924

ANSWER 24

Duhem Ltd
Cash flow statement for the year ended 30 September 2002

		£000	£000
Net cash inflow from operating activities			4,658
Returns on investments and servicing of finance			
	Interest paid		(513)
Taxation			(618)
Capital expenditure			
	Payments to acquire tangible fixed assets (W1)	(6,900)	
	Proceeds from sale of fixed assets (W2)	666	
			(6,234)
Equity dividends paid (W3)			(710)
			(3,417)
Financing			
	Loan	1,600	
	Issue of ordinary share capital	1,600	
			3,200
Decrease in cash			(217)

Workings

(All figures £000)

(W1)

Tangible fixed assets

Balance b/f	12,710	Depreciation	1,906
Additions (bal fig)	6,900	Disposal (980 – 420)	560
		Balance c/f	17,144
	19,610		19,610

(W2)

Disposal of fixed assets

Cost	980	Accumulated depreciation	420
Profit on disposal	106	Proceeds (bal)	666
	1,086		1,086

(W3)

Dividends

Cash paid (bal)	710	Balance b/f	500
Balance c/f	590	Profit and loss	800
	1,300		1,300

Chapters 7, 8 and 9

Consolidated accounts

ANSWER 25

Consolidated balance sheet

Dunsley Ltd and its subsidiary undertaking, Ravenscar Ltd, as at 31 December 20X1

	£000s	£000s
Fixed assets		
Intangible asset: goodwill (W3)		447
Tangible assets (5,210 + 1,750)		6,960
Current assets		
Stocks (1,520 + 610)	2,130	
Debtors (1,120 + 520)	1,640	
Cash at bank (120 + 85)	205	
	3,975	
Less current liabilities (1,610 + 710)	2,320	
Net current assets		1,655
		£9,062
Capital and reserves		
Share capital		3,000
Share premium		1,000
Profit and loss account		4,160
Minority interest (W4)		902
		£9,062

Workings

(W1) Group structure:

D
| 60%
R

$\frac{300,000}{500,000}$ = 60% holding

(W2) Net assets of Ravenscar Ltd:

	At acquisition date = balance sheet date £000s
Per balance sheet	1,755
Fair value adjustment (1,750 – 1,250)	500
	2,255

(W3) Goodwill:

	£000s
Price paid	1,800
Less: Net assets acquired (60% × 2,255 (W2))	(1,353)
	447

(W4) Minority interest:

	£000s
40% × 2,255 (W2)	902

ANSWER 26

Consolidated balance sheet as at 31 December 20X1

	£000s	£000s
Fixed assets		
Intangible asset (W3)		1,944
Tangible assets (17,500 + 5,750 + 400)		23,650
Current assets (4,750 + 1,520)	6,270	
Less current liabilities (2,250 + 940)	3,190	
Net current assets		3,080
Total assets less current liabilities		28,674
Less creditors falling due after one year:		
Debentures (4,100 + 1,000)		5,100
		£23,574
Share capital and reserves:		
Share capital		8,000
Share premium		1,500
Profit and loss account (W4)		11,782
Minority interest (W5)		2,292
		£23,574

Workings

(W1) Group structure:

S
|
| 60%
|
H

(W2) Net assets of Harkhill Ltd:

	At date of acquisition £000s	*At balance sheet date £000s*
Share capital	1,000	1,000
Share premium	500	500
Profit and loss account	3,000	3,830
	4,500	5,330
Fair value adjustment (3,500 – 3,100)	400	400
	4,900	5,730

(W3) Goodwill:

	£000s
Price paid	5,100
Less: Net assets acquired (60% × 4,900 (W2))	(2,940)
	2,160
Less: Amortisation to date (10%)	(216)
	1,944

(W4) Consolidated profit and loss account:

	£000s
Shireoaks Ltd	11,500
Harkhill Ltd 60% × (3,830 – 3,000)	498
Less: Goodwill amortisation to date	(216)
	11,782

(W5) Minority interest:

	£000s
40% × 5,730 (W2)	2,292

Question 27 - P.380 (Task 2.2)

ANSWER 27

	£000
Price paid	5,000
Less: Net assets acquired 75% × (4,800 + 1,000 fair value adjustment)	(4,350)
Goodwill arising	650

ANSWER 28

Norman Ltd
Consolidated balance sheet as at 31 March 2000

	£000	£000
Fixed assets		
Intangible assets: goodwill (W3)		414
Tangible assets (12,995 + 1,755 + 400)		15,150
		15,564
Current assets		
Stocks	4,098	
Debtors	2,575	
Cash	188	
	6,861	
Creditors: amounts falling due within one year		
Trade creditors	2,193	
Proposed dividend	160	
Taxation	863	
	3,216	
Net current assets		3,645
Total assets less current liabilities		19,209
Creditors: amounts falling due after more than one year		
Long-term loan		(400)
		18,809
Capital and reserves		
Called up share capital		2,000
Profit and loss account (W4)		16,238
		18,238
Minority interest (W5)		571
		18,809

Workings

(W1) Group structure:

N

75% $\frac{750,000}{1,000,000}$ = 75% holding

S

(W2) Net assets of Saxon Ltd:

	At date of acquisition £000	*At balance sheet date £000*
Share capital	1,000	1,000
Share premium	200	200
Profit and loss account	424	684
	1,624	1,884
Fair value adjustment	400	400
	2,024	2,284

(W3) Goodwill:

	£000
Price paid	1,978
Less: Net assets acquired (75% × 2,024 (W2))	(1,518)
Goodwill	460
Less: Amortisation to date (10%)	(46)
Net book value of goodwill	414

(W4) Consolidated profit and loss account:

	£000
Norman Ltd	16,089
Saxon Ltd (75% × (684 – 424))	195
Less: Goodwill amortised to date	(46)
	16,238

(W5) Minority interest:

	£000
25% × 2,284 (W2)	571

ANSWER 29 (Dec. 1999 Exam paper)

Task 29.1
(Task 2.1)

Shopan Ltd
Consolidated balance sheet as at 30 September 1999

	£000	£000
Fixed assets		
Intangible assets: goodwill (W2)		222
Tangible assets (6,273 + 1,633 + 400)		8,306
		8,528
Current assets		
Stocks	2,766	
Debtors	2,102	
Cash	288	
	5,156	
Current liabilities		
Trade creditors	1,973	
Taxation	619	
	2,592	
Net current assets		2,564
Total assets less current liabilities		11,092
Long-term loan		(3,270)
		7,822

Capital and reserves	
Called up share capital	2,000
Share premium	950
Profit and loss account	4,246
	7,196
Minority interest (25% × (2,104 + 400))	626
	7,822

Workings

(1) Shopan Ltd holding in Hower Ltd:

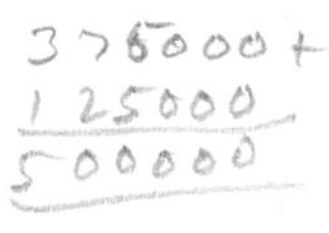

$\frac{375,000}{500,000} = 75\%$

Minority interest:

$\frac{125,000}{500,000} = 25\%$

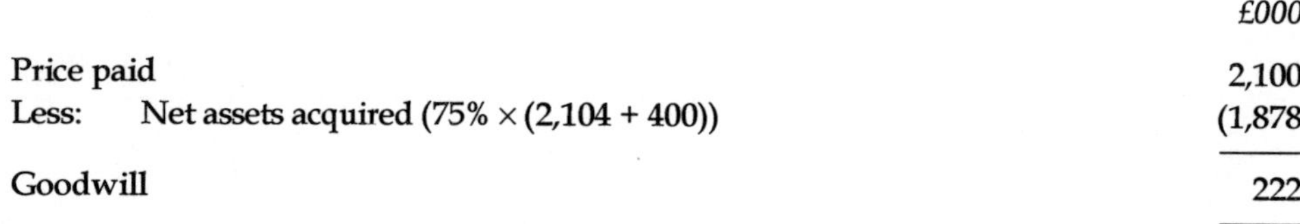

(2) Goodwill:

	£000
Price paid	2,100
Less: Net assets acquired (75% × (2,104 + 400))	(1,878)
Goodwill	222

Task 29.2

An undertaking is the parent undertaking of another undertaking (a subsidiary undertaking) according to FRS 2 if any of the following apply:

- It holds a majority of the voting rights in the undertaking.
- It is a member of the undertaking and has the right to appoint or remove directors holding a majority of the voting rights at meetings of the board on all, or substantially all, matters.
- It has the right to exercise a dominant influence over the undertaking.
- It is a member of the undertaking and controls alone, pursuant to an agreement with other shareholders or members, a majority of the voting rights in the undertaking.
- It has a participating interest in the undertaking and:
  - it actually exercises a dominant influence over the undertaking; or
  - it and the undertaking are managed on a unified basis.

A parent undertaking is also treated as the parent undertaking of the subsidiary undertakings of its subsidiary undertakings.

ANSWER 30

Minority interest = 25%.

Minority interest in the consolidated balance sheet as at 30 September 1998 would be 25% × (2,280 + 200 fair value adjustment) = £620,000.

The minority interest on the consolidated balance sheet of Fun Ltd would be shown after share capital and reserves attributable to the group.

Minority interest is that proportion of the subsidiary undertaking's share capital which is not held by the parent company, Fun Ltd.

ANSWER 31

Task 31.1

Goodwill on acquisition:

	£000
Price paid	1,716
Less: Net assets acquired (75% × (1,708 + 400 fair value adjustment))	(1,581)
Goodwill arising	135

Task 31.2

FRS 10 states that positive goodwill should be capitalised and classified as an intangible asset on the balance sheet.

There is a rebuttable presumption that the useful economic life of purchased goodwill should not normally exceed 20 years.

Where the life is believed to be 20 years or less, the carrying value should be amortised to the profit and loss account on a systematic basis, using the straight line method, over the useful economic life.

If the life is assumed to be more than 20 years and the value is significant, it should be amortised over its useful life, but must also be reviewed for impairment on an annual basis.

ANSWER 32

Calculation of goodwill as at 31 March 2002

	Total equity	*Attributable to Fertwrangler (60%)*
Net assets at acquisition date	*£000*	*£000*
Share capital	2,000	1,200
Share premium	1,000	600
Revaluation reserve (4,455 – 4,055)	400	240
Profit and loss – at acquisition	1,350	810
		2,850
Consideration		3,510
Goodwill arising on consolidation		660
Less: Goodwill written off (10%)		66
Goodwill as at 31 March 2002		594

Workings

(i) Fertwrangler Ltd holding in Voncarryon Ltd:

$$\frac{1,200,000}{2,000,000} = 60\%$$

(ii) Revaluation of assets in Voncarryon Ltd to fair value at date of acquisition:

DR	Fixed assets	£400,000	
CR	Revaluation reserve		£400,000

This is the fair value adjustment necessary to restate the fixed assets on acquisition from their book value of £4,055,000 to their fair value of £4,455,000.

ANSWER 33

Consolidated profit and loss account for the year ended 31 December 20X1

	£000s
Turnover (W1)	18,400
Cost of sales (W2)	9,100
Gross profit	9,300
Distribution costs	2,050
Admin costs	1,825
Profit on ordinary activities before interest	5,425
Interest paid	885
Profit on ordinary activities before tax	4,540
Tax on profit on ordinary activities	1,600
Profit on ordinary activities after tax	2,940
Minority interest (W3)	200
Profit for the financial year	2,740
Dividends	800
Retained profit for the financial year	1,940

Workings

		£000s
(1)	Turnover:	
	Malton Ltd	14,100
	Whitby Ltd	5,100
	Less inter-company sales	(800)
		18,400
(2)	Cost of sales:	
	Malton Ltd	7,150
	Whitby Ltd	2,750
	Less inter-company purchase	(800)
		9,100
(3)	Minority interest:	
	20% of £1,000	200

ANSWER 34

Skuhn plc
Consolidated profit and loss account for the year ended 30 September 2002

	£000
Turnover (W1)	32,700
Cost of sales (W2)	14,055
Gross profit	18,645
Distribution costs	4,640
Administrative expenses	3,050
Profit on ordinary activities before interest	10,955
Interest payable	2,500
Profit on ordinary activities before taxation	8,455
Tax on profit on ordinary activities	2,565
Profit on ordinary activities after taxation	5,890
Minority interests (W3)	932
Profit for the financial year	4,958
Dividends	2,100
Retained profit for the financial year	2,858

Workings

All figures £000

(1) **Turnover**

Skuhn sales	25,300
e-Lakatos sales	8,600
Less intercompany sale	(1,200)
	32,700

(2) **Cost of sales**

Skuhn cost of sales	11,385
e-Lakatos cost of sales	3,870
Less intercompany purchase	(1,200)
	14,055

(3) Minority interests: 40% × 2,330 = 932

Chapter 10

Reporting financial performance (FRS 3, SSAP 25, FRS 14)

ANSWER 35

Whitby and Sandsend Ltd – Profit and loss account for the year ended 31 December 20X1

	£000s	£000s
Turnover:		
Continuing operations	40,910	
Acquisitions	2,850	
	43,760	
Discontinued operations	1,240	
		45,000
Cost of sales		19,500
Gross profit		25,500
Distribution costs	5,950	
Administrative expenses	3,469	
		9,419
Operating profit:		
Continuing operations	15,361	
Acquisitions	710	
	16,071	
Discontinued operations	10	
		16,081
Loss on disposal of discontinued operations		480
Profit on ordinary activities before interest		15,601

ANSWER 36

Bay Ltd – Statement of total recognised gains and losses for the year ended 31 March 20X1

	£000s
Profit for the financial year	1,320
Unrealised surplus on revalued land	600
Total gains and losses since last annual report	1,920

ANSWER 37

Task 37.1

Mattesich Ltd
Profit and loss account for the year ended 30 September 2000

	£000	£000
Turnover		
Continuing operations (W1)	36,521	
Acquisitions	2,714	
	39,235	
Discontinued operations	1,213	
		40,448
Cost of sales (W2)		18,173
Gross profit		22,275
Distribution costs		5,863
Administrative expenses		3,469
Operating profit		
Continuing operations (W3)	12,327	
Acquisitions	603	
	12,930	
Discontinued operations	13	
		12,943
Loss on disposal of discontinued operations		(473)
Profit on ordinary activities before interest		12,470
Interest payable		544
Profit on ordinary activities before taxation		11,926
Tax on profit on ordinary activities		3,813
Profit on ordinary activities after taxation		8,113
Dividends (W4)		4,900
Retained profit for the financial year		3,213

Workings

W1 *Turnover*

	£000
Sales per ETB	40,448
Less acquisitions	(2,714)
Less discontinued operations	(1,213)
Turnover from continuing operations	36,521

W2 *Cost of sales*

	£000
Opening stock	12,973
Purchases	18,682
Closing stock	(13,482)
	18,173

W3 *Operating profit from continuing operations*

	£000
Gross profit	22,275
Less distribution costs	(5,863)
Less administration expenses	(3,469)
Operating profit	12,943
Less operating profit from acquisitions	(603)
Less operating profit from discontinued operation	(13)
Operating profit from continuing operations	12,327

W4 *Dividends*

	£000
Final dividend (14,000,000 shares @ 20p per share)	2,800
Interim dividend	2,100
Total dividends	4,900

Task 37.2

NOTES FOR THE BOARD MEETING

(a) FRS 15 requires that where a policy of revaluation is adopted, it should be applied to individual classes of tangible fixed assets.

If a policy is adopted to revalue land and buildings, then all the assets included in land and buildings would have to be the subject of revaluation. It is not possible under the standard to show some at cost and others at valuation.

(b) FRS 15:

(i) states that where a tangible fixed asset is subject to revaluation, the carrying amount should be its current value on the balance sheet date.

(ii) states the basis of valuation for non-specialised properties should be existing use value.

(iii) states that any gain or loss on revaluation should be shown in the statement of total recognised gains and losses.

ANSWER 38

Task 38.1

			£000	£000
(1)	DR	Final dividend (8,000 × 10p)	800	
	CR	Dividends payable		800
(2)	DR	Tax charge	972	
	CR	Corporation tax payable		972
(3)	DR	Interest charges (3,600 × 8% × $\frac{1}{12}$)	24	
	CR	Interest charges		24

Task 38.2

Fun Ltd
Profit and loss account for the year ended 30 September 1998

	£000
Turnover	
Continuing operations (W1)	14,363
Cost of sales (W2)	6,464
Gross profit	7,899
Distribution costs	2,669
Administrative expenses	2,042
Operating profit	
Continuing operations	3,188
Interest payable and similar charges	324
Profit on ordinary activities before taxation	2,864
Tax on profit on ordinary activities	972
Profit for the financial year	1,892
Dividends (W3)	1,280
Retained profit for the financial year	612

Workings (all figures £000)

1 Sales 14,595 - returns inwards 232 = 14,363

2 Calculation of cost of sales:

Opening stock	1,893	
Purchases	6,671	
Plus carriage inwards	87	
Less returns outwards	(146)	
	8,505	
Less closing stock	2,041	
Cost of sales		6,464

3 Dividends:

Interim dividend	480
Final dividend proposed	800
	1,280

Task 38.3

(a) Share premium arises when shares are issued at a price more than their nominal value.

For example, if 50,000 ordinary shares of £1 each were issued at £1.50 then the accounting procedure would be:

Dr	Cash/bank	£75,000	
Cr	Share capital		£50,000
Cr	Share premium		£25,000

The revaluation reserve represents the excess of the valuation of an asset over its book value.

For example, an asset with a NBV of £250,000 might have its market value to be considered to be £400,000 established by valuation.

The accounting procedure would be:

Dr	Fixed assets	£150,000	
Cr	Revaluation reserve		£150,000

(b) SSAP 21 deals with the way in which leased assets are accounted for.

The accounting treatment depends on whether the lease is a finance lease or operating lease.

The standard defines a finance lease as one which transfers substantially all the risks and rewards of ownership to the lessee.

An operating lease is a lease other than a finance lease.

An asset acquired under a finance lease should be recorded in the lessee's balance sheet as an asset and also as an obligation to pay future rentals. If the asset was leased on an operating lease it would not be shown as an asset on the lessee's balance sheet.

Chapters 11 to 17

Accounting standards

ANSWER 39

Notes for meeting with the Chief Accountant

(a) Entities should comply with the requirements of accounting standards, Urgent Issues Task Force Abstracts (UITF Abstracts) and companies legislation.

Where compliance with accounting standards or UITF Abstracts is inconsistent with the requirement to give a true and fair view, they should be departed from to the extent necessary to give a true and fair view.

(b) The objectives are:

- Relevance
- Reliability
- Comparability
- Understandability

(c) The two concepts are:

- Going concern
- Accruals

Chapter 18

Interpretation of accounts

ANSWER 40

(a) **Return on capital employed**

$$\frac{\text{Profit before interest and tax}}{\text{Total assets less current liabilities}} \times 100\%$$

(If the balance sheet had included long-term debt then this figure of total assets less current liabilities would comprise 'capital and reserves' plus 'long-term debt'.)

$\frac{0.82}{3.49} \times 100\%$ = 23.50%

Asset turnover

$$\frac{\text{Turnover}}{\text{Total assets less current liabilities}}$$

$\frac{6.90}{3.49}$ = 1.98 times

% net profit before tax to sales

$\frac{0.82}{6.90} \times 100\%$ = 11.88%

Current ratio

Current assets : current liabilities

2.49 : 1.90 = 1.31 : 1

Liquidity ratio/acid test

Current assets less stocks : current liabilities

1.89 : 1.90 = 0.99 : 1

Debtors collection period

$\frac{\text{Debtors}}{\text{Sales}} \times 365$ days

$\frac{1.84}{6.90} \times 365$ = 97 days

Cost of sales to finished goods

6.08 : 0.40 = 15.2

Labour cost % of sales

$\frac{1.26}{6.90} \times 100\%$ = 18.26%

Operating costs as % of sales

$$\frac{6.08 - 0.88}{6.90} \times 100\% \quad = \quad 75.36\%$$

Distribution and admin costs % of sales

$$\frac{0.88}{6.90} \times 100\% \quad = \quad 12.75\%$$

(b) **Comparison of Fylingdales Quarries Ltd with sector as a whole**

Ratio	*Fylingdales*	*Sector*	*Comment*
Return on capital employed	23.50%	25.60%	Marginally less than sector as a whole but still giving a more than adequate return on investment.
Asset turnover	1.98	1.80	The company is generating more volume of output per '£' worth of investment than its competitors.
% net profit to sales	11.88%	14.22%	The company is less profitable than the sector as a whole. It seems to be achieving volume at the expense of profitability.
Current ratio	1.31 : 1	1.50 : 1	The company has a sound level of liquidity, but marginally less than the sector.
Acid test	0.99 : 1	1.02 : 1	An ideal ratio here would be 1 : 1, the company has almost achieved this desired level of liquidity; again marginally less than the sector.
Debtors collection period	97 days	82 days	Tighter controls are required here. The collection period is typically high for the sector but the company needs to review its position. There is always the danger of the incidence of bad debts.
Cost of sales to finished goods	15.2	8.10	The company is turning over its finished goods stocks faster than the industry as a whole. It is holding approx 0.8 months compared with 1.48 months for the sector.
Labour costs as % of sales	18.26%	18.10%	Almost in line with the industry average.
Operating costs % of sales	75.36%	72.10%	The lack of profitability is highlighted here. Costs may need review and control or selling prices may need revising.
Distribution and admin cost % of sales	12.75%	14.12%	More favourable than the sector as a whole.

Overall the company performance is marginally worse than the average performance for the sector.

The lack of profitability as highlighted in the % of operating costs to sales is the significant factor which affects the return on capital. The company is achieving a good level of activity but is marginally less profitable.

ANSWER 41

Ocean Motors

		20X8	*20X7*
(i)	Return on capital employed	78.4%	81.0%
(ii)	Asset turnover	2.9	2.4
(iii)	Net profit margin	26.7%	34.0%
(iv)	Gross profit margin	53.3%	70.0%
(v)	Stock turnover	1.4	1.5
(vi)	Current ratio	0.75	0.74
(vii)	Acid test ratio	0.41	0.44
(viii)	Stocks to (gross) current assets	45.5%	40.0%
(ix)	Average debtors' collection period	146 days	109 days
(x)	Debt to equity ratio	76.5%	26.2%

NB: If the bank overdraft were treated as a long-term borrowing, the current and acid test ratios would be as follows:

	20X8	20X7
Current ratio	1.02	0.88
Acid test ratio	0.56	0.53

ANSWER 42

Wodehouse

(a) **Accounting ratios**

Profitability

Ratios			*Pelham Ltd*	*Grenville Ltd*
(i)	Gross profit margin	$\frac{\text{GP}}{\text{Sales}}$	$\frac{230}{840} = 27.4\%$	$\frac{257}{762} = 33.7\%$
(ii)	Net profit margin	$\frac{\text{Op profit}}{\text{Sales}}$	$\frac{85}{840} = 10.1\%$	$\frac{144}{762} = 18.9\%$
(iii)	ROCE	$\frac{\text{Op profit}}{\text{Cap employed}}$	$\frac{85}{422} = 20.1\%$	$\frac{144}{272} = 52.9\%$
(iv)	Asset turnover	$\frac{\text{Sales}}{\text{Cap employed}}$	$\frac{840}{422} = 2.0$	$\frac{762}{272} = 2.8$
(v)	Stock turnover	$\frac{\text{Cost of sales}}{\text{Stock}}$	$\frac{610}{104} = 5.9$	$\frac{505}{80} = 6.3$

Liquidity

(i)	Current ratio	$\frac{\text{CA}}{\text{CL}}$	$\frac{347}{141} = 2.5$	$\frac{169}{165} = 1.0$
(ii)	Quick ratio	$\frac{\text{CA - Stock}}{\text{CL}}$	$\frac{243}{141} = 1.7$	$\frac{89}{165} = 0.5$
(iii)	Average collection period	$\frac{\text{Debtors}}{\text{Av daily sales}}$	$\frac{38}{2.3} = 16\frac{1}{2}$ days	$\frac{86}{2.1} = 41$ days

(b) **Comments**

Profitability

(1) Fairly large difference in both GP and NP margins between two companies in same retailing sector. Grenville is much better than Pelham.

Possible reasons:

- Grenville may have shops in better positions than Pelham.
- Pelham may have a higher proportion of cash sales or prompt payment discounts.
- Grenville may simply be more effective in its control of costs.
- Pelham's comparatively low NBV of fixed assets could indicate a need for high maintenance costs.

(2) ROCE much lower for Pelham: high cash balance may point to under-use of resources. With a lower gross margin, Pelham's asset turnover should be considerably higher than Grenville's to compensate. More sales volume is needed by Pelham.

Liquidity

(1) Pelham's large cash balance makes its current ratio unnecessarily high: it could afford an increase in capital expenditure, leading potentially to increased production and sales.

(2) Grenville's liquidity looks alarming but may not be if the amount of the bank loan can be increased and if debtors will pay promptly. Its credit period of 41 days is somewhat high, and there could be a problem here. Further information needed as to the ageing of debtors and the terms of the bank loan.

(c) **Comparison of two companies as investments**

Pelham: could be said to be ripe for a takeover as it appears to be under-using its assets. A safe but unexciting performance which could be improved with more dynamic management.

Grenville: more of a risk. Needs an injection of cash for security, but given a state of continued solvency it has the potential to make high profits and a good return on investment.

ANSWER 43

REPORT

To: Duncan Tweedy

From: A Student

Subject: Assessment of relative profitability of Byrne Ltd and May Ltd

Date: X - X - XX

Introduction

This report has been prepared to assist in determining the relative profitability and performance of Byrne Ltd and May Ltd and is based on the information you supplied on both companies.

Ratios

	Byrne Ltd	*May Ltd*
Return on capital employed	21.5%	32.1%
Gross profit percentage	59.0%	67.0%
Net profit percentage	25.0%	36.0%
Earnings per share	47p	82p

Explanation and comment

- *Return on capital employed*

  This measure shows the percentage of operating profit to capital employed in the business. It is a prime measure of profitability. It is expressed as:

  $$\frac{\text{Operating profit before interest and tax}}{\text{* Capital employed}} \times 100\%$$

  *Capital employed is defined here as share capital and reserves plus long-term debt.

  May Ltd shows the higher return than Byrne Ltd and is thus generating more profit per '£' of capital employed than Byrne.

- *Gross profit percentage*

  This measure is often referred to as the gross margin and represents the percentage of gross profit in relation to sales. It is expressed as:

  $$\frac{\text{Gross profit}}{\text{Sales}} \times 100\%$$

  May Ltd shows a higher gross profit to sales ratio and is therefore generating more gross profit per '£' of turnover than Byrne Ltd which indicates they are achieving higher margins.

- *Net profit percentage*

  This measure of profitability shows the percentage of net profit in relation to sales and is directly affected by the gross margin and levels of other expenses in the accounting period. It is expressed as:

  $$\frac{\text{Net profit}}{\text{Sales}} \times 100\%$$

May Ltd also has a higher net profit ratio to sales than Byrne Ltd as it is generating more net profit per '£' of sales than Byrne which is influenced by both the gross margin and the level of other costs in relation to turnover.

- *Earnings per share (EPS)*

  This measure considers the earnings attributable to ordinary shareholders in relation to the number of shares issued. It is expressed as:

  $$\frac{\text{Net profit after tax and preference dividend}}{\text{Number of ordinary shares in issue}}$$

  May Ltd's earnings per share is approximately double that of Byrne Ltd. However, the EPS of two different companies are not directly comparable since they may have different numbers of shares in issue.

Conclusion

In terms of profitability, May Ltd has a much higher level of performance than Byrne Ltd as indicated by both the profitability measures calculated.

ANSWER 44

Task 44.1

REPORT

To: Magnus Carter

From: A Student

Subject: Interpretation of financial statements

Date: 23 June 2000

This report has been prepared to support the interpretation of the financial statements of Baron Ltd and to compare and contrast the company performance over the two year period.

(a) **Calculation of the ratios**

	2000		*1999*	
Gross profit percentage	$\frac{1,204}{1,852}$	= 65%	$\frac{1,116}{1,691}$	= 66%
Net profit percentage	$\frac{519}{1,852}$	= 28%	$\frac{592}{1,691}$	= 35%
Debtor turnover in days	$\frac{319}{1,852} \times 365$	= 63 days	$\frac{236}{1,691} \times 365$	= 51 days
Creditor turnover in days	$\frac{48}{648} \times 365$	= 27 days	$\frac{44}{575} \times 365$	= 28 days
Stock turnover in days	$\frac{217}{648} \times 365$	= 122 days	$\frac{159}{575} \times 365$	= 101 days

(b) **Explanation and comment**

- *Gross profit percentage*

  This measure of profitability shows the percentage of gross profit in relation to sales, it is often termed the gross margin.

  The ratio has remained fairly constant over the two year period with only a marginal decrease from 66% to 65%. It is expressed as:

  $$\frac{\text{Gross profit}}{\text{Sales}} \times 100\%$$

  The company has achieved a greater volume of business without having to reduce its margins.

- *Net profit percentage*

  This measure of profitability shows the percentage of net profit in relation to sales. It is influenced by the gross margin and the level of other costs in relation to sales. There has been a significant fall in the net return over the period. The gross margin has only fallen marginally, however the expenses in relation to turnover have increased from 31% to 37% over the period and this has had an adverse effect on the performance.

  This indicates that the company is generating less net profit per '£' of turnover than previously achieved.

- *Debtor turnover*

  This is a measure of management control as it relates to the effectiveness of the credit control policy.

  The ratio shows the average number of days it takes to collect debts. It is expressed as:

  $$\frac{\text{Debtors}}{\text{Sales}} \times 365 \text{ days}$$

  The debtor days have increased over the two year period and it is taking 12 days longer to collect debts than previously experienced. This may be due to either customer cash flow problems or poor and less effective credit control.

- *Creditor turnover*

  This ratio shows the average days it takes for the company to pay its suppliers. This period has remained similar over the two years.

  It indicates that the company can meet its demands from creditors on a timely and regular basis.

- *Stock turnover*

  This is a measure of the effectiveness of the inventory control policy. It shows the average number of days it takes to turn over the stock.

  There has been a deterioration in this control over the two years as it is taking a further 21 days to turn over the stock than previously experienced.

Task 44.2

(a) The accounting equation is:

Assets - Liabilities = Ownership interest

In a not-for-profit entity, funds given to the organisation by donors and those generated from within are utilised to meet the entity's objective. Such funds are equivalent to the ownership interest element of the accounting equation.

In a company's balance sheet the ownership interest of the shareholders is represented by the share capital and reserves of the company.

(b) Examples of outside users and uses:

User	**Uses**
Potential investors	To decide whether to invest in the company.
Bank	To decide whether to grant a loan to the company.
Creditors	To decide whether to supply goods or services to the company.

Other reasonable examples of outside users are also acceptable.

(c) **Areas for improvement**

The measures of performance and other ratios indicate that Baron Ltd should focus on the control of expenses, debtors and stock.

The gross margin and creditor payment periods have remained similar to the previous year, but there has been a decline in the net profit percentage due to a more than proportional increase in the level of expenses to turnover, which suggests controls are needed.

The credit control policy and procedures need review and there is also the danger of bad debts occurring. The stock holding policy needs considering with a full analysis of both moving and slow moving stock.

ANSWER 45

Notes to Jonathan Fisher

(a) A balance sheet shows the net worth of an entity. It lists the values of assets, liabilities and ownership interest at a certain date in time.

A profit and loss account is a statement which shows revenue income and expenditure, the difference between these elements being profit over the accounting period.

(b) The accounting equation is:

Assets - Liabilities = Ownership interest

Figures in £000s at 30 September 1999

Assets	(£4,214 + £1,341	=	£5,555)
Liabilities	(£838 + £2,500	=	£3,338)
Ownership interest	(£5,555 - £3,338	=	£2,217)

(c) **Calculation of ratios**

The following ratios for the company have been computed:

		1999		*1998*	
(i)	*Gearing*				
	Debt/capital employed	$\frac{2,500}{4,717}$	= 53%	$\frac{1,000}{2,703}$	= 37%
	or				
	Debt/equity	$\frac{2,500}{2,217}$	= 113%	$\frac{1,000}{1,703}$	= 59%
(ii)	*Net profit percentage*	$\frac{668}{3,183}$	= 21%	$\frac{689}{2,756}$	= 25%
(iii)	*Current ratio*	$\frac{1,341}{838}$	= 1.6 : 1	$\frac{1,284}{611}$	= 2.1 : 1
(iv)	*Return on equity*	$\frac{356}{2,217}$	= 16%	$\frac{471}{1,703}$	= 28%

(d)

- *Gearing ratio*

  This measure represents the company's reliance on debt in relation to total capital employed. The gearing has increased over the two years and the company is now a 'high geared' organisation. There is a greater reliance on borrowed funds in the second year. This increases shareholder risk as when profits reduce, interest payments must still be met.

- *Net profit percentage*

  The net return to sales has fallen over the period. This is a result of a fall in the gross margin from 63% to 58%, the level of expenses to sales remaining fairly constant.

- *Current ratio*

  There has been a reduction in this measure of liquidity over the period, there has been a deterioration in the cash position and the acid test ratio has fallen significantly from 0.97 to 0.65. The business now has less current assets per '£' of current liabilities than previously.

- *Return on equity*

  The return has fallen over the two year period which has been influenced by the overall reduction in profitability as shown in the net profit percentage to sales.

  The company is not generating as much profit for each '£' worth of equity investment as it did in the previous year.

(e) The decrease in both profitability and liquidity indicates that the company is a worse prospect for investment than it was in the previous year.

ANSWER 46

Task 46.1

REPORT

To: Directors of Machier Ltd

From: AAT Student

Date: 17 June 1999

Re: Analysis of Machier Ltd financial statements

Introduction

The purpose of this report is to analyse the company financial statements for 1998 and 1999 and comment on its profitability, liquidity and financial position and assess the likelihood of the bank providing a substantial loan to fund future business strategy.

(a) *Calculation of ratios*

The following ratios for the company have been computed:

	1999		*1998*	
Return on equity	$\frac{321}{1,708}$	= 18.8%	$\frac{266}{1,227}$	= 21.7%
Net profit percentage	$\frac{738}{2,636}$	= 28%	$\frac{523}{1,687}$	= 31%
Quick ratio/acid test	$\frac{527}{749}$	= 0.7 : 1	$\frac{423}{359}$	= 1.2 : 1
Gearing ratio:				
Debt/capital employed	$\frac{2,800}{4,508}$	= 62%	$\frac{1,500}{2,727}$	= 55%
Interest cover	$\frac{738}{252}$	= 2.9 times	$\frac{523}{120}$	= 4.4 times

(b) *Comment and analysis*

The company profitability has fallen over the two year period.

The return on equity has decreased from 21.7% to 18.8%. This indicates that the company is generating less profit per '£' of equity investment than before.

The percentage of net profit to sales has also fallen; the gross margin remained fairly constant but the relationship of expenses to sales increased from 34% to 37%, the influencing factor being the additional depreciation incurred on the extra investment in fixed assets.

The company liquidity also deteriorated in the year with the acid test showing that the business has only 70p worth of liquid assets for each '£' worth of current liabilities. The business may be entering a period of cash flow difficulty.

The business has a high level of gearing, 62% in the current year compared with 55% previously.

High gearing is a risk to shareholders as, in periods of reduced profit, interest charges still have to be met and the company may struggle to pay this obligation.

This increase in gearing also reflects in the fall in the interest cover.

(c) *Conclusion*

The additional investment in fixed assets, funded mainly by the increased debt, has not resulted in a proportional increase in turnover but may achieve a higher volume in future years.

Based on this information and assessment it is unlikely that the bank will agree to further funding in the form of a substantial loan. The company is already highly geared and profitability has fallen.

I hope that this assessment and review is meaningful and useful to you.

Task 46.2

Notes for the directors

(a) The elements in a balance sheet and those in Machier Ltd comprise:

Elements	*Balances*
Assets	Fixed assets and current assets
Liabilities	Current liabilities Long-term loan
Ownership interest	Capital and reserves

(b) The accounting equation shows (figures in £000 at 31 March 1999):

Assets	(£4,282 + £975)	= £5,257
Liabilities	(£749 + £2,800)	= £3,549
Ownership interest	(£5,257 - £3,549)	= £1,708

ANSWER 47

REPORT

To: Managers of Bimbridge Hospitals Trust

From: AAT Student

Date: 3 December 1998

Re: Analysis of Patch Ltd's financial statements

Introduction

The purpose of this report is to analyse the financial performance of Patch Ltd for 1998 and 1997 to consider it as a major supplier of bandages and dressings to the Trust.

The following are key financial ratios together with industry benchmarks.

	1998	*Industry average 1998*	*1997*	*Industry average 1997*
Return on capital employed	$\frac{552}{5,334}$ = 10.3%	9.6%	$\frac{462}{5,790}$ = 8.0%	9.4%
Net profit percentage	$\frac{552}{2,300}$ = 24%	21.4%	$\frac{462}{2,100}$ = 22%	21.3%
Quick ratio/acid test	$\frac{523}{475}$ = 1.1 : 1	1.0 : 1	$\frac{418}{465}$ = 0.9 : 1	0.9 : 1
Gearing:				
Debt/capital employed	$\frac{1,654}{5,334}$ = 31%	36%	$\frac{2,490}{5,790}$ = 43%	37%

Comment and analysis

Overall company profitability has improved over the two years with return on capital employed strengthening from 8% to 10.3%.

The company is generating more net profit per '£' of investment in 1998 than in the previous year.

Compared with the sector average their performance was adverse in 1997 but more favourable in 1998.

The percentage of net profit to sales also increased over the period increasing from 22% to 24%.

The company is therefore more profitable in the current year and is performing more favourably than the sector as a whole and a good indicator for the future.

Company liquidity has shown an improvement with a slightly stronger acid test ratio than the sector as a whole.

The company currently has £1.10 worth of liquid assets for each '£' worth of current liabilities. This appears to be a sound liquidity position.

There has been a reduction in gearing over the two year period, with a much less reliance on debt than previously experienced.

High geared companies increase shareholder risk in times of profit decline. The company is moving to a 'lower' geared structure and to a position less than the industry average.

The company is considered to be a lower risk than previously.

Conclusion

Based on this assessment of the financial statements provided, it is recommended that Patch Ltd can be used as a supplier to the Trust.

Its profitability, liquidity and gearing suggest that the company is financially sound.

ANSWER 48

REPORT

To:	Michael Beacham	**From:**	Accounting Technician
Subject:	Interpretation of ratios	**Date:**	21 June 2002

Introduction

This report has been prepared to assist in the interpretation of the accounting ratios of Goodall Ltd, the company that you are considering making a loan to. It analyses the financial position and performance of the company over the years 2001 and 2002 and compares the results with the industry averages.

Explanation and comment

Gearing ratio. The gearing ratio measures the percentage of debt finance and preference share finance to total capital employed. The ratio is higher in 2002 than 2001, which suggests that the company is becoming riskier than in the previous year. Lending money to this company will increase the risk of failure to meet interest payments unless increased profits earned by the use of the loan are generated. In comparison with the industry average, the company is highly geared. This means that there is a higher than average risk in lending money to the company.

Interest cover. This ratio shows how many times the company could meet its interest payments out of operating profit. The interest cover has decreased from last year. This means that it is more difficult for the company to meet interest payments out of profits than last year. The ratio is very low in comparison with the industry average, which means that the company is earning considerably less profit in relation to the interest payments than other companies. This, again, makes it a riskier company to lend to.

Quick ratio/acid test. This ratio measures the extent to which the company has sufficient current assets that are quickly convertible into cash to meet its current liabilities. This ratio has decreased between the two years. In neither year did it have sufficient quick current assets to meet its current liabilities. The ratio is significantly worse than the industry average. This suggests that it has more of a liquidity problem when compared with other companies within the industry and hence that it is a riskier prospect.

Return on equity. This ratio measures the percentage of profit available for equity shareholders that is generated by the use of equity finance. The return on equity has fallen during the year. This means that there is less profit available for equity shareholders and makes it less likely that additional investment will be made in the company to enable additional profits to be made or to cover liquidity shortfalls. The return on equity is substantially less than the industry average, which makes it a less attractive prospect for investment than other companies within the sector.

Conclusion

The fact that Goodall Ltd is already highly geared and has deteriorating interest cover suggests that it is a risky prospect for a loan. It is riskier than other companies in its sector. The liquidity problems it is experiencing suggest that it may be unable to meet its interest payments in the future and it is unlikely, given the poor performance in profitability for equity investors, that they would be willing to meet any shortfall. It would not be advisable to lend money to Goodall Ltd.

ANSWER 49

AAT Student
Address
X December 2002

Dear Mr Popper

As requested, I am writing to you about the liquidity and financial position of Zipps Ltd. In this letter, I analyse the financial statements and conclude as to whether it is likely that the bank will lend the company money. My analysis is based solely on the financial statements of the business for the two years 2001 and 2002.

I have calculated the following ratios of the company for each of the years ending 30 September 2001 and 2002:

Ratios			*2002*		*2001*	
Current ratio	=	$\frac{\text{Current assets}}{\text{Current liabilities}}$	$\frac{1{,}430}{650}$	= 2.2 : 1	$\frac{1{,}302}{620}$	= 2.1 : 1
Quick ratio (acid test)	=	$\frac{\text{Current assets less stocks}}{\text{Current liabilities}}$	$\frac{585}{650}$	= 0.9 : 1	$\frac{682}{620}$	= 1.1 : 1
Gearing ratio	=	$\frac{\text{Long term debt}}{\text{Long term debt + Ordinary shareholders' funds}}$	$\frac{1{,}300}{2{,}000}$	= 65%	$\frac{900}{1{,}800}$	= 50%
[Alternative ratio]						
Debt/equity ratio	=	$\frac{\text{Long term debt}}{\text{Ordinary shareholders' funds}}$	$\frac{1{,}300}{700}$	= 186%	$\frac{900}{900}$	= 100%
Interest cover	=	$\frac{\text{Profit/(loss) before interest and tax}}{\text{Interest charges}}$	$\frac{(46)}{104}$	= - 0.4 times	$\frac{270}{77}$	= 3.5 times

My comments on the ratios are set out below:

Current ratio

The current ratio measures the extent to which the company has sufficient current assets to meet its current liabilities. It gives an indication of the liquidity of the company. Companies with low ratios may have difficulty in meeting creditor payments next year without a further injection of finance, and if this is not forthcoming it might be difficult to continue to trade. The ratio has increased during the year, which should mean that the company has better liquidity. However, if the increase in the ratio is due to increases in current assets that are not easily convertible to cash, the company may have poorer liquidity despite the increase in the ratio. A better test of liquidity in such a situation is given by a quick ratio or acid test.

Quick ratio/acid test

This ratio measures the extent to which the company has sufficient current assets that are quickly convertible into cash to meet its current liabilities. This ratio has decreased in the year from a position where it had more than enough quick current assets to meet its current liabilities to a position where there is a shortfall. The improvement in the current ratio seems to have come about due to an increase in stock and not an increase in quick assets. This means that the company has worse liquidity than last year. However, it still has almost enough quick assets to meet current liabilities and so may be able to continue trading.

Gearing ratio

The gearing ratio measures the percentage of debt finance and preference share finance to total capital employed (the debt/ capital employed ratio) or to total equity (the debt/equity ratio). A high ratio increases the risk that if profits reduce, the company may not be able to meet its interest payments or borrow further funds to overcome any liquidity problems. The ratio is higher in 2002 than in 2001. The company is highly geared and hence would be considered a risk by a lender.

Interest cover

This ratio shows how many times the company could meet its interest payments out of operating profit. Low levels of cover may make it difficult for the company to borrow more funds. Ordinary shareholders are unlikely to invest further funds in a company whose profits are reduced by interest costs leaving no return for them. The interest cover has significantly decreased from last year to the point where there are no available profits to cover the interest payments.

Given the difficulty in covering interest out of profits, the bank may well look at the profitability ratios of the company. These might include the net profit and gross profit ratios. It is clear that profits are substantially down on last year and the bank is likely to want to know why this is the case. Calculating those ratios might assist them in understanding why this is the case. They will want to know whether this is likely to continue in the future and hence whether the company is likely to be able to cover interest out of profits and eventually have enough funds to pay back the loan.

In conclusion, the company has poorer liquidity this year than last. The increase in the current ratio seems attributable to an increase in stock rather than an increase in cash or near cash current assets. The quick ratio shows relatively less quick assets to meet current liabilities. This is already a highly geared company and it is not making sufficient profits to cover its interest payments. Its financial position has deteriorated and looks insecure. A loan to the company would be risky and the bank is unlikely to lend money to the company on the basis of the ratios and analysis alone.

Yours sincerely

AAT Student

Mock Examination Answers

SECTION 1

TASK 1.1

LETTER

AAT Student
Any Road
Anytown
Anywhere

22 June 2001

Dear Ms Grieg

I write to you in regard to the financial position of Gint Ltd. I have analysed the financial statements using a number of ratios and below I show the results of this analysis.

Key measures of financial performance include:

Ratio	*2001*			*2000*		
Current ratio	$\frac{1,663}{723}$	=	2.3	$\frac{1,301}{650}$	=	2.0
Quick ratio/acid test	$\frac{506}{723}$	=	0.7	$\frac{585}{650}$	=	0.9
Gearing ratio						
Debt/capital employed	$\frac{600}{5,312}$	=	11.3%	$\frac{500}{4,992}$	=	10.0%
Or						
Debt/equity	$\frac{600}{4,712}$	=	12.7%	$\frac{500}{4,492}$	=	11.1%
Interest cover	$\frac{552}{46}$	=	12	$\frac{410}{41}$	=	10

My comments on the ratios are:

Current ratio

This is a measure of company liquidity. It is calculated as current assets : current liabilities. If current assets exceed current liabilities then the company has sufficient current assets to meet its current liabilities.

Gint's ratio has increased during the year from 2.0 to 2.3 which should indicate a strengthening of liquidity. However, the speed at which stock can be converted to cash flow is such that it is prudent not to regard stock as available to cover creditors. A second ratio in terms of liquidity is the quick ratio or acid test.

Letter (continued)

Quick ratio/acid test

This measures the relationship of liquid or near liquid assets to current liabilities. It is a measure of how well the business can cover its short-term demands from creditors. It is calculated as (current assets – stocks) : current liabilities. In most businesses, although there are exceptions, the ratio should be maintained around 1 : 1.

Gint's ratio has fallen over the two years from 0.9 to 0.7 which indicates that the company may be facing a shortage of cash flow and needs an injection of cash. It has only 70p worth of liquid assets to cover each £1 worth of current liabilities. It has tied up excess cash flow in the form of stock.

Gearing ratio

This is a measure of debt and preference share finance to total capital employed. It considers the reliance on debt finance to total investment.

The company is 'low geared' in both years but with a marginal increase in year two.

A company which is high geared increases risk to shareholders if profits fall, as interest charges must be paid irrespective of performance.

The company currently does not have a heavy reliance on debt to total investment.

Interest cover

There is a link here with gearing. The interest cover ratio measures the number of times the operating profit covers the interest payable. Low levels of cover may indicate a high geared structure and make it difficult for a company to borrow further funds to increase liquidity. Shareholders are unlikely to invest if profits for distribution are severely restricted by high interest payments leaving little or no return for them.

Gint's interest cover has strengthened over the two years and can comfortably cover its interest payments out of profits.

In conclusion, the company's liquidity is weaker than the previous year. Its increase in the current ratio is attributable to the extra investment in stocks. The company is low geared and has the ability to cover its interest payments.

The financial position seems reasonably sound. A loan would ease the short-term liquidity needs but we would need to consider future business volume. On the basis of these ratios I would recommend a loan is made to Gint Ltd.

TASK 1.2

(a) 'Assets' are rights or other access to future economic benefits controlled by an entity as a result of past transactions or events. Plant and machinery fit this definition of an asset in that:

(i) there has been a past transaction, the investment in the plant and machinery.

(ii) as a result of this past transaction, the entity will use the plant and machinery to manufacture products.

(iii) the manufacture and sale of these products will generate future economic benefits if they are profitable.

(b) 'Liabilities' are obligations of an entity to transfer economic benefits as a result of past transactions or events. The bank loan fits the definition of a liability in that:

(i) there has been a past transaction, the receipt of funds from the bank.

(ii) as a result of this past transaction, the bank is a loan creditor.

(iii) the obligation of the entity is to transfer economic benefits in the future, in that the loan has to be repaid and the interest on the loan has to be paid.

(c) (i) The figure of 'retained profit for the year' in the profit and loss account is the amount of profit retained in the company relating to the current financial year. The balance for the profit and loss account on the balance sheet represents the accumulated undistributed retained profit to date.

(ii) The retained profit for the year in the profit and loss account is added to the retained profits brought forward from the previous year. This gives the figure for the retained profits carried forward which is shown in the balance sheet of the company.

Note that the definitions of assets and liabilities are taken from the ASB's 'Statement of Principles'.

SECTION 2

TASK 2.1

Jake Ltd - Consolidated balance sheet as at 30 September 2001

	£000	£000
Fixed assets		
Intangible assets (W1)		477
Tangible assets (18,104 + 6,802 + 600 reval)		25,506
Investments		-
		25,983
Current assets	7,247	
Current liabilities	2,923	
Net current assets		4,324
Total assets less current liabilities		30,307
Less creditors: amounts falling due after more than one year		
Long-term loan		5,500
		24,807
Capital and reserves		
Called up share capital		5,000
Share premium		3,000
Profit and loss account (W2)		13,507
		21,507
Minority interest (W3)		3,300
		24,807

WORKINGS

(W1) Goodwill:

	£000
Price paid	5,000
Less: Net assets acquired (60% × (1,000 + 400 + 5,450 + 600 reval))	(4,470)
Goodwill	530
Less: Amortised to date (10%)	(53)
	477

(W2) Consolidated profit and loss account:

	£000
Jake Ltd	13,080
Dinos Ltd (60% × (6,250 – 5,450))	480
Less: Goodwill amortised to date	(53)
	13,507

(W3) Minority interest:

	£000
40% × (7,650 + 600 fair value adjustment)	3,300

TASK 2.2

NOTES

FRS 10 states that where goodwill is considered to have an indefinite useful economic life, it should not be subject to amortisation.

It would, however, be dealt with by the provisions of FRS 11 *Impairment of Fixed Assets and Goodwill*. The goodwill would be shown on the balance sheet at the cost of acquisition and reviewed for impairment at the end of the year of acquisition and at the end of each reporting year.

An impairment write-down is necessary when the recoverable amount of the asset is considered to be less than its carrying value.

TASK 2.3

NOTES

- The company's cash flow statement shows that there has been a reduction in cash balances of £1,609,000; a significant fall from £1,843,000 to only £234,000.

- The net cash flow from operating activities was £5,959,000, although the profit together with the adjustment for depreciation – the non-cash item, had generated £10,610,000.

  This difference was caused by a significant rise in debtors for the period £3,584,000 together with a decrease of £1,031,000 in creditors. Both these factors create a fall in cash balances. It is noted that both sales and purchases were at a similar level for both years and therefore suggests that the debtors collection period needs review. The decrease in creditors indicates that the company is paying creditors more quickly than before. To comment further on these issues it would be useful to know the actual collection and payment periods. The total effect on cash flow was a decrease of £4,615,000.

- The interest charge needs to be paid to service the finance and is an unavailable cash outflow, as in taxation. A further significant cash outflow is the capital expenditure which seems to have been funded by the increase in debt.
- The net cash flow from operating activities less the outflows for interest and taxation leaves a surplus of £3,400,000 before the positive effects of financing. Dividend payments were however £5,000,000 and thus had an adverse effect on cash reserves. This suggests that, if business volume is similar in the coming year, that dividend policy needs review. However, if debtor and creditor policy had remained at a similar level of control as before then there would have been sufficient cash flow to cover the dividend payment.

TASK 2.4

Leger Ltd - Profit and loss account for the year ended 30 September 2001

	£000	£000
Turnover		
Continuing operations	21,324	
Acquisitions	-	
Discontinued operations	-	
		21,324
Cost of sales (W1)		9,383
Gross profit		11,941
Distribution costs	3,415	
Administrative expenses	2,607	
		6,022
Operating profit		
Continuing operations	5,919	
Acquisitions	-	
Discontinued operations	-	
Profit on ordinary activities before interest		5,919
Interest payable (W2)		360
Profit on ordinary activities before taxation		5,559
Tax on profit on ordinary activities		1,567
Profit on ordinary activities after taxation		3,992
Dividends (W3)		675
Retained profit for the financial year		3,317

WORKINGS

(1) **Cost of sales**

	£000
Opening stock	3,127
Purchases	11,581
Carriage inwards	83
	14,791
Less closing stock	5,408
	9,383

(2) **Interest** (9% debentures)

£4m × 9% × ½ = £180,000 per trial balance.
Therefore accrual £180,000.
Total interest per profit and loss account £360,000.

(3) **Dividends**

Final dividend 2.5m shares × £0.15 = £375,000.
Interim dividend £300,000.
Total dividend for year £675,000.

TASK 2.5

Note on historical cost profits and losses per FRS 3

	£000
Reported profit on ordinary activities before taxation	5,559
Difference between historical cost depreciation and actual charge for year	10
Historical cost profit on ordinary activities before taxation	5,569

TASK 2.6

LETTER

AAT Student
Address

X December 2001

Dear Directors

I write in reply to your question concerning the regulatory framework and structure for the setting and enforcing of accounting standards within the UK.

The standards are now referred to as FRSs – Financial Reporting Standards - but there are still some older SSAPs – Statements of Standard Accounting Practice - still in use.

The structure comprises:

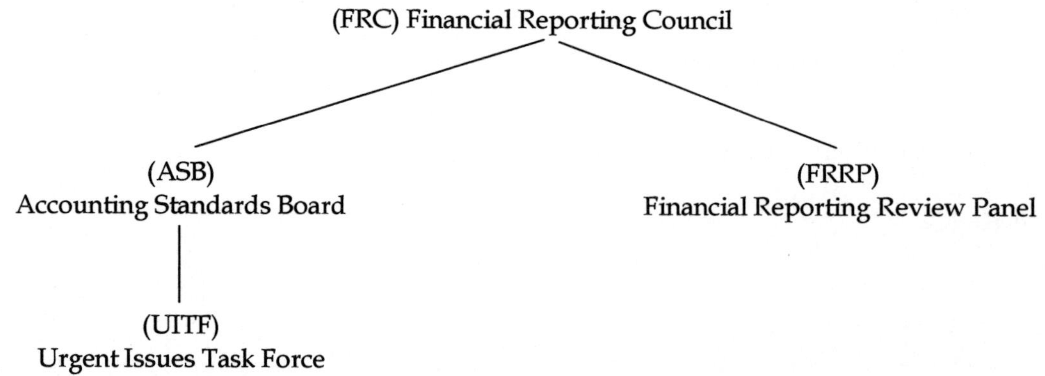

The role of the 'umbrella' body, the FRC, is to promote best practice and advise the government on accounting legislation and its improvement. It governs the work of the ASB and FRRP, both of which are operational bodies of the FRC, the members of which are appointed by the FRC. It also ensures that their operations are properly funded.

Letter (continued)

The ASB's primary role is the setting of accounting standards (FRSs). It adopts a consultation process when developing a new standard, by issuing for consultation an exposure draft (FRED), the responses to which influence the form of a new FRS before it is issued.

The UITF is a sub-committee of the ASB. It deals with urgent matters not covered by current standards in issue which cannot wait for the normal standard-setting process to deal with the issue.

The FRRP reviews departures from the requirements of the standards by companies in order to determine whether the financial statements give a true and fair view despite the departure. Where such departures do not lead to a 'true and fair view', the FRRP would seek an agreement from the company to review and revise their accounts. Failing this they have the powers to seek a court order compelling the revision.

Yours sincerely

A Student

TASK 2.7

JOURNAL

			Dr £	*Cr* £
1	DR	Dividend	300	
	CR	Dividend payable		300
2	DR	Stock (balance sheet)	5,346	
	CR	Stock (profit and loss account)		5,346
3	DR	Taxation	1,473	
	CR	Taxation payable		1,473
4	DR	Depreciation	1,115	
	CR	Buildings - accumulated depreciation		65
	CR	Fixtures and fittings - accumulated depreciation		217
	CR	Motor vehicles - accumulated depreciation		648
	CR	Office equipment - accumulated depreciation		185
5	DR	Land	850	
	CR	Revaluation reserve		850
6	DR	Damages	250	
	CR	Provisions for damages		250

Workings:

Dividend:	3,000,000 × 10p	=	£300,000
Revaluation:	£6,000,000 - £5,150,000	=	£850,000

SPECIMEN PAPER

Specimen Paper Questions

This examination paper is in TWO sections.

You have to show competence in BOTH sections.

You should therefore attempt and aim to complete EVERY task in BOTH sections.

You should spend about 125 minutes on Section 1 and 55 minutes on Section 2.

The answer booklet includes:

- A Companies Act 1985 consolidated balance sheet proforma (format 1).
- A proforma for journal entries.
- A proforma profit and loss account (format 1 as supplemented by FRS 3).
- A proforma cash flow statement (FRS 1 revised).

SECTION 1

You should spend about 125 minutes on this section.

This section is in three parts.

PART A

You should spend about 45 minutes on this part.

Data

You have been asked to assist in the preparation of the consolidated accounts of the Jake Group. Set out below are the balance sheets of Jake Ltd and Dinos Ltd as at 30 September 2002:

	Jake Ltd		*Dinos Ltd*	
	£000	*£000*	*£000*	*£000*
Tangible fixed assets		18,104		6,802
Investment in Dinos Ltd		5,000		
Current assets	4,852		2,395	
Current liabilities	(2,376)		(547)	
Net current assets		2,476		1,848
Long-term loan		(4,500)		(1,000)
		21,080		7,650
Share capital		5,000		1,000
Share premium		3,000		400
Profit and loss account		13,080		6,250
		21,080		7,650

You are given the following further information:

(i) The share capital of both Jake Ltd and Dinos Ltd consists of ordinary shares of £1 each. There have been no changes to the balances of share capital and share premium during the year. No dividends were paid or proposed by Dinos Ltd during the year.

(ii) Jake Ltd acquired 600,000 shares in Dinos Ltd on 30 September 2001.

(iii) At 30 September 2001 the balance on the profit and loss account of Dinos Ltd was £5,450,000.

(iv) The fair value of the fixed assets of Dinos Ltd at 30 September 2001 was £3,652,000 as compared with their book value of £3,052,000. The revaluation has not been reflected in the books of Dinos Ltd. (Ignore any depreciation implications.)

(v) Goodwill arising on consolidation is to be amortised using the straight-line method over a period of 10 years.

Task 1.1

Using the proforma provided in the answer booklet, prepare the consolidated balance sheet of Jake Ltd and its subsidiary undertaking as at 30 September 2002.

Task 1.2

Prepare notes for the directors of Jake Ltd to answer the following questions:

(a) What difference would it make to the accounting treatment of goodwill if, instead of having a useful life of 10 years, the goodwill was regarded as having an indefinite useful economic life?

(b) If so, what would be the appropriate accounting treatment?

Your answer should make reference, where relevant, to accounting standards.

PART B

You are advised to spend 50 minutes on this part.

Data

You have been asked to help prepare the financial statements of Hightink Ltd for the year ended 30 September 2002. The trial balance of the company as at 30 September 2002 is below:

Hightink Ltd
Trial balance as at 30 September 2002

	Debit	*Credit*
	£000	*£000*
Interest	240	
Distribution costs	6,852	
Administration expenses	3,378	
Trade debtors	5,455	
Trade creditors		2,363
Interim dividend	400	
Ordinary share capital		4,000
Sales		31,170
Long-term loan		6,000
Land - cost	5,000	
Buildings - cost	3,832	
Fixtures and fittings - cost	2,057	
Motor vehicles - cost	3,524	
Office equipment - cost	2,228	
Purchases	15,525	
Cash at bank	304	
Profit and loss account		6,217
Stock as at 1 October 2001	6,531	
Share premium		2,000
Buildings - accumulated depreciation		564
Fixtures and fittings - accumulated depreciation		726
Motor vehicles - accumulated depreciation		1,283
Office equipment - accumulated depreciation		463
	55,326	55,326

Further information:

- The authorised share capital of the company, all of which has been issued, consists of ordinary shares with a nominal value of £1.
- The company paid an interim dividend of 10p per share during the year but has not provided for the proposed final dividend of 15p per share.
- The stock at the close of business on 30 September 2002 was valued at cost at £7,878,000.
- The corporation tax charge for the year has been calculated as £1,920,000.
- Credit sales relating to October 2002 amounting to £204,000 had incorrectly been entered into the accounts in September 2002.
- Interest on the long-term loan has been paid for six months of the year. No adjustment has been made for the interest due for the final six months of the year. Interest is charged on the loan at a rate of 8% per annum.
- On 21 October 2002 there was a fire at the company's premises that destroyed fixed assets and stock. The losses from the fire amounted to £487,000 and they were not covered by the company's insurance. This amount is considered by the directors to constitute a material loss to the company.

Task 1.3

Using the proforma in the answer booklet, make the necessary journal entries for the year ended 30 September 2002 as a result of the further information given above. Dates and narratives are not required.

Notes:

1 You must show any workings relevant to these adjustments.

2 Ignore any effect of these adjustments on the tax charge for the year given above.

Task 1.4

Using the proforma provided in the answer booklet, and making any adjustments required as a result of the further information provided, draft a profit and loss account for the year ending 30 September 2002 for Hightink Ltd.

Task 1.5

Prepare a memo for the directors of Hightink Ltd to cover the following matters:

(a) Explain what is meant by a 'post balance sheet event'.

(b) Distinguish between a post balance sheet event that is an 'adjusting event' and one that is a 'non-adjusting event'.

(c) Explain your treatment of the losses that arose from the fire on the company's premises on 21 October 2002.

PART C

You are advised to spend 30 minutes on this part.

DATA

You have been asked to prepare a cash flow statement for Stringberg Ltd for the year ended 30 September 2002. The profit and loss account and balance sheets of Stringberg Ltd are set out below:

Stringberg Ltd
Profit and loss account for the year ended 30 September 2002

	£000
Turnover	9,047
Cost of sales	(4,939)
Gross profit	4,108
Profit on the sale of fixed assets	93
Distribution costs	(1,013)
Administrative expenses	(722)
Profit on ordinary activities before interest	2,466
Interest payable and similar charges	(243)
Profit on ordinary activities before taxation	2,223
Tax on profit on ordinary activities	(509)
Profit for the financial year	1,714
Dividends	(630)
Retained profit for the financial year	1,084

Stringberg Ltd
Balance sheet as at 30 September 2002

	2002		2001	
	£000	£000	£000	£000
Fixed assets		5,366		4,075
Current assets				
Stocks	3,016		2,284	
Trade debtors	1,503		1,394	
Cash	23			
	4,547		3,678	
Current liabilities				
Trade creditors	(1,372)		(930)	
Dividends payable	(420)		(380)	
Taxation	(509)		(492)	
Bank overdraft			(137)	
	(2,301)		(1,939)	
Net current assets		2,246		1,739
Long-term loan		(3,038)		(3,324)
		4,574		2,490

Capital and reserves		
Called up share capital	2,500	1,900
Share premium	400	-
Profit and loss account	1,674	590
	4,574	2,490

Further information:

- A fixed asset costing £363,000 with accumulated depreciation of £173,000 was sold during the year. The total depreciation charge for the year was £505,000.
- All sales and purchases were on credit. Other expenses were paid for in cash.

Task 1.6

Prepare a reconciliation of operating profit to net cash flows from operating activities for Stringberg Ltd for the year ended 30 September 2002.

Task 1.7

Using the proforma in the answer booklet, prepare a cash flow statement for Stringberg Ltd for the year ended 30 September 2002 in accordance with the requirements of FRS 1 (Revised).

SECTION 2

You are advised to spend approximately 55 minutes on this section.

Data

Tom Matease plans to invest in Fauve Ltd. This is a chain of retail outlets. He is going to meet the Managing Director of Fauve Ltd to discuss the profitability of the company. To prepare for the meeting he has asked you to comment on the change in profitability of the company. He also has some questions about the balance sheet of the company. He has given you the profit and loss accounts of Fauve Ltd and the summarised balance sheets for the last two years. These are set out below:

Fauve Ltd
Summary profit and loss accounts for the year ended 30 September

	2002	*2001*
	£000	*£000*
Turnover	4,315	2,973
Cost of sales	(1,510)	(1,189)
Gross profit	2,805	1,784
Distribution costs	(983)	(780)
Administrative expenses	(571)	(380)
Operating profit	1,251	624
Interest payable and similar charges	(45)	(27)
Profit on ordinary activities before taxation	1,206	597
Tax on profit on ordinary activities	(338)	(167)
Profit for the financial year	868	430
Dividends	(340)	(300)
Retained profit for the financial year	528	130

Fauve Ltd
Balance sheets as at 30 September

	2002		2001	
	£000	£000	£000	£000
Fixed assets		6,663		4,761
Current assets	3,503		2,031	
Current liabilities	(1,736)		(1,387)	
Net current assets		1,767		644
Long-term loan		(500)		(300)
		7,930		5,105
Called up share capital: ordinary shares of £1 each		4,000		1,703
Profit and loss account		3,930		3,402
		7,930		5,105

Task 2.1

Prepare a report for Jake Matease that includes the following:

(a) A calculation of the following ratios of Fauve Ltd for each of the two years:

(i) return on capital employed
(ii) net profit percentage
(iii) gross profit percentage
(iv) asset turnover (based on net assets)

(b) An explanation of the meaning of each ratio and a comment on the performance of Fauve Ltd as shown by each of the ratios.

(c) A conclusion on how the overall performance has changed over the two years.

Task 2.2

Prepare notes for a meeting with Tom that answers the following questions relating to the balance sheet of Fauve Ltd:

(a) Why is the plant and machinery included in the fixed assets of the company classified as an 'asset' of the business?

(b) Why is the bank loan classified as a 'liability' of the business?

(c) (i) Why is the final figure of 'retained profit for the year' in the profit and loss account not the same figure that appears in the balance for the profit and loss account on the balance sheet of the company?

(ii) Is there any connection between the two figures?

Specimen Paper Answer Book

SECTION 1

PART A

Task 1.1

Jake Ltd

Consolidated balance sheet as at 30 September 2002

	£000	*£000*
Fixed assets		
Intangible assets		
Tangible assets		
Current assets		
Creditors: amounts falling due within one year		
	———	
Net current assets		
Creditors: amounts falling due after more than one year		
Long-term loan		
		———
		———
Capital and reserves		
Called up share capital		
Share premium		
Profit and loss account		
		———
Minority interest		
		———
		———

Task 1.2

Notes for the directors

PART B

Task 1.3

	£000	£000
1		
2		
3		
4		
5		

Task 1.4

Hightink Ltd

Profit and loss account for the year ended 30 September 2002

	£000	£000
Turnover		
Continuing operations		
	———	
Cost of sales		
		———
Gross profit		
Distribution costs		
Administrative expenses		
		———
Operating profit		
Continuing operations		
	———	
Profit on ordinary activities before interest		
Interest payable and similar charges		
		———
Profit on ordinary activities before taxation		
Tax on profit on ordinary activities		
		———
Profit on ordinary activities after taxation		
Dividends		
		———
Retained profit for the financial year		
		———

Task 1.5

MEMO

PART C

Task 1.6

Stringberg Ltd

Reconciliation of operating profit to net cash inflow from operating activities

Task 1.7

Stringberg Ltd

Cash flow statement for the year ended 30 September 2002

	£000	£000
Net cash inflow from operating activities		
Returns on investments and servicing of finance		
Interest paid		
Taxation		
Capital expenditure		
Payments to acquire tangible fixed assets		
Proceeds from sale of fixed asset		
	———	
Equity dividends paid		
		———
Financing		
Repayment of loan		
Issue of ordinary share capital		
	———	
		———
Increase in cash		
		———

SECTION 2

Task 2.1

REPORT

To:	**Subject:**
From:	**Date:**

Task 2.2

Notes for meeting

Specimen Paper Answers

SECTION 1

PART A

Task 1.1

Jake Ltd

Consolidated balance sheet as at 30 September 2002

	£000	£000
Fixed assets		
Intangible assets		477
Tangible assets		25,506
Current assets	7,247	
Creditors: amounts falling due within one year	(2,923)	
Net current assets		4,324
Creditors: amounts falling due after more than one year		
Long-term loan		(5,500)
		24,807
Capital and reserves		
Called up share capital		5,000
Share premium		3,000
Profit and loss account		13,507
		21,507
Minority interest		3,300
		24,807

Workings

(i) **Jake Ltd holding in Dinos Ltd**

$$\frac{600,000}{1,000,000} = 60\%$$

Minority interest:

$$\frac{400,000}{1,000,000} = 40\%$$

(ii) **Revaluation of assets in Dinos Ltd to fair value at date of acquisition**

DR	Fixed assets	£600,000
CR	Revaluation reserve	£600,000

(iii) **Calculation of goodwill arising on consolidation and minority interest**

All £000s	*Total equity 100%*	*{Attributable to Jake Ltd} At acquisition 60%*	*Since acquisition 60%*	*Minority interest 40%*
Share capital	1,000	600		400
Share premium	400	240		160
Revaluation reserve	600	360		240
Profit and loss:				
- at acquisition	5,450	3,270		2,180
- since acquisition	800		480	320
	8,250	4,470		3,300
Consideration		5,000		
Goodwill arising on consolidation		530		
Profit and loss account of Jake Ltd			13,080	
Less goodwill written off			(53)	
Profit and loss account of Jake Ltd			13,507	

(iv) **Goodwill arising on consolidation**

Goodwill arising on consolidation	530
Written off during year	(53)
	477

Task 1.2

Notes for the directors

(a) According to FRS 10, where goodwill is regarded as having an indefinite useful economic life, it should not be amortised.

(b) If goodwill is not amortised then it should be shown at the cost of acquisition. However, if goodwill is not amortised then it should be reviewed for impairment at the end of each reporting period in accordance with FRS 11 *Impairment of Fixed Assets and Goodwill*. Impairment of a fixed asset occurs when there has been a reduction in the recoverable amount of a fixed asset below its carrying amount.

PART B

Task 1.3

			£000	£000
1	DR	Dividend	600	
	CR	Dividend payable		600
2	DR	Stock (balance sheet)	7,878	
	CR	Stock (profit and loss account)		7,878
3	DR	Taxation	1,920	
	CR	Taxation payable		1,920
4	DR	Sales	204	
	CR	Debtors		204
5	DR	Interest	240	
	CR	Interest payable		240

Workings

Dividend:	£4,000,000 × 15p	=	£600,000
Interest:	£6,000,000 × 8% × ½	=	£240,000

Task 1.4

Hightink Ltd

Profit and loss account for the year ended 30 September 2002

	£000	£000
Turnover		
Continuing operations	31,506	
		31,506
Cost of sales		(14,178)
Gross profit		17,328
Distribution costs		(6,852)
Administrative expenses		(3,378)
Operating profit		
Continuing operations	7,098	
Profit on ordinary activities before interest		7,098
Interest payable and similar charges		(480)
Profit on ordinary activities before taxation		6,618
Tax on profit on ordinary activities		(1,920)
Profit on ordinary activities after taxation		4,698
Dividends		(1,000)
Retained profit for the financial year		3,698

Workings

W1 Turnover

	£000
Sales per TB	31,710
Less credit sales in wrong period	(204)
	31,506

W2 Cost of sales

	£000
Opening stock	6,531
Purchases	15,525
Closing stock	(7,878)
	14,178

W3 Interest paid

	£000
Interest per TB	240
Accrued interest	240
	480

W4 Dividends

	£000
Final dividend	600
Interim dividend	400
Total dividends	1,000

Task 1.5

MEMO

(a) A 'post balance sheet event' is an event either favourable or unfavourable that occurs between the balance sheet date and the date on which the Board of Directors approves the financial statements.

(b) An 'adjusting event' is an event that provides additional evidence of conditions existing at the date of the balance sheet. A 'non-adjusting event' is an event that arises after the balance sheet date that relates to conditions that did not exist at the date of the balance sheet.

(c) The losses that arose from the fire on the company's premises on 21 April 2002 constitute a 'non-adjusting' post balance sheet event. The condition did not exist at the balance sheet date, but came into existence after that date. No adjustment is required for the event as the conditions did not exist at the balance sheet date and thus do not constitute an adjusting event. However, the event is so material that failure to disclose may render the financial statements misleading. Hence, this non-adjusting event should be disclosed by way of a note to the accounts.

PART C

Task 1.6

Stringberg Ltd

Reconciliation of operating profit to net cash inflow from operating activities

	£000
Operating profit	2,466
Depreciation charges	505
Profit on sale of tangible fixed assets	(93)
Increase in stock	(732)
Increase in debtors	(114)
Increase in creditors	442
Net cash inflow from operating activities	2,474

Task 1.7

Stringberg Ltd

Cash flow statement for the year ended 30 September 2002

	£000	£000
Net cash inflow from operating activities		2,474
Returns on investments and servicing of finance		
Interest paid		(243)
Taxation		(492)
Capital expenditure		
Payments to acquire tangible fixed assets	(1,986)	
Proceeds from sale of fixed asset	283	
		(1,703)
Equity dividends paid		(590)
		(554)
Financing		
Repayment of loan	(286)	
Issue of ordinary share capital	1,000	
		714
Increase in cash		160

Workings (all figures £000)

(i) **Fixed asset additions**

Opening balance £4,075 - Depreciation £505 - Net book value of asset sold £190 + Additions ? = Closing balance £5,366

Therefore ? = £1,986

(ii) **Dividends paid**

Dividends

Cash	590	Balance b/f	380
Balance c/f	420	Profit and loss	630
	1,010		1,010

SECTION 2

Task 2.1

REPORT

To: Tom Matease **Subject:** Interpretation of financial statements

From: A Student **Date:** December 2002

This report has been prepared to assist in the interpretation of the financial statements of Fauve Ltd. It considers the profitability and return on capital of the business over 2001 and 2002.

(a) **Calculation of the ratios**

	2002	*2001*
Return on capital employed (Shareholders' funds plus long-term liabilities)	$\frac{1,251}{8,430}$ = 4.9%	$\frac{624}{5,405}$ = 11.5%
Net profit percentage	$\frac{1,251}{4,315}$ = 29%	$\frac{624}{2,973}$ = 21%
Gross profit percentage	$\frac{2,805}{4,315}$ = 65%	$\frac{1,784}{2,973}$ = 60%
Asset turnover (based on net assets)	$\frac{4,315}{8,430}$ = .51	$\frac{2,973}{5,405}$ = .55

(b) **Explanation and comment**

Return on capital employed

- This ratio shows in percentage terms how much profit is being generated by the capital employed in the company.
- The company is showing a higher return on capital employed in 2002 compared to 2001 and hence is generating more profit per £ of capital employed in the business.

Net profit percentage

- This ratio shows in percentage terms how much net profit is being generated from sales
- The ratio has increased over the two years.
- This could be explained either by an increase in the sales margins or by a decrease in expenses, or both.
- It is also the case that the percentage of expenses to sales has decreased from 39% in 2001 to 36% in 2002.

Gross profit ratio

- This ratio shows in percentage terms how much gross profit is being generated by the sales of the company and thus indicates the gross profit margin on sales.
- The ratio has improved over the two years with an increase in the percentage from 60% to 65%.
- The company is increasing its sales while increasing its margins.
- This may be due to increasing its sales price or reducing the cost of sales or both.

Asset turnover

- This ratio shows how efficient the company is in generating sales from the available capital employed/net assets.
- The ratio has deteriorated between the two years and less sales are generated from the available capital employed/net assets in 2002 than in 2001.
- Considerable new investment has been made in fixed assets and current assets in 2002 and it may be that the investment has yet to yield the expected results.

(c) **Overall**

The ratios show that the return on capital employed has improved in 2002 and that the company is generating more profit from the capital employed/net assets. This is due to increased margins and to greater control over expenses, perhaps brought about by economies of scale. However, the efficiency in the use of assets has deteriorated in 2002 and this has reduced the increase in return on capital employed. It may be that the increased investment in assets that has taken place in 2002 has yet to yield benefits in terms of a proportionate increase in sales and that the situation will improve when the assets are used to their full potential.

Regards

AAT Student

Task 2.2

Notes for meeting

(a) 'Assets' are rights or other access to future economic benefits controlled by an entity as a result of past transactions or events. Plant and machinery fit this definition of an asset in that:

(i) there has been a past transaction: the purchase of the plant and machinery.

(ii) as a result of this past transaction, there is a right of the entity to use the plant and machinery to manufacture products.

(iii) these products will generate future economic benefits when they are sold at a profit.

(b) 'Liabilities' are obligations of an entity to transfer economic benefits as a result of past transactions or events. The bank loan fits the definition of a liability in that:

(i) there has been a past transaction: the receipt of money from the lender.

(ii) as a result of this past transaction, there is an obligation to the lender.

(iii) the obligation of the entity is to transfer economic benefits in the future in that the loan has to be repaid and the interest on the loan paid.

(c) (i) The figure of 'retained profit for the year' in the profit and loss account is the amount of profit retained in the company for the current financial year. The balance for the profit and loss account on the balance sheet represents the accumulated retained profit of the company since its inception.

(ii) The retained profit for the year in the profit and loss account is added to the retained profits brought forward from previous years in order to get the retained profits carried forward which is shown in the balance sheet of the company.

Index

Textbook and Workbook Review Form

AAT UNIT 11- DRAFTING FINANCIAL STATEMENTS

We hope that you have found this Textbook and Workbook stimulating and useful and that you now feel confident and well-prepared for your examinations.

We would be grateful if you could take a few moments to complete the questionnaire below, so we can assess how well our material meets your needs. There's a prize for four lucky students who fill in one of these forms from across the Syllabus range and are lucky enough to be selected!

	Excellent	*Adequate*	*Poor*
Depth and breadth of technical coverage			
Appropriateness of coverage to examination			
Presentation			
Level of accuracy			

Did you spot any errors or ambiguities? Please let us have the details below.

Page	**Error**

Thank you for your feedback.

Please return this form to:

The Financial Training Company Limited
Unit 22J
Wincombe Business Park
Shaftesbury
Dorset SP7 9QJ

Student's name: ....

Address: ....

....

....

AAT Publications Student Order Form

o order your books, please indicate quantity required in the relevant order box, calculate the amount(s) in the column provided, and add postage to etermine the amount due. Please then clearly fill in your details plus method of payment in the boxes provided and return your completed form with ayment attached to:

The Financial Training Company, Unit 2, Block 2, Wincombe Conference Centre, Wincombe Business Park, Shaftesbury, Dorset SP7 9QJ or fax your order to 01747 858821 or Telephone 01747 854302

FOUNDATION LEVEL

		TEXTBOOK		WORKBOOK		FOCUS NOTE		AMOUNT
Unit	Title	Price £	Order	Price £	Order	Price £	Order	£
2 & 3	Receipts, payments & initial trial balance	20.00		20.00		6.00*		
		COMBINED TEXT & WORKBOOK						
	Supplying information for management & control	15.00						
,22 &23	Personal effectiveness & working with computers	15.00						

INTERMEDIATE LEVEL

		COMBINED TEXT & WORKBOOK		FOCUS NOTE		AMOUNT
Unit	Title	Price £	Order	Price £	Order	£
	Maintaining financial records and preparing accounts	20.00		6.00		
	Evaluating costs and revenues	20.00		6.00*		
	Preparing reports and returns	20.00				

TECHNICIAN

		COMBINED TEXT & WORKBOOK		FOCUS NOTE		AMOUNT
Unit	Title	Price £	Order	Price £	Order	£
9	Management of performance, value and resource	20.00		6.00		
)	Managing systems & people	15.00				
	Drafting financial statements	20.00		6.00		
5	Cash management & credit control system	15.00		6.00		
7	Implementing auditing procedures	15.00		6.00		
3 (02)	Preparing Business Tax Computations FA2002	15.00				
3 (03)	Preparing Business Tax Computations FA2003	15.00		6.00		
9 (02)	Preparing Personal Tax Computations FA2002	15.00				
9 (03)	Preparing Personal Tax Computations FA2003	15.00		6.00		

Jnits 1, 2, 3 & 4 are in one Focus Note. Units 6 & 7 are in one Focus Note.

PAYROLL

		COMBINED TEXT & WORKBOOK		AMOUNT
Level	Title	Price £	Order	£
evel 2	Payroll Administration 2002	20.00		
evel 2	Payroll Administration 2003	20.00		
evel 3	Payroll Administration 2002	20.00		
evel 3	Payroll Administration 2003	20.00		

Sub Total £

Postage and packing – please note a signature is required on delivery

	First book	Each additional book
UK/N Ireland	£5*	nil (up to 10 books)
Europe	£25	£3
Rest of World	£40	£4

£

Focus notes to UK and NI £1 each max £5 TOTAL PAYMENT £

he following section **must be filled in clearly** so that your order can be despatched without delay.

TO PAY FOR YOUR ORDER TICK AN OPTION BELOW

. I WISH TO PAY BY MASTERCARD ❑ VISA ❑ DELTA ❑ SWITCH ❑

ARD NO. All cards last 3 digits on signature strip (Switch only)

XPIRY DATE ISSUE No. (Switch only) **Cardholder's Signature**

ardholder's Name & Address:

Cardholder's Tel. No. (Day):

. I WISH TO PAY BY CHEQUE ❑ **Cheques should be made payable to *The Financial Training Company Ltd*** and must be attached to your rder form. **Personal cheques cannot be accepted without a valid Banker's Card number written on the back of the cheque.**

TUDENT NAME: TEL NO. (Day)

ELIVERY ADDRESS: (Must be the same as cardholder's address. Please contact us if you wish to discuss an alternative delivery address).

POST CODE:

pril 2003 (This order form replaces any previous order forms.)